D1707505

GANDHI

GANDHI

BEHIND the MASK
of DIVINITY

G. B. SINGH

Prometheus Books
59 John Glenn Drive
Amherst, New York 14228-2197

Published 2004 by Prometheus Books

Inquiries should be addressed to
Prometheus Books
59 John Glenn Drive
Amherst, New York 14228–2197
VOICE: 716–691–0133, ext. 207
FAX: 716–564–2711
WWW.PROMETHEUSBOOKS.COM

08 07 06 05 04   5 4 3 2 1

Library of Congress Cataloging-in-Publication Data

Singh, G. B., 1954–
    Gandhi : behind the mask of divinity / G. B. Singh
        p. cm.
    Includes bibliographical references and index.
    ISBN 1–57392–998–0 (cloth : alk. paper)
    1. Gandhi, Mahatma, 1869–1948. 2. Statesmen—India—Biography.
3. Nationalists—India—Biography. I. Title.

DS481.G3 S5325 2002
954.03'5'092—dc21
[B]   2002068083

Printed in the United States of America on acid-free paper

Dawn of the Civil Rights Movement
with
GURU NANAK
(1469–1539)

Of a woman are we conceived,
Of a woman we are born,
To a woman are we betrothed and married,
It is a woman who keeps the race going,
Another companion is sought when the life-partner dies,
Through woman are established social ties.
Why should we consider woman cursed and condemned,
When from woman are born leaders and rulers.
From woman alone is born a woman,
Without woman there can be no human birth.
Without woman, O Nanak, only the True One exists.
Be it man or be it woman,
Only those who sing His glory
Are blessed and radiant with His Beauty,
In His Presence and with His grace
They appear with a radiant face.

—*Guru Granth*, p. 473

Today, in retrospect, may we proclaim:

Without women, there wouldn't have been
the American Civil Rights Movement.

Therefore, this book is dedicated to one who epitomized
the conscience of the American Civil Rights Movement

Miss Ella J. Baker
(1903–1986)

CONTENTS

7

ACKNOWLEDGMENTS

My work on *Gandhi: Behind the Mask of Divinity* was sustained by several of my friends scattered throughout the world serving in myriad assignments. These honorable men and women, whom I have been associated with over the past twenty years, have contributed to this book either directly or indirectly. I am particularly indebted to the thousands of African Americans who took the time to share their inner feelings with me and, in the process, sharpened my focus on the issues of racism and race relations. Richard Grenier, who was once a columnist for the *Washington Times*, will always occupy a special place within my heart for bringing to my attention a different Gandhi story from the one that I grew up with. Also, this book would not have been thorough if it wasn't for Dr. James D. Hunt and Dr. Maureen Swan. Both have contributed scholarly works on Gandhi and his relationship to black people in South Africa. I am particularly grateful to them for their dedicated efforts.

Another person who is close to my heart is Dr. Velu Annamalai, a brave man born and raised as an Untouchable and who, with hard work, made his way to the United States. Since then, he has pursued a commendable drive to educate the West on the true nature of Gandhi and his cruel hoax on the poorest people on the face of the globe—the Untouchable community. Dr. Annamalai's campaigns of highlighting human rights abuses in India compelled me to take another look at Gandhi and what he did to the Untouchables. I thank him for introducing to me a great personality—Dr. B. R. Ambedkar, a contemporary of Gandhi.

I am in debt to the staff of the Tutt Library at Colorado College for providing me with unrestricted access to the Gandhi literature. Similarly, I must mention the names of Perkins Library and the Divinity School Library at Duke University in Durham, North Carolina, for accumulating excellent Gandhi resource materials—which I used without reservation.

Ms. Lattie C. Smith of the John L. Throckmorton Library in Fort Bragg, North Carolina, deserves a special mention here. She spent numerous hours on the interlibrary loan system hunting for the old Gandhi literature. For her services, I am thankful.

Also, I am indebted to the modern skeptical movements presently under way in the United States. Through them, I acquired the modern analytical and intellectual skills necessary to study the often puzzling Gandhi subject matter. My special acknowledgment goes out to Dr. Paul Kurtz and Steven L. Mitchell of Prometheus Books, who courageously showed the fortitude to bring this explosive book to the public eye. My editors, Meghann French, Mary Read, and Benjamin Keller, deserve a special mention. Their expertise has streamlined and corrected the imperfections in the text, polishing it into fine readability. I owe my gratitude to friends such as John Frazier, Craig Patterson, Kerri Jamison, Tito Quiroz, Lee Mayfield, C. T. Urugodawatte, Dr. Krishnamurthy Ajjarapu, and Robert Lane, who were kind enough to proofread this book and to provide valuable guidance and suggestions.

I take full responsibility for the material produced in this book. Because of the nature of the subject matter dealing with racism, I chose to hone my research references, primarily focusing on this facet only. If, in the process, I unintentionally failed to quote any of the more relevant references, the inadequacies reflect upon me and not on anybody else.

INTRODUCTION
WHY ANOTHER BOOK on GANDHI?

If I can say so without arrogance and with due humility, my message and methods are, indeed, in their essentials for the whole world and it gives me keen satisfaction to know that it has already received a wonderful response in the hearts of a large and daily growing number of men and women in the West.

—Mahatma Gandhi
Young India, August 11, 1920

As a full-grown fetus in my mother's womb, I had no choice but to land on this planet, at least somewhere on it. That "somewhere," as it turned out, was called *Bharat* by many, with reverence—best known to the rest of the world as *India*. Due to this early upbringing, *Bharat* took on a special meaning—it entered into our psyche by some mystical osmosis—as a part of the larger Hindu memory bank.[1] And nobody was going to dissuade us—we little patriots were that certain of our past heritage. Only well into my adulthood did I realize that I was born in the Republic of India, a product and leftover entity of British colonialism. I received my early education, college education, and professional education in India before emigrating to the United States in 1976. I remember vividly that during this entire studentship sojourn in India, my colleagues and I received numerous school-setting formal and informal lessons concerning the "father of the nation," called Mahatma Gandhi; *Mahatma* means, simply, "great soul."

Since we were spoon-fed very carefully by the Indian educational bureaucracy, we were naturally led to believe that our Mahatma was indeed a Great

Being. To be more exact, we were indoctrinated to believe that God had taken birth in a human form to liberate us from the British, albeit nonviolently. Not only that, we believed that the British Empire—the greatest empire in the human history—was no match for our Mahatma. He uprooted the British with his spiritual powers, and they had no choice but to leave *Bharat*. We sincerely believed that the future of humankind was safe only if we all followed in the Great Soul's footsteps. And to search for his footsteps, one need not go too far. Our Indian government leaders—appointed by the Mahatma himself before the Constitution of the Republic of India came into effect—were nearby to emulate him. Frankly, there were quite a few of these Gandhi apostles on the landscape. Two were somehow more emphasized to us than others. One was Pandit Nehru. We youngsters reverently called him *chacha*, meaning "uncle." The other was Vinoba Bhave, a distantly placed holy man in a rural setting. The former was designated as the political heir and the latter as the spiritual heir to Mahatma Gandhi, according to our teachers, the media, and many of the elders surrounding us. And all the Gandhi apostles were exhausting their Mahatma-bestowed talents to restore and usher *Bharat* to its indescribably glorious past. Rather than getting better, ironically, the conditions surrounding us just kept deteriorating. We couldn't figure out why. The British were already gone! We were given license to a fertile imagination and we used it quite well. But, somewhere in the back of my mind, a problem was beginning to brew. This was as a result of a few adults who lived in our neighborhood in New Delhi who had the luxury of having lived in both British and post-British India. They had seen the British rule firsthand and had known about Mahatma Gandhi. They were not enthused with the history we were learning in our schools. They couldn't provide specific information on Gandhi, because they had none—but they were certain that we were not learning the truth. In this manner, the first post-British generation in India grew to accept what was spoon-fed to them. And if anyone of us had any doubts, there were no other channels of information available to us. We could fall back on only the information that we already were accustomed to hearing.

I grew up in such an environment. But once in the United States, in the midst of a strange, new world, I began to question some of the history that I "knew." In February 1983 I saw *Gandhi*, a movie that, I must say, had a tremendously positive effect upon me. The very next month I encountered and read Richard Grenier's article, "The Gandhi Nobody Knows."[2] It, too, had a profound effect upon me, although much of it was painful.

I learned that, officially, the government of India under Prime Minister Indira Gandhi (not a blood relative to the Mahatma) paid one-third the financing of the movie in return for its portrayal of Mahatma Gandhi as an absolute pacifist. Then, in June 1984, came another painful jolt: The same prime minister ordered the Indian Army to invade the Sikh religion's most sacred shrine, the Golden Temple, and thirty-eight other Sikh temples under the pretext of combating terrorism. The army killed thousands of innocent men, women, and children who had earlier assembled in the temple precincts in observance of an annual religious event. Justifying her actions in an interview with *Time* magazine, she stressed, "Mahatma Gandhi, in his time, accepted that necessity."[3] In other words, the prime minister was trying to tell us that her bloody actions against the Sikhs were, in a sense, justifiable because she had exhausted all other available options—and in the end she invoked one of Mahatma Gandhi's teachings to show that she had no choice but to resort to a military option. Because of this, within two years after I had viewed the internationally acclaimed film, I came to see two images of Mahatma Gandhi: one as an absolute pacifist and the other as a typical shrewd politician. Both images, of course, originated from the same source—the prime minister! Which of these two images was the correct one? Soon, the pain and anguish gave way to a strong will to thoroughly research the life and work of Gandhi to find out for myself.

At this juncture, let me digress a little to lay out some pertinent background information for the benefit of the readers, with a hope that this book will in no way be construed as a result of the "strained, bickering relationships" between the Hindus and the Sikhs that we have often heard the Western media report in the last twenty years. The fact is that before the twentieth century, the Sikh and the Hindu communities had lived in peace ever since the inception of the Sikh religion in the early sixteenth century. Historically, the Sikh people have willingly sacrificed their lives for the protection of Hindus and their human rights, precisely at the crossroads of several centuries of bloody history when there were no other groups with an appreciation for such basic, yet revolutionary, humanistic values. This is remarkable and is a testament to the tenets of Sikh religious teachings—to honor fundamental values of human rights, civil rights, and equality of all human beings, including that of women, irrespective of any differences. Because of spatial constraints, this is not the place to explore that history. Suffice it to say that even in today's political India, with all the bloodshed, in the villages of the Punjab region, where the Sikh population is by far the majority, there has not been a single riot in which the Sikh population unleashed its fury on the Hindu minority. That feature of India's bloody modern existence is more commonly associated with the Hindu-Muslim conflicts, in which the members of one civil community go after the throats of another—but even this is not that old in its genesis. I hate to point my finger here, but there is more of this to come in this book: it was Gandhi himself and his politics that injected the poisonous dose of hatred into British India's relatively peaceful society of multiple communities and their affairs.

My own background, as it pertains to these conflicts, is a bit unusual. I was born into an upper-caste, patriarchal Hindu extended family, a firstborn son to my non-Hindu parents, and a secondborn grandson to my paternal Hindu grandparents. In my younger years, I was the apple of my elders' eyes—a boy who recited intricate details of various Hindu scriptures—and my paternal side of the family tree knew that I, the darling boy, was on the right track, with the aim of nothing less than embodying the pinnacle of the best thing ever known to humankind, Hinduism. Circumstances changed, though, and even as a grown man and as a Sikh, my yearning to study Hinduism never left me; it only intensified with time. With the passage of time and the smattering of education that has come my way in the United States, I have become a professional student of Hinduism (more on this is presented briefly in part 6). So one can appreciate that I myself am a product of that very harmonious state of affairs that existed between the Sikhs and the Hindus before the end of the colonial period. And I am proud of that heritage. I hope that readers will bear this fact in mind and will not look with a jaundiced eye upon my arguments as a result.

Over the years I have discussed Gandhi with many Americans, both formally and informally. I recall a conversation in one of the major cities of the Rocky Mountain region of the United States with a highly cultured woman who had lived in the literary world for at least forty years and had come to greatly admire Gandhi. I presented the information I had gathered on Gandhi, which she scrutinized thoroughly before conceding: "Another hero down the tube." She was appalled at the number of her heroes that had already fallen from their pedestals. Some folks, in moments of heated debate, had quarreled with me. Some would sputter about, saying, "When we acquire nonviolence for the greater betterment of society, by learning from admittedly false Gandhi, what wrong does that do? After all, we all benefit. What harm does it do? No one is hurt." Such talk is pervasive in our culture. If we accept such notions, then, may I ask, where is the fruit? There is no evidence to prove that Gandhi's "nonviolent" image has brought about peace. Our societies continue to inflict violence on each other. Nowhere is this more true than in India, home of the Mahatma, a focal point of unending violence in spite of going the extra mile to commemorate him. Mahatma Gandhi is a revered hero to much of humankind. Ironically, his most ardent followers are not in India—they are here in the West, which came as a surprise to me.

Take, for example, the case of Hillary Rodham Clinton, the former First Lady of the United States. On July 14, 1995, at the Kennedy Center in Washington, D.C., she illumined one of Gandhi's hypes: "Gandhi gave us principles for behaving and living that not only enable us to improve ourselves, but also to improve our societies." In support, she endorsed what is purported to be Gandhi's saying, "Violence springs from seven root causes, or 'blunders.'" She listed them as:

- Wealth without work
- Pleasure without conscience

- Knowledge without character
- Commerce without morality
- Science without humanity
- Worship without sacrifice
- Politics without principles

In all likelihood, she mentioned the above quote in good faith, out of sheer ignorance. But by her action, she unknowingly imparted authenticity to a concept that cannot be validated as being Gandhi's.[4] A slightly different rendition of these "blunders" under the heading of "seven social sins," inscribed on a silk scroll, was presented to then President Bill Clinton on March 21, 2000, upon his official visit to India. Equally profound is a recent example of Gandhi image making in which he was exalted as a "secular humanist" and ranked high in the prestigious company of such stalwarts as Mark Twain, Thomas Jefferson, James Madison, Alexander Hamilton, Abraham Lincoln, Ralph Waldo Emerson, Henry David Thoreau, Bertrand Russell, and William McNeile Dixon.[5]

On December 26, 1999, *Time* magazine declared Albert Einstein its Person of the Century. Mahatma Gandhi was one of *Time*'s two runners-up, because he "symbolize[d] the ability of individuals to resist authority to secure civil rights and personal liberties." To see highly educated, supposedly rational-minded people in the West following Gandhi has often left me in an awkward predicament and forced me to pause to reassess my initial impressions of the Western world. I can easily understand the East harboring false heroes. But to see educated Westerners as the mirror of the East is simply not what I was prepared to face. Today, the West is just as vulnerable as the East. However, there is a difference: In much of the East, the environment is admittedly not conducive to critical thinking. The West has been more than benevolent in offering the best resources and educational facilities to those who choose them. What continues to irk me is the amount of Gandhi "propaganda material" that has flooded our libraries and bookstores. For an unsuspecting Westerner, the reading of Gandhi as he is portrayed on these shelves can bring about the intended result. That is understandable. This book is an attempt to close the gap between the popularized Gandhi and the historical Gandhi. This book will incite readers to be more openminded and to seek to validate the "truths" presented. My hope is that it will provoke honest, healthy, and open dialogue and foster more critical scrutiny about him. That is the least I would expect from the West. When the East decides to follow the West in its pursuit of intellectual analysis of our heroes, it will be a day of reckoning.

The genesis of this book dates back to January 24, 1998, when something unthinkable happened. On this Saturday evening, a large statue of Mohandas K. Gandhi was erected at the Martin Luther King Jr. National Historic Site, in Atlanta, Georgia. Andrew Young, former mayor of Atlanta, former U.S. Ambassador to the United Nations, and, above all, a close associate of Dr. King, unveiled the life-size statue. The government of India procured and paid for the statue, donated through the hands of a politically active United States–based Hindu group calling itself the National Federation of Indian-American Associations.

Now why do we need a statue of Gandhi at the Martin Luther King Jr. National Historic Site? At the King Center located at the site, there is already a large room dedicated to Gandhi. In addition, as visitors walk into its Freedom Hall, they encounter Gandhi sketches, one of which even shows Gandhi and Dr. King together. *The truth is, they never met each other.* In addition, the Atlanta-based Hindu propagandists regularly conduct "Gandhi sermons" celebrating Gandhi's birth and death anniversaries; these are often attended by a dignitary from the Indian embassy in Washington, D.C. And now, thanks to them, we have a huge Gandhi statue.

There is another catch. All the Gandhi memorabilia at the Martin Luther King Jr. National Historic Site is housed at the King Center—a private property owned by the King family. But this Gandhi statue stands on a public place, on the grounds of John Hope Elementary School of the Atlanta Board of Education. In 1996 the board granted an easement for a walkway to the National Park Service (NPS), only to be surprised later on with a permanent fixture—the Gandhi statue—on the easement tract. This was placed with the full knowledge and consent of senior NPS officials.[6] Months after the Gandhi statue was placed, I carried on discussions with these NPS officials, concentrating on the issue of black people and what the historical Gandhi did to them. As a result, there was a consensus that the factual information on Gandhi and the black people must be brought out for the public to study. Years of dedicated research on Gandhi convinced me that our hero was fundamentally a *racist*. In this book, I present the facts. The evidence presented here is not a matter of speculation or distorted interpretation. Much of the irrefutable evidence lay buried beneath a mountain of Gandhi's own writings—in his own words, which I have uncovered—comments that will be difficult to dispute once they are read. In this book you will read the evidence in its entirety. My primary intention is to untangle the web that Gandhi weaved—and his followers are still weaving—for many years. Only through a methodical probing can we expose Gandhi's campaign of deception: the lies, the propaganda, the misinformation, the half-truths, and the efforts to hide behind religion. Where Gandhi left off, his followers have picked up, and they continue their own sophisticated campaigns, both in India and abroad. This book should not be looked upon as another Gandhi biography. Rather, it should provide a standard by which to weigh the Gandhian literature for accuracy and objectivity. Also, this book, though narrowly focused, should stand as a guide alerting us to how thoroughly the Gandhi propagandists and others have succeeded in deceiving us.

To begin, we will take a close look at the Gandhi propaganda machine (part 1) and what it would like us to believe about Gandhi's participation in a 1906 war against blacks in South Africa. Then we will thoroughly analyze little-known historical documents (part 2) in which Gandhi himself put pen to paper concerning the 1906 conflict. Part 3 is provocative. It reassesses the very roots of *Satyagraha*—Gandhi's concept of nonviolent resistance—and its underlying association with racism. In part 4, we will confront the facts of Gandhi's racist practices before and after the Boer War. This section concludes with an overview of Gandhi's remaining time in South Africa. Beginning with part 5, we will explore Gandhi's activities during World War I, mainly in India, and thereafter the consequences of his 180-degree turn—becoming anti-British.

To gain a proper perspective on Gandhi, we must open our ears to what Dr. B. R. Ambedkar had to say concerning Gandhi's anti-Untouchable practices and the ugly subject of caste. This is in sharp contrast to the image of Gandhi projected to the world at large. This issue is addressed in part 6. We then will explore Gandhi's role in the murder of William Francis Doherty, a white American. Assessing the cover-ups and Gandhi's tactical racism against whites and his view of ethnic cleansing is no easy task, given the lack of readily available information. Part 7 should open the door for further investigative work on Gandhi. The final analysis in my conclusion chronologically integrates Gandhi's history of cover-ups, his tragic death, and the further consequences of his bitter legacy in the form of *nuclear Satyagraha*—the pronounced public policy currently in effect by the present-day Indian leaders.

Note: In this book I make extensive use of *The Collected Works of Mahatma Gandhi* (by Mohandas K. Gandhi, 100 vols. [Delhi: Government of India, Ministry of Information and Broadcasting, Publications Division, 1958–1994]). References are abbreviated CWMG and include volume, document, and page numbers (e.g., CWMG 5, #283, p. 379).

NOTES

1. The Constitution of India has labeled the Republic of India with another Hindu name, *Bharat*.

2. Richard Grenier, "The Gandhi Nobody Knows," *Commentary* 75, no. 3 (March 1983): 59–72.

3. "The Roots of Violence," *Time*, July 2, 1984, p. 36.

4. *The Gandhi Message* 29, no. 1 and 2 (1995): 5–10. Other references of note are:

    a. Betty Cannon and Sanford Krolick have described the seventh deadly sin as "science and technology without humanity"; *Gandhi in the Postmodern Age: Issues in War and Peace* (Golden: Colorado School of Mines Press, 1984), p. xviii.

    b. Arun Gandhi, Mahatma Gandhi's grandson, has added to the list "rights without responsibilities" as the eighth blunder of the world; *World without Violence: Can Gandhi's Vision Become Reality?* (New Delhi: New Age International, 1994), p. 15.

c. Swami Dwiroopanand described the second of the "Seven Great Sins and Sinners" as "Pleasure (Sex-Joy) without consciousness of duty"; *Mahatma Gandhi: Ambassador of God for Mankind in the 21st Century* (Ahmedabad, India: Adhyatma Vignan Prakashan, 1992), p. 117.

d. A highly specialized health care journal, *TMDiary: News Journal of the American Academy of Head, Neck and Facial Pain*, in its spring/summer 1995 issue published the seven blunders—and then suggested to the readers, "seems as if this great pacifist had one eye on the future" (p. 4).

e. *Awake!* a periodical by the Watchtower Bible and Tract Society of New York, published the seven blunders followed by an interesting paragraph:

> Maybe you could suggest a few more, but this list is certainly thought-provoking. The Bible's answer to these "blunders" is condensed into two commandments: "'You must love Jehovah your God with your whole heart and with your whole soul and with your whole mind.' This is the greatest and first commandment. The second, like it, is this, 'You must love your neighbor as yourself.' On these two commandments the whole Law hangs, and the Prophets."—Matthew 22:37–40. (January 8, 1997, p. 20)

f. Steven R. Covey, author of *Principle-Centered Leadership* (New York: Simon & Schuster, 1991), devoted an entire chapter to the "Seven Deadly Sins." In the last paragraph, he made a suggestion that is somewhat mind-boggling:

> The Seven Habits will help you avoid these Seven Deadly Sins. And if you don't buy into the Seven Habits, try the Ten Commandments. (p. 93)

g. It is not clear when and how Gandhi received these "seven deadly sins." Most likely, the source was some Christian contact. Perhaps the reader should consult another parallel article by Paul Jordan-Smith, who elaborated, "Early and medieval Christianity expressed the sevenfold division of vicious human inherencies as the Seven Deadly Sins, or the Seven Capital (or Cardinal, or Principal) Vices," *Parabola* 10, no. 4 (November 1985): 34.

5. Paul D. Simmons, ed., *Freedom of Conscience: A Baptist/Humanist Dialogue* (Amherst, N.Y.: Prometheus Books, 2000), p. 15.

6. In order to fully comprehend the extent of the National Park Service and its willingness to go beyond the dictates of the establishment of the Martin Luther King Jr. National Historical Site, Public Law 96-428, *U.S. Statutes at Large* 94, part 2 (1981), and to violate the agreement with the board, I recommend the readers to procure, under the Freedom of Information Act, the following documents: (1) the "Memorandum of Understanding" between the NPS and the Atlanta Board of Education (signed March 13, 1996) and (2) the "Walkway and Landscape Easement Agreement" between the NPS (identified as the United States on the document) and the board, June 5, 1996.

PART 1

THE GANDHI
PROPAGANDA MACHINE

The highest honour that my friends can do me is to enforce in their own lives the programme that I stand for or resist me to their utmost if they do not believe in it.

—Mahatma Gandhi
Young India, June 12, 1924

1

INTRODUCTION

I have titled part 1 of this book "The Gandhi Propaganda Machine" for many reasons. Some of these will become clearer as you read further into this book.
Today, the men and women who are involved in promoting Gandhi in the West
follow somewhat similar tactics of "active measures" that were once employed by
the former Soviet regime in furtherance of communist ideals. These followers of
Gandhi pursue a methodical propagation, using all the avenues at their disposal to
spread the name of Gandhi and the ideals he is purported to have cherished. The
relentless and repetitive nature of their "Gandhi witnessing" on the horizon accelerated further scrutiny on my part. It leaves no doubt that there is a machine under
way, supported by the government of India, to nourish, export, and propagate
Gandhi, especially in the West. The men and women involved in the propaganda
process, at present as well as in the past, are the ones whom I call "Gandhi propagandists." Some of them I have met, and many others I have conversed with on
the telephone and via e-mail. They parrot Gandhi's supernatural and other plau-
sible stories, and pass out the literature concocted to back up their claims. However, a few have confessed to me that they know next to nothing about Gandhi but
still like to participate in the witnessing because they feel it is the "right thing" for
them to do. These are the latest actors in the propaganda drive in a long series that
began to take shape in the very early 1920s. Today it is the old actors who were
once engaged in this momentous drive, though many of them are dead, who
deserve our attention. They were the "true champions" who dedicated their time
to writing books and other materials that helped to disseminate the Gandhi story
that we have come to accept as truth. Some of those important figures, through
their works, will be introduced here in the next few chapters.

Understandably, Gandhi is a more famous and respected figure today, more than fifty years after his assassination, than when he was alive. He is a favorite topic among the peace movements; he continues to be revered alongside Christ among many churchgoers—a hero of the freedom fighters and a background lamppost to the American civil rights movement. How do we account for this? Perhaps the answer is buried in a phenomenon not widely appreciated in the West: the Hindu propaganda machine. This may come as a surprise to many, but the Hindu propaganda machine is a real phenomenon and nobody knew the extent of this better than former British prime minister Winston Churchill. He considered Hindus a "foul race."[1] In 1945, while on board HMS *Orion* and after reading Beverley Nichols's *Verdict on India*,[2] he wrote to his wife, confessing:

> Meantime we are holding on to this vast Empire, from which we get nothing, amid the increasing criticism and abuse of the world and our own people and increasing hatred of the Indian population, who receive constant and *deadly propaganda* to which we make no reply. (my italics)[3]

Here is a leader of the British Empire (with India under its control) confessing his helplessness in the face of the deadly Hindu propaganda! There is no doubt that Winston Churchill is referring to the "Hindu propaganda" as opposed to a relatively more soothing expression, "Indian propaganda." Winston Churchill had an astonishing insight into the world of Hindus and modern Hinduism.

Let me add a few words on the background of the Hindu propaganda machine, a phenomenon that was created in a long, drawn-out process, largely a result of historical settings thrust upon Hindus by the colonial foreigners. As a result, generic Hinduism was compelled to interface with the "creation of British India," a piecemeal expansionist process lasting roughly two centuries; the Western educational system; Western technology; and, most important of all, buffeted by the various Christian missionary movements that flooded British India. The interrelationship between these historical factors, dynamic though they were, brought about the birth of *modern Hinduism*, whose main purpose was to reinterpret Hinduism using the jargon of the Bible believers and then to spread that new creed to the world, especially to the Christian West, using Christian missionary tactics and vocabulary. A number of Christian missionaries themselves, with the help of few senior British officials, helped in this process and were instrumental to bringing about *missionary Hinduism*, a subset of modern Hinduism, which, to its credit, employed and perfected propaganda and disinformation tactics to achieve its goals. By the late 1800s Hindu missionaries reached the Western countries, even though modern Hinduism had already landed in the West about one hundred years earlier. Modern Hinduism had its own line of prophets and the figure of Gandhi, who surfaced almost at the tail end of this incredible phenomenon. He benefited like no other prophet before him from the Western contacts. The Hindu institutions that were already in place propelled him to the political forefront, and he took full advantage. There, he further refined and organized institutions to spread the gospel of modern Hinduism in this long, evolutionary chain of events. With Gandhi as the leader of the Congress Party, there arose a number of breathtaking transformations, particularly the convergence of religious and political goals and their propagation under one roof. The rudimentary propaganda machinery continued to make headway and expanded both vertically and horizontally. British officials, including Winston Churchill, knew the gravity of this burgeoning machine, which often manifested itself in religious phraseology, but felt helpless to counter it. The circumstances after the Second World War pressed, and the British, before departing from the subcontinent in 1947, transferred all the organs of their modern state to the children of modern Hinduism under Gandhi's leadership. For the British, it was good riddance. But the transfer of power into Hindu elite hands accelerated the machine's maturation, since the sophisticated propaganda tools and the institutional infrastructures that the British left behind fell to the bosom of the modern Hindu state. The result, as observed over the last fifty years, is a phenomenal growth, both qualitatively and quantitatively, that has taken place to turn the Hindu propaganda machine into a force to be reckoned with.[4]

Today, the Gandhi propaganda machine is a vital component of the Hindu propaganda machine, run under the aegis of the government of India. This machine has perfected the art of deception, relentless repetition, and deliberate misuse of Gandhi's "holy" image to employ and exploit Hindus settled abroad as the instrument of Gandhi propaganda. There is also an active media inside and outside India that uses the gullible foreign press, who are too willing to participate in promoting this Hindu messiah figure. Modern Gandhi propaganda is an intricate two-stage process in which the impregnable apparatus (a stimulus finely calculated to open our hearts and minds to accept Gandhi willingly) has been designed to penetrate the intended audience's absorption screen, concentrating on building up positive images of post-British India by presenting wonderful, peaceful, "holy" Gandhi, hailed as the "father of the nation." By controlling our attitudes and aims, this apparatus, once successful, opens the door for its operational side to fetch positive results for bigger projects and synchronizes these two stages to facilitate the government of India's foreign-policy objectives. Moreover, India's promotion of Gandhi's image in the West is a strategic move to sell its cultural image. At a certain stage of the process, Gandhi in some ways loses his personhood and becomes a strategy. Just as the West uses the democratic medium to promote its consumerism, the Hindu imperialists deploy Gandhi and other necessary tools to alter the Western conscious about India and Hinduism.

Gandhi propaganda has been delivered quite effectively by ways of cultural exchanges, friendship societies promoting India, front groups, Gandhi exhibitions, Gandhi literature, Gandhi tourism, and films. The operational arm of the Gandhi propaganda machine aims at producing specific, action-oriented results. It is connected with specific issues, raises questions relating to those issues, recommends the answers, shows the way and the time of action, and guides the audience to seek refuge in Gandhi. For example, following school shootings in the United States, a number of Gandhi propagandists tried to seize the golden opportunity to deliver Gandhi "peace prescriptions." The unveiling of Gandhi statues and memorials, especially in the West, is by far the best example of successful actions. Another recent prize—the first of its kind—is the very ambitious Gandhi Institute for Reconciliation at Morehouse College in Atlanta, Georgia. Successful results are feasible only once the targeted audience becomes receptive to the believable story that is being promulgated. In the case of Gandhi, the reader will learn in this book how lengthy this process was, and in the end, how it was successful.

There is no doubt that the market is flooded with Gandhi literature. The magnitude of Gandhi reading material, even for a Gandhian scholar, is overwhelming. Because of its incredible bulk, the Gandhi literature has been collectively named *Gandhiana*. In 1955 Jagdish S. Sharma cataloged 3,349 entries published by and about Gandhi in ten European languages.[5] By his second edition in 1968, the number of entries had swelled to 3,671. In 1995 Ananda M. Pandiri compiled much of the Gandhian material published in English, listing references for 985 Gandhi biographies.[6] The number of articles published on Gandhi is mind-boggling, as are the number of speeches about him by pastors, politicians, academicians, journalists, and others. The Gandhi literature comes in many shapes, sizes, and formats: some designed for juveniles, some for intellectuals, and much for the innocent adult population. It is spread all over the world by Gandhi propagandists. I will concentrate here on only the literature and the films in order to explore biographies, especially those that are known to have left an impact on their audiences. Since I am investigating a particular Gandhi trait—racism—I will target my search on Gandhi's role toward the black people of South Africa, where he lived almost twenty-one years. It does make sense to scrutinize him as he is depicted in these important biographies with regard to the Zulu rebellion in 1906. I offer a fair selection of biographies and other important articles related to this period, ranging from the earliest ones in South Africa, Gandhi's autobiographical accounts, early biographies written in the West (considered to be the most famous), and those authored by reputable scholars. Given the incredible number of biographies available and the different publication times, it is easy to get confused while delving deep in the comprehension process. The solution to prevent such confusion and to aid understanding when reading the biographical materials laid out in chapters 2 through 7 is to juxtapose them in the timeline in the appendix. This will help the reader gain a better appreciation and comprehension of its historical settings and sequences.

For our discussion, the most important feature in the timeline—and the one often ignored—is the 1906 incident: "June–July: Gandhi participates in war against blacks." This incident is paramount for those of us who wish to understand Gandhi's core. Only once we have studied this can we move outward to untangle the rest of Gandhi's mystery. Unfortunately, what we know of Gandhi is either through the eyes of the apologists or through the scholars. Collectively, they took the information about the 1906 incident from the pages of Gandhi's autobiographical accounts penned in the mid-1920s, in this case a flawed method. We need to study Gandhi's behavior toward blacks before, during, and just after the 1906 incident. Much of this book is woven around studying this phase before we study Gandhi during 1908–1909 and other time periods, including his thirty-two years in India.

At this early stage of our analysis and investigation, let me make one point clear: It was the white minority government of Natal colony in southern Africa that declared war against blacks. Gandhi, like many others, participated in it. We are investigating his role. At no point here am I alleging that Gandhi exercised racism.

Another parallel point I must emphasize here is that the reading materials contained in chapters 2 through 8 are not intended in any fashion to prove that Gandhi was a racist. These chapters are absolutely necessary in that they provide a groundwork on which the reader will be able to walk with a grasp of the important Gandhi literature that was published well after the 1906 episode. Only by absorbing what is contained in the rest of part 1 will we begin to appreciate the gravity of the matter that deals with cover-up, deception, racism, and so forth. Then and only then will the racial drama begin to unfold, as detailed in part 2 and onward. However, in the rest of part 1, as we read, we will learn what the famous biographies tell about our man Gandhi, what "pressing factors" led him to participate in the 1906 war, and his leadership role in it.

NOTES

1. Martin Gilbert, *Winston S. Churchill* (Boston: Houghton Mifflin, 1986), p. 1232.
2. Beverley Nichols, *Verdict on India* (New York: Harcourt, Brace, 1944).
3. Gilbert, *Winston S. Churchill*, p. 1166.
4. I recognize that the above analysis is too brief a report of an otherwise huge project. I also realize that the phenomenon of "Hindu propaganda machine" may be new to the reader. This book is not the place to explore its background and other facets, and the grave consequences for the future if it is left to operate untouched, unanalyzed, and unhindered. Here are some references that I believe deliver some historical background information to expound upon the subject matter (other references throughout the book will also help) Swami Dharma Theertha, *History of Hindu Imperialism* (Madras, India: Dalit Educational Literature Center, 1992); E. B. Havell, *The History of Aryan Rule in India: From the Earliest Times to the Death of Akbar* (New York: Frederick A. Stokes, 1918); Charles Wilkins, *The Bhagavat-Geeta or Dialogues of Kreeshna and Arjoon in Eighteen Legtures, with Notes* (London: C. Nourse, 1785); P. J. Marshall, ed., *The British Discovery of Hinduism in the Eighteenth Century* (London: Cambridge University Press, 1970); Katherine Mayo, *Mother India* (New York: Harcourt, Brace, 1927); Zuhair Kashmeri and

Brian McAndrew, *Soft Target: How the Indian Intelligence Service Penetrated Canada* (Toronto: James Lorimer, 1989); Wendell Thomas, *Hinduism Invades America* (New York: Beacon Press, 1930); Elizabeth A. Reed, *Hinduism in Europe and America* (New York: G. P. Putnam's Sons, 1914); Ram Narayan Kumar and Jean Ecalle, *Confronting the Hindu Sphinx: Dialogues on the Indian Tangle* (Delhi: Ajanta Publications, 1992); Chaman Lal, *Hindu America?* (Bombay: Bharatiya Vidya Bhavan, 1940); Patricia Kendall, *Come with Me to India* (New York: Charles Scribner's Sons, 1931); Swami Dayananda Saraswati, *Light of Truth, or An English Translation of the Satyarth Prakash* (1882); Lise McKean, *Divine Enterprise: Gurus and the Hindu Nationalist Movement* (Chicago: University of Chicago Press, 1996); R. C. Zaehner, *Our Savage God: The Perverse Use of Eastern Thought* (New York: Sneed and Ward, 1974); Nirad C. Chaudhuri, *The Continent of Circe: An Essay on the Peoples of India* (New York: Oxford University Press, 1966); Marlin Maddoux, *Free Speech or Propaganda? How the Media Distorts the Truth* (Nashville, Tenn.: Thomas Nelson, 1990); Neville Maxwell, *India's China War* (New York: Pantheon Books, 1970), and *China's "Aggression" of 1962* (Oxford: Court Place Books, 1999).

5. Jagdish S. Sharma, *Mahatma Gandhi: A Descriptive Bibliography* (Delhi: S. Chand, 1955).

6. Ananda M. Pandiri, *A Comprehensive Annotated Bibliography on Mahatma Gandhi*, Vol. 1 (Westport, Conn.: Greenwood Press, 1995).

2

Three biographies were written between 1893 and 1914, when Gandhi was in South Africa. I have added two more to the list because of their direct bearing on Gandhi's South African experience.

M. K. GANDHI: AN INDIAN PATRIOT IN SOUTH AFRICA
by Joseph J. Doke (1909)

This is the first Gandhi biography covering his life from October 2, 1869 to October 28, 1909. In this sense it is truly historic. Rev. Joseph J. Doke (1861–1913) came to Johannesburg in 1907 and worked there as Minister of the Central Baptist Church. As fate would have it, the ongoing Indian passive resistance movement and other events led him to meet Gandhi in person. Further events set the stage for Rev. Doke to write the biography, as explained by Bishop James K. Mathews in his dissertation at Columbia University:

> He was really "tricked" into allowing this to be done. Mr. Doke came to his office one day in about 1908, asking Gandhi if he were ready to be a martyr. The ready reply was, "I am nothing. I am willing to die at any time or to do anything for the cause." The "martyrdom" consisted in allowing the biography to be written, for the minister felt that it would help the cause of the Indians for their leader to be known in England.[1]

Keep in mind that no written or oral biographical information on Gandhi existed before this book was written. It was the first-ever biography of Gandhi, who largely dictated the account himself. Then he took the manuscript with him on his way to London for the second deputation, as part of his ongoing *Satyagraha* campaigns, in June 1909. He somehow convinced Lord Ampthill (senior British official as former governor of Madras and governor general of India, who had Indian sympathies) to write the introduction, and by October 1909 Nasarwanji M. Cooper, editor of *Indian Chronicle*, published the book. While in London, Gandhi did his best to extract mileage out of this biography, and he brought back with him about 700 copies for distribution. Of these, 24 copies were sent to Dr. P. J. Mehta in Rangoon, Burma; 250 copies to the manager of G. A. Natesan & Company in Madras, India; and another 250 copies to the International Printing Press in Durban, Natal, South Africa. He mailed one copy to Leo Tolstoy in Russia, emphasizing the uniqueness of his *Satyagraha* struggle depicted in the book. Remember, this is the first book that explained Gandhi's historical participation in the 1906 war incident, incidentally the same episode that we are studying:

In 1906, just before the Asiatic Law Amendment Ordinance was passed by the Provisional Government, the Zulu Rebellion began, and an offer was made by the Natal Indian Congress, at Mr. Gandhi's suggestion, to raise a Stretcher-bearer Corps for service with the troops, as had been done in the late Boer War. . . .

In June, owing to the uncertainty of the political situation, Mr. Gandhi broke up his home, and took his wife and family to Natal. Somewhat to his surprise, on reaching Durban, he found that the offer of a Bearer Corps had been accepted, and the men were waiting for him to take command. The Corps numbered twenty free Indians. Mr. Gandhi was offered the rank of Sergeant-Major, with three Sergeants and one Corporal under him.

With his usual wholeheartedness, he threw himself into the work, and during the month that followed, he and his men were present at nearly all the engagements. The supposed work of the Corps was to carry the wounded; but early in the campaign, other duties were pressed upon them.

Dr. Savage, who was in charge of the ambulance, asked if they objected to enlarge the scope of their work. When they replied that they were willing to do all they could, he placed the sanitation of the camp in their hands, and employed them as nurses to those Zulus who had been lashed.

Mr. Gandhi speaks with great reserve of this experience. What he saw he will never divulge. I imagine it was not always creditable to British humanity. As a man of peace, hating the very thought of war, it was almost intolerable for him to be so closely in touch with this expedition. At times, he doubted whether his position was right. No one besides his men, however, was prepared to do the work, and sheer pity for the sufferers forbade them to relinquish it. Not infrequently, the condition of the lashed men, who were placed in their charge, was appalling, the wounds filthy, their lives hanging in the balance. Dr. Savage won the unstinted praise of all. To the native patients he was invariably humane. But among the Europeans, apparently, he was the exception. So these Indians toiled at their irksome tasks day after day, cleansing wounds, binding up rents which the lash had made, carrying the helpless men behind the cavalry, up and down the hills for twenty and twenty-five miles at a stretch, or attending to the sanitation of the camp.

It was a month of hard, self-sacrificing toil. Nor was it a light thing for these Indians to do this work. They were members of a sensitive and cultured race, with elements of an ancient civilisation going to make up their characters—men from whose fathers the world has received portions of its finest literature, and examples of its greatest thought. It was no trifle for such men to become voluntary nurses to men not yet emerged from the most degraded state.[2]

M. K. GANDHI: A SKETCH OF HIS LIFE AND WORK
by Henry S. L. Polak (1910)

This is the second Gandhi biography, authored by a very close disciple who happened to be with Gandhi in South Africa during the war period. It is believed that this book was written at the request of the publisher G. A. Natesan & Company. On close inspection it is apparent that much of the information originated from the first biography, with one exception. Mr. Polak continued to update the Gandhi story with the latest editions. This book at one point changed its title to *Mahatma Gandhi: The Man and His Mission*. More editions were published; the eighth edition (1930) carried the narrative of the 1906 incident under the heading "Leading a Stretcher-Bearer Corps":

In 1906, a native rebellion broke out in Natal due to many causes, but realising that bloodshed was imminent and that hospital work would necessarily ensue therefrom, Mr. Gandhi offered, on behalf of the Natal Indians, a Stretcher-Bearer Corps, which, after some delay, was accepted. Meanwhile, he had sent his family in Phoenix, where he thought it was most proper that they should live, rather than in the dirt, noise, and restlessness of the town. He himself volunteered to lead the Corps, which was on active service for a month, being mentioned in despatches and publicly congratulated and thanked by the Governor for the valuable services rendered. Each member of the Corps has had awarded to him the medal especially struck for the occasion, and as an indication of the manner in which the Transvaal Government appreciated the work so selflessly performed by Mr. Gandhi and his Corps, it may be noted that, together with at least three other members of the Corps, as well as some who belonged to or helped to fit out the old Ambulance Corps, he was flung into gaol, to associate with criminals of the lowest type.

The work of the Corps was, besides that of carrying stretchers and marching on foot behind mounted infantry, through dense bush, sometimes thirty miles a day, in the midst of a savage enemy's country unarmed and unprotected, to perform the task of hospital assistants and to nurse the wounded natives, who had been callously shot down by the colonial troopers, or had been cruelly lashed by military command. Mr. Gandhi does not like to speak his mind about what he saw or learnt on this occasion. But many times he must have had searchings of conscience as to the propriety of his allying himself, even in that merciful capacity, with those capable of such acts of revolting and inexcusable brutality. However, it is well to know that nearly all his solicitude was exercised on behalf of aboriginal native patients, and one saw the Dewan's son ministering to the needs and allaying the sufferings of some of the most undeveloped types of humanity, whose odour, habits and surroundings must have been extremely repugnant to a man of refined tastes—though Mr. Gandhi himself will not admit this.[3]

MAHATMA GANDHI
by Henry S. L. Polak, H. N. Brailsford,
and Lord Pethick-Lawrence (1949)

After Gandhi's assassination in 1948, a new biography surfaced. In this book, Mr. Polak wrote of Gandhi's life in South Africa. With respect to 1906 incident, he wrote:

> Early in 1906 came the news of the Zulu Rebellion. Regarding himself still as a Natal citizen, with duties to the State, he immediately wrote to the Governor, offering to form a volunteer Indian stretcher-bearer company for service with the Natal forces. The offer was promptly accepted and Gandhi was appointed leader of the new unit, with the honorary rank of sergeant-major. The Indian company undertook the task of nursing the wounded Zulus—rebels and loyalists alike—back to health. In addition, Gandhi acted as compounder and dispenser to the white soldiers. On several occasions the Indian stretcher-bearers had to march forty miles a day to the nearest camp, often through hilly and sparsely populated country. Among the Natal commanding officers were some who had bitterly opposed Gandhi on his return from India ten years earlier. They were surprised at his devotion to this new task, and called upon him to thank him. The campaign was of short duration, and the stretcher-bearer company was soon discharged, with a letter of thanks for its services from the Governor.[4]

M. K. GANDHI AND THE
SOUTH AFRICAN INDIAN PROBLEM
by P. J. Mehta (1912?)

Gandhi knew P. J. Mehta from his days in London, India, and South Africa. Later on, Mehta settled in Rangoon, Burma—precisely the same place to which Gandhi had mailed 24 copies of Doke's text. Dr. Mehta wrote his own dissertation (as he called it, rather than a biography) based upon Rev. Doke's work. In India, G. A. Natesan & Company, which earlier received 250 copies of Doke's biography, published Mehta's book. This publisher also mounted a propaganda blitz to spread Gandhi's good name. Oddly, Mehta's dissertation treats the 1906 Zulu War incident as if it never took place. As it turned out, Mehta's account was nothing more than a service to promote Doke's narrative.[5]

MR. GANDHI: THE MAN
by Millie G. Polak (1931)

Millie Polak, who would later be the wife of Henry S. L. Polak, met Gandhi upon her arrival in Johannesburg, South Africa in December 1905. Her account of Gandhi is not hagiographic at all, but is rather a frank, honest, candid portrayal. She is unique among Gandhi's associates in that she never let Gandhi trample over her independent thinking. Based upon the Polaks' visit to India in 1917–18, Mrs. Polak provided the best narrative available on record analyzing Gandhi's psychologically impaired health during his war promotion endeavor of World War I. However, with respect to the 1906 incident, Mrs. Polak writes:

> After a very few weeks of my stay at Phoenix the Natal Native rebellion broke out and a great deal of unrest was felt by us all. . . . Mr. Gandhi made an offer to the Government to take a stretcher-bearer company to the scene of action, and though the offer was not accepted at the time, the knowledge that at any moment he might be called away added to the feeling of unrest in the community. . . .
>
> Soon after we left Phoenix, Mr. Gandhi's offer of a stretcher-bearer company was accepted, and he left for the front with a small contingent of his countrymen that he had himself collected together and whom he had instructed in their duties. Mrs. Gandhi was naturally rather worried at this new step in her husband's life. But he was not away long. The rebellion was soon over, and Mr. Gandhi returned to Phoenix, but not to stay.[6]

* * *

It is evident from the above biographies (except Mrs. Polak's account) that from the oldest sources of biographical materials available, it is Gandhi himself telling us his war story while hiding behind other names. I had high expectations from Mr. Polak, a close lieutenant of Gandhi and historically located closest to Gandhi's war efforts, to provide us an independent, in-depth, and honest account of Gandhi's role in the war. Unfortunately, he provided no new material. In the earliest edition authored by Polak in 1910, he relied almost exclusively on Doke's biography, which remained the standard story line in all his subsequent editions until 1943. In the 1949 edition he discarded the old story line and switched to a new Gandhi story line, disseminated under the cover of Gandhi's autobiography (detailed in the next chapter). Millie Polak failed to mention her husband's 1910 book in all of her writings. In fact, nowhere in his later writings does Mr. Polak mention his 1910 biography or its subsequent ten editions. This is odd. Is it possible that he never wrote it and perhaps never even knew of its existence? If so, who wrote it, and why? If someone else authored it, why was Mr. Polak's name used? Did it serve some useful purpose?

NOTES

1. James K. Mathews, *The Matchless Weapon: Satyagraha* (Bombay: Bharatiya Vidya Bhavan, 1989), p. 12.

2. Joseph J. Doke, *M. K. Gandhi: An Indian Patriot in South Africa* (London: Indian Chronicle, 1909), chap. 17.

3. Henry S. L. Polak, *M. K. Gandhi: A Sketch of His Life and Work* (Madras: G. A. Natesan & Company, 1910). Subsequent editions after 1922 were published under the title *Mahatma Gandhi: The Man and His Mission*. The narrative quoted is taken from the eighth edition (1930), pp. 15–16. The title in question is not to be confused with another somewhat similar biographical title, *Mohandas Karamchand Gandhi: A Sketch of His Life and Career*. This biography, written by an unidentifiable person, was not published independently, but as part of another book titled *Mahatma Gandhi: His Life, Writings, and Speeches* (India: Ganesh & Company, 1917–1923).

4. Henry S. L. Polak, H. N. Brailsford, and Lord Pethick-Lawrence, *Mahatma Gandhi* (London: Odhams Press, 1949), p. 51.

5. P. J. Mehta, *M. K. Gandhi and the South African Indian Problem* (Madras: G. A. Natesan & Company, [1912]).

6. Millie G. Polak, *Mr. Gandhi: The Man* (London: George Allen & Unwin, 1931), chap. 6.

3

GANDHI'S AUTOBIOGRAPHICAL WRITINGS

SATYAGRAHA IN SOUTH AFRICA

Convicted of sedition (for inciting crowds against the government) in 1922 and sentenced to six years in prison, Gandhi actually served only two years at Yeravda Central Jail. There, in 1923, he commenced writing a book, dictating to another inmate in his native tongue. By November 22, 1925, the newspaper *Navajivan* completed the serial publication of this work, better known as *Satyagraha in South Africa*. The English translation appeared in 1928, though it was never published serially or published in the United States during this time period. Chapter 11 of this book, titled "The Reward of Gentleness—The Black Act," must be reproduced here at length to show what Gandhi himself would like us to believe about what happened in the war against blacks in 1906:

> The Zulu "rebellion" broke out in Natal just while attempts were thus being made to impose further disabilities upon Indians in the Transvaal. I doubted then and doubt even now if the outbreak could be described as a rebellion, but it has always been thus described in Natal. Now as in the Boer War, many European residents of Natal joined the army as volunteers. As I too was considered a resident of Natal, I thought I must do my bit in the war. With the community's permission, therefore, I made an offer to the Government to raise a Stretcher-bearer Corps for service with the troops. The offer was accepted. I therefore broke up my Johannesburg home and sent my family to Phoenix in Natal where my co-workers had settled and from where *Indian Opinion* was published. I did not close the office as I knew I would not be away for long.
>
> I joined the army with a small corps of twenty or twenty-five men. Most of the provinces of India were represented even on this small body of men.

35

The corps was on active service for a month. I have always been thankful to God for the work which then fell to our lot. We found that the wounded Zulus would have been left uncared for, unless we had attended to them. No European would help to dress their wounds. Dr Savage, who was in charge of the ambulance, was himself a very humane person. It was no part of our duty to nurse the wounded after we had taken them to the hospital. But we had joined the war with a desire to do all we could, no matter whether it did or did not fall within the scope of our work. The good Doctor told us that he could not induce Europeans to nurse the Zulus, that it was beyond his power to compel them and that he would feel obliged if we undertook this mission of mercy. We were only too glad to do this. We had to cleanse the wounds of several Zulus which had not been attended to for as many as five or six days and were therefore stinking horribly. We liked the work. The Zulus could not talk to us, but from their gestures and the expression of their eyes they seemed to feel as if God had sent us to their succour.

The work for which we had enlisted was fairly heavy, for sometimes during the month we had to perform a march of as many as forty miles a day.

The Corps was disbanded in a month. Its work was mentioned in dispatches. Each member of the Corps was awarded the medal especially struck for the occasion. The Governor wrote a letter of thanks. The three sergeants of the Corps were Gujaratis, Shris Umiashankar Manchharam Shelat, Surendra Bapubhai Medh, and Harishankar Ishvar Joshi. All the three had fine physique and worked very hard. I cannot just now recall the names of the other Indians, but I well remember that one of these was a Pathan, who used to express his astonishment on finding us carrying as large a load as, and marching abreast of, himself.

While I was working with the Corps, two ideas which had long been floating in my mind became firmly fixed. First, an aspirant after a life exclusively devoted to service must lead a life of celibacy. Secondly, he must accept poverty as a constant companion through life. He may not take up any occupation which would prevent him or make him shrink from undertaking the lowliest of duties or largest risks.[1]

AN AUTOBIOGRAPHY, OR THE STORY OF MY EXPERIMENTS WITH TRUTH

Gandhi's autobiography has another strange facet. He himself tells us in the introduction:

[It] is not my purpose to attempt a real autobiography. I simply want to tell the story of my numerous experiments with truth, . . . as my life consists of nothing but those experiments. . . . But I should certainly like to narrate my experiments in the spiritual field which are known only to myself, and from which I have derived such power as I possess for working in the political field.[2]

Though the "vision" originated somewhat earlier, the roots of the idea to write an autobiography came while he was in prison, and he continued to work on it after his release. He wrote weekly narratives in his native Gujarati language, which were then published in weekly installments in Gandhi's paper, *Navajivan*, from November 29, 1925, to February 3, 1929. A carefully revised English translation (done by his close disciples Mahadev Desai, Pyarelal Nayar, and Miss Slade) appeared later, simultaneously, in *Indian Opinion* in South Africa and *Young India* in India beginning on December 3, 1925. Four months later, *Unity* in the United States began to serially publish the "autobiography" for 135 weeks, beginning April 5, 1926. Gandhi himself was an active participant in decisions, making sure that his weekly installments received widespread publicity. It is no accident that his autobiography received instant exposure almost all over the world. In 1927 and 1929, Macmillan published the autobiography in two volumes. The second edition, published in 1940, came out in one big volume. This book has been translated into numerous languages, including Hindi, Kannada, Malayalam, Marathi, Oriya, Punjabi, Tamil, Telugu, Urdu, Sanskrit, Spanish, Portuguese, French, German, Polish, Russian, Swedish, Arabic, Turkish, Serbocroat languages, Japanese, Korean, Nepalese, Tibetan, and Swahili. The autobiography, though it covers Gandhi's life only until December 1920, is definitely the most widely read of his works. And, of course, it is the most quoted in the literature.

Concerning the 1906 incident, this is what Gandhi himself wrote in a chapter titled "The Zulu 'Rebellion'":

Even after I thought I had settled down in Johannesburg, there was to be no settled life for me. Just when I felt that I should be breathing in peace, an unexpected event happened. The papers brought the news of the outbreak of the Zulu "rebellion" in Natal. I bore no grudge against the Zulus, they had harmed no Indian. I had doubts about the "rebellion" itself. But I then believed that the British Empire existed for the welfare of the world. A genuine sense of loyalty prevented me from even wishing ill to the Empire. The rightness or otherwise of the "rebellion" was therefore not likely to affect my decision. Natal had a Volunteer Defence Force, and it was open to it to recruit more men. I read that this force had already been mobilized to quell the "rebellion."

I considered myself a citizen of Natal, being intimately connected with it. So I wrote to the Governor, expressing my readiness, if necessary, to form an Indian Ambulance Corps. He replied immediately accepting the offer.

I had not expected such prompt acceptance. Fortunately I had made all the necessary arrangements even before writing the letter. If my offer was accepted, I had decided to break up the Johannesburg home. Polak was to have a smaller house, and my wife was to go and settle at Phoenix. I had her full consent to this decision. I do not remember her having ever stood in my way in matters like this. As soon, therefore, as I got the reply from the Governor, I gave the landlord the usual month's notice of vacating the house, sent some of the things to Phoenix and left some with Polak.

I went to Durban and appealed for men. A big contingent was not necessary. We were a party of twenty-four, of whom, besides me, four were Gujaratis. The rest were ex-indentured men from South India, excepting one who was a free Pathan.

In order to give me a status and to facilitate work, as also in accordance with the existing convention, the Chief Medical Officer appointed me to the temporary rank of Sergeant Major and three men selected by me to the rank of sergeants and one to that of corporal. We also received our uniforms from the Government. Our Corps was on active service for nearly six weeks. On reaching the scene of the "rebellion," I saw that there was nothing there to justify the name of "rebellion." There was no resistance that one could see. The reason why the disturbance had been magnified into a rebellion was that a Zulu chief had advised non-payment of a new tax imposed on his people, and had assailed a sergeant who had gone to collect the tax. At any rate my heart was with the Zulus, and I was delighted, on reaching headquarters, to hear that our main work was to be the nursing of the wounded Zulus. The Medical Officer in charge welcomed us. He said the white people were not willing nurses for the wounded Zulus, that their wounds were festering, and that he was at his wits' end. He hailed our arrival as a godsend for those innocent people, and he equipped us with bandages, disinfectants, etc., and took us to the improvised hospital. The Zulus were delighted to see us. The white soldiers used to peep through the railings that separated us from them and tried to dissuade us from attending to the wounds. And as we would not heed them, they became enraged and poured unspeakable abuse on the Zulus.

Gradually I came into close touch with these soldiers, and they ceased to interfere. Among the commanding officers were Col. Sparks and Col. Wylie, who had bitterly opposed me in 1896. They were surprised at my attitude and specially called and thanked me. They introduced me to General Mackenzie. Let not the reader think that these were professional soldiers. Col. Wylie was a well-known Durban lawyer. Col. Sparks was well known as the owner of a butcher's shop in Durban. General Mackenzie was a noted Natal farmer. All these gentlemen were volunteers, and as such had received military training and experience.

The wounded in our charge were not wounded in battle. A section of them had been taken prisoners as suspects. The General had sentenced them to be flogged. The flogging had caused severe sores. These, being unattended to, were festering. The others were Zulu friendlies. Although these had badges given them to distinguish them from the "enemy," they had been shot at by the soldiers by mistake.

Besides this work I had to compound and dispense prescriptions for the white soldiers. This was easy enough for me as I had received a year's training in Dr. Booth's little hospital. This work brought me in close contact with many Europeans.

We were attached to a swift-moving column. It had orders to march wherever danger was reported. It was for the most part mounted infantry. As soon as our camp was moved, we had to follow on foot with our stretchers on our shoulders. Twice or thrice we had to march forty miles a day. But wherever we went,

I am thankful that we had God's good work to do, having to carry to the camp on our stretchers those Zulu friendlies who had been inadvertently wounded, and to attend upon them as nurses.[3]

During the early twentieth century, when Gandhi himself was involved in two wars, a consideration of possible psychological side effects from these wars was not in vogue. Gandhi's war role was not stressful, at least compared with others under combat conditions. But by now he had had enough, and so, it seems, time had come for some soul searching. Therefore, in the very next chapter of his autobiography, Gandhi pours out his heart:

The Zulu "rebellion" was full of new experiences and gave me much food for thought. . . . To hear every morning reports of the soldiers' rifles exploding like crackers in innocent hamlets, and to live in the midst of them was a trial. But I swallowed the bitter draught, especially as the work of my Corps consisted only in nursing the wounded Zulus. . . . This work, therefore, eased my conscience. . . . I pondered over *brahmacharya* and its implications, and my convictions took deep root. . . . I too took the plunge—the vow to observe *brahmacharya* for life. . . . I saw that *brahmacharya*, which is so full of wonderful potency, is by no means an easy affair. . . . A true *brahmachari* will not even dream of satisfying the fleshly appetite. . . . This is the teaching of every great book of religion, and I am realizing the truth of it every moment of my striving after that perfect *brahmacharya*. . . . The very first change I made in my mode of life was to stop sharing the same bed with my wife or seeking privacy with her. Thus *brahmacharya*, which I had been observing willy-nilly since 1900, was sealed with a vow in the middle of 1906.[4]

In the West, we are accustomed to relying upon the autobiographies to provide us firsthand, reliable information. Unfortunately, with Gandhi, that's not easy. *Satyagraha in South Africa* must be addressed as an indispensable supplement to the *Autobiography*. Robert Payne describes the autobiography as an "erratic and disturbing work. . . . He [Gandhi] occupies the center of the stage, and has no gift for bringing any other characters to life. . . . In the autobiography he paints himself as the hero; in the second book *Satyagraha* is the heroine, and he is her chief companion-in-arms."[5] Although *Autobiography* was and still is hailed a great spiritual masterpiece, it was not without critics, Robert Payne being one of them. *Autobiography* shocked Millie G. Polak. She let it be known in the preface to her own book that she was somewhat hesitant to write something on Gandhi:

And in the discussions that resulted, some of the incidents related in the following pages have been recalled by me. "Why don't you write that down?" was the frequent comment. But I had always refused to do so. The sacredness of the intimate talk of friendship would, it seemed to me, have been violated by publication. Then came the *Autobiography*, and, with something of a shock, I realized that Mr. Gandhi himself had not hesitated to strip the veil off everything that he had thought or experienced, and that I need not have been hypersensitive about recording my own recollections of those days.[6]

Louis Fischer, the author of Gandhi's most famous biography, considered *Autobiography* "indispensable" but also "inadequate." He is on the record as stating his reservations that the twenty-one crucial years Gandhi spent in South Africa are "covered so poorly as to be unintelligible without an earlier book by Gandhi, *Satyagraha in South Africa*." "The autobiography," Fischer wrote, "was written and published to preach morals to the Mahatma's followers, and it suffers from all the disadvantages of that approach."[7]

The renowned psychoanalyst Erik H. Erikson, in his *Gandhi's Truth: On the Origins of Militant Nonviolence*, devoted his talents to psychoanalyzing Gandhi using his own writings. Somewhat bewildered with *Autobiography* and *Satyagraha in South Africa*, Erikson wrote:

> Neither of the two books alone gives an adequate account. Furthermore, one feels that in spite of all the Mahatma's candor, some connecting themes are missing which fit neither into the style of the *Experiments* nor into that of *Satyagraha*. These themes, were they to be clarified, might more directly connect the two decisions of avoiding both sexual intercourse and killing. For it would seem that the experience of witnessing the outrages perpetrated on black bodies by white he-men aroused in Gandhi both a deeper identification with the maltreated, and a stronger aversion against all male sadism—including such sexual sadism as he had probably felt from childhood on to be part of all exploitation of women by men.[8]

Throughout the book it seems that Erikson is out to grab something important. But he can't get his hands on it, even after performing a feat no other Gandhian scholar had attempted before: "For those who would wish to study this whole period in Gandhi's life more comprehensively than is possible here, it would be necessary to compare *The Story of My Experiments with Truth* with *Satyagraha in South Africa*, to see what the Mahatma selected for one or the other publication and in what sequence."[9] Erikson compared Gandhi's own two biographical accounts and, although he couldn't get the missing link (or links) he was looking for, the impression among those of us who evaluate Gandhi's literature critically is that he compared the wrong two documents. There was a third document—Gandhi's letters—available, which he should have delved into. I plan to pick up right where Erikson left off. In her *Gandhi: The South African Experience*, Maureen Swan bluntly stated that both *Satyagraha in South Africa* and *Autobiography* were "historically inaccurate."[10]

If anyone lashed out at *Autobiography* with no holds barred and freely expressed his disappointment, it was V. S. Naipaul. He poured out his feelings in a beautifully written book, *India: A Wounded Civilization*:

Gandhi, maturing in alien societies, defensively withdrawing into the self, sinking into his hard-won convictions and vows, becoming more obstinate with age, and always (from his autobiography) seemingly headed for lunacy, is constantly rescued and redefined by external events, the goadings of other civilizations: the terror and strangeness of England, the need to pass the law examinations, the racial pressures of South Africa, British authoritarianism in India (made clear by his experience of the democratic ways of South Africa). . . .

It was in South Africa that he became the Mahatma, the great-souled, working through religion to political action as leader of the Indian community, and through political action back to religion. The adventure never ceased to be internal: so it comes out in the autobiography. And this explains the most remarkable omission in Gandhi's account of his twenty active years in South Africa: Africans.

Africans appear only fleetingly at a time of a "rebellion," when for six weeks Gandhi led an Indian ambulance unit and found himself looking after wounded Africans. He says his heart was with the Africans; he was distressed by the whippings and unnecessary shootings; it was a trial, he says, to have to live with the soldiers responsible. But the experience did not lead him to a political decision about Africans. He turned inward and, at the age of thirty-seven, did what he had been thinking about for six years: he took the Hindu vow of brahmacharya, the vow of lifelong sexual abstinence. And the logic was like this: to serve humanity, as he was then serving the Africans, it was necessary for him to deny himself "the pleasures of family life," to hold himself free in the spirit and the flesh. So the Africans vanish in Gandhi's heart-searchings; they are the motive of a vow, and thereafter disappear.[11]

Using Swan's analysis, I ask: Why would Gandhi use historically inaccurate facts to write his autobiography? Erikson suggests that they were meant to convey certain moral lessons to the readers. Swan blames it on memory lapse and the time factor, since they were written years after the events they describe. Only Naipaul is bold enough to diagnose Gandhi as "headed for lunacy." No doubt some will agree with him that in *Autobiography*, Gandhi is seemingly headed for lunacy. Even though Gandhi gives that appearance, in reality he was not. Although Gandhi himself stated that his autobiography is not a "real autobiography," Naipaul seems to have disregarded this fact. The correspondence between Gandhi and Rev. John Haynes Holmes in the United States regarding *Autobiography* reveals that Gandhi was astutely negotiating the business contract for his writings to be published in the United States.[12] He couldn't have been headed for lunacy. Instead of a real autobiography, Gandhi wrote something else. Investigating that "something else," if possible, would be the hallmark of investigative research on him. Gandhi knew well that he would not waste his time writing something for a number of years (more than three years, in this case) just to show his propensity for lunacy. In *Autobiography*, Gandhi took shelter behind much of the religious verbiage that has given message of "preach morals" among his followers, including Fischer, whose biography of Gandhi will be discussed in chapter 5. The Indian government official entourage, responsible for compiling his huge *Collected Works*, believed rather proudly that *Autobiography* may be regarded on par "as a modern contribution to the dialogue between Pilate and Jesus" (CWMG 39, p. vi) as depicted in the Gospel of Saint John (18:36–38). The religious hue and cry surrounding *Autobiography* is largely responsible for protecting Gandhi from further analysis. It will be demonstrated in part 5 that Gandhi's purpose in writing *Autobiography* was essentially to cover up his past activities, especially those he expounded in South Africa.

NOTES

1. Mohandas K. Gandhi, *Satyagraha in South Africa* (1928; reprint, Ahmedabad: Navajivan Publishing House, 1972), pp. 90–91.

2. Mohandas K. Gandhi, *An Autobiography, or The Story of My Experiments with Truth* (1927, 1929; reprint, Boston: Beacon Press, 1957), p. xii.

3. Ibid., pp. 313–15.

4. Ibid., pp. 315–18.

5. Robert Payne, *The Life and Death of Mahatma Gandhi* (New York: Konecky & Konecky, 1969), pp. 376–77.

6. Millie G. Polak, *Mr. Gandhi: The Man* (London: George Allen & Unwin, 1931), preface.

7. Louis Fischer, *The Life of Mahatma Gandhi* (New York: Harper & Brothers, 1950), p. 510.

8. Erik H. Erikson, *Gandhi's Truth: On the Origins of Militant Nonviolence* (New York: W. W. Norton, 1969), p. 194.

9. Ibid., pp. 192–93.

10. Maureen Swan, *Gandhi: The South African Experience* (Johannesburg: Raven Press, 1986), preface.

11. V. S. Naipaul, *India: A Wounded Civilization* (New York: Vintage Books, 1978), pp. 104–105, 117.

12. S. P. K. Gupta, *Apostle John and Gandhi: The Mission of John Haynes Holmes for Mahatma Gandhi in the United States of America* (Ahmedabad: Navajivan Publishing House, 1988); check the Gandhi-Holmes correspondence section. The *New York Times* reported on January 31, 1948, a day after Gandhi's assassination, that sixteen years earlier (in 1932) Gandhi had signed a contract worth $200,000 with Columbia Phonograph Company for recording a record titled *Justification of God.*

4

In 1922 Edmund Candler astutely observed the budding American perception of Gandhi:

> Probably there is no figure in contemporary history who means so many different things to so many different people. To the incurious Westerners, the name of Gandhi calls up the picture of a saint, or a charlatan, an ascetic, fanatic, or a freak. If he reads many newspapers, the Mahatma will appear in turn as patriot, martyr, high-souled idealist, and arch traitor; evangelist, pacific quietist, and truculent tub-thumper and revolutionist, subverter of empires and founder of creeds, a man of tortuous wiles and stratagems, or, to use his own phrase, "a single-minded seeker after truth"; generally, in the eyes of the tolerant who are without prejudice, a well-meaning but misguided politician. Certainly a complex figure. Probably very few, even of the Anglo-Indian community on whom his personality impinges directly, a very substantial incubus, have made up their minds which of these things he is.[1]

The early 1920s also gave birth to a breed of "Gandhi apologists" who, just like the Christian apologists, were numerous and diverse. They still are. They come from India as well as from the West, consisting of educated Hindus living abroad or Christians of the liberal missionary type. The aim of Gandhi apologists was to present Gandhi to the world disguised in religious clothing. In other words, they used religious propaganda to promote Gandhi. Religious appeal was their ticket, and they did a wonderful job. In India they tenaciously held a relentless propaganda drive, using Hindu vocabulary, depicting him as an incarnation of a particularly Hindu, Vishnu variety of the deity. Outside India, his liberal Christian apologists made use of their respective Christian organizations to depict Gandhi as either a Christian saint or the Jesus Christ of the twentieth century. These persons utilized their pulpits to deliver sermons to their congregations and used their Christian printing presses to promote Gandhi. In this way, Gandhi's name began to take hold on churchgoing Westerners. Through these propagandists' years of hard labor, we in the post–World War II generation received the message often camouflaged in an existing, changeable political set of circumstances. Strange as it may sound, various diverse groups imbibed Gandhi to suit their own narrowly focused milieu, thereby renovating him with an attractive appeal for all, molding him to adapt to different religious and non-religious ideals. Religionists love him for simply advancing religion. Spiritualists adore him for exuding the highest spiritual values. Freedom fighters emulate him for providing a technique and commitment for freedom. Civil rights advocates look to Gandhi as a role model. Politicians mention him adoringly for being a politician par excellence. Economists delve into him to learn how to implement economic ideas of national simplicity and frugality. The list goes on and on. In almost all instances, his image today is infinitely more exalted than it was in the early 1920s.

Gandhi himself was well aware of what his apologists were doing, and he took full advantage of the situation. In time, his religious image became so entrenched that it could never be dislodged. In India he became an avatar and prophet of modern Hinduism. Outside India, his Christian followers portrayed him in the Christ image. But Gandhi espoused a different and bigger role for himself—he had set his eyes on being a prophet of *Oceanic Hinduism*, in which all religions would merge, as he wished, in their mother source: Hinduism. In a speech on December 4, 1947, Gandhi said:

> It cannot be said that Sikhism, Hinduism, Buddhism, and Jainism are separate religions. All these four faiths and their offshoots are one. *Hinduism is an ocean into which all the rivers run. It can absorb Islam and Christianity and all other religions and only then can it become the ocean. Otherwise it remains merely a stream along which large ships cannot ply.* (my italics)[2]

What follows is a brief look at what various Gandhi apologists, who spared no effort to turn the man into a Messiah figure, enumerate, with a focus on the 1906 incident.

MY GANDHI
by John Haynes Holmes (1953)

The one person who can be called the father of Gandhi apologists and the central force in turning Gandhi into a famous figure in the West is Rev. John H. Holmes (1897–1964). He was the pastor of the Community Church of New York, a Unitarian church. This New York minister promulgated Gandhi's image through his magazine, *Unity*, publishing not only Gandhi's autobiography but also accounts of him as if Gandhi was a de facto correspondent for *Unity*. In his sermon delivered in 1921 titled "Who Is the Greatest Man in the World Today?" the pastor described his unique experience of meeting Gandhi:

> I heard of him first in 1917, through an article by Professor Gilbert Murray in the *Hibbert Journal* [a British Unitarian paper]. I did not learn anything of him again until a few months ago, when there came to my desk a little paper-covered pamphlet containing extracts from his speeches and writings. This is meager information; but when I read it, I felt as did John Keats when he first read Chapman's translation of the Iliad—
>
>> Then felt I like some watcher of the skies
>> When a new planet swims into his ken;
>> Or like stout Cortez when with eagle eyes
>> He stared at the Pacific—and all his men
>> Looked at each other with a mild surmise—
>> Silent, upon a peak in Darien.[3]

During this sermon, he told his congregation about the 1906 incident with these words:

> In 1906, there was a native rebellion in Natal. Again the strike was suspended, while Gandhi raised and personally led a corps of stretcher-bearers, whose work was dangerous and painful. On this occasion he was publicly thanked by the Governor of Natal.[4]

There is no doubt that the pastor borrowed the above information (without paying attention to details) from the *Hibbert Journal*.

In *My Gandhi*, Holmes states that he read the *Hibbert Journal* in 1918 at the New York Public Library. He wrote prolifically on Gandhi. Some of his writings and sermons had titles such as, "Gandhi: The Modern Christ," "Mahatma Gandhi: The Greatest Man since Jesus Christ," "Mahatmaji: Reincarnation of Christ," and "Gandhi before Pilate: A Sermon on the Indian Revolution." Years later, after Gandhi's death, the pastor wrote *My Gandhi*, the opening of which begins with another spiritual sermon:

> In my extremity I turned to Gandhi, and he took me in his arms, and never let me go. Away across the globe he cared for me, and taught me, and reassured me. In London, in 1931, I met him and found him indeed my saint and seer. When I saw him in India, only a few weeks before his assassination, in 1947, he was as wonderful as ever. Had the Mahatma not come into my life, I must sooner or later have been lost. As it was, he saved me. He gave me a peace of mind and a serenity of soul which will be with me to the last. Even when he died, I gave way only for a time. Then the tears flowed with a passion of grief which there

was no controlling. But the Mahatma did not fail me. I called to him, and I am persuaded that he answered. My real life as a teacher began with Gandhi, and it ended with his end. I should have retired when he died, for all through these latter months, I have been but an echo of my true self. If I have been content to stay on till now, it is because I could the longer bear witness to Gandhi.[5]

Based upon *Autobiography* and Louis Fischer's account of Gandhi, Holmes recorded the following on the 1906 incident:

Thus, during the Boer War and the later Zulu rebellion, while ardently in sympathy with the natives, Gandhi organized neutral relief units and led them to the front, to bury the dead and minister to the wounded.[6]

It is no surprise that Holmes transformed "medic Gandhi" into a "chaplain Gandhi."

GANDHI THE APOSTLE: HIS TRIAL AND HIS MESSAGE
by Haridas T. Muzumdar (1923)

Haridas Muzumdar (1900–?) came to the United States in 1920 to pursue higher education and to "interpret India and Mahatma Gandhi to the American public." He wrote this Gandhi biography in 1921–22, with encouragement from others, most notably John H. Holmes. In 1923 Muzumdar published *Gandhi the Apostle: His Trial and His Message*, the first Gandhi biography published in the United States. So committed was Muzumdar that he helped establish the Universal Publishing Company in Chicago to publish the Gandhi materials. After finishing his higher education and the academic tenure at the University of Arkansas at Pine Bluff, the author never lost his love for Gandhi: He created a think tank named the Gandhi Institute of America in Little Rock, Arkansas. His book opens with a poem dedicated to Gandhi, taken from Chicago-based Unitarian magazine *Unity*, and authored by Benjamin C. Woodbury.

When shall there be again revealed a Saint,
A holy man, a Savior of his race,
When shall the Christ once more reveal His face?
Gautama left his bode without complaint,
Till weary, hungered, desolate and faint.
He sank beneath the bo-tree with his load,
As on the Path of solitude he stood;
And Jesus died to still the sinner's plaint.
Lives there a man as faithful to his vow?
Mahatma to a bonded race of men?

Aye, Gandhi seeks his nation's soul to free:
Unto the least, ye do it unto Me!
Hath Buddha found in peace Nirvana now;
Or doth a Christ walk on the earth again?[7]

Since Holmes wrote in April 1921 that "Mahatma Gandhi is the greatest man in the world today," Muzumdar dedicated his book to Holmes. About the questionable 1906 incident, he wrote:

> Of a similar nature are the services rendered by Mr. Gandhi to the government, when the Zulus rebelled against it. At his suggestion, the Natal Congress offered the services of a stretcher Bearer Corps, as in the late war. The corps consisted of twenty "free" Indians; Gandhi acted as Sergeant-Major, and was assisted by three Sergeants and one Corporal.
>
> The Zulus, struggling for justice and for right in their own land, came in for a severe lashing at the hands of the British troops. The supposed work of Gandhi's Corps was to carry the wounded but early in the campaign other duties were pressed upon them. It meant a month of hard, self-sacrificing toil, involving the most gruesome of tasks. "Mr. Gandhi speaks with great reserve of this experience. What he saw he will never divulge. I imagine it was not always creditable to British humanity. As a man of peace, hating the very thought of war, it was almost intolerable for him to be so closely in touch with this expedition. At times, he doubted whether his position was right. No one besides his men, however, was prepared to do the work, and sheer pity for the sufferers forbade them to relinquish it. Not infrequently, the condition of the lashed men, who were placed in their charge, was appalling, the wounds filthy, their lives hanging in the balance. So these Indians toiled at their irksome tasks day after day, cleansing wounds, binding up rents which the lash had made, carrying the helpless men behind the cavalry, up and down the hills for twenty and twenty-five miles at a stretch, or attending to the sanitation of the camp"—thus, the late Rev. Joseph J. Doke, Gandhi's biographer.[8]

The above account was taken from Doke's biography. However, the author failed to duplicate correctly word for word what was recorded in Doke's version.

MAHATMA GANDHI: THE MAN WHO BECAME ONE WITH THE UNIVERSAL BEING
by Romain Rolland (1924)

Romain Rolland (1866–1944) was well known in Europe for his novel *Jean Christophe* and received the Nobel Prize in Literature in 1915. Rolland wrote books on few other modern Hindu saints, so a book about the budding Mahatma Gandhi, which he authored before his works on other saints, should come as no surprise. After all, Rolland not only looked at Gandhi as a Hindu saint, but also as "another Christ." Initially, Gandhi came to Rolland's attention accidentally, when the Indian publisher S. Ganesan asked him for an introduction to an English edition of Gandhi's selected writings. After gathering data from his own acquaintances in India, Rolland began a new biography of Gandhi covering his life from birth to his incarceration in 1922. Written in French, it was soon translated into several European languages and had a wide circulation—this was virtually the first time Gandhi was presented to European readers. In 1924 this book made it to the United States. It opens with this stanza:

> He is the One Luminous, Creator of All, Mahatma,
> Always in the hearts of the people enshrined,
> Revealed through Love, Intuition, and Thought,
> Whoever knows Him, Immortal becomes. . . .

However, with respect to the 1906 incident, we learn very little:

> In 1908 the natives in Natal revolted. Gandhi organized and served at the head of a corps of *brancardiers*, and the Government of Natal tendered him public thanks.[9]

Here, *brancardiers* mean the stretcher bearers. However, the incident described was not in 1908 but in 1906.

THE MAHATMA AND THE WORLD
by Krishnalal Shridharani (1946)

Prior to his arrival in the United States in 1934, Krishnalal Shridharani (1911–1960) was a student at Gujarat Vidyapith (a type of Gandhi university) and, as he himself claimed, participated in Gandhi's historic Salt March to Dandi in 1930 intended to symbolically break the government's monopoly and tax on salt. In the United States, he established contacts with a few African Americans to bring Gandhi to them. Suffice to say, he had seen Gandhi from a unique setting. He became Gandhi's spokesman in the United States along with Muzumdar, Syud Hossain, and Anup Singh, who were promoting Gandhi in America. Before his biographical sketch of Gandhi, the author begins with a chapter called "Inspiration for a Portrait." The very first page makes it clear that in the author's mind the importance of Gandhi's underlying religious image equated him with the seventh reincarnation of Vishnu, Lord Rama:

> The Lord Supreme and Parvati I praise,
> The parents of all worlds, close-joined in one
> As word with sense, and pray for gift of speech
> With mighty meaning fraught. How else could I,

Weak-witted, dare to hymn the kingly race
Descended from the Sun—daring not less
Than one who ventures on a raft to cross
Some pathless sea? [10]

With respect to the 1906 incident, the author made no reference to it.

GANDHI: PORTRAYAL OF A FRIEND
by E. Stanley Jones
(Reprint of Mahatma Gandhi: An Interpretation; 1948)

The Christian literature proudly proclaims E. Stanley Jones to be the "greatest missionary since St. Paul." As expected from a Christian missionary, Jones tried to convert Gandhi to Christianity. Alas, he failed. He opted for second best—he presented Gandhi as a Christianized Hindu or, even better, as a Hinduized Christian. Nevertheless, from his writings, a case can be ascribed that Jones himself got converted to Gandhism: "I bow to Mahatma Gandhi, but I kneel at the feet of Christ and give him my full and final allegiance. . . . On the day that Mahatma Gandhi was killed, I arrived in Delhi just an hour and a quarter before the tragedy, . . . the greatest tragedy since the Son of God died on the cross. . . ."[11]

Jones wrote his book based upon his thirty years of "friendship" with Gandhi, and it never occurred to him that the book might one day have a decidedly unintended impact. A few years later, Jones told the editors of *Time* magazine:

> When I published my book *Mahatma Gandhi—An Interpretation*, I thought it a comparative failure. It didn't seem to do much. But when I saw Dr. Martin Luther King for the first time, he greeted me with this: "It was your book . . . which gave me my first inkling of the method and spirit of nonviolence. This is the method, I said to myself, to apply to the freedom of the Negro in America. I will use this method of nonviolence instead of the method of violence. So it was your book that started us on this path of matching soul force against physical force. We will match our capacity to suffer against the other man's capacity to inflict the suffering. And we will wear down opposition by goodwill. . . ."[12]

According to Eunice Jones Mathews, Jones's daughter: "Martin Luther King, Jr., told me he owed a debt to my father for his book on Mahatma Gandhi. He had read many books on Gandhi, read his writings, but it was that particular book of my father's that had triggered his decision to use the method of . . . nonviolence in his civil rights movement for his people."[13] Mrs. Mathews further recalled in November 1998 that she had met Dr. King in 1964 while standing in a reception line at Boston University during Dr. King's visit after he received the Nobel Peace Prize.

Although privy to Gandhi's autobiography, Jones failed to mention anything about the 1906 incident. However, on pages 91–94, the missionary reproduced

Gandhi's statement delivered in court during his trial of 1922, in which Gandhi mentioned in passing the 1906 incident, easy to miss even for a careful reader. In the missionary's mind, Gandhi's statement in court brought about some vivid memories of Jesus Christ—and that's what he intended to share in this book. Unless we reject Jones's and his daughter's statements as self-serving, we have no choice but to conclude that, based upon what has been reported, it is clear that Jones's book had a unique impact on Rev. Martin Luther King Jr. Yet this same book is conspicuously absent from the list of ten books that affected Dr. King's thinking the most![14]

THAT STRANGE LITTLE BROWN MAN GANDHI
by Frederick B. Fisher (1932)

Frederick B. Fisher (1882–1938), bishop of the Methodist Church in India, met Gandhi in 1917. Based upon his personal testimony with Gandhi, Fisher wrote:

> Gandhi knew war. I have heard from his lips the most graphic descriptions of the battlefields, troops, spoils, victories, and defeats. He had proved himself no coward. He refused from principle to carry arms, but he had carried a stretcher through the thick of the fighting during the Boer War when the Englishman was fighting the Boer. Also during the Zulu rebellion, when the white man was fighting the black, Gandhi often walked twenty to thirty miles a day under the blazing sun of Africa, carrying the wounded, patching up the destruction that the war had made. He knew the cold singing of bullets, the scream of the dying. He had received the Kaiser-i-Hind medal, and other honors from the British Government for his African services.[15]

Here is a rather very brief account taken from neither Doke's biography nor Gandhi's autobiography. What is written is directly from Gandhi's mouth as communicated to Fisher. Exactly when Gandhi told his "war stories" to the author is not known, but it is safe to assume that Gandhi narrated his story before he penned his autobiographical writings. However, as expected, Gandhi would not divulge his real historical past to anyone voluntarily (more on this in part 2).

MAHATMA GANDHI—HIS OWN STORY
Edited by C. F. Andrews (1930)

Charles F. Andrews (1871–1940), an Englishman, was an ordained priest. In 1914, after years of missionary work in India, on the advice of an elderly Indian leader, Gokhale, Andrews went to South Africa. On reaching Durban and upon seeing Gandhi, Andrews swiftly bent down and touched Gandhi's feet. That was their first meeting. A Christian missionary meeting a Hindu saint! Hindu saint won without uttering a single word! Others have looked at Andrews as a man with "somewhat eccentric views." By the late 1920s full-length books on Gandhi were coming on the market and becoming available to the West. Andrews was not going to be left behind. He edited three of them: *Mahatma Gandhi—His Own Story* is really Andrews's edition of Gandhi's *Autobiography*, an adaptation in the third person for the Western audience.[16] To understand Andrews's affinity toward Gandhi, one has to turn once again to Jesus Christ, as Andrews witnessed in South Africa:

> All that long day, I watched the behavior of the crowd and their attitude towards Mahatma, their leader. It was there for the first time that I could understand the secret of his amazing influence with his fellow countrymen and the reason for their devotion to him. I can only describe this briefly by saying that my thoughts went back to the Gospel story for an analogy. He was there, in the heart of that multitude that pressed upon him. They had come to him without anything to eat; and he was busy providing for their needs. An infinite tenderness and compassion shone from his eyes, while the mothers brought their little children to him, so that he might lay his hands upon them and bless them. . . . As I have often in memory looked back upon that scene and afterwards recalled many other pictures also of similar character I have been able from time to time to find the parallels I needed in history. . . .[17]

Andrews essentially repeated Gandhi's autobiographical version of the 1906 incident word for word, which is why I will not quote it here.

MAHATMA GANDHI: HIS LIFE, WORK, AND INFLUENCE
by Jashwant Rao Chitambar (1933)

Jashwant Rao Chitambar (1879–1940), a converted Indian Christian, was the first of his kind to attain the prestigious status of bishop within the Methodist church. True to his faith, he visited North America in 1932 and for the next six months he wholeheartedly devoted his time to introduce Gandhi to his spellbound audiences in fully packed churches, colleges, universities, and Rotary and Kiwanis clubs. His rationale was simple: By serving the *living* Gandhi, he was indeed serving his Christ. With respect to the 1906 incident:

> In 1906 the Zulus in Natal rebelled against the Natal government and again the *Satyagraha* movement was called off. Gandhi offered to organize an Indian ambulance corps and his offer was accepted by the Governor. A corps of twenty-four was formed and a hospital for the wounded was improvised. Thus the Indians, with Gandhi as their sergeant major, rendered invaluable service for six weeks at this time of need.[18]

Here the bishop blended the textual version as described by Romain Rolland with that of Gandhi's *Autobiography*, a feat singularly well executed in the Gandhian literature.

MAHATMA: LIFE OF
MOHANDAS KARAMCHAND GANDHI
by D. G. Tendulkar (1951)

D. G. Tendulkar dedicated several years researching and compiling Gandhi's biographical data in eight hefty volumes. His research included reviewing newspapers from more than fifty years, obtaining information from important people known to Gandhi, visiting numerous places associated with Gandhi, and even consulting Gandhi personally about several facts and details. A major portion of the narrative is in Gandhi's own words. Hence, this work reads like an extended version of Gandhi's *Autobiography*. In a foreword to the first edition, Mr. Jawaharlal Nehru stated, "It brings together more facts and data about Gandhi than any book that I know." Volume 1 covers 1869 to 1920, including a chapter called "Zulu Rebellion and After (1906)," in which the author states:

> In April 1906 the so-called Zulu Rebellion broke out. At Gandhi's suggestion the Natal Congress made an offer to the Governor to raise an Indian Ambulance Corps for service with the troops. Gandhi had doubts about the "rebellion" itself, but he believed that the British Empire existed for the welfare of the world.
>
> In June, owing to the uncertainty of the political situation, Gandhi decided to break up his home at Johannesburg and take his family to Natal. On reaching Durban, he found that the offer of the Indian Ambulance Corps was accepted. Gandhi at once sent his family to the Phoenix Settlement and he collected twenty-four volunteers consisting of nineteen ex-indentured men, one Pathan and four Gujaratis. The chief medical officer appointed Gandhi to the temporary rank of sergeant-major. The Indian Ambulance Corps received uniforms from the Government and was hurriedly dispatched to the front.
>
> On reaching the scene of "rebellion," Gandhi realized that it was in fact a no-tax campaign. His sympathies now were with the Zulus and the main work of the Indian corps, to Gandhi's delight, was to be the nursing of the wounded rebels. Gandhi and his men were attached to a swift moving column of mounted infantry and they had to follow it on foot, sometimes forty miles a day, with stretchers on their shoulders. The wounded Zulus in charge of Gandhi were not wounded in battle but were innocent villagers, who were flogged severely, on being suspected of their participation in the "rebellion."
>
> The Zulu "rebellion" was an eye-opener to Gandhi. He saw the naked atrocities of the whites against the poor sons of the soil. The whites flogged the Zulus, but they were unwilling to nurse their festering wounds and also did not favor the Indian Ambulance Corps attending them. The Zulus were grateful to the Indians for having come to their help. Besides the ambulance work, Gandhi

had to compound and dispense prescriptions for the white soldiers, the work he used to do in Dr. Booth's little hospital.

The "rebellion" ended by July 1906. The Indian Ambulance Corps was on active service for nearly six weeks. Its work was mentioned in dispatches. Each member was awarded a medal especially struck for the occasion.

Marching through the hills and dales of Zululand, Gandhi often fell into deep thought. Two ideas which had been floating in his mind became fixed. First, an aspirant after a life exclusively devoted to service must lead a life of celibacy. Secondly, he must accept voluntary poverty.[19]

There is nothing new in the above narrative; it is the same repetition of Gandhi's autobiographical accounts.

GANDHI, SOLDIER OF NONVIOLENCE: AN INTRODUCTION
by Calvin Kytle (1969)

This is a reprint (with slight revisions) of an earlier book that was published under the title *Gandhi, Soldier of Nonviolence: His Effect on India and the World Today*. Calvin Kytle, former acting director of a federal conciliation agency, describes the Zulu War of 1906 as follows:

In May of 1906, Gandhi's routine was shattered by news of the Zulu Rebellion in Natal. Although the causes were vague, the British were mobilizing and Gandhi, who still considered himself a loyal subject of the Crown, promptly volunteered to organize the Indian Ambulance Corps.

In Durban, Gandhi recruited twenty-four men, mostly former indentured servants from South India. On induction, the corps was assigned to a fast-moving column of mounted infantry and ordered to nurse wounded Zulus, a duty that white corpsmen had refused. The infantrymen were under orders to move on a moment's notice, to whatever native village was reported to be in a state of incipient revolt. Once camp was struck, Gandhi and his stretcher-bearers followed on foot.

For a good part of his six weeks' service, Gandhi was in motion, sometimes marching as much as forty miles a day. On these long, silent marches through the sparsely populated land Gandhi fell to thinking about the purpose of life, the senseless war that he was in, the meaning of renunciation, the nature of God, and his own future in South Africa. The marches usually led to some simple *Kraal* of "uncivilized" Zulus where the soldiers rarely met any resistance but invariably shot off their rifles anyway. The marches brought Gandhi to a turning point.

The rebellion, as he saw it, was a sham. There had indeed been a disturbance. A Zulu chief had resisted payment of a newly imposed tax and had speared a sergeant who had come to collect. The British had responded by magnifying a manhunt into a war of counter-revolution, the main casualties of which were innocent black villagers. Gandhi was appalled to discover that of the wounded in his charge not one had been hurt in battle. About half had been taken prisoner and flogged so badly that they were left with festering sores; others were "friendlies" who, although given badges to distinguish them from the "enemy," had been shot by mistake. His respect for Europeans was not enhanced by the fact that white soldiers habitually stood on the other side of the fence that surrounded the nursing compound, alternately swearing at the suffering Zulus and urging the Indian medics to "let the savages die."

His experience brought home the horrors of war more vividly than anything he had seen during the Boer War. Violence, he decided irrevocably, was an insult to God's intent for man. He could ease his conscience only with the thought that if it had not been for him the Zulus would not have been cared for at all.

In the midst of these pitiful, frightened, and dying black men—in the employment of men who seemed to value life only if it came packaged in a white skin—Gandhi came to equate life with time and to see the acceptance of death as a condition of freedom. . . . From this moment of resolution, Mohandas Gandhi became the most believing, the most living man of the twentieth century.[20]

Again, nothing of substance is presented. The author transformed Gandhi's autobiographical account into an attractive story with supposedly far-reaching consequences for Gandhi and humankind! But he didn't answer two questions: Why did Gandhi consider himself a British loyalist? What were Zulus considered?

MAHATMA GANDHI, VOLUME 3: *THE BIRTH OF SATYAGRAHA— FROM PETITIONING TO PASSIVE RESISTANCE* by Pyarelal (1986)

Pyarelal (1900–1982) is purported to be the best of all Gandhi biographers; after all, he was Gandhi's personal secretary for twenty-eight years. Shortly after Gandhi's assassination in 1948, the Hindu leaders—Nehru included—invited Pyarelal to undertake the project of writing his official biography. He started, but never completed it. How reliable is Pyarelal's account of Gandhi's South African tenure? Not very, considering: "Gandhiji's work in South Africa can be properly studied only as a prelude to and in the perspective of India's struggle for independence—both before and under his leadership."[21] After Pyarelal's death in 1982 his sister, Sushila Nayar, took over the huge project. After several years, she produced Gandhi's life from his birth to 1948 in ten hefty volumes. Readers ought to be cautious: These exhaustive volumes look like a gigantic historical work. But on close inspection, alas, much of it is hagiographic and intensely boring. Another alert: Sushila Nayar, who happened to be Gandhi's personal physician, once confessed to Ved Mehta, "I used to sleep with him [Gandhi]. . . . He was a god. I have always been drawn to the supernatural."[22] Like any other biography authored by an apologist, this one spurts out a religious theme for its attraction among wide-spread Gandhi-prone Christians. For volume 4, R. Venkataraman, president of the Republic of India at that time, wrote a foreword, stating:

> Hundreds of books have been written on Gandhiji and doubtless many more will be written. Some of these are factual, some interpretive. But while valuable insights have and may continue to come from other pens, there will be one and only one definite biography of Gandhiji and that will be Pyarelal's, now being completed by his sister, Dr. Sushila Nayar. This work, being based on original documentation and total fidelity to fact, can only be ranked to the direct accounts of the Saints: John, Matthew, Mark and Luke whose records of the Life of Jesus comprising the New Testament can never be dislodged by any other.[23]

Volume 3 covers Gandhi's life from January 1902 to September 11, 1906. Dr. James D. Hunt, who at the time was a professor of religion at Shaw University in Raleigh, North Carolina, was invited by Nayar to write a few sections. Of his writings, chapter 20, "The Zulu Rebellion," is of particular interest—by far the best biographical material ever written, though incomplete, of Gandhi's participation in the war of 1906 in South Africa.[24] The chapter on Gandhi and the details of his participation in war are handled commendably because of their reliance on the original 1906 historical documents, which will be explored further in part 2.

NOTES

1. Edmund Candler's quote cited in James R. Mitchell, "The Gandhi Image in the American Mind: 1921–1941" (master's thesis, University of Virginia, 1967).
2. CWMG 90, p. 177.
3. John Haynes Holmes, "Who Is the Greatest Man in the World Today?" Sermon delivered April 10, 1921, to the Community Church, New York. The "little paper-covered pamphlet" that Holmes received on his desk was probably *Speeches and Writings of Mahatma Gandhi*, either the 1917 or 1919 edition. It was by no means a pamphlet. To date, the mechanism by which the "pamphlet" made it to Holmes remains a mystery.
4. Ibid.
5. John Haynes Holmes, *My Gandhi* (New York: Harper & Brothers, 1953), p. 1.
6. Ibid., p. 70.
7. Haridas T. Muzumdar, *Gandhi the Apostle: His Trial and His Message* (Chicago: Universal Publishing, 1923), p. iv.
8. Ibid., pp. 112–13.
9. Romain Rolland, *Mahatma Gandhi: The Man Who Became One with the Universal Being* (New York: Century, 1924), p. 18. It seems that Rolland also received *Speeches and Writings of Mahatma Gandhi*, most probably the 1922 edition, but never wrote the introduction.

10. Krishnalal Shridharani, *The Mahatma and the World* (New York: Duell, Sloan and Pearce, 1946), p. vii.

11. E. Stanley Jones, *Gandhi: Portrayal of a Friend* (Nashville, Tenn.: Abingdon Press, 1983), p. 8. This book surfaced after the movie *Gandhi* was released in 1982. This book is actually a reprint of *Mahatma Gandhi: An Interpretation*, published in 1948.

12. Norman Cousins, ed., *Profiles of Gandhi: America Remembers a World Leader* (Delhi: Indian Book Company, 1969), p. 130.

13. Quoted in Jones, *Gandhi*, on an unnumbered page at the beginning of the book.

14. *Christian Century* 79 (May 23, 1962): 661.

15. Frederick B. Fisher, *That Strange Little Brown Man Gandhi* (New Delhi: Orient Longmans, 1970), p. 62. This book was published in the United States in 1932.

16. C. F. Andrews, ed., *Mahatma Gandhi—His Own Story* (New York: Macmillan, 1930).

17. Kirby Page, "Is Mahatma Gandhi the Greatest Man of the Age?" in *The Americanization of Gandhi: Images of the Mahatma*, ed. Charles Chatfield (New York: Garland Publishing, 1976), p. 691.

18. Jashwant Rao Chitambar, *Mahatma Gandhi: His Life, Work, and Influence* (Chicago: John C. Winston, 1933), pp. 61–62.

19. D. G. Tendulkar, *Mahatma: Life of Mohandas Karamchand Gandhi* (Bombay: Vithalbhai K. Jhaveri and D. G. Tendulkar, 1951), vol. 1, pp. 91–92.

20. Calvin Kytle, *Gandhi, Soldier of Nonviolence: An Introduction*, rev. ed. (Washington, D.C.: Seven Locks Press, 1982), pp. 85–87. Kytle was a member of the planning committee in the United States that celebrated the one hundredth anniversary of Gandhi's birth. Incidentally, the late U.S. Senator Hubert H. Humphrey was the chairman of the U.S. Committee on the Gandhi Centennial.

21. Pyarelal, *Mahatma Gandhi*, vol. 2, *The Discovery of Satyagraha—on the Threshold* (Bombay: Sevak Prakashan, 1980), p. vii.

22. Ved Mehta, *Mahatma Gandhi & His Apostles* (New Haven, Conn.: Yale University Press, 1993), pp. 203–204.

23. R. Venkataraman, Foreword to *Mahatma Gandhi*, vol. 4, *Satyagraha at Work*, by Sushila Nayar (Ahmedabad: Navajivan Publishing House, 1989), p. vii.

24. James D. Hunt, "The Zulu Rebellion," in Pyarelal *Mahatma Gandhi*, vol. 3, *The Birth of Satyagraha—from Petitioning to Passive Resistance* (Ahmedabad: Navajivan Publishing House, 1986), pp. 465–83.

5

THE LIFE OF MAHATMA GANDHI
by Louis Fischer (1950)

Louis Fischer (1896–1970) was an experienced and well-respected American journalist in the field of international affairs. He authored several books, four of which were on Gandhi. Fischer yearned to seek answers for the betterment of humankind, which brought him to adopt Communism, championing the cause of Soviet Russia and, later, of Republican Spain. Personal agony and revulsion later caused him to reject Communism and join the ranks of ex-Communists.

He met Gandhi in 1942 and stayed with him as his guest for a week, and Fischer finally found the "messiah" he was looking for. In 1946 he again spent eight days in Gandhi's company. Fischer remained Gandhi's steadfast admirer till the end. *The Life of Mahatma Gandhi* is, without a doubt, the most famous Gandhi biography ever written. What did Fischer write about the 1906 incident? The same story that appears in Gandhi's autobiographical writings:

> Nevertheless, Gandhi forsook the political arena when the Zulu "rebellion" occurred in the first half of 1906, and joined the British army with a small group of twenty-four Indian volunteers to serve as stretcher bearers and sanitary aids. Gandhi said he joined because he believed that "the British Empire existed for the welfare of the world"; he had a "genuine sense of loyalty" to it.
>
> The "rebellion" was really a punitive expedition or "police action" which opened with the exemplary hanging of twelve Zulus and continued to the last as a ghastly procession of shootings and floggings. Since white physicians and nurses would not tend sick and dying Zulus, the task was left to the Indians who witnessed all the horrors of black men whipped till their skin came off in strips.

Gandhi's party sometimes came on the scene five or six days after the British had passed by and found the victims suffering agony from open, suppurating wounds. The Indians marched as many as forty miles a day.

After a month's service, the Indian unit was demobilized and each man honored with a special medal. Gandhi had held the rank of sergeant major. All members wore khaki uniforms, this time with puttees. . . . The suppression of the tribesmen, with its insane cruelty of man to man, depressed him. The long treks to the hamlets of the suffering Negroes afforded ample opportunity for self-analysis; he must do more to make a better world. . . .[1]

But, if this is at all historically accurate, why did Gandhi forsake his political arena?

GANDHI: A MEMOIR
by William L. Shirer (1979)

William L. Shirer (1904–1993), author of many fiction and nonfiction books, attained distinction for his books around the time of the Second World War. While employed as a foreign correspondent for the *Chicago Tribune*, he covered Gandhi and his activities after having met him in February 1931 for the first time. When *Gandhi: A Memoir*[2] was published almost fifty years later—in spite of the benefit of time and other resources—it included nothing about Gandhi's South African experience, particularly in the 1906 war. Nonetheless, this book is a famous reference text, and Shirer was presented as a composite character—along with Vincent Sheean and Louis Fischer—in the movie *Gandhi*, a role played by Martin Sheen.

LEAD KINDLY LIGHT: GANDHI & THE WAY TO PEACE
by Vincent Sheean (1949)

Vincent Sheean (1899–1975) started his career as a foreign correspondent for the *Paris Herald*. Regarding the question of Gandhi and blacks in 1906, he wrote:

The Phoenix Settlement flourished for years on the principles of its foundation, but Gandhi could not live there himself for long at a time: his work in Johannesburg was now approaching a climax and was about to demand his fullest attention. But before this could come about the final step of his self-purification, as he saw it, had to take place. He took the vow of chastity for life in 1906, when he was thirty-seven years old.[3]

Lead Kindly Light is a very famous biography, yet it provides no information on the issue of the war against blacks in 1906. However, another Sheean book—*Mahatma Gandhi: A Great Life in Brief*, published in 1955—provides a little more description:

> The hour of Gandhi's renunciation (his rather gradual renunciation) was at hand. No doubt the Zulu War, like everything else, had something to do with it, as did [British writer John] Ruskin, Tolstoy, Jesus, Buddha, and the Hindu Scriptures. The moment the Zulu "rebellion" broke out in Natal, Gandhi offered his services with an Indian ambulance corps, and to his astonishment, the Governor of Natal accepted at once (no doubt remembering the services given in the Boer War). In actual fact Gandhi's sympathies were with the Zulus, but he felt his loyalty to the British Empire to override everything else. He organized a corps of twenty-four Indian volunteers, who served through the Zulu War, and to his delight their task was to care for wounded or sick or injured Zulus.[4]

Here the author relied upon Gandhi's autobiographical account, rendering a somewhat spiritual disposition to it.

MAHATMA GANDHI: A BIOGRAPHY
by B. R. Nanda (1958)

B. R. Nanda (1917–) was director of Nehru Memorial Museum and Library, New Delhi and national fellow of the Indian Council of Social Science Research. As he was employed with the government of India and had written a number of books, his book on Gandhi carried considerable authority. Regarding the event of 1906, he wrote:

> The occasion for the *Brahmacharya* vow was the Zulu rebellion in 1906, in which Gandhi had led an Indian volunteer ambulance unit. During the strenuous marches through the "solemn solitudes" of the Kraals of Zululand, it was borne in upon him that if he was to repeat the service of the kind he was rendering, he would find himself unequal to the task if he were engaged in the pleasures of family life and in the propagation and rearing of children. . . .[5]

This biography is often quoted in the literature, but on the question of the Zulu War it provides hardly anything of substance.

GANDHI
by Geoffrey Ashe (1968)

English scholar Geoffrey Ashe (1923–) observed in his biography:

> A Zulu rising broke out in Natal. Or so the authorities viewed it. Gandhi liked the Zulus, but, as with the Boers, a question arose as to whether Indians could

agitate for citizenship if they did not show willingness to perform civic duties. He raised a party of twenty-four stretcher-bearers and gave up his Johannesburg house, though not his office. Kasturbai [Gandhi's wife] and the boys stayed at Phoenix during his month or so of service. He was given the rank of sergeant-major (a strange thought) and the whole corps was put in uniform. His stamina was boundless; he could march forty miles a day, and get his men to do like-wise. As it turned out, the rising was minimal. A chief had advised his tribe not to pay a new tax, and run an assegai through the tax-collector. Most of the work consisted in nursing Zulus who had been flogged or shot, often by mistake, during the restoration of order. Some had hideous wounds, but the white staff would do nothing. Idle soldiers watched the Indians at their task, jeered at them for taking such trouble over niggers, and abused the patients.[6]

While somewhat puzzled at Gandhi's military rank, it appears Ashe reluctantly accepted the account enumerated in Gandhi's autobiography.

NOTES

1. Louis Fischer, *The Life of Mahatma Gandhi* (New York: Harper & Brothers, 1950), pp. 57–58.

2. William L. Shirer, *Gandhi: A Memoir* (New York: Simon & Schuster, 1979).

3. Vincent Sheean, *Lead Kindly Light: Gandhi & the Way to Peace* (New York: Random House, 1949), p. 103.

4. Vincent Sheean, *Mahatma Gandhi: A Great Life in Brief* (New York: Alfred A. Knopf, 1955), p. 71.

5. B. R. Nanda, *Mahatma Gandhi: A Biography* (1958; reprint, Oxford: Oxford India Paperbacks, 1996), pp. 83–84.

6. Geoffrey Ashe, *Gandhi* (New York: Stein and Day, 1968), p. 93.

6

THE MYTH OF THE MAHATMA: GANDHI, THE BRITISH, AND THE RAJ
by Michael Edwardes (1986)

Michael Edwardes (1923–) is a noted historian of British India. The book was written in response to *The Jewel in the Crown* (a TV reworking of Paul Scott's novels), *Jewel* (a screen adaptation of E. M. Forster's *A Passage to India*), and, of course, the movie *Gandhi*. With respect to Gandhi and blacks, two short paragraphs appear:

> Gandhi arrived in South Africa in 1893, still behind the mask of a lawyer, though a little uneasy in the role. When he returned to India for the last time in 1915, he was almost ready to assume the mask of freedom fighter, and the mantle of holy man; to move from barrister-at-law to Mahatma.
>
> The details of Gandhi's life in South Africa are well known, the myth-makers defining the period as a sort of preparation in the desert for the real work to come. Glossed over is his failure to achieve anything of lasting value for the Indian community and his indifference to the plight of the indigenous African majority. . . .[1]

We learn nothing about the 1906 war, but the author is correct about Gandhi's indifference to the plight of blacks. More on this is discussed in parts 2, 3, and 4.

61

MAHATMA GANDHI & HIS APOSTLES
by Ved Mehta (1977)

When he wrote this book, Ved Mehta (1934–) was a staff writer for the *New Yorker*. This is a remarkable book examining Gandhi's preoccupation with human excreta, enemas, and sleeping naked with women, including young girls. More than that, this book also provides a biographical glimpse concerning the 1906 incident.

> Early in 1906, a Zulu chieftain threw an assagai and killed a tax collector in Zul-uland. The incident set off violent disturbances. The British had annexed Zulu-land to Natal in 1887, and the spirited Zulus—whose main occupation was farming—did not like the arrangement. The Natal government now mounted a punitive expedition to put down what it called a Zulu Rebellion. As in the Boer War, Gandhi believed that Indians, as loyal subjects of the Empire, must side with the British, and he organized another volunteer ambulance corps.
>
> When Gandhi and his corps got to Zululand, however, they discovered that the expeditionary force was quelling the "rebellion" by public hangings and public floggings. The wounded nursed by the corps were mostly Zulus. "We found that the wounded Zulus would have been left uncared for if we had not attended to them," Gandhi writes. "No European would help to dress their wounds. . . . We had to cleanse the wounds of several Zulus which had not been attended to for as many as five or six days and were therefore stinking horribly. We liked our work. The Zulus could not talk to us, but from their gestures and the expression of their eyes, they seemed to feel as if God had sent us to their succour." The conduct of the expeditionary force was such a scandal that the expedition was quickly called off, and Gandhi and his corps were returned to Johannesburg within six weeks.
>
> Gandhi says that the suffering he witnessed in Zululand caused a profound and permanent change in his life, making him resolve to serve humanity with all his soul. To this end, within a few months of his return from Zululand he adopted three principles by which to live: brahmacharya, or celibacy, which was an ancient Hindu vow; satyagraha, or the force of truth and love, which was his own invention; and ahimsa, or nonviolence to all living things, which was an ancient Jain commandment. . . .[2]

This, again, is the story taken from Gandhi's autobiography. Mehta's narra-tive gives fresh momentum to the existing notion that Gandhi joined the army for humanitarian purposes.

THE LIFE AND DEATH OF MAHATMA GANDHI
by Robert Payne (1969)

Of all the biographies available, this is the best and least hagiographic of full-length Gandhi studies. This book includes a chapter, appropriately titled "Sergeant Major Gandhi," detailing Gandhi's role during the war in 1906. This is a well-balanced chapter in which the author brings into focus information other than the mythology presented in Gandhi's autobiographical writings:

> In his articles in *Indian Opinion* Gandhi called upon the Indians to fight on the side of the British. He pointed out that the Europeans had always distrusted the fighting prowess of the Indians in Natal; at the first sign of danger they would desert their posts and make their way back to India. "We cannot meet this charge with a written rejoinder," he wrote. "There is but one way of disproving it—the way of action." He asked the Indians to join the Volunteer Corps. They should not be afraid of war. Wars are relatively harmless. There was nothing to fear, and everyone at the front was perfectly happy.[3]

In part 2 we will discuss in detail other articles about the 1906 war published in the *Indian Opinion*.

GANDHI: PRISONER OF HOPE
by Judith M. Brown (1989)

Judith M. Brown (1944–) is a professional historian and a well-respected Gandhian scholar at Oxford University. Her book is the result of two decades of dedicated research on India and on the career of Gandhi. What happened in 1906?

> He used his medical skills more publicly on two occasions when he organized an Indian Ambulance Corps in South Africa, once in the Boer War and again in the Zulu Rebellion of 1906. The latter brought home to him particularly vividly the horrors of war, as he nursed Zulus whom no white men were willing to tend. Such war work demanded courage and physical strength as well as humanitarian dedication. . . . Although his personal sympathies lay with the Boers and the Zulus in each case he felt that if he demanded rights as a citizen of the empire so it was his duty to participate in its defence. . . . Reflecting on this after a decade's work in India and a significant shift in his attitude to the British empire, he had no regrets, and he wrote in his detailed account of satyagraha in South Africa that he would do the same again if he still had the faith he had then in the empire, and the hope that Indians would achieve liberty within it.[4]

The account quoted above is a wonderful blend of Gandhi's *Autobiography* with *Satyagraha in South Africa*.

MAHATMA GANDHI: AN ESSAY IN POLITICAL BIOGRAPHY
by Dietmar Rothermund (1991)

Dietmar Rothermund (1933–) is the head of the Department of History at the South Asia Institute in Heidelberg, Germany. In 1989 he authored a comprehensive Gandhi biography in the German language, after reading complete Gandhi literature. He tells us:

> In 1906 Gandhi's life was transformed by a series of crucial decisions. The Zulu uprising saw him once more in the field, leading a medical corps, the commander under whom he served was the butcher who had once led the mob which nearly lynched Gandhi. He now highly appreciated Gandhi's services. Before joining duty Gandhi had dissolved his household in Johannesburg and had sent his family to live in Phoenix Farm. It seemed as if he knew in advance about his transformation. The fight against the Zulus was an eye-opener for him. It was not an ordinary war, but a vicious manhunt in which he was on the wrong side. He sympathised with the Zulus and his only consolation was that he was not one of the hunters, but that he had to nurse the wounded of both sides. The uprising had started when a Zulu had speared a tax collector and spears were the only weapons the Zulus could wield against the superior forces of their oppressors. Serving under the butcher who had once persecuted him must have appeared as a strange irony of fate to Gandhi. He brooded during the nights in the field and finally decided that he should devote the whole of his life to public work and should give up his legal profession as well as the life of an ordinary householder. . . .[5]

Here the author paints a picture of Gandhi as a victim of circumstance, doing honorable work under compelling conditions.

NOTES

1. Michael Edwardes, *The Myth of the Mahatma: Gandhi, the British, and the Raj* (London: Constable, 1986), p. 187.
2. Ved Mehta, *Mahatma Gandhi & His Apostles* (1977; reprint, New Haven, Conn.: Yale University Press, 1993), pp. 117–18.
3. Robert Payne, *The Life and Death of Mahatma Gandhi* (New York: Konecky & Konecky, 1969), p. 154.
4. Judith M. Brown, *Gandhi: Prisoner of Hope* (New Haven, Conn.: Yale University Press, 1989), pp. 61, 64.
5. Dietmar Rothermund, *Mahatma Gandhi: An Essay in Political Biography* (Delhi: Manohar Publishers, 1991), pp. 18–19.

7

MISCELLANEOUS ARTICLES

The first article known to have triggered a reaction of support for Gandhi among the Christian clergy was titled "The Soul As It Is, and How to Deal with It," by the Oxford classicist Prof. Gilbert Murray. Why would Murray depict Gandhi in such "glowing spiritual" terms? His answers are not surprising. When Murray met Gandhi in England in 1914, he noticed that Gandhi ate only rice, drank only water, and slept on the bare wooden floorboards. Gandhi's conversation was that of a cultivated and well-read man, with a certain indefinable suggestion of saintliness. Quite a qualification for higher spiritualism! The truth is, the reality was quite different for Gandhi in the very early phase of World War I in 1914. Anyone who has read his literature from the World War I period in England should come to the conclusion that I reached: Gandhi would have benefited had he sought psychiatric intervention and therapy! Professor Murray was off by a mile. About the 1906 incident, we read the following: "In 1906 there was a Native rebellion in Natal: Gandhi raised and personally led a corps of stretcher-bearers, whose work seems to have proved particularly dangerous and painful. Gandhi was thanked by the Governor of Natal."[1]

* * *

In an article titled "Non-violence As a Political Strategy: Gandhi and Western Thinkers," Hugh Tinker wrote:

> In 1906, there was a revolt among the Zulus of Natal, and once again Gandhi raised an Indian ambulance unit. However, the experience proved traumatic. It was a very minor revolt, but it brought white troops with modern weapons up

65

against African guerrillas, and as so often in this situation the tactics of overkill were employed. Gandhi was horrified. His reaction was similar to that of Tolstoy in the Crimean war. But whereas Tolstoy took many years to reach his final renunciation, Gandhi's response had all the signs to total and almost "instant" conversion.[2]

* * *

In a paper titled "Gandhi in South Africa: A Study in Social Accounting," presented at the National Seminar on Gandhi and South Africa, held in Bombay, May 22–24, 1993, Prof. R. R. Ramchandani, former director of the Centre of African Studies at Bombay University, commented:

> It is true Gandhi did not espouse the cause of indigenous Africans, even though he saw that their suffering and their plight was pitiable indeed; and that Indians in South Africa certainly received far better treatment. But, then, reasons for Gandhi's aloofness in this respect are not far to seek: (1) Gandhi had known little about South Africa before he went there; (2) he had a first brush with blatant racial discrimination against Indians on his being thrown out of a first-class compartment even when he had a valid first-class ticket; (3) As a lawyer he was familiar with the "rule of law" as it prevailed in Britain from where he had acquired his law degree and where he had seen that law made no distinction against Indians on racial or colour grounds; (4) The post-1857 Victorian proclamation had assured that the Indian subject of the Empire will not be cultural ethos of the Indians and could easily appreciate their predicament. Moreover, being new to South Africa he could easily mingle with them and establish more meaningful communication channels much faster; (5) He had just started his experimentation in social accounting and it was relatively easier to awaken the conscience of his own countrymen who were also settlers, like the Whites, but who too, belonged to the ancient civilisation of no mean consequence; and Gandhi had high ideas of Indian cultural traditions as also of Indian value systems including dominant religions in India, be it Hinduism or Islam. On the other hand, Gandhi was yet unfamiliar with the earlier civilisational thrust of the "native" Africans and their cosmological ideas.[3]

* * *

Another famous Gandhian scholar, P. S. Joshi, wrote *Mahatma Gandhi in South Africa*. Just in case readers expected an objective work, its opening statement is startling: "To thousands of all races, of all colours and creeds, who have died in, been exiled or deported from, South Africa, and to all those who have languished and are still languishing in prison for the attainment of a society for the evolution of which Mohandas Karamchand Gandhi consecrated his life."

Joshi arrived in South Africa in 1920 and stayed there for a protracted thirty-seven years. According to Joshi, he gathered "relevant material from every available source and from persons close to Mahatma Gandhi then alive." On the issue of blacks, this is what we learn:

> The violent revolt in Bengal and militant no-tax campaign of the Zulus in Natal brought home to Gandhi the desirability of liberation of the oppressed from the oppressor. But his method of organizing the movement for freedom differed fundamentally from the orthodox conception of the age. He believed neither in war nor armed warfare. His was the path of non-violence and truth. His armoury was soul force, and ammunition suffering. To achieve the ideal, he had prepared himself for the supreme sacrifice. He had adopted the motto of non-possession. He said the universe was his family and it existed through the grace of God. He led an ascetic's life with little love for worldly enjoyments. The house-work was shared by the inmates. He practised celibacy, experimented in dietetics and ate very simple food. He was beginning to realise the power of the soul.[4]

* * *

Dr. S. Radhakrishnan, at the time president of the Republic of India, wrote a preface to Pyarelal's *Mahatma Gandhi: The Early Phase*:

> In South Africa, Gandhiji struggled to remove race discrimination. Though South Africa is still dominated by race prejudice and *apartheid*, other parts of Africa have attained liberation from colonial bondage. Large parts of Africa are now in a position to shape their future according to their own will and genius. In the United States, the Civil Rights Bill has been passed into Law. American Negroes are getting into their own. Gandhiji's influence has been, to some extent, responsible for this increasing recognition of equality of races. It is very much to be hoped that even the rulers in South Africa will understand their own enlightened self-interest, recognise the winds of change that are blowing over the whole world and work for greater equality among its citizens.[5]

* * *

In *Freedom at Midnight*, Larry Collins and Dominique LaPierre write:

> The scar left by his father's death, a desire to have no more children, his rising religious consciousness—all drove him toward his decision. One summer evening in 1906 Gandhi solemnly announced to his wife, Kasturbai, that he had taken the vow of Brahmacharya. Begun in a joyous frenzy at the age of thirteen, the sexual life of Mohandas Gandhi had reached its conclusion at the age of thirty-seven.[6]

* * *

In the superbly written article "Gandhi and the Black People of South Africa," James D. Hunt had the audacity to tell with a ring of truth, at least in the last line:

On the other hand, many Africans would not forget that Gandhi joined in the bloody suppression of the Zulu Rebellion in Natal in 1906. Though Gandhi had doubts concerning the justice of the Government's case, he believed that in a crisis Indians should rally along with the troops. Actually he treated Native victims more than Whites, but his purpose had been to suppress the revolt.[7]

* * *

In the much-acclaimed book *Gandhi in South Africa: British Imperialism and the Indian Question, 1860–1914*, author Robert A. Huttenback wrote:

> In 1906 he again led a stretcher company during the Bambata Rebellion in Zululand. Even the anti-Indian governor of Natal, Sir Henry McCallum, felt constrained to write a letter of thanks to "Sergeant-Major Gandhi."[8]

* * *

In the strangely titled *Mahatma Gandhi: The Great Rogue of India?* author Govind Dass Consul tells us:

> He suffered personal insults, humiliations, hardships, sufferings, tortures, imprisonment and almost death in his struggle for the removal of social and political disabilities and inequalities of his countrymen and the amelioration and redress of the misery of the natives of South Africa.[9]

This book was written as a part of larger celebration of Gandhi's seventieth birthday on October 2, 1939. Ironically, Gandhi responded to the book with a statement on his own somewhat exotic letterhead with a red-colored inscription: "MAHATMAJI'S ACKNOWLEDGMENT." As expected, Gandhi never corrected the mistakes (as will become apparent in part 2) committed by the author about his South African adventures.

* * *

Fatima Meer, a well-known Gandhi scholar in South Africa, addressed the issue in a chapter titled "The Making of the Mahatma: The South African Experience":

> Gandhi's personal preparation for satyagraha occurred on the war plain of the so-called Zulu Rebellion. Gandhi, still a loyal British subject, once more answered the call of "king and country." But he soon realised that he was on the wrong side, that this was no rebellion but stark repression, that justice was on the side of the Zulus who were treated with inhumanity for doing no more than resisting a poll tax similar to that imposed on the Indians. The Indian stretcher-bearers redeemed themselves by nursing the Zulu prisoners of war abandoned

by the British. For Gandhi, the brutality against the Zulus roused his soul against violence as nothing had been done up to then; he sought answers and found them in his traditional scriptures. He returned from the war determined to give himself wholly to serving the people.[10]

* * *

In an article "To the American Negro: A Message from Mahatma Gandhi," there appeared alongside a brief biographical sketch of Gandhi for the benefit of African Americans:

> Mohandas Karamchand Gandhi, the greatest colored man in the world, and perhaps the greatest man in the world, was born October 2, 1869 in India. He finished High School and then studied for three years in England at London University, and at the Law School of the Inner Temple. Returning, he began to practice law in Bombay, but not being successful, he went to South Africa in 1893, and there his public life began. He gave up the law and devoted himself to the Indian people who were being persecuted along with the natives in that land. He served with the Red Cross during the Boer War, attending friend and foe alike. For twenty years he toiled in South Africa to remove race prejudice. He led his people; he went to jail; he agitated; and finally triumphed by gaining for the Indians of South Africa a large measure of freedom. At the outbreak of the Great War, he returned to India, and although a Pacifist, aided the great war. But when after the war there came repression, the massacre of Amritsar, and the infamous Rowlatt bills, Gandhi was disillusioned. He came out for Home Rule and announced his great Gospel of conquest through peace. Agitation, non-violence, refusal to cooperate with the oppressor, became his watchword and with it he is leading all India to freedom. Here and today, he stretches out his hand in fellowship to his colored friends of the West.[11]

Dr. W. E. B. Du Bois, editor of *Crisis*, completely ignored Gandhi's participation of the 1906 war! Why? Perhaps Rev. John Haynes Holmes provided the sanitized version above, since he was closely allied with the National Association for the Advancement of Colored People (NAACP).

* * *

Dr. Martin Luther King Jr. listed *The Power of Nonviolence* by Richard B. Gregg[12] as one of the ten books that affected his thinking. Reading this book from cover to cover, one learns nothing about the 1906 incident; it is as if it never took place. Another book, *The Gandhi Reader: A Source Book of His Life and Writings*, edited by Homer A. Jack,[13] a prominent member of the Congress of Racial Equality (CORE), is equally worth pointing out. In this book, the reader likewise learns nothing about the Zulu rebellion. This book is known to have crossed Dr. King's study table. Mary E. King, in her *Mahatma Gandhi and Martin Luther King Jr: The Power of Nonviolent Action*,[14] failed to make even a single mention of the Zulu rebellion.

* * *

Gandhi's historical saga as presented by Indian Christian scholarship falls acutely short of the facts: "Gandhi's war services (in the Boer War and the Zulu rebellion—1899) were yet another attempt to make his faith effective at the social level. . . ."[15] Similarly, Dr. Ignatius Jesudasan, an Indian Jesuit, paints a Gandhi story highly deficient of facts and rich in religious propaganda.[16] As of lately, the Christian propaganda on "Saint Gandhi" has not abated even slightly; rather, it continues to reach for new heights for the new audience:

> [Gandhi] was one of those examples of unquestioned holiness—St. Francis comes to mind as another—whose challenge transcends the limits of his age and culture. It is the example of someone like Gandhi that makes it impossible for most Christians to maintain the notion that salvation is restricted to the visible church. Indeed, Gandhi is a powerful argument for the capacity of non-Christians to function for Christians as saints—living icons of the invisible God.[17]

* * *

In "Gandhi and Black South Africans," Sushila Agarwal, professor of political science at Jaipur University in India, halfheartedly concedes Gandhi's involvement in the Zulu rebellion. But she cautions us not to get carried away: "A correct assessment of Gandhi's work during the Zulu rebellion is to evaluate him as a 'Mahatma and *Satyagraha* in the Making' and realise that his spirit was revolting against the injustice done to the Zulus but he felt helpless."[18]

* * *

In *The Good Boatman: A Portrait of Gandhi*, Rajmohan Gandhi (Mahatma's grandson) manipulates the war issue in a way that guarantees the reader more confusion. The author has jumbled so many historical events, criss-crossing Mahatma's years in South Africa with those in India, without any sense of clarity and thought.[19]

* * *

In *Mohandas Gandhi: The South Africa Years*, Mahatma's granddaughter Ela Gandhi reports the war incident, with a unique twist at the end:

When the Bambatha rebellion broke out, Gandhi felt that he should offer his services in the same way as in the Anglo-Boer war seven years earlier. He wrote to the government offering to form an Indian Ambulance Corps. About 24 men volunteered to join Gandhi and helped nurse the wounded. Dr Savage was the medical doctor in charge of the ambulance corps. He was unable to persuade white ambulancemen to attend to the African wounded, but Gandhi and his band of volunteers attended to them. . . . Now they found that in some cases the wounded had to remain unattended for up to six days as they had to be carried on stretchers to the hospital 64 km away.[20]

* * *

Many years after the fact, Albert West, a close lieutenant of Gandhi, reported:

Early in 1906 I began to consider the possibility of visiting my home in England, from which I had been absent for nearly four years. I discussed it with Gandhi, and he encouraged me in my resolve to sail for England in June. Arrangements were made and the passage booked, when there came a bolt from the blue. The Zulu "rebellion" was reported in the papers and this looked like war. Gandhi thought it his duty to offer his services to the Government in forming an Indian Ambulance Corps, as he had done in the Boer War. His offer was promptly accepted and he at once began preparations.[21]

* * *

It is truly amazing to read what the majority of writers have written on the subject of Gandhi and the Zulu rebellion. Mostly, we see that Gandhi's war activities have been turned into religious propaganda, be it from members of the Christian faith or others. Among the scholars, the narrative may not be religious propaganda, but it is certainly Gandhi propaganda in disguise because it relies on his questionable autobiographical accounts. (This will become more evident in part 2.) Even his most recently published biographies—*Gandhi: A Life* and *Gandhi's Passion: The Life and Legacy of Mahatma Gandhi*[22]—are woefully inadequate. Prof. James D. Hunt, who lamented in one of his papers on the overall deficiency of well-researched Gandhi biographies and the sorry state of his story (especially as portrayed in the movie), shares my view:

If we look for detailed monographic studies of well-defined aspects of Gandhi's life and career we find a similarly depressing prospect, for these are likewise few, especially for the early period. Full-length biographies have been the favored genre; there seems to be a compulsion to tell the sacred drama in its entirety, as in Richard Attenborough's film (1982). None of these biographies has a proper foundation in critical monographic studies. They are condemned to repeat the same ritualized and mythologized versions of familiar incidents, with perhaps a new detail here and there and a sprightly bit of debunking to indicate that the author has originality. The film does them all one better by inflating the old myths into powerful new images that are in some instances not only mistaken but perverse. . . . In the film for example, one of the most memorable scenes shows the young Gandhi beaten by the police as he attempts to burn passes. Not only was he never, in his whole life, beaten by the police—indeed his relations with them were most respectful—but the scene suggests that Gandhi foolishly rushed into defiant challenge of the law before doing his careful legal work. It therefore distorts his character. Later he is shown frightening horses in a scene which has no basis in history or nature. The printed media are generally more modest in their additions to historical truth, but they are rarely any more helpful in penetrating the myths.[23]

NOTES

1. Gilbert Murray, "The Soul As It Is, and How to Deal with It," *Hibbert Journal* 16, no. 2 (January 1918): 201.

2. Hugh Tinker, *Gandhi Marg* (August 1980): 247. Tinker was once a professor of political science at the School of Oriental and African Studies, University of London.

3. R. R. Ramchandani, "Gandhi in South Africa: A Study in Social Accounting," paper presented at the National Seminar on Gandhi and South Africa, Bombay, May 22–24, 1993; quoted in *India Quarterly: A Journal of International Affairs* (October–December 1993): 42.

4. P. S. Joshi, *Mahatma Gandhi in South Africa* (Rajkot, Gujarat: Author, 1980), p. 55.

5. S. Radhakrishnan, preface to *Mahatma Gandhi: The Early Phase*, vol. 1, by Pyarelal (Ahmedabad, India: Narajivan Publishing House, 1965), p. ix.

6. Larry Collins and Dominique LaPierre, *Freedom at Midnight* (New York: Simon & Schuster, 1975), p. 57.

7. James D. Hunt, "Gandhi and the Black People of South Africa," *Gandhi Marg* (April/June 1989): 11.

8. Robert A. Huttenback, *Gandhi in South Africa: British Imperialism and the Indian Question, 1860–1914* (Ithaca, N.Y.: Cornell University Press, 1971), p. 125.

9. Govind Dass Consul, *Mahatma Gandhi: The Great Rogue of India?* (Delhi: Garcon National Publishers, 1939), pp. 21–22.

10. Fatima Meer, "The Making of the Mahatma: The South African Experience," in *Mahatma Gandhi: 125 Years*, ed. B. R. Nanda (New Delhi: Indian Council for Cultural Relations and New Age International Publishers, 1995), pp. 48–49.

11. "To the American Negro: A Message from Mahatma Gandhi," *Crisis* 36, no. 7 (July 1929): 225.

12. Richard B. Gregg, *The Power of Nonviolence*, 2d rev. ed. (New York: Schocken Books, 1966).

13. Homer A. Jack, ed., *The Gandhi Reader: A Source Book of His Life and Writings* (1956; reprint, New York: AMS Press, 1970).

14. Mary E. King, *Mahatma Gandhi and Martin Luther King Jr.: The Power of Nonviolent Action* (Paris: UNESCO, 1999).

15. George Pattery, *Gandhi—The Believer: An Indian Christian Perspective* (Delhi: Indian Society for Promoting Christian Knowledge, 1996), p. 15.

16. Ignatius Jesudasan, *A Gandhian Theology of Liberation* (Maryknoll, N.Y.: Orbis Books, 1984).

17. Robert Ellsberg, *All Saints: Daily Reflections on Saints, Prophets, and Witnesses for Our Time* (New York: Crossroad, 1997), pp. 54–55.

18. Sushila Agarwal, "Gandhi and Black South Africans," in *Gandhi and South Africa*, ed. Shanti Sadiq Ali (Delhi: Hind Pocket Books, 1994), p. 182.

19. Rajmohan Gandhi, *The Good Boatman: A Portrait of Gandhi* (New York: Viking, 1995).

20. Ela Gandhi, *Mohandas Gandhi: The South Africa Years* (Cape Town: Maskew Miller Longman, 1994), p. 40.

21. Albert West, "In the Early Days with Gandhi," *Illustrated Weekly of India*, October 3, 10, 17, and 31, 1965.

22. Yogesh Chadha, *Gandhi: A Life* (New York: John Wiley, 1997); Stanley A. Wolpert, *Gandhi's Passion: The Life and Legacy of Mahatma Gandhi* (New York: Oxford University Press, 2001).

23. James D. Hunt, "Gandhi in South Africa," in *Gandhi's Significance for Today*, ed. John Hick and Lamont C. Hempel (New York: St. Martin's Press, 1989), pp. 61–63.

8

I have been known as a crank, faddist, madman. Evidently the reputation is well deserved. For wherever I go, I draw to myself cranks, faddists, and madmen.

—Mahatma Gandhi
Young India, June 13, 1929

At least twenty-six films have been released on Gandhi. Of these, only three were major production undertakings worth mentioning. The first of these films—*Mahatma*—was released in India in 1969 during the official celebration of Gandhi's centenary year. *Mahatma* took nearly seven years to make, was thirty thousand feet long rolled in thirty-three reels, and ran for nearly five hours. Whether it made any lasting impression on the viewers, one would not know today.

The Making of the Mahatma, which centers on the twenty-one years Gandhi lived in South Africa, was released in October 1996. A joint Indo–South African venture funded the production of this film. The film, based on Fatima Meer's *Apprenticeship of a Mahatma*,[1] was intended for a general audience on a worldwide scale. It flopped. Indians were sold on the need to see this movie, and they bought overpriced tickets.

But the story of the 1982 movie *Gandhi* is quite different. This movie was a long one—it ran over three hours (188 minutes)—but it proved to be a blockbuster. *Gandhi* was nominated for eleven Academy Awards, of which it won eight, including Best Picture, Best Director, Best Actor, Best Screenplay, Best Cinematography, Best Art/Set Direction, Best Film Editing, and Best Costume Design.

Without a doubt the one thing that truly made Gandhi famous in the West is this film. Many Americans bought *Gandhi* on videocassette for their home video libraries. In school, especially high school, students learn the art of nonviolent conflict resolution by watching *Gandhi*. In some middle schools, teachers take special delight in showing *Gandhi* to young, impressionable students so that they may emulate the higher morals practiced by Mahatma Gandhi. It has been said that some Christian churches show *Gandhi* in lieu of Bible classes. The Catholic Church classified *Gandhi* as offering "good social lessons for young adults," thereby wholeheartedly recommending it to the lovers of the faith. On February 1, 1986, during his ten-day visit to India, Pope John Paul II laid a wreath at the *samadhi* (cremation place) of Mahatma Gandhi and hailed him the "apostle of non-violence" and the "hero of humanity."[2] This would have been inconceivable, at least in a logical sense, if someone from the church hierarchy had taken time to examine its own historical pages. In fact, in December 1931 Pope Pius XI refused audience with Gandhi—not once, but twice—when the latter paid a holy visit to the Vatican.[3] Commenting on the apologetic nature of *Gandhi*, Mark Juergensmeyer, a professor at the University of California, wrote, "In short, the movie was an advertisement for a global saint, and it succeeded for a time in rekindling the flame of Gandhiolatry. Attenborough's film was an authentic recreation of the hagiography of Andrews, Holmes, and Oldfield. Like them, Attenborough fastened onto Gandhi's Christ-like charisma and his masterful actions."[4]

In his book *In Search of Gandhi*, the film's director, Sir Richard Attenborough, described his twenty-year obsession with the project. In the end, he spent $22 million to make the movie, one-third paid for by the government of India. The movie tells nothing about Gandhi's role during the Zulu rebellion in South Africa; one can simply walk out of the movie theater thinking the Zulu rebellion never took place. In his book, however, Attenborough writes, "Although having great sympathy for those opposed to the British during the Boer War and the Zulu Rebellion, Gandhi felt that if Indians were to attain equality and claim the benefits of British citizenship, they must also accept the incumbent responsibilities. He therefore formed volunteer ambulance corps, whose bravery tending the wounded in battle cost many Indian lives."[5]

Cost many Indian lives? That's positively unhistorical! Why did Attenborough's film not show scenes of Gandhi in the Zulu rebellion? Perhaps the answer is simple: The movie script had to be okayed by such Gandhian stalwarts as B. R. Nanda, Pyarelal, Sushila Nayar, D. G. Tendulkar, and, of course, Prime Minister Indira Gandhi. There were a few scattered protests in India by India's Untouchable community toward *Gandhi*. There were none abroad, except for a few brave souls who took time to put the *Gandhi* and Gandhi record straight. Among them was Richard Grenier, who, in his article "The Gandhi Nobody

Knows," provided the best critique on the movie. With regard to the black issue, Grenier summarized Gandhi's war efforts:

> The film, moreover, does not give the slightest hint as to Gandhi's attitude toward blacks, and the viewers of *Gandhi* would naturally suppose that, since the future Great Soul opposed South African discrimination against Indians, he would also oppose South African discrimination against black people. But this is not so. While Gandhi, in South Africa, fought furiously to have Indians recognized as loyal subjects of the British empire, and to have them enjoy the full rights of Englishmen, he had no concern for blacks whatever. In fact, during one of the "Kaffir Wars" he volunteered to organize a brigade of Indians to put down a Zulu rising, and was decorated himself for valor under fire.[6]

The Gandhi apologists who read "The Gandhi Nobody Knows" were incensed at Grenier for having sullied the image of their hero, and they responded in kind. Lloyd I. Rudolph and his wife, Susanne H. Rudolph, at the time both full professors of political science at the University of Chicago, rebutted in their letter to the editor in *Commentary*:

> It is true that Gandhi raised a volunteer brigade during the Zulu war but, like the brigade he raised during World War I, it was an ambulance corps to care for the wounded and sick. He meant to nurture, not kill, while being loyal to an empire whose laws he hoped to change.[7]

Martin E. Marty writing for *The Christian Century* was even more blunt.[8] In India, Western critiques on the film attracted some attention, at least within the Gandhi elite propagandists' circle. Mr. B. R. Nanda, world renowned for his own Gandhi biography, couldn't help but write another book, appropriately titled *Gandhi and His Critics*. Here he did a bit better in explaining the 1906 incident:

> In 1906 while Gandhi was practising as a barrister at Johannesburg, he had led—with the rank of Sergeant-Major—a group of twenty Indian stretcher-bearers to nurse Africans wounded during the operations against "the Zulu Rebellion" in Natal; it was a mission of mercy, all the more valuable because the British soldiers and doctors were reluctant to attend on the unfortunate victims of the military expedition. Seven years earlier, in 1899 during the Boer War, Gandhi raised a 1200-strong ambulance corps from among Indian residents of Natal. On both these occasions, he had argued that since the Indian community claimed equality in rights with the Europeans in Natal and Transvaal, it must also accept equal obligations; and one of the obligations of citizenship was participation in the defence of the country. To equate Gandhi's ambulance work with "war-mongering" is absurd. . . .[9]

Another author worth mentioning is the highly distinguished Indian-born, U.K.-based scholar Nirad C. Chaudhuri (1897–1999). While in India years ago, he was presented the unique opportunity of having personally seen Gandhi in rather close quarters. He was not at all happy to see Gandhi portrayed as he was in the movie *Gandhi*. He responded in his book *Thy Hand, Great Anarch!: India, 1921–1952*:

> As if that was not enough, a further outrage on the martyrdom of Gandhi has been perpetrated by an Englishman through a film he has made. . . . [T]he film made him a vulgar posturing demagogue, which he most emphatically was not.
>
> An Englishman making such a film had to eat every word about Gandhi uttered not only by those Englishmen who were openly and honestly hostile to him, as were Churchill and Archbishop Cosmo Lang, but also by every English Viceroy of India who had to deal with him, had personal firsthand knowledge of him, and were also respectful of him; he would give a wholly false historical view of the Indian nationalist movement; he would libel a great political phenomenon which, with all its faults and even evils, did greater good to India than Gandhi did or could have done; and, last of all, he would become an accomplice in the exploitation of the simple Indian people by the most cunning and persistent exploiters they have known even in all their unhappy existence. . . .
>
> But the film-maker . . . has become without being aware of it an agent of the present Indian ruling class. I can understand why the Government of India supported him. It took advantage of his naïveté to make him play their game. In the first place, they knew that a film on Gandhi according to the evangel preached by it would be technically better if made by an Englishman than an Indian; and, what was more important, coming from an Englishman it would carry greater conviction, as indeed it did.
>
> The interested diffusion of the false Gandhi legend reminds me of a tale by Edgar Allan Poe. In it a man who is a mesmerist wants to make an experiment in order to find out what would happen to a man if he is mesmerised in articulo mortis, just at the point of death. . . .
>
> They watched the [mesmerized] body for seven months and no change came over it. At last the mesmerist decided to release M. Valdemar from his mesmeric trance and see what happened. After some time the same hideous voice broke forth: "For God's sake!—Quick, quick—put me to sleep, or quick! Awaken me! Quick! I say to you that I am dead."
>
> The mesmerist went on with his passes and all those who were in the room were prepared to see M. Valdemar awaken. But something quite unforeseeable happened. The mesmerist describes that:
>
> "As I rapidly made the mesmeric passes, amid ejaculations of 'dead! dead!' absolutely bursting from the tongue and not from the lips of the sufferer, his whole frame at once—within the space of a single minute, or less, shrank—crumbled—absolutely rotted away beneath my hands. Upon the bed, before the whole company, there lay a nearly liquid mass of loathsome—of detestable putrescence."
>
> Will the hand of truth at any time reduce the vile myth of Gandhi to the putrid mass it deserves to be? That is not likely. All over the world too many people are doing too well out of Gandhi, above all financially, for that to be pos-

sible. As Sir Thomas Browne said: "Mummy is become merchandise, Mizraim cures wounds, and Pharaoh is sold for balsams."[10]

It was reported that *Gandhi* was shown with Arabic subtitles on the Jordanian television during the *intifada* when the Palestinians in the Israeli-occupied West Bank and Gaza rebelled nonviolently.[11] The political purpose of showing the film was obvious.

The earliest known film that Americans viewed about India was Thomas A. Edison's documentary reel *Hindoo Faqir*, first shown in 1902. A few more films followed. However, in 1939 Hollywood introduced to Americans a movie by the name of *Gunga Din*[12] and from there on Gunga Din, as a figure, was the Indian name best known to Americans until the advent of Gandhi.[13] The moviegoers watching *Gunga Din* witnessed a pathetic creature whose doglike devotion and ultimate sacrifice for his British masters was obvious. Incredibly, in the movie, the leader of a band of thugs remarkably resembled the Gandhi we know.

NOTES

1. Fatima Meer, *Apprenticeship of a Mahatma* (Durban, South Africa: Institute for Black Research/Madiba Publishers, 1994).

2. *The Pope Speaks to India* (Bombay: St. Paul Publications, 1986), pp. 15–16.

3. "Gandhi Quits Rome; Fails to See Pope," *New York Times*, December 14, 1931.

4. Mark Juergensmeyer, "Saint Gandhi," in *Saints and Virtues*, ed. John Stratton Hawley (Berkeley: University of California Press, 1987), p. 202.

5. Richard Attenborough, *In Search of Gandhi* (Piscataway, N.J.: New Century Publishers, 1982), p. 91.

6. Richard Grenier, "The Gandhi Nobody Knows," *Commentary* 75, no. 3 (March 1983): 62.

7. Lloyd and Susanne Rudolph, "Letter to the Editor," *Commentary* 76, no. 7 (July 1983): 12.

8. Martin E. Marty, "Richard, Stay Home!" *Christian Century*, August 17–24, 1983, p. 759.

9. B. R. Nanda, *Gandhi and His Critics* (Delhi: Oxford University Press, 1993), p. 115.

10. Nirad C. Chaudhuri, *Thy Hand, Great Anarch! India, 1921–1952* (New York: Addison-Wesley, 1988), pp. 881–85.

11. James W. Douglass, *The Nonviolent Coming of God* (New York: Orbis Books, 1991), p. 191.

12. *Gunga Din*, a movie produced by RKO Radio Pictures, Inc., was released in 1939. The movie was later banned in India.

13. Harold R. Isaacs, *Scratches on Our Minds: American Images of China and India* (New York: John Day, 1958), p. 241.

PART 2

*My life is one indivisible whole, and all my activities run into
one another, and they all have their rise in my insatiable love
for mankind.*

—Mahatma Gandhi
Harijan, March 2, 1934

9

It has always been a mystery to me how men can feel them-selves honoured by the humiliation of their fellow-beings.

—Mahatma Gandhi
An Autobiography

Wars simply do not pop up out of the blue. They are premeditated, and the Zulu rebellion was no exception. Modern nations (also once the aggressive colonial powers of an earlier era) that commit themselves in pursuit of war, whether defensively or offensively, employ their sovereign right to engage in war exercises, just in case. We should know that. Such was the case with the white minority government against the majority blacks of South Africa. Similarly, since Gandhi participated in the conflict in 1906, we can reasonably assume he, too, had a track record in war preparations, which we will examine in this chapter. Keep in mind that in Gandhi's own biographical writings we learn very little about his activities in the months before he volunteered for the war. Did he prepare for the war? If so, how and in what manner? Why didn't he elaborate in his autobiographical writings? Is it possible that he didn't want us to know about his questionable past and went about covering it up? The answer is *yes*. Here is the evidence:

In his *Satyagraha in South Africa*, Gandhi mentioned that sometime in 1910, while on the Tolstoy Farm, he destroyed papers. Exactly which ones, he didn't mention. In my opinion, this action of his should catch our attention. According to Gandhi:

I have thrown away or burnt such things in my life. I destroyed such papers as I felt it was not necessary to preserve them or as the scope of my activities was extended. I am not sorry for this, as to have preserved all of them would have been burden-some and expensive. I should have been compelled to keep cabinets and boxes, which would have been an eyesore to one who has taken the vow of poverty.[1]

Placing the above statement within the context of the Gandhi story line is easy. After all, in 1906, after the Zulu rebellion, Gandhi had taken the vow of poverty. And now in 1910, in the midst of the heavy-duty Satyagraha campaign, it is only natural to suppose that any reasonable person in that situation would destroy the papers. Who wants to carry that extra burden when one is under the vow of poverty while fighting a Satyagraha war? But, there is a problem! We know Pyarelal had been Gandhi's secretary for twenty-eight years; of which the last four and a half-years were as the chief secretary. After Gandhi's death, he was handpicked to write the official biography. We find that in the introduction to *Mahatma Gandhi: The Early Phase*, he brings this to our attention:

Luckily Gandhiji had brought with him from South Africa a boxful of corre-spondence and other documents relating to his work there. . . . He had also maintained a systematic and fairly exhaustive record of clippings from contem-porary newspapers for the period 1889–1900 in thirteen scrapbooks. He [Gandhi] had spoken to me about them. . . .[2]

What happened to the paperwork from 1900 onward, in particular the period covering the 1906 Zulu rebellion? Can we safely infer that Gandhi himself destroyed these documents? There is another twist: Ananda M. Pandiri in *A Com-prehensive, Annotated Bibliography on Mahatma Gandhi* recorded that Gandhi, upon returning from South Africa to India in 1915, donated around fifteen thou-sand of his books to Sheth Maneklal Jethabhai Pustakalya, a library located in Ahmedabad, Gujarat.[3] This fact alone highlights his apparent inconsistencies and contradictions. At this stage, there are two options left for us to make some sense out of Gandhi's actions:

- Follow the Gandhi story line. After the Zulu rebellion in 1906, Gandhi searched his soul. He took vows of celibacy and poverty. And in 1910 he destroyed documents that could be a source of embarrassment later on. To account for the historical gap for the period of 1893 to 1914 in South Africa later on, he wrote his biographical data, describing and giving a new account. Years later, as an old man, Gandhi clearly instructed his close disciples to destroy all his writings. Who will know the truth other than him? He was mistaken. He didn't know that after his death his die-hard followers, with the state's treasury in their grips, would go to extraor-dinary lengths to dig up his past, hoping to create an even better Gandhi image through Pyarelal's "official" biography and the *Collected Works of Mahatma Gandhi* (CWMG).[4] It is worth recording here what the first president of the new Republic of India wrote in the opening pages of *Collected Works*: "Let me close this with the assurance that no one who takes a dip into Gandhiji's stream of life as represented in this series, will emerge disappointed, for there lies in it buried a hidden treasure out of which everyone can carry as much as he likes, according to his own capacity and faith" (CWMG 1, p. viii).

- Don't accept the Gandhi story line. In 1906, after the Zulu rebellion, Gandhi had no soul searching, maybe a vow of celibacy, and certainly no vow of poverty. He destroyed no documents as he says he did in *Satyagraha in South Africa*. In 1915 he brought with him to India all the paperwork he had. Upon return, he donated fifteen thousand books to the library and kept the important documents to himself. Sometime between 1921 and 1925, when he was already against British rule and his name was gaining worldwide attention, he apparently thought it was time to clean the past. What would be better than to first destroy documents, especially those dealing with the 1906 incident? Then, rewrite the missing times in two new biographical accounts. In other words, a cover-up. Nobody will know.

I believe Gandhi exercised this option. I have researched the literature and in all honesty I cannot find any evidence that he lived in poverty after the Zulu rebellion. As far as his celibacy goes, Mrs. Gandhi might have left an answer, certainly not the one I heard in the *Gandhi* movie but somewhere else in the vast literature.

Now, the evidence destroyed, Gandhi was walking on safe territory. He had become world famous. Various Christian Churches proclaimed him as a new Messiah. Many Hindus adored him as a new avatar. Gandhi was on the high road and he was not going to let anybody bring him down. After his death, his own handpicked Hindu leaders of India, over the head of Vinoba Bhave's objections, created a new bureaucracy dedicated to research Gandhi and write books. The one hundred volumes of the *Collected Works of Mahatma Gandhi*, especially volume 5, cast a startling light on the 1906 Zulu rebellion. This is a highly prized product delivered by this public by paid group. Gandhi himself would have been appalled and might have resorted to another hunger strike to stop it, had he lived.

I contend Gandhi left several gaps uncovered in his efforts to cover up his past, one of which was *Indian Opinion*, a weekly newspaper of his own creation with a first issue that surfaced on June 4, 1903. *Indian Opinion* had sections in four languages—English, Gujarati, Hindi, and Tamil. Shortly after the first issue, the Hindi and Tamil sections were dropped. Only the English and Gujarati sections remained, Gujarati being Gandhi's mother tongue. Whatever Gandhi wrote concerning the 1906 incident in *Indian Opinion* was disseminated with the paper's circulation. His strong beliefs on the Zulu rebellion were printed not only in English but also largely in the Gujarati language—a vernacular known only to the majority of the Indian trading community who had their roots originally in Gujarat, similar to Gandhi. The majority of other Indians could not read, write, or understand the Gujarati language. Beginning in the early 1920s, Gandhi decided to cover up his past—he was safe since he had destroyed the selective documents he possessed under the umbrella of "poverty vow." But he could not retract the old issues of *Indian Opinion* that had already been circulated. It was that information which worried him later in his life. I contend he had wished his followers to destroy the information, but it didn't happen. Those letters of Gandhi printed in *Indian Opinion* concerning the Zulu rebellion are the focus of attention in this chapter. These letters or commentaries are reprinted here in their entirety for one reason: I do not wish to be accused of having presented the information out of context. Each letter of his is followed by my brief explanation.

INDIAN OPINION, NOVEMBER 18, 1905, "AN INDIAN VOLUNTEER CORPS"

Last week we reproduced, from *The Natal Witness*, some questions and answers at a political meeting in Newcastle with reference to the liability of Indians to serve during the time of war.

> Mr. Thorold urged that some arrangement should be made whereby the Arabs and Indians should be called upon to assist in case of the calling out of the first line of defence. It would be manifestly unfair to allow the Arabs to sit in their stores and to do business while the Europeans were fighting at the front.

Had Mr. Thorold known the inner working of the Government, he would not have made the remarks attributed to him. The Government simply *do not wish* to give the Indians an opportunity of showing that they are as capable, as any other community, of taking their share in the defence of the Colony. At the time of the Boer War, it will be remembered, the Indians volunteered to do any work that might be entrusted to them, and it was with the greatest difficulty that they could get their services accepted even for ambulance work. General Buller has certified as to what kind of work the Natal Indian Volunteer Ambulance Corps did. If the Government only realised what reserve force is being wasted, they would make use of it and give Indians the opportunity of a thorough training for actual warfare. There is, too, on the Statute-book, a law for the purpose, which has been allowed to fall into desuetude from sheer prejudice. We believe a very fine volunteer corps could be formed from Colonial-born Indians that would be second to none in Natal in smartness and efficiency, not only in peace but in actual service also. (CWMG 5, #150, p. 134).

* * *

The reasons Gandhi offered as to why Indians should participate in the coming Zulu War are: (1) Indians are capable of defending the colony (2) It makes sense to use the reserve force, (3) There is an old law allowing it. In Gandhi's eyes, the colonial-born Indians should get the first honor to be selected for military service!

INDIAN OPINION, DECEMBER 2, 1905, "INDIAN VOLUNTEERING"

Our note on the subject of Indian volunteering, we are glad to notice, has been warmly taken up by *The Natal Witness*, and some correspondence has appeared on the subject. We hope, now that the matter has been taken up by the Press, that it will not be allowed to die out without an expression of opinion from the Government as to its policy. Law No. 25 of 1875 was specially passed to increase "the maximum strength of the Volunteer Force in the Colony by adding thereto a force of Indian Immigrants Volunteer Infantry". Under the Law, the Governor is authorised "to accept, with the consent of the employer, the services of any Indian Immigrants who may be willing to be formed into a Volunteer Corps." The limit of the strength of the force was, in *those* days confined to one thousand three hundred men. Any planter could raise such a corps, and, subject to the approval of the Governor, be appointed Captain of the same. A capitation grant of twenty shillings per man is made for every efficient volunteer and no volunteer

> Shall count as efficient who shall not attend a minimum of twelve days' drill of four hours per diem, or twenty-four days' drill of two hours per diem, or forty-eight days' drill of one hour per diem in each year, and no drill shall count which is not of an hour's duration.

Provision is made also for compensation to any member of the Indian Immigrants Volunteer Force whilst engaged in actual military service, should he be wounded or otherwise seriously injured, and for pensions to the widows and children left in Natal of any such volunteer killed in action, or who shall die of wounds received while so engaged. Here, then, if the Government only wanted the Indian immigrant to take his share in the defence of the Colony, which he has before now shown himself to be quite willing to do, there is legal machinery ready made for it (CWMG 5, #164, p. 154).

* * *

Gandhi's sole reason why the Indians should participate in the Zulu War was simply to advocate law number 25 of 1875 as a way for Indians to participate.

INDIAN OPINION, MARCH 17, 1906, "A PLEA FOR INDIAN VOLUNTEERING"

The Natal Native trouble is dragging on a slow existence. There can be no doubt that the imposition of the poll-tax is itself the immediate cause, though probably the trouble has been brewing for a long time. Whosesoever the mistake may be, report has it that it is costing the Colony two thousand pounds per day. The white colonists are trying to cope with it, and many citizen-soldiers have taken up arms. Today, perhaps, no further assistance is necessary, but this trouble ought to suggest reflections to the Government, as also to every thinking colonist. There is a population of over one hundred thousand Indians in Natal. It has been proved that they can do very efficient work in time of war. The suspicion that they were worthless in emergencies has been dispelled. In the face of these incontrovertible facts, is it prudent for the Government to allow a source of strength, which always lies at its disposal, to run to waste? Our contemporary, *The Natal Witness*, has recently written a very thoughtful editorial on the Indian question, and has shown that, some day or other, the question of Indian representation must be seriously taken up by the colonists. We agree with the view, though Indians do not aspire to any political power in the Colony. All they require is a guarantee of full civil rights under the general laws of the Colony. This should be the birthright of every British subject living in a British territory. Refusal to accept anybody as an immigrant is, in certain circumstances, justifiable, but imposition of disabilities upon well-behaved and physically sound immigrants can never be justified either on economic or political grounds. Whilst, therefore, the question of Indian representation is undoubtedly very important, we consider that the question of Indian volunteering is more important because it is more practicable. There is, it is nowadays fully recognised, work in the field which does not require the bearing of arms, but which is just as useful and quite as honourable as the shouldering of a rifle. If the Government, instead of neglecting Indians, were to employ them for volunteering work, they would add appreciably to the utility of the Militia, and would always be able in times of trouble to rely upon Indians giving a good account of themselves. The Government, we doubt not, recognise that it is impossible for them to drive Indians out of the country. Why not, then, make the best of the material at hand, and convert a hitherto neglected community into a permanent and most valuable asset of the State (CWMG 5, #250, pp. 233–34)?

* * *

Gandhi certainly placed quite a few general persuasive arguments to the government to make his case strong for Indians to participate in the war, first as noncombatants and then hopefully as a permanent force after receiving the required combat training.

INDIAN OPINION, MARCH 31, 1906, "INDIAN VOLUNTEERING"

Mr. Watt, the Minister of Defence, has been "letting himself go" at a recent meeting which was held in connection with the militia. In reply to a question:

> Do the Government propose to make Arabs, in possession of stores in various parts of the Colony, join the militia reserves, and if so, will they provide them with rifles?

the answer, we are told, which Mr. Watt gave, drew forth a round of applause. "I am pleased," he is reported to have said,

> to say that the militia is composed entirely of Europeans. I should be sorry indeed if I should have to depend for the defence of myself and family on Arabs, but the Government, I am glad to say, has power in time of war to turn out all the Coloured population—Indians, Natives and Arabs—for any service which may be necessary.

The following further question was then put:

> Does the Government recognise that when the Europeans are called out, the Arabs will obtain the trade in all districts? What do they propose doing in regard to this?

Mr. Watt's reply was in keeping with the first:

> That is a matter in which I think the leaders should have a voice. If I were a leader, I should advise the Government to regulate the opening and closing times of shops. I should see that Europeans were not treated worse than Arabs, and I should see that the Arabs had their share of the work, if not in carrying rifles, in digging trenches.

We have no doubt that, as Defence Minister, Mr. Watt knows that digging of trenches is just as necessary in warfare as the shouldering of a rifle. If, then, he would not depend for his own and his family's defence on Arabs, why will he have the latter to dig trenches? Either work, we have it from the late Mr. Harry Escombe, who, too, was a Minister of Defence, is equally honourable. Whether Mr. Watt, on reconsideration, would have himself or the Colony defended by Arabs and Indians or not, by the work of digging trenches or other work, how does he expect them to do any work in connection with warfare unless previous training is given? Even the camp-followers in any army require proper discipline, otherwise they are, instead of being a help, a positive nuisance. But we despair of having either common sense or justice at the hands of a Minister who so far forgets himself as to offer an unwarranted insult to a whole class of inoffensive people.

In contradistinction to the attitude shown on various occasions by the Minister of Defence—whose business it is as a Minister, we might remark, to put his personal prejudices in his pocket—we welcome an editorial in *The Natal Advertiser* of the other day, which we reprint elsewhere. Our contemporary rightly gives Indians and Coloured people the credit due to them. It also points out that Section 83 of the Militia Act states that no ordinary member of a Coloured contingent shall be armed with weapons of precision, *unless such contingents are called out to operate against [persons] other than Europeans.* Now it is evident that, in the unfortunate event of such a state of affairs arising as to necessitate the arming of an Indian contingent, the arms would be useless in the hands of inexperienced men. Why will not the authorities adopt the suggestion we made some time ago, and raise a volunteer corps from amongst Indians? We feel sure the Colonial-born Indians especially—Natal's own children equally with the whites—would give a good account of themselves. Why do not the Colonists insist on these, at all events, being given a chance to prove their mettle (CWMG 5, #267, pp. 251–52)?

* * *

Here Gandhi has advanced the legal reasoning on a higher plateau—direct reference to then current minister of defense, Mr. Watt, and the former defense minister, Mr. Escombe. He now specifically cites section 83 of the Militia Act to force Mr. Watt to act; this also questions the wisdom of training Indians for military purposes.

INDIAN OPINION, APRIL 7, 1906, "THE POLITICAL TURMOIL IN NATAL"
Translated from Gujarati

Important events, the effects of which will not be forgotten for many years, took place in Natal last week. As a result of these, Natal has gained in stature. The cause of self-government has triumphed; but the British Empire has received a set-back.

The Kaffirs in Natal rose in revolt against the poll-tax. Sergeants Hunt and Armstrong were killed in the revolt; martial law was declared in Natal and the Kaffirs were severely dealt with. Some Kaffirs were prosecuted under the martial law, and twelve of them were condemned to death and blown up at the mouth of a cannon. The Kaffirs from neighbouring areas and their Chief were invited to witness the execution, which was to take place on March 29.

Meanwhile, Lord Elgin sent a cablegram from England to the Governor of Natal, asking him to suspend the execution of the sentence. The executive councillors of the Natal Government resented this and tendered their resignations to the Governor. The Governor asked them to wait until a further communication was received from Lord Elgin, and to this they agreed.

As soon the full story became known, a wave of excitement swept over the whole of South Africa. The Press protested vehemently, arguing that the constitution of self-governing Natal was violated by Lord Elgin's intervention. They said that, as Natal was a self-governing Colony, the Imperial Government could not interfere in its administration. Congratulations were showered from every side on the executive councillors for having resigned. Meetings were held at many places, and speeches made against the Imperial Government.

The Imperial Government believed that, since they had helped Natal to put down the rebellion, it was their duty to see that justice was done to the Kaffirs; and hence they saw nothing improper in asking the Natal Government to put off execution of the sentence. But South Africa became excited, the arguments of the Imperial Government proved unavailing, and Lord Elgin had to bow down before Natal opinion.

Lord Elgin has written to the Governor that, on inquiry, it was found that justice had been done in the case of the Kaffirs, that the Imperial Government did not now wish to interfere in the administration by the executive councillors of Natal, and that they could do what they deemed proper. Lord Elgin has, however, put the entire blame on the Governor. He further says that no intervention by the Imperial Government would have taken place if the Governor had supplied all the facts of the case at the outset. Twelve lives have been taken for two. The twelve Kaffirs were blown to death at the mouth of a cannon on Monday.

During all this excitement, only one man kept a cool head, and that was Mr. Morcum. At a meeting in Maritzburg, he declared that Lord Elgin's move was quite proper. It was a matter of saving human life, and there was no need for the executive to resign. Hunt and Armstrong were killed before martial law was declared; and hence the Kaffirs ought to have been tried by the Supreme Court. The whole meeting was against him, and though they hissed and hooted at him, the brave Mr. Morcum had his way.

What is the outcome of all this? That some Kaffirs were killed will soon be forgotten. We cannot say for certain whether or not they have received justice. But wherever self-government has been granted, a people became overweening. They will take undue liberties, and the Imperial Government will hesitate to intervene. It will seldom do so, for, as the saying goes, a man once bitten by a serpent dreads even a length of rope. It is only the Coloured people who stand to lose by this. They have no vote. Where they have it, they cannot use it effectively, so that the Colonial authority will place greater restrictions on them, and they alone will get justice who ingratiate themselves with it. Great changes are likely to take place in South Africa during the coming years. The Indians and other Coloured people have much to ponder and they must act with circumspection (CWMG 5, #285, pp. 266–67).

* * *

Here is the first letter about the impending conflict printed in the Gujarati language. It provides a brief history, but does not tell Gandhi's Gujarati-only readers that he had been importuning the government for Indians to serve in the coming Zulu war. Also, it seems like Gandhi is making a case against the idea of self-government.

INDIAN OPINION, APRIL 14, 1906, "THE NATAL REBELLION"
Translated from Gujarati

The twelve Kaffirs sentenced to capital punishment have been shot dead. The Colonists of Natal are pleased. Mr. Smythe's prestige has been vindicated. The Imperial Government have had to climb down. Mr. Churchill made a very good speech in this connection. He showed that the Imperial Government were entitled to an explanation from Natal. For, if the Kaffirs did not remain under proper control, the Imperial Government were bound to send an expeditionary force. Incidents that followed, like Mr. Smythe's resignation, are to be ascribed solely to the speeches made by Mr. Chamberlain's partisans and to the fact that all the newspapers in South Africa are controlled by that party. Mr. Churchill pointed out that, if Mr. Smythe's act should become a precedent, the good feeling between England and the Colonies would not endure.

While Mr. Churchill was speaking thus, the third chapter of this woeful tale was being written. Though twelve Kaffirs were put to death, the rebellion, instead of being quelled, has gathered strength. Bambata, the Kaffir Chief, was deposed and another installed in his place, because the behaviour of the former was not satisfactory. Seizing the right opportunity, Bambata kidnapped the new Chief and rose in revolt. And the disturbance continues in Grey Town. The region in which Bambata is operating as an outlaw is in difficult terrain full of bushes and trees, where the Kaffirs can remain in hiding for long periods. To find them out and force a fight is a difficult job.

The small party of soldiers that was on Bambata's trail included the Englishmen who had shot the twelve Kaffirs. Bambata and his men encircled the party and, though they fought very bravely, the soldiers were defeated in the end and managed to escape with great difficulty. Some of them were killed. The dead included those who had shot the twelve Kaffirs. Such is the law of God. The executioners met their death within two days.

At the time of writing, Bambata is at large. Meanwhile, his followers go on increasing. There is no knowing how all this will end.

What is our duty during these calamitous times in the Colony? It is not for us to say whether the revolt of the Kaffirs is justified or not. We are in Natal by virtue of British power. Our very existence depends upon it. It is therefore our duty to render whatever help we can. There was a discussion in the Press as to what part the Indian community would play in the event of an actual war. We have already declared in the English columns of this journal that the Indian community is ready to play its part; and we believe what we did during the Boer War should also be done now. That is, if the Government so desires, we should raise an ambulance corps. We should also agree to become permanent volunteers, if the Government is prepared to give us the requisite training.

Such a step would be considered proper, even if we viewed it from the standpoint of our own interests. The case of the twelve Kaffirs shows us that whatever justice we may seek is to be had ultimately from the local Government. The first step in trying to get it is to do our own duty. The common people in this country keep themselves in readiness for war. We, too, should contribute our share (CWMG 5, #297, pp. 281–82).

* * *

Here is a second letter about the impending conflict printed in the Gujarati language. It provides another brief on the Kaffirs. Now Gandhi begins to importune his Gujarati readers to serve in the coming Zulu War. Also, he cautions them to be realistic for their self-interests. However, he begins with a brainwashing tactic: "It is not for us to say whether the revolt of the Kaffirs is justified or not."

INDIAN OPINION, APRIL 28, 1906

This issue carried a report in English attesting to the fact that on April 24, 1906, about 250 Indians gathered under the auspices of Natal Indian Congress for a meeting in the Congress Hall, Durban, to consider appropriate Indian response to the Zulu rebellion. Apparently, there were different opinions floating around as to the cause of black revolt. Gandhi made clear his position by being adamant that the duty of Indians was "not to be prejudiced by any such thoughts." Here is another of his brainwashing tactics. He also introduced another strange notion that, "if [Indians] claimed rights of citizenship, they were bound to take their natural share in the responsibilities that such rights carried with them" (CWMG 5, #309, p. 291). That is, to defend the Colony from its rightful owners, the blacks! Anyway, the resolution to help the white government passed unanimously in the end.

In all probability, after this meeting, Natal Indian Congress dispatched the Pledge of Allegiance to the Natal government. This pledge was printed in *Indian Opinion* dated June 16, 1906, once the offer was accepted.

> We, the undersigned, solemnly and sincerely declare that we will be faithful and bear true allegiance to His Majesty King Edward the Seventh, His Heirs and Successors, and that we will faithfully serve in the supernumerary list of the Active Militia Force of the Colony of Natal as Stretcher-Bearers, until we shall

lawfully cease to be members thereof, and the terms of the service are that we should each receive Rations, Uniform, Equipment and 1s. 6d. per day.

> M. K. Gandhi, U. M. Shelat, H. I. Joshi, S. B. Medh,
> Khan Mahomed, Mahomed Shaikh, Dada Mian,
> Pooti Naiken, Appasamy, Kunjee, Shaikh Madar,
> Mahomed, Alwar, Muthusamy, Coopoosamy, Ajodhyasing,
> Kistama, Ali, Bhailal, Jamaludin (CWMG 5, #379, p. 357)

* * *

Gandhi was indeed jubilant in his English column—"An Indian Offer"—in the April 28, 1906, issue of *Indian Opinion*:

> The meeting held under the auspices of the Natal Indian Congress the other day is to be congratulated on having passed a resolution offering the services of Indians in connection with the Native revolt. The offer is a complete answer to the many correspondents in the local Press, who have been worrying themselves over the prospect, should the rebellion spread, of having to defend themselves and also Indians in the Colony. Those Indians who packed the Congress Hall last Tuesday evening have shown that they possess the faculty of discrimination in an eminent degree, and that they are capable of forgetting personal grievances when the common good of the body politic, of which they form a part, is concerned. We trust that the Government will see their way to accept the offer, and give the Indian community the chance once more of proving its worth.
>
> But whether the offer is accepted or not, it shows most clearly the importance of the Government turning to good account the Indian willingness to take its share in the defence of the Colony by giving Indians a proper previous training. We have more than once pointed out the criminal folly of not utilizing the admirable material the Indian community offers for additional defensive purposes. If it is not possible to turn the present Indian population out of the Colony, it is surely elementary wisdom to give it an adequate military training. There is an expressive Indian proverb that you cannot start digging a well when a fire breaks out. Nor can you suddenly develop the Indians, however willing and capable they may be, into an efficient corps of even "trench-diggers". Will Mr. Watt and his fellow-ministers wake up to a sense of their duty in the matter? (CWMG 5, #312, p. 293)

Who would tell the good news to those readers who read only the Gujarati language? One can see Gandhi's influence on his fellow Indians of the merchant community. Apart from his standard propaganda rhetoric, Gandhi voices another reason to fight a war: as a logical Indian response to the concerns of white local press. Apparently at this meeting of the Natal Indian Congress, there were about forty Indians who had volunteered for the war services. In the Pledge of Allegiance, one can count a total of only twenty names. This wide discrepancy is not accounted for in the literature.

INDIAN OPINION, APRIL 28, 1906, "THE NATAL REBELLION AND AID TO NATAL"
Translated from Gujarati

Bambata is still at large, and it is reported that he has 300 men with him. Many speeches have been made on the armed encounters with him. The Natal cabinet has declared that it will not seek aid from England. Telegrams have been received which mention a large meeting held at Johannesburg and say that the people there are prepared to render all aid to Natal. All this means that the strength and the independence of Natal will increase. It was right and proper of the Indian community to have gone to the help of the Government at such a time. Had they not made the offer, a slur would have been put on our good name for ever. Those who have enlisted themselves for war have indeed shown great courage and enthusiasm. Most of them are Colonial-born. It is a matter of satisfaction to us that they have joined the other Indians and it is the duty of the leaders to encourage them to go forward (CWMG 5, #317, p. 297).

* * *

The latter portion is quite puzzling. Gandhi has supported the decision to render Indian help; otherwise he says a slur would have fallen on their good name. Gandhi mentioned that other Indians had enlisted for the war; this news that cannot be accounted for. Perhaps Gandhi is playing a game with his Gujarati readers to induce them to join him for the war by citing other fake Indians.

INDIAN OPINION, MAY 5, 1906, "OUR DUTY"
Translated from Gujarati

A correspondent who has signed himself "Ajax" has addressed a letter to *The Advertiser*. We print a translation elsewhere in this issue. The letter deserves to be pondered over by all Indians. It is intended to stir up public feeling against us. All of it is written in an ironical manner, the purport being that Indians are useless in times of war.

We should give this accusation earnest thought. In sending an offer of help to the Natal Government we took the right step. Because of this, we can face others with some measure of confidence. But that is not enough. We should strive harder with a view to playing [a more direct] part in times of war. Under the Militia Law, enlisting is compulsory for whites when war breaks out. If we can also prove our willingness and ability to fight, our disabilities may possibly disappear. But whether these are removed or not, we Indians in South Africa ought to hold ourselves in readiness to share in the adversity that might befall Natal or any other part of South Africa. If we fail to do so, we shall be found wanting to that extent.

There is rumour of a revolt in Swaziland. The Natal Government has ordered huge quantities of ammunition. All this goes to show that the Natal rebellion will last many more days. And if it spreads further, it might affect the whole of South Africa. This time help from the Transvaal has already reached Natal. The Cape has promised aid, and an offer has been made by England also. If we keep aloof at such a time, it is bound to create a bad impression about us. It is necessary for every Indian to consider this matter very seriously (CWMG 5, #326, pp. 302–303).

* * *

His Gujarati readers are presented with another emotional appeal. He apprised them of the potentially developing danger from blacks, which if left unchecked may adversely affect Indians. He is hammering his propaganda talk along the lines already written earlier.

INDIAN OPINION, MAY 12, 1906, "INDIAN VOLUNTEERING"

Correspondence has appeared in *The Natal Advertiser* on the offer of the Indian community, in connection with the Native rebellion, which ordinarily we should not feel justified in noticing. As, however, the subject discussed by the correspondents of our contemporary is of such vital importance both to the Indian community and to the Colony, we make no apology for dealing with the points raised by them. We have no concern with the reckless abuse indulged in by some of the correspondents.

One of them has satirically suggested that Indians, so that they may not run away, should be placed in the front-line, and that then the fight between them and the Natives will be a sight for the gods. We propose to take the correspondent seriously, and venture to suggest that, if such a course were adopted, it would be undoubtedly the very best that could happen to the Indians. If they be cowardly, they will deserve the fate that will overtake them; if they be brave, nothing can be better than for brave men to be in the front-line. But the pity of it is that the Government, and the European Colonists who have dictated the policy to the Government, have not taken the elementary precaution of giving the necessary discipline and instruction to the Indians. It is, therefore, a matter of physical impossibility to expect Indians to do any work with the rifle; or, for that matter, to do any work in connection with war with much efficiency. The Indian Ambulance Corps, at the time of the late war, did excellent work, without the necessary instruction and discipline, only because the Indian leaders who joined the Corps had previously been instructed and prepared under Dr. Booth.

Another correspondent has suggested that Indians should not be armed, because if they were, they would sell their arms to the Natives. This is a suggestion which is made wickedly, and without any foundation in fact. Indians have never been armed; it is, therefore, sheer folly to say that, if they were, they would act in a particular direction. It has also been suggested that the offer has been made to gain cheap applause, and also to gain something not made apparent in the proceedings of the Congress meeting. The first statement is slanderous, and the best way to disprove the stricture is for these correspondents to make the Government accept the offer, and to see whether the response is adequate or not. The second statement is difficult to understand. If it is intended to convey the impression that Indians, by serving during war time, hope to obtain a redress of their wrongs, the statement is true, and no Indian should be ashamed of such a motive. What can be better and more praiseworthy than that Indians, by standing shoulder to shoulder with their fellow-Colonists in the present trouble, should show that they are not unworthy of the ordinary rights of citizenship which they have been claiming all these years? But it is equally true also that the offer has been made unconditionally, as a matter of simple duty, and irrespective of whether there is any redress of the grievances granted or not. We, therefore, consider it to be the special aim of every Colonist to support the Indian community in the offer it has made, and thereby to show prudence and foresight, for it cannot be seriously argued that there is any wisdom or statesmanship in blindly refusing to make use of, for purposes of war, one hundred thousand Indians who are perfectly loyal, and who are capable of good training (CWMG 5, #334, pp. 311–12).

* * *

This is Gandhi's classic example of bluffing. He heightens his military service response to these alleged white correspondents who continue to challenge Gandhi and others. Gandhi no doubt is trying to arouse his readers to enlist. Along with pursuing the old propaganda lines, Gandhi throws the biggest stake to his readers to grab: Indians are described as "fellow-Colonists" who must stand by their fellow white brothers to continue colonialism over blacks and their land! The timing is perfect! He has pumped the Indian ego by throwing to them the attractive impression of being "fellow-Colonists." Then, on May 29, 1906, he let the South African authorities know that he and the British Indian Association have always "admitted the principle of white predominance and has, therefore, no desire to press, on behalf of the community it represents, for any political rights for the sake of them" (CWMG 5, #364, p. 335).

INDIAN OPINION, JUNE 2, 1906, "THE NATAL REBELLION"
Translated from Gujarati

We publish elsewhere a translation of a letter an old Colonist has addressed to *The Times of Natal.* The substance of it is that the Indians are not able to go to the battle-field, but they can assist the men at the front with the requisite amenities. It is necessary that Indians help in the way they did when a fund was started at the time of the Boer War. It will be good to collect some money and send it to the Government or to some Fund that might have been started. We shall then be considered to have done our duty to that extent. We hope the leaders of the community will take up this matter (CWMG 5, #370, p. 347).

* * *

Now he makes another demand of these Gujarati-reading "fellow-Colonists"— to collect money for the purposes of conducting the war.

INDIAN OPINION, JUNE 9, 1906, "INDIANS AND THE NATIVE UNREST"

The Government have at last accepted the offer of the Indian community, and put it upon its mettle. By way of experiment, they want a corps of twenty stretcher-bearers. The Natal Indian Congress has sent in a prompt reply. We think the Congress has done well in offering to defray the wages of the bearers, so long as the corps remains in the experimental stage.

The acceptance by the Government synchronizes with the amendment of the Fire-Arms Act, providing for the supply of arms to Indians, and the statement made by Mr. Maydon to the effect that the Government intended to give Indians an opportunity of taking their share in the defence of the Colony.

Indians have now a splendid opportunity for showing that they are capable of appreciating the duties of citizenship. At the same time, the fact of the corps being raised is nothing to be unduly proud of. Twenty Indians, or even two hundred, going to the front is a flea-bite. The Indian sacrifice will rightly be considered infinitesimal. But it is the principle involved which marks the importance of the event. The Government have, by accepting the offer, shown their goodwill. And if Indians come successfully through the ordeal, the possibilities for the future are very great. Should they be assigned a permanent part in the Militia, there will remain no ground for the European complaint that Europeans alone have to bear the brunt of Colonial defence, and Indians will cease to feel that, in not being allowed to participate in it, they are slighted (CWMG 5, #376, p. 353).

* * *

Sometime in the very early part of June 1906, the offer for a stretcher-bearer corps comprising twenty Indian "soldiers" was accepted. Gandhi seems to be pleased with this amendment to the Fire-Arms Act. Gandhi is saying that now is the opportunity to enlist and cement future foundations to get the prized military training with arms! Gandhi knows the art of war and his Indians are a natural ally to the war-making apparatus.

INDIAN OPINION, JUNE 9, 1906, "SOLDIERS' FUND"
Translated from Gujarati

The Durban Women's Association has started a special fund for the soldiers who have gone to the front to fight the Kaffirs. All leading men have contributed to the Fund and some Indian names are seen among the contributors. It is our advice that more Indians, traders and others, should subscribe to the Fund. We mentioned last time how a correspondent had advised us to raise such a fund in Maritzburg. He says that, since we cannot bear our full share of the burden in the war, it is better that we help in this manner.

The soldiers' life is a hard one. The salary and allowances that the Government pay them are not always enough. Those, therefore, who do not go to the front should, in order to express their sympathy, raise a fund for the purpose of sending the soldiers fruits, tobacco, warm clothing and other things that they might need. It is our duty to subscribe to such a fund (CWMG 5, #377, pp. 353–54).

* * *

Cigarettes (tobacco) for Indian soldiers! For white soldiers! This is not the same Gandhi we have heard of! Gujarati readers knew their man! Apparently, in South Africa it was no surprise to the Indians that Gandhi would go for using cigarettes.

INDIAN OPINION, JUNE 23, 1906, "INDIAN VOLUNTEERS"
Translated from Gujarati

Much discussion has been carried on in this journal regarding whether or not the Indians should participate in the war. The Government has agreed to accept a corps of twenty stretcher-bearers, and the Congress has got that number together. This has produced a very favourable impression on the minds of prominent whites. Some leading members of the community have, because of this, formed the opinion that we must have innate ability for such work; and they advise us that we should accordingly ask for a permanent place in the Volunteer Corps.

Between this proposal and the Stretcher-Bearer Corps that has already been raised, there is much difference. The Stretcher-Bearer Corps is to last only a few days. Its work will be only to carry the wounded, and it will be disbanded when such work is no longer necessary. These men are not allowed to bear arms. The move for a Volunteer Corps is quite different and much more important. That Corps will be a permanent body; its members will be issued weapons, and they will receive military training every year at stated times. For the present they will not have any fighting to do. Wars are not fought all the time. A war breaks out, roughly speaking, once in twenty years. It is now more than twenty years since the last Kaffir rebellion broke out. There is, therefore, absolutely no risk in joining the Volunteer Corps. It can be looked upon as a kind of annual picnic. The person joining it gets enough exercise and thus keeps his body in good trim and improves his health. One who enlists as a volunteer is much respected. People love him and praise him, calling him a civilian soldier.

If the Indians are given such a status, we believe it would be a very good thing. It is likely to bring in some political advantage. Whether or not any advantage is to be derived, there is no doubt that it is our duty to enlist. Hundreds of leading whites enlist themselves and take pride in doing so. Under the prevailing law, it is open to the Government to enlist compulsorily. We ought to obey the laws designed for the defence of the country we live in. Therefore, considering the matter from any point, it is clear that, if we are able to join the Volunteer Corps, the reproach against us would be lived down, once and for all.

For fifteen years now the whites have accused the Indians that, if it came to giving one's life in defence of Natal, they would desert their posts of duty and flee home. We cannot meet this charge with a written rejoinder. There is but one way of disproving it—the way of action. The time to act appears to have come now. But how is it to be done? Not by making volunteers out of the poor labourers freed from their indentures. It is the duty of the trading community to take part in the movement themselves. Many men can be trained up even if each shop offers only one man. Trade will not suffer. The condition of those who join will improve. They will gain in strength and energy and will be deemed to have done their duty as citizens.

It is sheer superstition to believe, as some appear to do, that there is greater risk to life in going to the battle-field or preparing for it. Next week we intend to adduce examples in support of this.

Meanwhile, we are placing these thoughts before the leaders of the community and we hope that they will receive due consideration (CWMG 5, #385, pp. 361–62).

* * *

If this letter is not an outright bluff (a part of some Hindu brainwashing mechanism), then I don't know what is. It is written in Gujarati for a purpose: he is encouraging his own merchant community to get ready to join the Volunteer Corps. The stretcher-bearer corps is a small achievement, a stepping-stone to a permanent place in the military hierarchy. Gandhi seems to know much more about the Kaffirs' history.

INDIAN OPINION, JUNE 23, 1906, "INDIAN STRETCHER-BEARER CORPS"
Translated from Gujarati

Mr. Omar Haji Amod Johari and Mr. Mahomed Cassim Anglia, the joint Honorary Secretaries of the Congress, have received from the Government a reply to their letter offering to pay the salary of the members of the Stretcher-Bearer Corps. The Government have accepted the offer.

Mrs. Nanji and Mrs. Gabriel have together prepared Red Cross badges for the members of the Corps. These badges are worn on the left arm and identify those who are engaged exclusively in attending to the wounded. These badges cannot be very important in the Kaffir rebellion; but among European nations there is a convention that arms cannot be used against persons wearing such badges (CWMG 5, #388, pp. 363–64).

* * *

Gandhi not only wanted Indians to go to war but also wanted to pay them through the coffers of the Natal Indian Congress. Red Cross badges are not very important while fighting the Kaffirs. The suggestion is that Kaffirs are backward savages. Then why wear those badges?

INDIAN OPINION, JUNE 30, 1906, "SHOULD INDIANS VOLUNTEER OR NOT?"
Translated from Gujarati

We commented on this subject in our last issue. Towards the end of that article, we had said that most of us held back only because of fear. There is, however, no cause whatever for fear, as should be evident from the examples we propose to give for the benefit of those who believe that we should be ever ready to participate in war if we want to live happily and respectably in Natal, in South Africa or, for that matter, in any part of the British Empire. The Crimean War caused heavy casualties; yet it has been estimated that fewer men died from bayonet or bullet wounds in that war than through sheer carelessness or perverse living. It was calculated that, on an average, more men died of fever and other diseases during the attack on Ladysmith than by Boer bullets. The experience in every war has been similar.

Moreover, those who can take care of themselves and lead regular lives while at the front can live in health and happiness. The training such men receive cannot be had elsewhere, that is, if they do not go to the front only to prove their valour or quench their thirst for blood. A man going to the battle-front has to train himself to endure severe hardships. He is obliged to cultivate the habit of living in comradeship with large numbers of men. He easily learns to make do with simple food. He is required to keep regular hours. He forms the habit of obeying his superior's orders promptly and without argument. He also learns to discipline the movement of his limbs. And he has also to learn how to live in limited space according to the maxims of health. Instances are known of unruly and wayward men who went to the front and returned reformed and able fully to control both their mind and body.

For the Indian community, going to the battle-field should be an easy matter; for, whether Muslims or Hindus, we are men with profound faith in God. We have a greater sense of duty, and it should therefore be easier for us to volunteer. We are not overcome by fear when hundreds of thousands of men die of famine or plague in our country. What is more, when we are told of our duty, we continue to be indifferent, keep our houses dirty, lie hugging our hoarded wealth. Thus, we live a wretched life acquiescing in a long, tormented process ending in death. Why, then, should we fear the death that may perhaps overtake us on the battle-field? We have to learn much from what the whites are doing in Natal. There is hardly any family from which some one has not gone to fight the Kaffir rebels. Following their example, we should steel our hearts and take courage. Now is the time when the leading whites want us to take this step; if we let go this opportunity, we shall repent later. We therefore urge all Indian leaders to do their duty to the best of their ability (CWMG 5, #391, pp. 366–67).

* * *

Another one of Gandhi's classic bluffs directed toward his own caste. This commentary should be a part of curriculum at our military schools. Amazingly, Gandhi had a tendency to mix religion and politics in any way that suited his ideology. Here also, religion is the backbone of his chilling arguments. Also, Indians can prove their patriotism by killing blacks. In the last portion he is sarcastic to his own caste colleagues, whether they picked it up or not. Is Gandhi learning about other wars also, such as the Crimean War? And how would he put this knowledge to use?

* * *

Let us now summarize Gandhi's statements to get a clear picture. Before joining the army, Gandhi had a total of about seven months at his disposal to make his case, starting with his first letter dated November 18, 1905. The first four letters are essentially addressed as a response to the white community, particularly the government leaders and the white print media. He starts off with a "defense of the colony" argument. He demands training in actual warfare, not for all Indians, only for ones who are colonial-born. He then makes a legal maneuver, resurrecting an old dormant law to convince Natal leaders of their legal obligations to train Indians militarily for defense of the colony. Then he puts forth his second-best option: to plead for Indians to aid the militia by doing fieldwork.

After laboring for about four months to justify the war preparations, Gandhi turns his attention to Indian readers of his *Indian Opinion*, in particular the Gujarati-speaking community. He writes in brief to "educate" them of the Kaffirs' revolt. While challenging their masculinity, he starts to implement mass brainwash techniques to absolve his readers from thinking about blacks and their struggle. He gets what he wants from the Natal Indian Congress. Presumably there were problems; not everyone agreed with Gandhi. He blurted out the notion that Indians claimed "rights of citizenship." Did Indians really claim themselves to be citizens of Natal? He tells Natal authorities it will be "criminal folly" if they don't take in Indians for the war. Not only is it the duty of Indians to enlist, but it is also the duty of Natal authorities to open doors for Indians to enlist. Then Gandhi begins to make use of the Indian pride issue and heightens the gravity of the blacks' revolt by predicting its likely spread. Gandhi is overly eager to see his Indians in a war against blacks. After all, he tells them rather frankly, they too are colonists over blacks and therefore, standing shoulder to shoulder with fellow white colonists is a natural progression. Indians, in addition to their military services, should also start a drive for money collection. And finally, he makes a last-ditch effort in a series of bluffs on the nature of the battleground: it's good for your health; no greater risk to life; a vacation time, as if going to some resort; a source of pride; you will learn to control your diet; to live in company; learn athletics and discipline; learn to adjust, to take orders from (white) superiors, and presumably from the sergeant-major without any argument! With this evidence of Gandhi's militarism, let's revisit Richard Grenier's 1983 statement:

> It is something of an anomaly that Gandhi, held in popular myth to be a pure pacifist (a myth which governments of India have always been at great pains to sustain in the belief that it will reflect credit on India itself, and to which the present movie adheres slavishly), was until fifty not ill-disposed to war at all. As I have already noted, in three wars, no sooner had the bugles sounded than Gandhi not only gave his support, but was clamoring for arms. To form new Regiments! To fight! To destroy the enemies of the empire! Regular Indian army

units fought in both the Boer War and World War I, but this was not enough for Gandhi. He wanted to raise new troops, even, in the case of the Boer and Kaffir Wars, from a tiny Indian colony in South Africa. British military authorities thought it not really worth the trouble to train such a small body of Indians as soldiers, and were even resistant to training them as an auxiliary medical corps ("stretcher bearers"), but finally yielded to Gandhi's relentless importuning.[5]

Looking at a bigger picture of what prompted the war in the first place, we are confronted with another question: What business did Gandhi have to go against blacks? Gandhi's activities were solely directed at protecting the economic well-being of the elite Indian classes; blacks likewise were engaged in preserving their rapidly shrinking economic base after having suffered so much already under the white colonists.

NOTES

1. Mohandas K. Gandhi, *Satyagraha in South Africa* (Ahmedabad: Navajivan Publishing House, 1972), p. 221.
2. Pyarelal, *Mahatma Gandhi: The Early Phase* (Ahmedabad: Navajivan Publishing House, 1986), vol. 1, p. xiv.
3. Ananda M. Pandiri, *A Comprehensive, Annotated Bibliography on Mahatma Gandhi* (Westport, Conn.: Greenwood Press, 1995), pp. 320–21.
4. Mohandas K. Gandhi, *The Collected Works of Mahatma Gandhi* (Delhi: Publication Division, Ministry of Information and Broadcasting, Government of India, 1958–1994).
5. Richard Grenier, "The Gandhi Nobody Knows," *Commentary* 75, no. 3 (March 1983): 64.

10

SERGEANT-MAJOR GANDHI

I may be a despicable person, but when Truth speaks through me I am invincible.

—Mahatma Gandhi
The Epic Fast, 1932

Gandhi's dream had been fulfilled. In the end, hard work had paid off. The Natal government had accepted Gandhi's offer for a stretcher-bearer corps. Like any army marching to the battle zone it is imperative to supply the citizens left behind with a progress report on the war front. War-assigned journalists come in handy for that purpose. But who was going to inform the Indians about the stretcher-bearer corps? Gandhi decided to act as a wartime journalist reporting for *Indian Opinion*. In addition, he was already an organizer, a leader, and the head of his corps.

The time had come to put on a new uniform. On June 16, 1906, Gandhi received a medical examination and was declared fit. On June 21 he received his marching orders and the next day the government bestowed upon him the rank of sergeant major. It seems Gandhi had pulled off another feat. After all, would-be artificial soldiers had already given their pledge of allegiance. But there were problems brewing which surfaced only as a direct result of Gandhi's "journalistic" insight. The following analysis is based upon the information Gandhi dispatched as a "journalist" reporting from the war front. Let us look at the composition of the corps printed in the July 21, 1906, *Indian Opinion* by Gandhi himself. This was written before July 19, 1906, under the subtitle: "Composition of the Corps."

> This Corps, which has been formed at the instance of the Natal Government by way of experiment, in connection with the operations against the Natives, consists of twenty Indians whose names are as follows: M. K. Gandhi (Sgt.-Major), U. M. Shelat (Sgt.), H. I. Joshi (Sgt.) S. B. Medh (Sgt.), Parbhu Hari (Corporal), Khan Mahomed, Jamaludin, Mahomed, Sheikh Madar, Sheik Dada Mia, Mahomed Essop, Puti Naiken, Appasamy, Kistama, Kupusamy, Bomaya, Kunji, Ajodhyasing.
>
> According to religion, the Corps is composed of six Mohamedans and fourteen Hindus. Geographically, there are five belonging to the Bombay Presidency, twelve to the Presidency of Madras, two to the Punjab, and one to the Presidency of Bengal. It may be added that one of the twelve Madrasis is Colonial-born.
>
> According to status, thirteen men have been, at one time or [an]other, under indenture in Natal, and are now working as free men, in the capacity of gardeners, domestic servants, etc. Two of them are engine-drivers by profession, one [is] a goldsmith, three are agents and book-keepers, having received higher education in India, and one is a barrister.
>
> It is now well known that the Government has provided uniforms and rations, and the Natal Indian Congress pays the salaries.[1]

Gandhi says his corps consists of twenty Indians, but cites only eighteen names. In the photograph of the corps, one can count twenty Indians, the correct number authorized by the Natal government. Gandhi had omitted the names of two Indians in his dispatch. Why? Perhaps it shows his lack of leadership skills. We are confronted with another problem: there is a discrepancy between those on the Pledge of Allegiance roster and those on the composition of the corps.

Most likely, the missing two names are out of the following—Ali, Muthusamy, Alwar, and Bhailal—who were a part of the Pledge of Allegiance roster but never made it to the action roster—the composition of the corps. Bomaya and Parbhu Hari, the corporal, were members of the corps who were conspicuously absent from the Pledge of Allegiance list. They started off with about forty Indian names, but only twenty signed in for the Pledge of Allegiance. The government set the corps' strength at twenty men.[3] There were dropouts, and at the eleventh hour Gandhi had to negotiate to get his magic twenty volunteers. Perhaps Parbhu Hari was lured in with a corporal rank. How Gandhi actually pulled it off will never be known. Another interesting feature of the corps is its leadership structure: All the three named sergeants of the corps were Gujaratis, as was the sergeant major and the corporal. It is reasonable to assume that the junior ranks were handed out by Gandhi himself. Did he exercise favoritism or even nepotism by assigning leadership positions to his caste Gujarati-speaking men and the "nonrank" jobs to Moslems, Madrasis, and Punjabis? The evidence

Composition of the Corps	Pledge of Allegiance[2]
1. M. K. Gandhi (Sgt.-Major)	M. K. Gandhi
2. U. M. Shelat (Sgt.)	U. M. Shelat
3. H. I. Joshi (Sgt.)	H. I. Joshi
4. S. B. Medh (Sgt.)	S. B. Medh
5. Parbhu Hari (Corporal)	
6. Khan Mahomed	Khan Mahomed
7. Jamaludin	Jamaludin
8. Mahomed	Mahomed Shaikh
9. Sheikh Madar	Sheikh Madar
10. Sheik Dada Mia	Dada Mian
11. Mahomed Essop	Mahomed
12. Puti Naiken	Pooti Naiken
13. Appasamy	Appasamy
14. Kistama	Kistama
15. Kunji	Kunjee
16. Ajodhyasing	Ajodhyasing
17. Kupusamy	Coopoosamy
18. Bomaya	
19.	Ali
20.	Muthusamy
21.	Alwar
22.	Bhailal

indicates that he did. What Gandhi alludes to in the composition of the corps— "five belonging to the Bombay Presidency,"— is in fact pointing to his caste Gujarati brothers. Just to add more confusion to the debate, Mahatma's U.S.-based grandson, Arun Gandhi, and his wife, in a 1998 book, claimed that the corps' size was twenty-four: one sergeant major, three sergeants, one corporal, and nineteen privates.[4]

From a military organizational point of view, the corps' chain-of-command structure is unusual, to say the least. Perhaps this peculiarity reflects Gandhi's lack of organizational skills. One thing is certain: there were dissidents within the Indian community. Some Indians did not agree with Gandhi and his response to blacks and their plight. If such was the case, we can't expect Gandhi to throw much light on such topics. However, we learn from Professor Hunt's account that there was another Indian named P. S. Aiyar who had started a rival paper, *The Indian World*, with a stated aim: "to save the Indian community from the insensate and short-sighted policy" of Gandhi and his friends.[5] Apparently, *The Indian World* never reached publication. Later on, Mr. Aiyar began *Colonial Indian News*, a weekly newspaper, published in English and Tamil. On June 20, 1906,

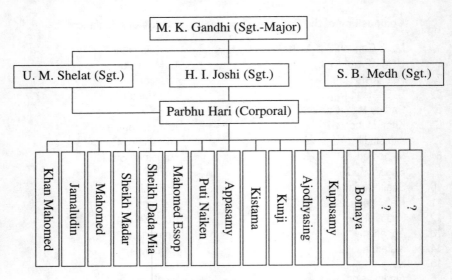

Organizational Chart—Stretcher-Bearer Corps

he started *African Chronicle*, a mouthpiece for the sector of colonial-born Indians and Tamil-speaking Indians who were opposed to Gandhi. Many years later, in 1914, Aiyar was joined by *Indian Views*, published by a Moslem group in Durban and exhibiting antagonism to Gandhi. Giving evidence before the Inquiry Commission set up by the South African government in 1914, which the pro-Gandhi Satyagrahis had boycotted, P. S. Aiyar described himself as chairman of the Indian Patriotic Union together with the Natal Indian Congress. But by then, Gandhi had already left or was about to leave South Africa for good. The damage was already done in the sense that the Indian community was deeply divided and more distanced from other nonwhite communities. Other foreign-based Indians were also critical of Gandhi. In New York, *Gaelic American* called Gandhi's volunteering "contemptible beyond expression." In London, *Indian Sociologist* of July 1906 found Gandhi's action "disgusting."[6]

Once the composition of the corps was in place, it was time to move (June 21) to the battle zone. Gandhi remained on active duty at the front from June 23 to July 18. In Gandhi's dispatch, printed in *Indian Opinion* of July 21 (composed sometime before July 19), there was published another subject category under the subtitle: "At the Front."[7] In the narrative that follows, I have added to Gandhi's description with material generously taken from Professor Hunt's chapter. Professor Hunt had additional information from Mr. Chhaganlal Gandhi, who authored a Gujarati manuscript on the Zulu rebellion.[8] Therefore, in the ensuing narrative the original sentence structures have been changed but not their direct and underlying meanings.

June 21: Before moving, the corps needed a hero's send-off and that was done at Mr. Omar Haji Amod Johari's house. Guests from the merchant community and other prominent Indian leaders assembled here. They opened a fund to be run under the supervision of Mr. Dawad Mahomed. They collected a bag of flour, twenty plates, and twenty pounds. The corpsmen received overcoats, socks, night-caps, plates, spoons, knives, and jugs from the fund. Mr. Odhav Kanji supplied the first round of fruits while other businessmen promised to maintain a steady fruit supply. Messrs S. P. Mahomed & Co. provided the men with tobacco and cigarettes.

June 22: The corps left Durban by train for Stanger, just forty-five miles to the north. Like true patriots on the march, the corpsmen were greeted on arrival by Mr. M. B. Sidat, Mr. Gokalbhai, Mr. Mani, and a few other local businessmen who served these budding heroes an ethnically palatable lunch, *doodhpak-puri*. They reported to Colonel Arnott, commander, squadrons of the Border Mounted Rifles (B.M.R.). After discussion with the regimental sergeant-major, Colonel Arnott gave orders for the corps to receive European rations, and rice and *dholl* with curry-powder in lieu of meat. Gandhi had carefully charted out the food logistic estimate information for his *Indian Opinion* readers.

The ration scale per man per day was determined to be: bread or biscuits, 1 lb.; sugar, 5 oz.; tea, ¼ oz.; coffee, ½ oz.; butter, 1 oz.; salt, ½ oz.; jam, 2 oz.; cheese, 2 oz.; potatoes, 4 oz.; onions, 2 oz.; mealie-meal (corn meal), 4 oz.; pepper; rice, 1 lb.; and lentils, ¼ lb.

Since there was no medical officer attached to Colonel Arnott's column, he authorized the corps to issue a small quantity of medical supplies in case of emergencies. The corps' medical service was soon put to work to the soldiers' benefit. Those who had either slight accidental injuries or were afflicted with malaria were the beneficiaries.

The night of the 22nd was passed in laager, a South African type of defensive camp, the layout of which Gandhi described: "They arrange themselves in strategic positions to defend themselves. On one side, they arrange carts. Then they have cavalry on the one hand and artillery on the other. At the centre are the tents of the officers. Unarmed personnel also sleep in that portion. This being the arrangement, the Indian Corps found a place to sleep in the middle of the laager." The corps slept in the open. And June being the first month of winter in South Africa, the government issued a single blanket to each corpsmen. This was not enough protection against cold. The overcoats, furnished from the Comforts Fund opened by the Indian community a day earlier, came in handy. Ironically, Gandhi's first letter from his foot-march to the battle was addressed not to the Indians in South Africa but rather to another India-based great leader, G. K. Gokhale, who happened to be at this time on a visit to England. Gandhi laid out to him the crucial nature of his role: "In any case, it was absolutely necessary for me to accompany the Corps if it was to be formed at all."

June 23: This Saturday morning, after sharing a common breakfast meal of mealie-meal with butter and sugar, the whole column moved forward to include the Durban Reserves, the Indian Corps, and an escort bringing up the rear. Each corpsmen carried his own kit (which included a water-can, a flask, a satchel, and bedding) on a mostly up-hill march, which exhausted some due to the heavy load. The stretchers were loaded on the wagons. After about eight miles and a climb of one thousand feet, the column reached Kearsney. There they were greeted by the sight of Sir James Hulett's garden, whose luscious naartjes (orange groves) were thrown open to the troops to help themselves liberally from, which they gladly did. The troops camped about a mile beyond the estate. Three kitchens were set up. In the first, eight Hindu Madrassis cooked rice and *dal*. In the second, Madrassis Moslems cooked rice and *dal* in their own way. In the third, they prepared *rotis*, *dal*, and vegetables shared by Punjabi Moslems and Gujarati Hindus, including Sergeant-Major Gandhi. This is the way lunch was prepared. The dinner meal was generally a *roti*, *paneer* (cheese), and coffee. The Indian merchants supplemented the diet with dried fruits. At Kearsney, another Indian Gujarati merchant, Mr. Narayan Desai, who owned a store nearby, looked after their needs. You can see the corps was taken care of quite well.

June 24: At 0630 hours the march commenced after the corpsmen loaded their kits onto the wagons, to their great relief. Late in the morning, they reached Thring's Post, where the rebels earlier had looted a store. Chhaganlal Gandhi's manuscript reported, "The whites as well as our own men looted the place again. As the store was unattended the whites picked up whatever they wanted. Some of us also followed suit and picked up handkerchiefs, cigarettes, caps, etc." Did Mahatma Gandhi loot that store too? In his dispatches, he never mentioned a thing about the store. In the afternoon, the columns encamped at the Otimati River crossing, on a hill in a beautiful valley, nearby where ran a sparkling stream. African huts were visible in the distance, many of them burned. Colonel Arnott established a fortified laager strengthened with barbed-wire entanglements. The site was now only a few miles from the black rebels. The column was not intended to go as far as Mapumulo, but was to operate from the Otimati River camp. The Indian Corps, however, had instructions to proceed with the first convoy to Mapumulo.

June 25: At midday, in the middle of luncheon being cooked, the corps received orders to march immediately with a column and some wagons farther up in the hills to Mapumulo. The corps left their food, packed up kits, and within a quarter of an hour were ready to move. They reached Mapumulo at about 1700 hours and reported to Captain Howden, the physician officer-in-charge of the dispensary. Captain Howden treated the corps very nicely and arranged for them to sleep in a tent. However, some white troops had been using the tent and refused to vacate it for the Indians. Captain Howden's assistant, Corporal Little, at last succeeded in evicting the white soldiers to make room for the corpsmen. The Indian soldiers slept under the tent in Mapumulo, with the exception of Gandhi, who volunteered to sleep outside in the open on the days it didn't rain. Why? Is it an example of excellence in leadership? Perhaps. Or possibly, Gandhi was on the lookout, pitching in to help the soldiers guarding the campsite from the neighborhood blacks!

In a second dispatch printed in the *Indian Opinion* dated July 28, 1906, Gandhi sent a lengthy report that he had written earlier, before July 19. He subtitled the report under six categories: Fatigue Duties, Heavy Work, Dead Tired, Weary and Footsore, Doing the Impossible, and Indian Resourcefulness.

June 26: Beginning on this Tuesday, the various tasks assigned to the corps fell into four broad categories: (1) Nine men of the corps were tasked to form a fatigue party to accompany the tank-wagon bringing water from an adjoining stream; (2) Some were detained to disinfect the whole camp under the superintendence of Dr. Savage, the District Surgeon for Mapumulo; (3) Three or four of the corpsmen were to dress the wounds on the backs of several native rebels who had received lashes; and (4) one corpsman assisted at entering up the daily roll of patients treated by Captain Howden.[9] Of the four categories, Gandhi didn't mention the task that he himself was assigned to. But he was clear what happened the next day on

June 27:

> Some of the above work was partially interrupted or suspended as a helio-message was received to forward a stretcher party to Otimati in connection with operations that were to be undertaken by the B. M. R. column at Thring's Post. Early on the morning of the 27th, therefore, one-half of the Corps, with two stretchers under Sgt.-Major Gandhi and Sgt. Joshi proceeded to Otimati, where instructions were received to take a stretcher to carry one of the troopers who was dazed. Fortunately, the trooper had recovered before the party reached Thring's Post. But by an unfortunate accident, another trooper, by name Forder, had received a bullet-wound in the thigh from a co-trooper. He, however, pluckily rode to the camp. The stretcher party had to assist Mr. Stokes, of the N. M. C. [the Natal Medical Corps], in treating the wounded trooper, and others, who had received slight injuries through accidents or otherwise, requiring medical help. (CWMG 5, #394, p. 370)

June 28: Continuing with the stretcher work, Gandhi narrated:

> The stretcher party at Otimati were to take to Mapumulo Private Sutton of the Durban Reserves, whose toe was crushed under a waggon wheel, and Trooper Forder. The latter had to be carried on a stretcher, as his wound was very deli-

cate. The work of carrying Trooper Forder proved to be much heavier than we had thought. The energy of all the available men had to be taxed to the utmost in carrying the wounded men, especially as it meant going uphill all the way. As we were nearing Mapumulo, the Captain of our escort sent word that, if it could be managed, Forder should be placed in the ambulance waggon, as the Natives about the hill might wrongly consider that the rebels had succeeded in wounding at least one of our men. Trooper Forder, on hearing the message, gladly volunteered to go into the waggon. And the fatigued bearers were equally glad to be relieved of the necessity of having to carry their charge up the very steep hill near Mapumulo. (CWMG 5, #394, p. 370)

Given the above account, we don't know what task Gandhi was specifically assigned among the four categories on June 26. But we know that on June 27, Sergeant-Major Gandhi and Sergeant Joshi, with one-half of the corps, were rushed with two stretchers to Otimati River to transport injured soldiers. This task also consumed the whole of June 28. After this brief interruption, the whole corps resumed its former work.

The work at Mapumulo continued for about four days, as troops from all over the Colony assembled to deliver a crushing blow to black rebels in the district. The Zulu chiefs, too, were gathering their forces: during the final week in June there was a mass exodus of Zulu workers from Durban. More than a thousand dock workers, about five hundred domestic workers, as well as rickshaw pullers and about 40 percent of the African Borough Police left their jobs in response to the call. At Thring's Post, Colonel McKenzie gathered about twenty-five hundred troops and developed an operations plan for striking at the three major bodies of rebels. Chief Meseni was south on the Umvoti River with the largest force, while Chief Matshwili was north-east in the Isinzimba Valley, and Chief Ndlovu was north in the Imati Valley. As the tension rose, Colonel Sparks wrote to the government asking for revolvers to be issued to the Indians for protection, but the action came before there could be an answer. The Indian Corps continued to work at Mapumulo till the morning of July 3, a day that would become memorable to the members of the corps.

July 3: On this Tuesday, the force was headed for the Umvoti Valley to attack Chief Meseni's Kraal. Gandhi described the day:

At 9 p.m. on the 2nd July, the Corps was ordered to follow a combined column at 2-30 a.m. the next morning which was to operate in the Umvoti Valley. We had to take two days' rations with us, our blankets, and five stretchers. We did so, and the march commenced at 3 a.m. on the 3rd. There were no waggons with the column, and, with the exception of the infantry, which had gone forward before, all were mounted men whom we had to follow. Men in the rear were to guard us. We were all unarmed. But as the troops galloped away in front of us and we followed them, we were quickly outdistanced. However, we marched on, trying, as far as possible, to overtake the column, but it was a hopeless task. There was, therefore, as a rule, considerable distance between the rear-guard and ourselves. At daybreak, the movement of the troops became naturally more rapid, and the distance between them and us began to increase. However, there was no prospect before us except that of running after the troops or of being assegaied by the rebels. Probably we had a narrow escape. At 7 o'clock troops were operating at some distance from us. As we were struggling along, we met a Kaffir who did not wear the loyal badge. He was armed with an assegai and was hiding himself. However, we safely rejoined the troops on the further hill, whilst they were sweeping with their carbines the bushes below. Thus, we had to perform what seemed to be a never-ending march. We had to cross and re-cross the Umvoti River, an operation that was difficult enough, seeing that we were obliged to take off our heavy boots and putties. One of the men narrowly escaped what might have been a very serious accident, and he only crossed the stream less his putties and with a bleeding toe. However, he marched bravely on with the rest of us. Towards evening, the column retired to a rise near the valley and pitched the camp. (CWMG 5, #394, pp. 370–71)

The casualties amounted to about four hundred rebels and the rest scattered. Gandhi continued:

All of us were dead tired, and it was a stroke of good luck that there were no casualties or accidents on our side. Had there been any, it is difficult to say how we would have discharged ourselves in carrying the wounded in such a fatigued condition, though the writer of these notes fully believes that, actuated as the Corps mainly was by a sense of duty, God would have given it sufficient strength to perform any such work. Anyhow, such was the answer given to the laughing troopers, who, half in pity and half in ridicule, inquired, as we were struggling along, what we should do if we had actually to carry some wounded. (CWMG 5, #394, p. 371)

July 4: On this Wednesday morning, the corps was divided into two parties to accompany the two divisions of the column, which were to operate in different parts in search of more rebels. The next day, on July 5, they returned to Mapumulo, many Indians with blisters and swollen legs, and all hungry because they had finished their two days' worth of carried rations.

July 6: Expecting a rest on this day, the corps was nevertheless ordered to march to Thring's Post along with the shifting camp. Sergeant-Major Gandhi appealed to Captain Howden and Colonel Sparks on behalf of nine or ten Indians who were unable to walk, asking that they be provided with wagon transport. The request was granted and the corps undertook the journey to Thring's Post. There they were attached to Captain Pearson, who treated the Indians with respect. After a day's rest (July 7) at Thring's Post they were ordered to join a column leaving camp at 3 a.m. on Sunday, July 8.

July 8: Colonel McKenzie moved against Chief Matshwili's Kraal at Isinzimba. It was a mild morning and the moon was brilliant, and the march seemed pleasant compared with the struggle through the Umvoti Valley. About 550 Africans, including the chief, were killed in the surprise attack at dawn, but the Indian Corps had a relatively easy day, marching about eight miles out and back. The troops rested the following day (July 9).

July 10: On this Tuesday the troops left the camp at 0230 hours to attack Chief Ndlovu and Chief Meseni in the Imati Valley. The Indian Corps accompanied a column that went down the Otimati River Gorge. They had taken two days' rations and the path lay through an essentially inaccessible valley. It was impossible for any ambulance to go down, and they had to descend steep precipices. Troopers had to lead their horses, and the route was so long that the corps never seemed to reach the bottom. However, at about 12 o'clock they finished the day's journey, with no Kaffirs to fight.

Then an incident happened way down the valley which was to test the corpsmen's ability to do stretcher-bearing work. A trooper under the belief shot a friendly Kaffir boy working as a guide. It was said that the native was misleading him. The African boy was badly wounded and required carrying, which was entrusted to the Indians. Orders were given to take him the same day back to Mapumulo. Four friendly Africans were assigned to assist this difficult transport. However, as soon as the troops were out of sight, three of them deserted, and the fourth, though he remained with the group, declined flatly to go to Mapumulo. Gandhi says that this fourth African "feared that, without an escort, we might be cut to pieces by the enemy. Fortunately, the troops were yet within reach" (CWMG 5, #394, p. 372). Sergeant-Major Gandhi reported the matter to the proper officer, and received fresh orders to transport the wounded Kaffir the next day. He received immediate nursing care and the entire troops and the corps encamped for the night in the valley.

July 11: With about twenty Kaffir levies assigned to help the Indians, the group started to move to Mapumulo along with the wounded African. Gandhi was not too pleased with these Africans' help; "They did so with much difficulty over part of the way, and then, too, because Doctor Savage happened to be with us. The Natives in our hands proved to be most unreliable and obstinate. Without constant attention, they would as soon have dropped the wounded man as not, and they seemed to bestow no care on their suffering countryman." The Indian bearers carried him to Mapumulo safely. Gandhi did not mince words about the Indian ingenuity, "All our resourcefulness was put to the test during the march. After we had finished the most difficult part of our journey along a narrow and steep pathway, the Japanese stretcher on which we were carrying the patient, who was very bulky, gave way, fortunately without hurting him. The railway stretcher, on which he was first carried, had already broken under his weight. What were we to do? Luckily, we had skilled men among us. We temporarily mended the railway stretcher, and took our charge safely to Mapumulo, reaching there about 4 p.m., a distance probably of over 15 miles" (CWMG 5, #394, p. 373).

July 12–14: On July 12 the corps took complete rest at Mapumulo. The next day (July 13), they returned to Thring's Post. Gandhi never told us why the corps went to Thring's Post. On the 14th, they retraced their steps back to a spot near Mapumulo, where they encamped. It seems that the two dispatches that Gandhi wrote for his *Indian Opinion* were written at this spot. The fleeing African chiefs soon surrendered to the authorities, and the troops were demobilized. The Indian Corps under orders was discharged on Thursday, July 19. Gandhi felt assured of the outcome of his corps' mission: "that the little band is capable of performing any work that may be entrusted to it."

NOTES

1. Mohandas K. Gandhi, *The Collected Works of Mahatma Gandhi* (Delhi: Publications Division, Ministry of Information and Broadcasting, Government of India, 1961), vol. 5 (1905–1906), document # 393. Hereafter cited as CWMG.

2. Ibid., 5, # 379, p. 357. From another undocumented source of reference, I learned the identities of all the soldiers lined up in the corps' photo (see photo insert):
Standing Row (left to right): Coopoosamy, Kunji, Ajodhyasingh, Alwar, Moothoosamy, Appasamy, Sheikh Dada Mia, Kistama, Mahomed Essop.
Middle Row (left to right): Jamaludin, Parbhu Hari, U. M. Shelat, M. K. Gandhi, H. I. Joshi, S. B. Medh, Khan Mahomed.
Sitting Row (left to right): Sheikh Madar, Mahomed, Bomaya, Pooti Naiken.
Based upon the above list, it is apparent that Gandhi had missed naming both Alwar and Muthusamy. In all probability, Appasamy, Kupusamy, and Muthusamy were individuals with some family ties.

3. J. L. Smail, *Those Restless Years: Dealing with the Boer and Bombata Rebellion* (Cape Town: Howard Timmins, 1971), p. 152.

4. Arun and Sunanda Gandhi, *The Forgotten Woman: The Untold Story of Kastur Gandhi, Wife of Mahatma Gandhi* (Huntsville, Ark.: Ozark Mountain Publishers, 1998), p. 137. In November 1998, I paid an unannounced visit to Arun Gandhi's office in Memphis, Tennessee. Though he was out of town on that day, I couldn't help but notice that his office accommodated the entire stack of the *Collected Works of Mahatma Gandhi*. I would hope that he had at least read them, particularly vol. 5. If he had, he would not have committed the blunder of repeating the strength of the corps' size as twenty-four, which he had taken from his grandfather's *Autobiography.*

5. Pyarelal, *Mahatma Gandhi: The Birth of Satyagraha—From Petitioning to Passive Resistance* (Ahmedabad: Navajivan Publishing House, 1986), vol. 3, pp. 63–64.

6. Ibid., p. 592, ref. 50.

7. CWMG 5, # 393, pp. 368–69.

8. Pyarelal, *Mahatma Gandhi*, vol. 3, chap. 20.

9. CWMG 5, # 394, pp. 369–70.

11

I make no distinction, from the point of view of ahimsa *between combatants and non-combatants. He who volunteers to serve a band of dacoits, by working as their carrier, or their watchman while they are about their business, or their nurse when they are wounded, is as much guilty of dacoity as the dacoits themselves. In the same way those who confine themselves to attending to the wounded in battle cannot be absolved from the guilt of war.*

—Mahatma Gandhi
An Autobiography

On July 19, the corps headed for Durban from Mapumulo. After trekking seventeen miles in five hours to reach Kearsney, they were greeted by Mr. Narayan Desai. The next day, they hiked to Stanger, where Mr. Sidat and other Indian merchants feasted the corps. From Stanger, the corps took the train, which passed through Tongaat where the corps received a heroes' welcome by the Indian community. At Durban, they were feasted at the home of Mr. Omar Hajee Amod Johari. At 8 P.M. on that day (July 20), the Natal Indian Congress, where Dawad Mahomed presided, convened a special meeting to welcome the members of the corps. They delivered a hearty vote of thanks on behalf of the British

117

Indian community of Natal. Guests delivered eulogistic speeches, warmly commending Gandhi's work in organizing and leading the corps to the front. Also expressed were words of praise for the men who accompanied Gandhi. Mr. Gandhi likewise delivered a speech in Gujarati which was reported in *Indian Opinion* on July 28:

> Thanking the organization on behalf of the Corps, Mr. Gandhi said that what the Corps had done was only its duty. If the Indians really wanted to show their appreciation of the work of the Corps, they should try through the Government to have a permanent Corps set up and should also exert themselves to improve their physique in order to qualify for admission. He said that if, for any reason, the traders could not enlist, other educated Indians as well as the servants and clerks of traders could easily do so. From experience gained during the fighting, he could say that the whites treated the Indians very cordially, and distinctions based on colour had ceased to exist. If a larger Indian Corps was formed on a permanent footing, such fellow-feeling would increase, and it was likely that in the process white prejudice against Indians might altogether disappear. He therefore very strongly recommended the formation of such a Corps.[1]

By a resolution, the Natal Indian Congress decided to present each member of the corps with a special silver medal in commemoration of the manner in which they had sustained the honor and dignity of the Indian community. This is particularly highlighted by the fact that the Indian grievances had been ignored for the moment, at a time of national danger from blacks.

On July 23, Mr. Peerum Mahomed banqueted the Indian stretcher-bearer corpsmen. Mr. Cassim Dowad presented each with a silk scarf while Dada Osman donated to each a packet of tobacco and smoker's requisites. Gandhi offered the host thanks on behalf of the guests. Later the Natal Indian Congress held a special meeting in the Congress Hall under the chairmanship of Dawad Mahomed. There the public votes of thanks were offered to various individuals who had aided the community in its recent task. Thanks were also given to Mrs. Nanji and Mrs. Bernard Gabriel for providing Red Cross badges and to all others who had rendered help or hospitality to the Indian Corps in one way or another.

On July 31, Gandhi addressed a letter from Johannesburg to Colonel Hyslop, Principal Medical Officer, Natal Militia, which was reprinted in *Indian Opinion*, August 11:

> The Indian Stretcher-Bearer Corps was disbanded on the 19th inst., and the Corps reached Durban on the 20th.
>
> The Corps was called upon to do the work of disinfecting the camp at Mapumulo, of dressing injuries and wounds, and of marching with the troops and doing stretcher work. Most of the bearers accompanied the troops during the operations at the Tugela, the Otimati and the Umvoti Valleys. In my humble opinion, the men did the work willingly and skillfully. The object of the Natal

Indian Congress, in offering to form the Corps, was to show that Indians recognized their responsibilities as settlers in Natal, and to induce the Government to utilize Indians as a permanent portion of the Natal Militia. I venture to think that my countrymen are essentially fit for ambulance and hospital work. Trooper Forder, whom we carried from Otimati, had, in addition to being carried, to be nursed by us, and he was so satisfied that he sought me out specially on his recovery to express his appreciation of the men's work.

The Corps consisted of some skilled English-educated Indians, as also of Indians of the labourer type, but all of them were intelligent workers, and capable in civil life of earning much more than what would be paid to them by the Indian community. As the community was anxious that its offer should be accepted, in order to avoid any difficulty, the men were induced to accept only one shilling and six pence per day, which they gladly did; but in my opinion, it is not possible to get intelligent men for less than £1 per week.

I also think that those who may be called leaders of stretcher parties should receive five shillings per day.

Members of the Corps were all untrained and untried men; they were called upon, too, to do responsible and independent work, and to face danger unarmed. If the Government would form a permanent Ambulance Corps, I think that special training is absolutely necessary, and that they should all be armed for self-protection.

As one who has been intimately connected with the Indian community for the last thirteen years, I have ventured to place the above views before you for your consideration.[2]

In his *Indian Opinion* dated August 4, Gandhi informed his readers from Johannesburg of another heroes' welcome under the title "The Return of T.M.R."

The contingent which was despatched from here to reinforce the units engaged in suppressing the Native revolt, namely, the Transvaal Mounted Rifles, has now returned. It was received with much pomp and *eclat* by the people of the Transvaal. Big meetings were held in its honour and grand banquets given. The celebrations still continue. Reuter messages about the discharge of the Indian Stretcher-Bearer Corps and the good work done by it have appeared in the local papers. [translated from Gujarati][3]

The post-war news clippings from the "local papers" in Transvaal are not to be found in the *Collected Works* or elsewhere. Perhaps they were destroyed by Gandhi. Neither are those from the newspapers based in Natal.

The Governor of Natal wrote to Gandhi on August 7 with the following kind words:

I cannot allow demobilization to take place without placing on record on behalf of the Government my appreciation of the patriotic movement made by the Indian community of Natal in providing a Bearer Company for service in the field during the rebellion.

The number of casualties in our forces have been providentially small and the labours of the company have not therefore been so heavy as they would otherwise have been.

At the same time mention has been made to me of the good services rendered by those who volunteered for this service and of the steadiness displayed by them. I should feel obliged if you will be good enough to convey to all ranks who served under your command my best thanks for the assistance they have given.[4]

While Gandhi was deployed at the front, a question then may be asked: How did his immediate family and others lodged at the Phoenix Settlement handle the stresses caused by the Zulu rebellion? Prabhudas Gandhi, son of Chhaganlal Gandhi, was only five years old at the time, but years later he vividly recalled:

I did not know what they talked about but I could sense that Kasturba [Gandhi's wife] was worried about Mohandas Kaka [Gandhi]. My father would come several times in the day from the press to give Kasturba the latest news. The talk then would centre on the activities of the Zulu people, how far they had reached and what they had done. I do not remember other things clearly but that atmosphere of fear is very vivid in my mind. Today when I read about the Zulu people's rebellion, the anxious face of Kasturba comes before my eyes.[5]

Arun and Sunanda Gandhi have recently reported that a few days after Gandhi's return from the Zulu conflict, Kasturba prepared a homecoming feast for her husband and several of his friends. The details of this feast are quite interesting, to say the least.[6]

Anti-African rumors infested the colony. Old Zulu wars were told and retold to the detriment of Africans. In spite of that, Africans deserved to be cited: they harmed not a single Indian, white woman, or child. blacks themselves suffered devastating losses in their own country. Many thousands were needlessly killed; many were left with physical pain, emotional scars beyond description, and their economy ruined. One author has reported that about four thousand blacks were killed, seven thousand went to jail, and over four thousand were subjected to lashing.[7] Not only that, with this defeat, blacks' efforts to maintain their economic independence from the demands of the white-dominated capitalist economy were doomed. Also, there were political repercussions: white factions felt the need for political unity to maintain control over the black population. The harsh suppression of the "rebellion" brought a storm of criticism on the Natal Colony from both England and South Africa. For example, J. C. Smuts described the military campaign as "simply a record of loot and rapine."[8] About twenty-four whites had lost their lives.[9] Yes, there were honorable whites who spoke up against the atrocities committed against blacks, and that didn't please Gandhi much. Here is an example. In the August 4, 1906, *Indian Opinion* under the title "Egypt and Natal—A Comparison: Is This Civilization?" Gandhi made clear his stand on torture and human-rights violations.

A controversy is going on in England about what the Natal army did during the Kaffir rebellion. The people there believe that the whites of Natal perpetrated great atrocities on the Kaffirs. In reply to such critics, *The Star* has pointed to the doings of the Imperial army in Egypt. Those among the Egyptian rebels who had been captured were ordered to be flogged. The flogging was continued to the limits of the victims' endurance; it took place in public and was watched by thousands of people. Those sentenced to death were also hanged at the same time. While those sentenced to death were hanging, the flogging of the others was taken up. While the sentences were being executed, the relatives of the victims cried and wept until many of them swooned. If this be true, there is no reason why there should be such an outcry in England against the Natal outrage. [translated from Gujarati][10]

If the above statement does not throw enough light on Gandhi's deranged thinking, I simply don't know what else will. Many years of hard work to raise the status of upper-caste Indians to the level of whites didn't bear fruit. This, of course, was of great consternation to Gandhi, whose often-repeated attempts to induce whites to treat Indians as brothers failed time and again, unless one counts the experience at the front. What he witnessed in the battlefield immensely satisfied him. In the Boer War, Indian and white soldiers drank from the same cup, shared the same tent, and ate the same food. This cordial "fellowship" was repeated again during the Zulu War when a "small band of Indian ambulance-bearers met Colonial soldier-citizen on terms of equality."[11] Gandhi's vision of "fellow-Colonists" working on equal footing for the betterment of the Empire dwelt only at the war fronts.

NOTES

1. Mohandas K. Gandhi, *The Collected Works of Mahatma Gandhi* (Delhi: Publications Division, Ministry of Information and Broadcasting, Government of India, 1961), vol. 5 (1905–1906), doc. 395. Hereafter cited as CWMG.

2. CWMG 5, # 400, pp. 376–77.

3. Ibid., 5, # 401, p. 378.

4. R. A. Huttenback, *Gandhi in South Africa: British Imperialism and the Indian Question, 1860–1914* (Ithaca, N.Y.: Cornell University Press, 1971), pp. 125–26.

5. Prabhudas Gandhi, *My Childhood with Gandhiji* (Ahmedabad: Navajivan Publishing House, 1957), p. 42.

6. Arun and Sunanda Gandhi, *The Forgotten Woman: The Untold Story of Kastur Gandhi, Wife of Mahatma Gandhi* (Huntsville, Ark.: Ozark Mountain Publishers, 1998), p. 141.

7. J. D. Omer-Cooper, *History of Southern Africa* (Portsmouth, N.H.: Heinemann Educational Books, Inc. 1987), p. 154.

8. Pyarelal, *Mahatma Gandhi: The Birth of Satyagraha—From Petitioning to Passive Resistance* (Ahmedabad: Navajivan Publishing House, 1986), vol. 3, p. 480.

9. Shula Marks, *Reluctant Rebellion: The 1906–8 Disturbances in Natal* (Oxford: Clarendon Press, 1970), p. xvi.

10. CWMG 5, # 404, p. 381.

11. Ibid., 11, # 88, p. 109. From *Indian Opinion*, June 17, 1911.

12

At the time of writing I never think of what I have said before. My aim is not to be consistent with my previous statements on a given question, but to be consistent with truth, as it may present itself to me at a given moment. The result has been that I have grown from truth to truth; I have saved my memory an undue strain; and what is more, whenever I have been obliged to compare my writing even fifty years ago with the latest, I have discovered no inconsistency between the two. But friends who observe inconsistency will do well to take the meaning that my latest writings may yield unless of course they prefer the old. But before making the choice, they should try to see if there is not an underlying and abiding consistency between the two seeming inconsistencies.

—Mahatma Gandhi
Mahatma, vol. 5, September 25, 1939

Reverend John H. Holmes never shrank from delivering "Gandhi sermons" to his congregation. The word spread. Other religious denominations picked up the idea for proclaiming a "new messiah of the twentieth century" by the name

123

of Mahatma Gandhi. By these means, Gandhi made a deep impression on a section of Americans. Many liberal Christian ministers borrowed materials from each other and passed them along to others. They were certain that the information in their hands was authentic; they received much of the material directly from India, from Gandhi's closed circles. We know many of these religious ministers were naïve on the one hand and on the other excelled in the art of religious propaganda. They were familiar with the New Testament's four Gospels and they knew the business side of their profession. No offense to the clergymen; after all, that was their trade and the art they mastered to earn their livelihood. If they were required to harmonize the inconsistencies and contradictions (or difficulties, Christian apologists would say) of the four Gospel stories, they did it quite well. When Gandhi's story echoed in their ears, they were joyful. Who would want to skip the Christ in action? Gandhi was their new Christ, not to replace the old one, but to complement him. Many years later, Reverend Martin Luther King Jr. compared Gandhi to Jesus Christ:

> Gandhi was probably the first person in history to lift the love ethic of Jesus above mere interaction between individuals to a powerful and effective social force on a large scale. Love for Gandhi was a potent instrument of social and collective transformation. It was in this Gandhian emphasis on love and nonviolence that I discovered the method for social reform that I had been seeking for so many months. The intellectual and moral satisfaction that I failed to gain from the utilitarianism of Bentham and Mill, the revolutionary methods of Marx and Lenin, the social-contracts theory of Hobbes, the "back to nature" optimism of Rousseau, and the superman philosophy of Nietzsche, I found in the nonviolent resistance philosophy of Gandhi. I came to feel that this was the only morally and practically sound method open to oppressed people in their struggle for freedom. . . . In other words, Christ furnished the spirit and motivation, while Gandhi furnished the method.[1]

Granted, Jesus Christ is a hero of the New Testament, and to those who believe in only the Old Testament, I suppose, Gandhi was not a suitable example. Pastor King, therefore, provoked another strong image, this one from the Hebrew Bible—Moses:

> In nearly every territory in Asia and Africa a courageous Moses pleaded passionately for the freedom of his people. For more than twenty years Mahatma Gandhi unrelentingly urged British viceroys, governors general, prime ministers, and kings to let his people go. Like the pharaohs of old, the British leaders turned deaf ears to these agonizing pleas.[2]

However, Gandhi, the new Christ, the new Moses, carried his own set of pitfalls. Likewise, his story had numerous inconsistencies and contradictions. He needed a face-lift and many Christian clergymen knew the art. Years of training and experience in harmonizing the Gospels now paid off when the holy Gandhi stories arrived in three packages, which I have labeled the "Gandhi gospels." To these three, I have added a fourth one, and the four Gandhi gospels parallel the four Jesus gospels. They are: (1) what he said, what he wrote, and how he acted during the South African times as depicted in *Indian Opinion*; (2) what Gandhi told Rev. Doke for his first biography in 1909; (3) *Satyagraha in South Africa*, written in 1924;[3] and (4) *An Autobiography, or The Story of My Experiments with Truth* (1925).[4] The truth is that this is all we possess of the authentic relevant documents. All other writings in the literature about the Zulu conflict are copied from these accounts either wholly or in part, except for a short independent account by Millie G. Polak.

The purpose of this chapter is to take a rather close look at Gandhi's utterances expressed at distinct times about his participation in the Zulu rebellion. Here I will compare, in a chronological order, his words from the four Gandhi gospels about the 1906 war. In some ways, I have continued the process that Professor Erikson started more than thirty years ago. When appropriate, I will address Mrs. Polak's writing. We will examine fourteen categories in this comparative analysis: (1) motivation, (2) Zulu rebellion, (3) sequencing, (4) rank, (5) number of soldiers, (6) composition of the corps, (7) duration, (8) hero, (9) Dr. Savage, (10) image of white soldiers, (11) Zulu categories, (12) work details, (13) washing his hands, and (14) after the war.

MOTIVATION

What prompted Gandhi to join the military? Are there any reasons for his action? In the letters and commentaries published in *Indian Opinion* during 1906, he projected himself as an unyielding imperialist. In 1909, in the biography by Rev. Doke, there is nothing mentioned on Gandhi's motivation for joining the military action. In his 1924 book, *Satyagraha in South Africa* (hereafter referred to as *Satyagraha*), he states that since many Europeans who considered themselves Natal residents had volunteered to join the army, he joined because he, too, considered himself a Natal resident. He thought he must do his "bit in the war." In other words, he simply copied the whites. In his *Autobiography* (1925), he is not copying the whites but participating as a citizen: "I considered myself a citizen of Natal, being intimately connected with it." To this he added, "But I then believed that the British Empire existed for the welfare of the world." Before the war, Gandhi was actually a Transvaal resident, not a Natal resident; he had lived and practiced law in Johannesburg since February 1903. One can understand if Gandhi had said that the British Empire existed for the welfare of the British Empire. But to say that the British Empire existed for the "welfare of the world" is somewhat difficult to swallow. Of these three new rationalizations, none can be found in his 1906 *Indian Opinion* columns, nor is any motivating factor jotted down in Mrs. Polak's narrative.

ZULU REBELLION

In the 1906 *Indian Opinion* columns, there is truly a Zulu rebellion. The blacks pose a significant threat, especially if the rebellion spreads. In the biography (1909) by Rev. Doke, the rebellion is also real. But it brought about anguish among the Indians, especially in Gandhi, who is a "man of peace, hating the very thought of war." In *Satyagraha* (1924), the Zulu rebellion is no longer entirely real. In fact, he casts doubt on it and labels it Zulu 'rebellion.' In *Autobiography* (1925), the doubt is complete: "On reaching the scene of the 'rebellion', I saw that there was nothing there to justify the name of 'rebellion.'"

SEQUENCING

Reading the biography by Doke, *Satyagraha*, and *Autobiography*, one gets the impression that with the outbreak of the Zulu rebellion, Gandhi broke up his house in Johannesburg, moved his family to the Phoenix Settlement in Natal (in the direction of the rebellion!), and then joined the army. Somehow, that is not the impression one gets reading Millie G. Polak's book. Who made the offer to the government for the Indian volunteer force? In the 1909 biography, the Natal Indian Congress made the offer, of course at Mr. Gandhi's suggestion. In *Satyagraha*, Gandhi says he himself made the offer after the Indian community gave that permission to him. In *Autobiography*, Gandhi says that he himself wrote to Natal's governor to express his eagerness to raise a force and the governor replied at once accepting the offer.

RANK

From the *Indian Opinion* columns, we know that Gandhi held a rank of sergeant major and by all accounts available, he was proud of the honor. *The Collected Works of Mahatma Gandhi*, volume 5, in its chronology section states very explicitly that the government bestowed that rank on Gandhi. In the 1909 biography, Gandhi was "offered the rank of Sergeant-Major." In *Satyagraha*, he fails to mention his rank, yet mentions his three subordinate sergeants. In *Autobiography*, he dampens his macho image and merely says he had "temporary rank of Sergeant Major" given out by an unnamed chief medical officer.

NUMBER OF SOLDIERS

In the *Indian Opinion* columns, there are exactly twenty comrades in the stretcher-bearer corps. That figure agrees with the description in the biography by Rev. Doke. In *Satyagraha*, Gandhi is undecided: it is twenty or twenty-five men. In *Autobiography*, he is no longer ambivalent: it is twenty-four. Should Gandhi be given the benefit of the doubt for possibly having suffered convenient memory lapses? After all, there is no great discrepancy between twenty or twenty-four or -five. Anyway, the correct figure is twenty. However, during World War I, Gandhi provided a significantly different figure. More on this can be found in part 5.

COMPOSITION OF THE CORPS

We learn from *Indian Opinion* columns that the corps was composed of five men from Bombay Presidency (which included Gujarat), twelve men from Madras Presidency, two men from Punjab Province, and one man from Bengal Presidency. Of these twenty men, six were Mohammedans and fourteen Hindus. The biography by Rev. Doke is silent on this topic. In *Satyagraha*, we are told the first and the middle names of his three lower-ranking sergeants, who are Gujaratis. On top of that he specifically added a newcomer, a Pathan who didn't exist in the 1906 composition group. In *Autobiography*, five men are from Gujarat, one man is a free Pathan, and the rest (which works out to be eighteen) are ex-indentured men from South India, which is Madras. Whatever happened to the two men from the Punjab and the one man from Bengal? Where and how did this Pathan enter into Gandhi's mind in the 1920s? Perhaps the events in India during the early 1920s muddled Gandhi's memory. Or perhaps, as was said earlier, Gandhi had already destroyed his important 1906 papers sometime during the very early 1920s. Therefore, by the time he wrote his autobiographical accounts, Gandhi had to rely solely on his unreliable memory. Or perhaps, Gandhi, by inducting Pathan, a Moslem match identity in the fake corps' list, is meddling willfully into Islam politics in North India during the first half of the 1920s.

DURATION

How long did the corps remain on active duty? In the *Indian Opinion* columns, the corps' active duty was from June 22 to July 19, 1906. In the biography by Rev. Doke, it is one month, similar to the figure referenced in *Satyagraha*. In *Autobiography*, it is nearly six weeks.

HERO

Who was the hero among the corpsmen and those who dealt with the corps? In the 1906 *Indian Opinion* narratives, indisputably, the true hero that emerges is none other than Sergeant-Major Gandhi himself. His corpsmen stand a distant second behind him. Then, in the biography by Rev. Doke, Dr. Savage is portrayed as a true hero, followed by Gandhi and the other corpsmen, who are barely at the back. In *Satyagraha*, Dr. Savage is again on a high pedestal. He can't get the medical-aid work from the whites and therefore, he goes out of his way to seek it from the Indians. In *Autobiography*, Dr. Savage's name is not located in the narrative. The hero image is back with Gandhi.

DR. SAVAGE

In the *Indian Opinion* columns, Dr. Savage was described as the "District Surgeon for Mapumulo." In the biography by Doke, Dr. Savage was "in charge of the ambulance." In *Satyagraha*, Dr. Savage was also "in charge of the ambulance." In *Autobiography*, he is not mentioned.

IMAGE OF WHITE SOLDIERS

Reading the 1906 columns of *Indian Opinion*, one gets hardly any information to discern anything about the white soldiers beyond their military performance. Three years later in the biography, Gandhi indirectly hints that the whites were not "prepared to do the work," that is, to provide first aid to the injured blacks and manage the camp's sanitation. In *Satyagraha*, according to Gandhi, Dr. Savage could not induce the whites to nurse the wounded blacks and it was beyond his power to give them orders. In *Autobiography*, the white soldiers took a big hit: "... the white people were not willing nurses for the wounded Zulus. . . ." The Medical Officer was "at his wits' end. He hailed our arrival as a godsend. . . ."

ZULU CATEGORIES

In the 1906 *Indian Opinion* columns, the following Zulu categories are described: (1) native rebels who had received the lashes; (2) a Kaffir who was "armed with an assegai [spear] and was hiding himself"; (3) a Kaffir (a friendly boy) who was wounded "accidentally"; (4) four friendly natives, among whom three deserted and one refused to move; and (5) twenty Kaffir levies, who under Gandhi's leadership "proved to be most unreliable and obstinate." In the biography, there is only one category: Zulus who earlier had been lashed. In *Satyagraha*, again, we detect only one category: wounded Zulus. In *Autobiography*, we learn of two categories: (1) Wounded Zulus who were (as it seems) neutral civilians and noncombatants—flogged in detention on mere suspicion, and (2) Zulu friendlies—shot at by the soldiers by mistake.

WORK DETAILS

We know from the biography (1909) that the corps' work details revolved around using stretchers to carry helpless men behind the cavalry, attending to the sanitation of the camp, and of course, nursing the wounded Zulus: "Not infrequently, the condition of the lashed men, who were placed in their charge, was appalling, the wounds filthy, their lives hanging in the balance." This entire work is described as inclusive for all the corpsmen. Exactly what Gandhi himself did is not revealed. In *Satyagraha*, we read, "We had to cleanse the wounds of several Zulus which had not been attended to for as many as five or six days. . . . The Zulus could not talk to us, but from their gestures and the expressions of their eyes they seemed to feel as if God had sent us to their succour." In addition, there was the stretcher-bearing work, "The work for which we had enlisted was fairly heavy, for sometimes during the month we had to perform a march of as many as forty miles a day." Again, the work details are inclusive of all corpsmen; the task breakdown is missing.

In *Autobiography*, the workload consists entirely of caring for the Zulus: "The wounded in our charge were not wounded in battle. A section of them had been taken prisoners as suspects. The general had sentenced them to be flogged. The flogging had caused severe sores. These, being unattended to, were festering." Gandhi then talks about the care provided to those Zulu friendlies who had been shot mistakenly by white soldiers. Up until this point the workload is inclusive of all corpsmen. After that, Gandhi mentioned specifically his job, "Besides this work I had to compound and dispense prescriptions for the white soldiers." Did Zulus get the medicine? If so, who prescribed it? If not, is there an explanation? Thereafter, Gandhi briefly mentioned the stretcher-bearing work, "But wherever we went, I am thankful that we had God's good work to do, having to carry to the camp on our stretchers those Zulu friendlies who had been inadvertently wounded, and to attend upon them as nurses."

Ironically, there are serious discrepancies between what Gandhi stated in his *Autobiography* when compared to the 1906 accounts of *Indian Opinion*. First, take the case of the corps' task assignments on June 26, 1906, which can be divided into four broad categories: (1) Nine men of the corps were tasked to form a fatigue party to accompany the tank-wagon bringing water from an adjoining stream; (2) Some were detained to disinfect the whole camp under the superintendence of Dr. Savage, the district surgeon for Mapumulo; (3) Three to four of the corpsmen were to dress the wounds on the backs of several native rebels who had received lashes; and (4) one corpsman assisted at entering the daily roll of patients treated by Captain Howden. Gandhi does not mention his own task, but he was most probably with Dr. Savage (since they conversed with each other) working on disinfecting the campsite. If Dr. Savage had such a pressing demand for medical care for the lashed Zulus, then why did he seek out only three or four of the corpsmen? The majority of the manpower was put to use to bring water. That much is quite clear from *Indian Opinion* columns. Incidentally, these Zulus are described as "native rebels" as opposed to the civilians or noncombatant types flogged in detention as described in *Autobiography*.

On the next day, June 27: "Some of the above work was partially interrupted or suspended as a helio-message was received to forward a stretcher party to Otimati in connection with operations that were to be undertaken by the B.M.R. column at Thring's Post. Early on the morning of the 27th, therefore, one-half of the Corps, with two stretchers under Sgt.-Major Gandhi and Sgt. Joshi proceeded to Otimati, where instructions were received to take a stretcher to carry one of the troopers who was dazed. Fortunately, the trooper had recovered before the party reached Thring's Post. But by an unfortunate accident, another trooper, by name Forder, had received a bullet-wound in the thigh from a co-trooper. He, however, pluckily rode to the camp. The stretcher party had to assist Mr. Stokes, of the N.M.C., in treating the wounded trooper, and others, who had received slight injuries through accidents or otherwise, requiring medical help." Were all the Zulus with lashes medically taken care of on June 26? Was there follow-up care? Note something of special interest here: "some of the above work was partially interrupted or suspended. . . ." Since one-half of the entire corps (ten soldiers) left on the morning of June 27 and some of the work was partially interrupted, can we presume reasonably that at least some work was completed or whatever that was unfinished was left for others to continue? I believe that of all the four task categories, the work least likely to have been left partially interrupted or suspended was the first-aid care to those festering wounds inflicted on the Zulus. In that case, we can say that those three or four corpsmen assigned to take care of the festering wounds continued with their work on June 27 and 28. One thing is unquestionably clear: since Gandhi left with the stretcher party on the early morning of June 27, he was probably not directly involved in rendering the first-aid care.

In *Autobiography*, Gandhi gives the impression that the stretcher bearing was used for only the Zulu friendlies. But in *Indian Opinion* that is not the case. Here we know the stretcher was used to transport a "Kaffir, being a friendly boy" (the only black) in addition to some whites, one of whom was named Forder. In *Autobiography*, Gandhi had to dispense prescriptions for the white soldiers. Strangely, he didn't mention this work of his anywhere else. If Gandhi's four gospels have left you in a state of confusion, then you are not alone.

The exhaustive analysis of these four Gandhi gospels trying to decipher the work details has by no means been a trouble-free undertaking. But, let there be a warning that the bottom line on these details is not conclusive at least up until this point simply because Gandhi has tried to bamboozle again by dropping another hoodwinking. In the chapter titled "Heart Searchings" after the Zulu "rebellion" chapter in *Autobiography*, Gandhi states: "The Zulu 'rebellion' was full of new experiences and gave me much food for thought. . . . To hear every morning reports of the soldiers' rifles exploding like crackers in innocent hamlets, and to live in the midst of them was a trial. But I swallowed the bitter draught, especially as the work of my Corps consisted only in nursing the wounded Zulus. . . . This work, therefore, eased my conscience. . . ." Now we are back to square one. The Indian corps' task was to nurse *only* the wounded Zulus. That corresponds to one of the duties chartered on June 26, 1906. After traveling full circle, we are left with no option but to finally conclude that the job descriptions narrated in the 1906 *Indian Opinion* columns are as close to the truth as possible.

WASHING HIS HANDS

In the 1906 accounts of *Indian Opinion*, there is no need for Gandhi to wash his hands. The same is true in the biography. However, in *Satyagraha*, the circumstances dictate a new setting: "I have always been thankful to God for the work which then fell to our lot. . . . We undertook this mission of mercy. We were only too glad to do this." In like fashion, in *Autobiography*, Gandhi reaches for the soap to wash his hands: "I bore no grudge against the Zulus, they had harmed no Indian. . . . At any rate my heart was with the Zulus, and I was delighted, on reaching headquarters, to hear that our main work was to be the nursing of the wounded Zulus . . . those innocent people. The Zulus were delighted to see us. The White soldiers . . . tried to dissuade us from attending to the wounds. And as we would not heed them, they became enraged and poured unspeakable abuse on the Zulus."

AFTER THE WAR

In the 1906 *Indian Opinion* columns, Gandhi is proud of his accomplishments. He looks forward to more military service. In the biography by Rev. Doke, his anguish is deep because the "Indians are coloured, and are accordingly classed with aboriginal natives." The Indians made sacrifices to nurse the blacks: "It was no trifle for such men to become voluntary nurses to men not yet emerged from the most degraded state." In *Satyagraha*, two ideas take hold in Gandhi—a life of celibacy and poverty. In *Autobiography*, he vowed to exercise *brahmacharya* and lead a celibate life.

During the first phase of Gandhi's introduction to the West by his Christian apologists, there was a conscious effort to polish him. After years of propaganda, we are on verge of the final stages: there is an unconscious amalgamation of variant accounts in these Gandhi gospels. Not only has the nonexpert reader lost the ability to detect variances or contradicting stories but it also has adversely affected the experts. Many Gandhi scholars fill in the lacunae of one Gandhi gospel story from another, and adopt harmonizing interpretations where contradictions appear to exist. And where the gap is unbridgeable they either skip it or concoct a story of their own. Some Gandhian authors turned to harmonizing the various accounts of the Zulu rebellion. They took information either from Gandhi's first biography and/or his two autobiographical accounts and then harmonized it with selections from the sixteen letters laid out in the previous chapter, "Getting Ready for the Zulu War." The following are ten examples that have seemingly paid off dividends.

Gandhi: A Life by Krishna Kripalani: Choosing selectively from sections from letter number # 10 (see chapter 9) and adding to it a juicy spice of his own, Mr. Kripalani conveniently lays the blame on whites and not on Gandhi:

> Though the offer was accepted by the authorities, the arrogant and graceless temper of the whites was indicated by a correspondent suggesting in the columns of the *Natal Advertiser* that "Indians, so that they may not run away, should be placed in the front-line, and that then the fight between them and the Natives will be a sight for the gods." Commenting on this in his *Indian Opinion*, Gandhi characteristically suggested that, "if such a course were adopted, it would be undoubtedly the very best that could happen to the Indians. If they be cowardly, they will deserve the fate that will overtake them; if they be brave, nothing can be better than for brave men to be in the front-line."[5]

"The Zulu Rebellion," authored by Professor James D. Hunt, chapter 20 in volume 3 of *Mahatma Gandhi: The Birth of Satyagraha—From Petitioning to Passive Resistance*: As affirmed earlier, Professor Hunt's account is definitely the best I have encountered. He has cited materials from almost all the sixteen letters and presented them in a manner as if harmonized from within. The tendency to harmonize from Gandhi's autobiographical account comes later in the chapter.

Gandhi on War and Peace by Rashmi-Sudha Puri: The author, on the faculty at the Department of Gandhian Studies at Punjab University, lumped elements from letter numbers # 7, 14, and 16 (see chapter 9) to provide a flowing rationale for Gandhi's "entanglements of war." Not necessarily a harmonizing effort but not truthfully forthcoming either.

Gandhi: Ordained in South Africa by J. N. Uppal: Here is a New Delhi–based Gandhian scholar who harmonized material taken from letter number # 6 with the autobiographical accounts.

Gandhi: A Life by Yogesh Chadha: This is one of the latest Gandhi biographies on the international market. As expected, Mr. Chadha likewise harmonized the materials from letter numbers # 14 and 16 with the autobiographical narratives.

The Forgotten Woman: The Untold Story of Kastur Gandhi, Wife of Mahatma Gandhi by Arun and Sunanda Gandhi: Here is a perfect example of a harmonization from letter number # 10.

> A correspondent commenting in the *Natal Advertiser*, for example, on what he viewed as the absurd idea of enlisting Indian soldiers to help fight Zulus, had slyly suggested that "the Indians, so that they may not run away, should be placed in the front line, and then the fight between them and the Natives will be a sight for the gods." How, Mohandas asked himself, could such venomous racial hatred be eradicated? How could such degrading stereotypes be dispelled? Perhaps he should advise his countrymen to volunteer for combat and ask for frontline duty. Yet, when he contemplated the conflict itself, his only reaction was misery at the thought of so much violence.[6]

The South African Gandhi: An Abstract of the Speeches and Writings of M. K. Gandhi, edited by Fatima Meer, the Director of the Institute for Black Research at the University of Natal. Chapter 24 is truly worth reading for its harmonization efforts. The selective contents from letter numbers # 5 and 6 were blended in with the selective narratives from *Autobiography*, *Satyagraha*, and Doke's biography.

Gandhiji's Vision of a Free South Africa by E. S. Reddy: The fourth chapter, "Gandhiji and Africans in South Africa," has a small section in which the author attempts to harmonize letter # 6 with that of Doke's biography.

The Great Indian Way: A Life of Mahatma Gandhi by Raja Rao: This is the latest Gandhi biography on the Indian market, written with a religious flavor. All the biographical material has been transformed to such an extent that it appears suitable for the religious ears in tune with Gandhi. Therefore, in that spirit and understandably, information about the Zulu War comes exclusively from *Autobiography*, and there is no need to harmonize with other accounts.

Mahatma Gandhi: An Essay in Appreciation by R. M. Gray and Manilal C. Parekh: This was, in all probability, the first book that benefited from selectively taking materials from *Autobiography* and combining it with much of the substance of Doke's biography.[7]

It is absolutely clear that Gandhi was hawkish during the 1906 Zulu rebellion. The evidence is that conclusive. However, by 1909, Gandhi is in the midst of an ongoing passive-resistance campaign and on his way to plead his case in England, where quite possibly there are British officials who harbor deep reservations about the Zulu rebellion. How can one appeal effectively to these officials? If Gandhi presents himself as a gung-ho soldier against blacks during the war, he may run the risk of jeopardizing his case in England. He is fully cognizant of the fact that there are a number of whites who voiced serious objections to the Natal government's antiblack military action. What do you do? What is your strategy? Gandhi utilized his time by twisting the truth in the biography by Reverend Doke. He rewrote the Indian Corps' role in the Zulu rebellion to create a more positive appeal to the British hierarchy. Gandhi and his caste Indians are presented as men from a great ancient civilization who had to really stoop so low (only for the British!) to provide medical aid to these otherwise savage Zulus. The result is the best of both worlds: Indians show their support for the British Empire against any threat. They also show their pity for the wounded, backward blacks. Conveniently and understandably, the motivation factor or factors to join the military are absent in this version. The injustice is perpetrated, not on blacks, but on Indians because of the manner in which whites treat them like niggers!

Now the time is the 1920s. Gandhi is in India, an internationally known figure. Besides being touted as the latest Hindu divine incarnation, he is also a focus for worship in selective Christian churches in the West. The future may hold promise of more. The time is ripe to rewrite the past to suit present and future needs. In *Satyagraha* Gandhi copies the whites in joining the army. However, once on the front lines and unlike the whites, he pursues a *mission of mercy* for the wounded Zulus. God comes into the picture and the Zulus, through their nonverbal communication, expressed thanks not only to Gandhi and Indians but also to God for having sent for them special assistance. Gandhi looks great! The whites begin to show in a less desirable light. The metamorphosis continues through the next stage, in *Autobiography*. Gandhi seems to do a somersault; he himself is a victim of circumstances when he joins the military action. The authentic, belligerent Gandhi of 1906 is replaced with a new man who is nothing short of a loving empathic fellow, whose heart is with the blacks. He was indeed a gifted humanitarian. If he had not joined the army, only God knows what would have happened to those innocent, helpless people, victims of the white aggression, called the Zulus. God in his infinite wisdom brought a miracle to these hapless blacks: Gandhi, who, standing tall, had his arms stretched out toward them with a bountiful love! Shame on the whites! Look at the greatness of Gandhi: In spite of what the whites had done to the blacks, Gandhi goes out, without any grumble, to discharge another one of his humanitarian tasks of dispensing medicines to these same racist white men! Isn't he great!

I have no doubt Gandhi was well aware of how difficult it was to rewrite history without leaving traces of the original story. One alteration always implies others; but like any storyteller, perhaps, he did not always think of the repercussions of alterations he had inserted in his new history, and so left the other parts of his work unaltered. Why would Gandhi resort to such low tactics? Was Gandhi running a pattern of cover-ups? If so, why?

NOTES

1. Martin Luther King Jr., *Stride Toward Freedom: The Montgomery Story* (New York: Harper & Row, 1958), chap. 6, "Pilgrimage to Nonviolence."

2. Martin Luther King Jr., *Strength to Love* (New York: Harper & Row, Publishers, 1963), chap. 8.

3. Gandhi dates the preface section of *Satyagraha in South Africa* as April 2, 1924. Therefore, I have used the year 1924 as a focus for analysis purposes only.

4. Gandhi dates the introduction section of *An Autobiography, or The Story of My Experiments with Truth* as November 26, 1925. Therefore, I have used the year 1925 as a focus for analysis purposes only.

5. Krishna Kripalani, *Gandhi: A Life* (New Delhi: Author, 1968), p. 67.

6. Arun and Sunanda Gandhi, *The Forgotten Woman: The Untold Story of Kastur Gandhi, Wife of Mahatma Gandhi* (Huntsville, Ark.: Ozark Mountain Publishers, 1998), pp. 133–34.

7. R. M. Gray and Manilal C. Parekh, *Mahatma Gandhi: An Essay in Appreciation* (Calcutta: Association Press [YMCA], 1931), p. 17. The first edition was published in 1924 and the second edition in 1925. It is highly likely that the information from *Autobiography* was selectively exploited before *Autobiography* itself was published. Mr. Parekh, in the early 1930s, visited Atlanta, Georgia, to establish holy alliances between Mahatma Gandhi and the church-based African Americans.

PART 3

THE LATENT PERILS
of SATYAGRAHA

I do not know what evil there is in me. I have a strain of cruelty in me, as others say, such that people force themselves to do things, even to attempt impossible things, in order to please me.

—Mahatma Gandhi
The Life and Death of Mahatma Gandhi

13

GETTING READY for SATYAGRAHA

*The world knows so little of how much my so-called great-
ness depends upon the incessant toil and drudgery of silent,
devoted, able and pure workers, men as well as women.*

—Mahatma Gandhi
Young India, April 26, 1928

In this chapter, I do not intend to dwell upon Satyagraha in its entirety. I will discuss it only to the extent that it may shed some light on an area that is hardly
talked about—racism—which was associated with Satyagraha. Satyagraha may be
variously designated as "truth-force," "soul-force," "a firm grasp upon truth,"
"insistence on truth," or "vindication of truth." The derivation is from *satya*, "truth,"
and *agraha*, "a steadfast grasping." It is referred to in English as passive resistance.
Gandhi did not like to define the term but explained it at the time he conceived it:

> The term denotes the method of securing rights by personal suffering; it is the
> reverse of resistance by arms. When I refuse to do a thing that is repugnant to
> my conscience, I use soul-force. For instance, the Government of the day has
> passed a law which is applicable to me. I do not like it. If by using violence I
> force the Government to repeal the law, I am employing what may be termed
> body-force. If I do not obey the law and accept the penalty for its breach, I use
> soul-force. It involves sacrifice of self.[1]

There is a Christian contention that claims that Gandhi acquired Satyagraha
straight out of the Bible. In one famous Christian scholarly work, we read:

139

As a devout practitioner of the Sermon on the Mount and the way of the cross, Gandhi knew that his term, *satyagraha*, was a re-creation of Jesus' "kingdom of God." He had derived his own initial understanding of non-violence from Leo Tolstoy's interpretation of Jesus' saying, "The kingdom of God is within your power" (Luke 17:21).[2]

The evidence rather suggests that Gandhi borrowed the concept of *dharna*—literally, to hold fast, or "sit tight"—from his Hindu background (which had evidence of few techniques of coercion). In *dharna*, an injured party would fast on the other party's doorstep, on the principle that if the fasting man died, his death was the responsibility of the other and would bring the wrath of the gods down upon him. Such a remote idea was to be applied in a public setting in South Africa. The time for such a Hindu spectacle came in 1906 after the sweet military victory over the blacks.

Most scholars have been led to believe that Satyagraha was born on September 11, 1906, within two months after Gandhi returned from his victorious military duty. Is that really accurate? Maureen Swan doesn't think so:

> Because the first declaration of passive resistance took place in September 1906, and because Gandhi has laid much stress on his activity as a stretcher bearer in the Zulu rebellion immediately before this, it is generally assumed that the critical turning point occurred during his military service. It should already be clear from what has been written above that most of the major elements of Gandhi's philosophy had already been thought out well before mid-1906. Indeed, Gandhi's first call for passive resistance took place not in September 1906, but in January 1904, a fact which seems to have been consistently overlooked.[3]

I plan to continue in this chapter as if the traditional Gandhi story line is accurate, which is that the Zulu War transformed his life and shortly after, the writing of *Satyagraha* resulted directly out of it. Gandhi himself pointed out in his *Autobiography* that he did some soul searching during the Zulu rebellion, which led him to take vows and pointed him to dedicate his life to, among other things, the "service of the community." One would also suppose, gleaning information from the *Autobiography*, that Mahatma Gandhi was going to do something to eradicate racism, not just against Indians but against the vast South African majority, the blacks. After all, one would think "service of the community" implies Indians, other Asians, blacks, and all others truly in need of help. However, there is a difference between "service of the community" and "service of the human community." Gandhi meant the Indian community. And within that he had specifically in mind the upper-caste brethren—the merchant community, the money earners.

After the Zulu War, it was time to take off the military uniform and put on the lawyer outfit. Back in Johannesburg, he was busy doing what he had done before going to the war: writing petitions to government leaders on familiar issues of the

Transvaal—continuing the effective use of the judicial system to obtain redress for Indian grievances. In Natal, the Natal Indian Congress did his bidding. Likewise in Transvaal, he had under control an organization called the British Indian Association (BIA). The documents in *Indian Opinion* compiled in *Collected Works* regarding the birth of *Satyagraha* are incomplete. In order to complete the story of what actually happened, I had no choice but to fill in the gaps with materials taken from *Satyagraha in South Africa* to some extent so that we get a complete story of what transpired with the passive resistance campaign of 1906.

In late August 1906, Gandhi read the updates of the ongoing debates on Asian immigration and other relevant issues in the August 22 *Transvaal Government Gazette*, which carried the draft of a bill called "Asiatic Law Amendment Ordinance 1906." Gandhi at once translated the draft ordinance into Gujarati for *Indian Opinion*. Years later, in *Satyagraha in South Africa*, he recalled the experience vividly:

> I shuddered as I read the sections of the Ordinance one after another. I saw nothing in it except hatred of Indians. It seemed to me that if the Ordinance was passed and the Indians meekly accepted it, that would spell absolute ruin for the Indians in South Africa. I clearly saw that this was a question of life and death for them. I further saw that even in the case of memorials and representations proving fruitless, the community must not sit with folded hands. Better die than submit to such a law. But how were we to die? What should we dare and do so that there would be nothing before us except a choice of victory or death? An impenetrable wall was before me, as it were, and I could not see my way through it.[4]

Again, my intention is not to exhaust the merits or flaws of this ordinance or even to explore its details, but only to analyze a few of the salient features from Gandhi's perspective and then move on quickly to the meat of my subject category, racism. Professor Hunt has summed up the offensive nature of the ordinance to the Indians as follows:

> Practically the whole text was given over to the registration procedures and penalties for non-compliance. The four supposed benefits were also there, plus one more: Asiatics travelling on temporary permits may, on the discretion of the Lt.-Governor be exempted from the provisions applying to coloured persons under the Liquor Licensing law. Other features of the new law became clear upon reading the draft:
> 1. The legal definition of an Asiatic in Law 3 of 1885 was continued: "persons belonging to any of the native races of Asia, including the so-called Coolies, Arabs, Malays, and Mohammedan subjects of the Turkish dominion."
> 2. Whereas under Law 3, and as reaffirmed in recent Supreme Court decisions, only male adults who intended to settle in the country must register, women were now required to register.

3. Every male and female above the age of eight, whether or not intending to settle, must register.
4. Only permits issued under the Peace Preservation Ordinance of 1902 would be honoured; previously the possession of old Dutch registration certificates was honoured at least by some magistrates.
5. Certificates were to be produced upon demand made by a police officer or any other person authorised thereto by the Colonial Secretary.
6. Stiff penalties were given for noncompliance, including fines, prison, and removal from the country. It was the clear authority to expel offenders, rather than authority to issue temporary permits, that the government had previously lacked.[5]

The Executive Committee of the British Indian Association met on August 24 to consider the draft ordinance. The members of the new Hamidiya Islamic Society were also present. Mr. Gandhi explained the Ordinance word by word in a highly charged atmosphere. He addressed the meeting:

This is a very serious crisis. If the Ordinance were passed and if we acquiesced in it, it would be imitated all over South Africa. As it seems to me, it is designed to strike at the very root of our existence in South Africa. It is not the last step, but the first step with a view to hound us out of the country. We are therefore responsible for the safety, not only of the ten or fifteen thousand Indians in the Transvaal but of the entire Indian community in South Africa. Again, if we fully understand all the implications of this legislation, we shall find that India's honour is in our keeping. For the Ordinance seeks to humiliate not only ourselves but also the motherland. The humiliation consists in the degradation of innocent men. No one will take it upon himself to say that we have done anything to deserve such legislation. We are innocent, and insult offered to a single innocent member of a nation is tantamount to insulting the nation as a whole. It will not, therefore, do to be hasty, impatient or angry. That cannot save us from this onslaught. But God will come to our help, if we calmly think out and carry out in time measures of resistance, presenting a united front and bearing the hardship, which such resistance brings in its train.[6]

Mr. Gandhi's friend, Mr. Reinhold Gregorowski, an attorney in Pretoria, was consulted to provide his views on the ordinance. He wrote:

The act is far more severe than the Dutch Law. There is not a single provision in it that is favourable to the Indians. The act makes the position of the Indian worse than that of the Kaffir. Not every Kaffir is required to carry a pass on him; but now every Indian will have to do so. Educated Kaffirs are exempt from such restrictive laws. But the Indian, whatever his education and standing, will have to carry a pass. The pass, it seems to us, will be like the one carried by prisoners, etc. Whatever loop-holes there existed in the Law [3] of 1885 have been closed in this Act. While Kaffirs can own land, Indians cannot. It does not seem probable that the Liberal Government will approve such a law.[7]

The red flag was raised: Indians worse than the Kaffirs! How could the upper-caste honorable brotherhood be humiliated in such a way? What followed next in the Satyagraha campaign was largely driven by propaganda which highlighted the blacks and the potential symbolic degrading of Indians to the levels of these blacks. No member of the Indian mercantile class could accept such an insult. To them it was perfectly okay to treat these blacks the way they were being treated—less than humans. The machine under Gandhi was set in full motion to stop the act. Gandhi's "service of the community" carried a heavy price tag, both in human and monetary terms, as will be seen shortly.

On September 8, 1906, the British Indian Association sent cables to the secretary of state for the colonies and the secretary of state for India, which read as follows:

> British Indians alarmed at haste with which Asiatic Ordinance is being rushed through Legislative Council. Ordinance reduces Indians to status lower than *Kaffirs* and much lower than that occupied under Dutch regime. British Indian Association request Imperial sanction be stayed pending deputation proceeding directly. Association requests reassuring reply.[8] [my italics]

Another cable, sent to the Viceroy of India, said:

> British Indians alarmed at Asiatic Ordinance passing through Legislative Council. Transvaal Ordinance degrading, insulting reduces Indians to a worse status than that of *Pariahs*. British Indian Association request the Viceroy's active intervention. His Excellency being directly responsible for their welfare.[9] [my italics]

Kaffirs! Pariahs! The Hindu mind had always equated the black people of Africa (Kaffirs) with their own serfs in India—the Untouchables, the pariahs, lowest of the low castes in Hinduism. These Untouchables are also known as the black people of India. You can see why these Indians didn't like the Ordinance. You can see why Gandhi didn't like the Ordinance. Among its many unacceptable provisions, the most humiliating to them was that they were about to be legally classified by the government on a par with blacks of Africa and Untouchables of India. That was unthinkable.

On September 9, the Hamidiya Islamic Society held a major conference in Johannesburg. More than eight hundred prominent Moslems attended. Gandhi addressed the meeting in Gujarati:

> We have received a reply to our cable to the Colonial Secretary. I have also cabled to London according to instructions. There is now no alternative to sending a deputation, because an intolerable and wicked law is being forced upon us; and we must not put up with it. As it is, our plight in the Transvaal is very bad, and now comes this vicious Draft Ordinance. My advice, therefore, is that we should not seek fresh registration.

Let the accusation of breaking the law fall on us. Let us cheerfully suffer imprisonment. There is nothing wrong in that. The distinctive virtue of the British is bravery. If therefore we also unite and offer resistance with courage and firmness, I am sure there is nothing that the Government can do. Even the half-castes and Kaffirs, who are less advanced than we, have resisted the Government. The pass law applies to them as well, but they do not take out passes. I do not want to say more. I would only advise you not to register yourselves again. If the Government sends us to gaol, I shall be the first to court imprisonment. And if any Indian is put to trouble because of his refusal to register afresh in accordance with the Draft Ordinance, I will appear in his case free of charge. On Tuesday next, we are holding a mass meeting. I expect you all to close your business on that day and attend it.[10]

Half-castes and Kaffirs again. Am I reading Gandhi correctly—that these "less advanced" people are already practicing Satyagraha and they are effective? Is Gandhi saying that if these "less advanced blacks" can practice Satyagraha, then why not us? Half-castes are the Hindu version of what we know as half-breeds. In all likelihood, Gandhi is referring to those born from the union of low-caste Indians in South Africa and Negroes.

Gandhi, to his credit, was always ahead of the game. Since he was going to commit himself to the "service of the community" somebody had to pay for the "service." So the decision was made to collect funds quickly through appointing a new committee consisting of the following persons: Abdul Gani, Ali Bhai Apuji, Mohammed Pirbhai Fancy, Ebrahim Coovadia, Essop Mian, Mohammed Essop Gatu, Ghulam Saheb, Musa Hapeji Balbolia, Gandhi, Bhikubhai Dahyaji, Ambaidu Parag, Dahya Ram, Lalaji P. V. Patel, and Makkan Master. Later, Gandhi exercised full control over the money.[11]

The idea of not registering really caught on quite early in the Satyagraha preparation. The linchpin of the entire protest movement on the horizon rested on the idea of refusing re-registration. Instead, the Gandhi-led Indians would go to prison in protest. In all honesty, the Asiatic Registration Certificate asked for trivial information: name, family, caste, father's name, thumbmark, height, occupation, address, place of issue, and age. At the bottom right it carried the signature block for the issuing officer. That was all. Gandhi didn't like it. It is not too hard to tell why. The time had come to implement "service of the community."

NOTES

1. Quoted in Michael Edwardes's *Myth of the Mahatma: Gandhi, the British, and the Raj* (London: Constable, 1986), pp. 187–88. Originally written in *Hind Swaraj*.

2. James W. Douglass, *The Nonviolent Coming of God* (Maryknoll, N.Y.: Orbis Books, 1991), pp. 30–31. Another interesting study to connect Satyagraha to Hinduism is Constance DeJong and Philip Glass's *Satyagraha: M. K. Gandhi in South Africa*

1893–1914: The Historical Material and Libretto Comprising the Opera's Book (New York: Tanam Press, 1983).

3. Maureen Swan, *Gandhi: The South African Experience* (Johannesburg: Raven Press, 1985), p. 117.

4. Mohandas K. Gandhi, *Satyagraha in South Africa* (1928; reprint, Ahmedabad: Navajivan Publishing House, 1972), pp. 91–92.

5. Pyarelal, *Mahatma Gandhi: The Birth of Satyagraha—From Petitioning to Passive Resistance* (Ahmedabad: Navajivan Publishing House, 1986), vol. 3, chap. 21, pp. 487–88.

6. Gandhi, *Satyagraha*, p. 94.

7. CWMG 5, # 442, p. 424.

8. Ibid., 5, # 437, p. 416.

9. Ibid., 5, # 438, p. 416.

10. Ibid., 5, # 440, p. 418.

11. Pyarelal, *Mahatma Gandhi: The Birth of Satyagraha*, p. 495.

14

*If I seem to take part in politics, it is only because politics
encircle us today like the coil of a snake from which one
cannot get out, no matter how much one tries. I wish therefore to wrestle with the snake.*

—Mahatma Gandhi
Young India, May 12, 1920

As decided earlier, an estimated three thousand Indians gathered on September 11, 1906, at the Empire Theatre in Johannesburg for a mass meeting. All the dignitaries of the British Indian Association (BIA) including Gandhi were present. Delegates, on invitation, from all parts of Transvaal had also gathered for the meeting. Mr. Abdul Gani, chairman of the BIA, presided over the meeting and promptly opened the proceedings at 3 P.M. Very early on he led the audience to a predetermined path: "whereby, we solemnly declare to the Government that, if our prayer is left unanswered, rather than submit to the indignity contemplated in the Ordinance, we shall go to gaol."[1] When he spoke of going to gaol, the crowd shouted in one voice, "We shall go to gaol; but will not register ourselves again."[2] This had been one of the most approved methods adopted by the British subjects, the chairman continued, whenever they had disapproved, with very considerable reason and as a matter of principle, with any legislation. Finally, he declared: "There are moments in the life of a community when resistance, especially of the above nature becomes a vital necessity and a sacred duty, and I think that such a moment is now at hand for us, if we would be called men. I have no doubt that if

147

you pass the resolution that will be submitted to you and carry it out, the Ordinance will be a blessing in disguise, for, has not Lord Selborne told us that oppression brings out the best, very often, in the oppressed? May God do so in us."[3] The chairman introduced the five resolutions to be passed. These resolutions were wholly the work of Gandhi. The five resolutions the chairman had already introduced were passed, one after the other (CWMG 5, #441, pp. 422–23).

Resolution I

This mass meeting of British Indians here assembled, respectfully urges the Honourable the President and Members of the Legislative Council of the Transvaal not to pass the Draft Asiatic Ordinance to amend Law No.3 of 1885, now before that Honourable House, in view of the facts that:

(1) It is, so far as the Indian community of the Transvaal is concerned, a highly contentious measure.

(2) It subjects the British Indian community of the Transvaal to degradation and insult totally undeserved by its past history.

(3) The present machinery is sufficient for checking the alleged influx of Asiatics.

(4) The statements as to the alleged influx are denied by the British Indian community.

(5) If the Honourable House is not satisfied with the denial, this meeting invites (an) open, judicial, and British enquiry into the question of the alleged influx.

Resolution II

This mass meeting of British Indians here assembled respectfully protests against the Draft Asiatic Law Amendment Ordinance now being considered by the Legislative Council of the Transvaal, and humbly requests the local Government and the Imperial Authorities to withdraw the Draft Ordinance, for the reasons that:

(1) It is manifestly in conflict with the past declarations of His Majesty's representatives.

(2) It recognises no distinction between British and alien Asiatics.

(3) It reduces British Indians to a status lower than that of the aboriginal races of South Africa and the Coloured people.

(4) It renders the position of British Indians in the Transvaal much worse than under Law 3 of 1885, and, therefore, than under the Boer regime.

(5) It sets up a system of passes and espionage unknown in any other British territory.

(6) It brands the communities to which it is applied as criminals or suspects.

(7) The alleged influx of unauthorised British Indians into the Transvaal is denied.

(8) If such denial is not accepted, a judicial, open and British enquiry should be instituted before such drastic and uncalled for legislation is enforced.

(9) The measure is otherwise un-British and unduly restricts the liberty of inoffensive British subjects and constitutes a compulsory invitation to British Indians in the Transvaal to leave the country.

(10) This meeting further and especially requests the Right Honourable the Secretary of State for the Colonies and the Right Honourable the Secretary of State for India to suspend the Royal sanction and to receive a deputation on behalf of the British Indian community of the Transvaal in connection with this Draft Ordinance.

Resolution III

This meeting hereby appoints a delegation with power from the Committee of the British Indian Association to add to its membership or to change its personnel, to proceed to England and to lay before the Imperial Authorities the complaint of the British Indian community of the Transvaal regarding the Draft Asiatic Law Amendment Ordinance.

Resolution IV

In the event of the Legislative Council, the local Government, and the Imperial Authorities, rejecting the humble prayer of the British Indian community of the Transvaal in connection with the Draft Asiatic Law Amendment Ordinance, this mass meeting of British Indians here assembled solemnly and, regretfully resolves that, rather than submit to the galling, tyrannous, and un-British requirements laid down in the above Draft Ordinance, every British Indian in the Transvaal shall submit himself to imprisonment and shall continue so to do until it shall please His Most Gracious Majesty the King Emperor to grant relief.

Resolution V

This meeting desires the Chairman to forward copy of the first resolution to the Honourable the President and Members of the Legislative Council, and copies of all the resolutions to the honourable the Colonial Secretary, to His Excellency the Acting Lieutenant-Governor, and to His Excellency the High Commissioner, and to request His Excellency the High Commissioner to cable the text of resolutions Nos. 2, 3 and 4 to the Imperial Authorities (CWMG 5, #442, pp. 425–26).

The fourth resolution described as the "Gaol Resolution" received the most attention. Mr. Hajee Habib introduced this resolution:

The Fourth Resolution is the most important of all. Everything depends upon it. There is no disgrace in going to gaol; rather it is an honour. Only a few people knew of Mr. Tilak before he went to gaol; today the whole world knows him.

We are not going to get justice at the hands of the British Government. It kills us with sweet words; we should not be deceived. They are always ready to appease the Christian peoples. Again in this country, the doors are open to the whites and Christians, even if they be foreign nationals. The Bill is most objectionable. If it is passed, I solemnly declare that I will never get myself registered again and will be the first to go to gaol. (Applause.) I recommend the same course to you all. Are you all prepared to take the oath? (The Assembly stood up to him and said, Yes, we will go to gaol!). (CWMG 5, #456, pp. 441–42)

Mr. Hajee Ojer Ally seconded the fourth resolution with a thundering speech hammering the point: "I, too, shall refuse to register myself and prefer to go to gaol and deem it an honor." All of the five resolutions were passed, with the fourth resolution receiving the greatest endorsement, hand clapping, and the final approval. The entire meeting adjourned at about 6 P.M. Before closing, Mr. Gandhi, honorary secretary of the BIA, brought the meeting to a climax, giving a long speech in his clear, low tones. His language was earnest, serious, and his words carefully chosen. His remarks, as he recalled them in *Satyagraha in South Africa*, were as follows:

> I wish to explain to this meeting that there is a vast difference between this resolution and every other resolution we have passed up to date and that there is a wide divergence also in the manner of making it. It is a very grave resolution we are making, as our existence in South Africa depends upon our fully observing it. The manner of making the resolution suggested by our friend is as much of a novelty as of a solemnity. I did not come to the meeting with a view to getting the resolution passed in that manner, which redounds to the credit of Sheth Haji Habib as well as it lays a burden of responsibility upon him. I tender my congratulations to him. I deeply appreciate his suggestion, but if you adopt it, you too will share his responsibility. You must understand what is this responsibility, and as an adviser and servant of the community, it is my duty fully to explain it to you.
>
> We all believe in one and the same God, the differences of nomenclature in Hinduism and Islam notwithstanding. To pledge ourselves or to take an oath in the name of that God or with Him as witness is not something to be trifled with. If having taken such an oath we violate our pledge we are guilty before God and man. Personally I hold that a man, who deliberately and intelligently takes a pledge and then breaks it, forfeits his manhood. And just as a copper coin treated with mercury not only becomes valueless when detected but also makes its owner liable to punishment, in the same way a man who lightly pledges his word and then breaks it becomes a man of straw and fits himself for punishment here as well as hereafter. Sheth Haji Habib is proposing to administer an oath of a very serious character. There is no one in this meeting who can be classed as an infant or as wanting in understanding. You are all well advanced in age and have seen the world; many of you are delegates and have discharged responsibilities in a greater or lesser measure. No one present, there-

fore, can ever hope to excuse himself by saying that he did not know what he was about when he took the oath.

I know that pledges and vows are, and should be, taken on rare occasions. A man who takes a vow every now and then is sure to stumble. But if I can imagine a crisis in the history of the Indian community of South Africa when it would be in the fitness of things to take pledges that crisis is surely now. There is wisdom in taking serious steps with great caution and hesitation. But caution and hesitation have their limits, and we have now passed them. The Government has taken leave of all sense of decency. We would only be betraying our unworthiness and cowardice, if we cannot stake our all in the face of the conflagration which envelops us and sit watching it with folded hands. There is no doubt, therefore, that the present is a proper occasion for taking pledges. But every one of us must think out for himself if he has the will and the ability to pledge himself. Resolutions of this nature cannot be passed by a majority vote. Only those who take a pledge can be bound by it. This pledge must not be taken with a view to produce an effect on outsiders. No one should trouble to consider what impression it might have upon the local Government, the Imperial Government, or the Government of India. Every one must only search his own heart, and if the inner voice assures him that he has the requisite strength to carry him through, then only should he pledge himself and then only will his pledge bear fruit.

A few words now as to the consequences. Hoping for the best, we may say that if a majority of the Indians pledge themselves to resistance and if all who take the pledge prove true to themselves, the Ordinance may not be passed and, if passed, may be soon repealed. It may be that we may not be called upon to suffer at all. But if on the one hand a man who takes a pledge must be a robust optimist, on the other hand he must be prepared for the worst. Therefore I want to give you an idea of the worst that might happen to us in the present struggle. Imagine that all of us present here numbering 3,000 at the most pledge ourselves. Imagine again that the remaining 10,000 Indians take no such pledge. We will only provoke ridicule in the beginning. Again, it is quite possible that in spite of the present warning some or many of those who pledge themselves may weaken at the very first trial. We may have to go to jail, where we may be insulted. We may have to go hungry and suffer extreme heat or cold. Hard labour may be imposed upon us. We may be flogged by rude warders. We may be fined heavily and our property may be attached and held up to auction if there are only a few resisters left. Opulent today we may be reduced to abject poverty tomorrow. We may be deported. Suffering from starvation and similar hardships in jail, some of us may fall ill and even die. In short, therefore, it is not at all impossible that we may have to endure every hardship that we can imagine, and wisdom lies in pledging ourselves on the understanding that we shall have to suffer all that and worse. If some one asks me when and how the struggle may end, I may say that if the entire community manfully stands the test, the end will be near. If many of us fall back under storm and stress, the struggle will be prolonged. But I can boldly declare, and with certainty, that so long as there is even a handful of men true to their pledge, there can only be one end to the struggle, and that is victory.

A word about my personal responsibility. If I am warning you of the risks attendant upon the pledge, I am at the same time inviting you to pledge yourselves, and I am fully conscious of my responsibility in the matter. It is possible that a majority of those present here may take the pledge in a fit of enthusiasm or indignation but may weaken under the ordeal, and only a handful may be left to face the final test. Even then there is only one course open to some one like me, to die but not to submit to the law. It is quite unlikely but even if every one else flinched leaving me alone to face the music, I am confident that I would never violate my pledge. Please do not misunderstand me. I am not saying this out of vanity, but I wish to put you, especially the leaders upon the platform, on your guard. I wish respectfully to suggest it to you that if you have not the will or the ability to stand firm even when you are perfectly isolated, you must not only not take the pledge yourselves but you must declare your opposition before the resolution is put to the meeting and before its members begin to take pledges and you must not make yourselves parties to the resolution. Although we are going to take the pledge in a body, no one should imagine that default on the part of one or many can absolve the rest from their obligation. Every one should fully realize his responsibility, then only pledge himself independently of others and understand that he himself must be true to his pledge even unto death, no matter what others do.[4]

Let us recapitulate the events at the Empire Theatre: By all the accounts available, the mass meeting was a success. They took the pledge to refuse the registration and gladly accept imprisonment. It seems they knew what to expect in prison. Their leader, Mr. Gandhi, attorney-at-law in Johannesburg, had already apprised them of all the eventualities to come: We may be insulted in the prisons! We may have to go hungry! We may suffer extreme heat or cold! Hard labor may be imposed! Rude wardens may flog us! We may be fined heavily! Our property may be attached and held up to auction! Opulent today we may be reduced to abject poverty tomorrow! We may be deported! Suffer from starvation! Some may fall ill and even die! We may endure every hardship that's imaginable! The BIA leadership, in Resolution II (3) had said "It reduces British Indians to a status lower than that of the aboriginal races of South Africa and the Coloured people." This clearly shows their ultimate disgust. Did Gandhi fail to inform his listeners as to who else they might encounter in prison? I am referring to the blacks. Could it be that if he had apprised them of blacks in prison, the Indians under his sway may have refused to go along with the Gaol Resolution? Did Gandhi even know of blacks being lodged in the prisons? He had to; after all, he was a lawyer in practice. I also believe he did not divulge that information to the Indians lest that would jeopardize the beginning of his long "service of the community."

As per Resolution III, a delegation to England was authorized to lay before the Imperial authorities the Indian community's complaints, hoping to prevent His Majesty's acceptance of the ordinance. It was not easy for Gandhi to collect the necessary fund from the supposedly enthusiastic Indians. Also, if we follow the traditional Gandhi story, at this stage of the game, he is already under the vow of poverty. Now, he demands that the delegation use first-class accommodation while representing the Indian community to England. Go high class! And he did. He and Mr. Ally left Johannesburg for London on October 1, 1906. While on board the S.S. *Armadale Castle*, he dispatched correspondences for *Indian Opinion*, resurrecting his old bluff tactics. In one, he hammered the point that if the Indians were to go for the new registration, they would lose "their good name" in the eyes of other Indians and their "condition will thereby become worse than that of the Kaffirs" (CWMG 5, #484, p. 475). In his second dispatch from the sea, as a follow-up to a certain Gujarati poem, he recorded these observations:

I find that the Englishman is not only full five cubits tall, a host in himself, match for five hundred but is capable in every other way. When he chooses to enjoy wealth and power, he excels in doing it and he makes the best of poverty, too. He alone knows how to give orders; and he knows too how to take them. In his behaviour he is great with the great and small with the small. He knows how to earn money and he alone knows how to spend it. He knows how to converse and move in company. He lives in the knowledge that his happiness depends on the happiness of others. The Englishman I observed during the war seems to be an altogether different person now. Then he did all his work himself, trekked over long distances and felt happy with dry bread. Here on board the ship he does not do any work. He presses a button, and an attendant stands before him. He must have nice dishes of all kinds to eat. Every day he puts on a new dress. All this becomes him, but he does not lose his balance. Like the sea, he can contain all within himself. Though, generally speaking, he has little sense of religion, yet living in society, he is disciplined and observes sabbath. Why indeed should such a people not rule? (CWMG 5, #479, pp. 469–70)

One can imagine the beauty of this narrative in its original Gujarati prose and its impact on the readers! Clearly, Gandhi has painted a beautiful image of whites, including their performance of duties during the war.

In England, Gandhi wrote petitions, met senior officials, and so forth to convince them to oppose the pending ordinance in Transvaal. One can read such details at other places. Here my concentration is on blacks only. In a number of petitions that Gandhi mailed to Lord Elgin, his latest curriculum vitae was incorporated, highlighting proudly his role during the Boer and Zulu wars (CWMG 6, #52, p. 46). In a similar petition to Lord Elgin, dated November 20, 1906, he carefully outlined his reason for joining the war against blacks: "to bring about such reconciliation, by showing that British Indians were not unworthy to be citizens of the Empire and were capable of recognizing their obligations if they also insisted on their rights" (CWMG 6, #227, p. 198). Here the "reconciliation" had a specific meaning. It is reconciliation between the Indians and the Europeans *only*—an avowed objective of the Natal Indian Congress (CWMG 1, #37, pp. 130–35). More on that topic will be dealt with in part 4. In his letter to the *Times*, dated November 12, 1906, Gandhi outlines problems the ordinance will cause: "The [poor Indians] would be hustled by the Kaffir Police at every turn, and not the better-class Indians!" (CWMG 6, #158, p. 147).

On December 1, 1906, the deputation left England for South Africa. On January 1, 1907, the Transvaal was granted self-government. On March 22, 1907, Transvaal parliament passed the Asiatic Registration Bill. By May, the royal king granted his assent and the law took effect July 1. Gandhi, in a bitter mood, continued to oppose to the government by resorting to strikes and other means of Satyagraha. The government was determined to make the Indians obey the law. To their credit, they extended the time limit for compliance to November 30. Ram Sundara Pandit became an instant hero by going to jail. He was given a hero's welcome when set free in December 1907. However, soon thereafter he left Transvaal for Natal, which elicited scathing remarks from Gandhi. A few days later, Gandhi himself became the focus of attention in court. From here on began a series of troubles with the authorities that landed him in prison several times. After his third incarceration, Gandhi and Haji Habib embarked (with a first-class ticket—so much for the poverty vow) on the R.M.S. *Kenilworth Castle* to England on a second deputation. The party reached England on July 10, 1909, and stayed there until November 13, 1909. During this time the team made numerous petitions outlining their cases point by point. One of the points was the status of the Indian prisoners being classed and lodged with blacks in South Africa, and the fact that two-thirds of their food was the same as that of the blacks (CWMG 9, #179, p. 297).

In 1909, at the time Gandhi was on his second deputation to England, there was another parallel movement under way in response to the movement for the South African Union. At this time the colored and Africans united amongst themselves in an attempt to amend the Union Bill. Gandhi did not participate and never saw any need for that. All nonwhite parties were in communication with each other when the Union Bill was placed before Parliament in London, at which time they decided to send the delegation to London. The Transvaal Native Congress did not send a delegation, but instructed the young African attorneys in London, Pixley Seme and Alfred Mangena, to work with the arriving delegations, which included Gandhi. Incidentally, the ship that Gandhi was on also carried Dr. Abdurrahman, W. P. Schreiner (nonwhite leaders in South Africa), and others of the delegation. Gandhi is known to have communicated with at least Dr. Abdurrahman and W. P. Schreiner while in London, but no record exists of his communicating with the London-based black delegates.[5]

At the height of the Satyagraha campaign, during the time when the resisters and their families took shelter at the Tolstoy Farm, there is a report that a black family squatted on the farm and did occasional labor. However, they were never invited to be a part of the community there.[6]

On April 19, 1911, with the Satyagraha saga continuing, Gandhi held a close meeting with General Jan Smuts, who at the time was the Union Minister for Interior, Mines and Defense. During the meeting, the General couldn't have been more blunt when he told Gandhi, ". . . this country is the Kaffirs'. We whites are a handful. We do not want Asia to come in" (CWMG 11, #37, p. 32). Here is an example of a senior South African official openly telling Gandhi that South Africa really belongs to blacks. Ironically, his words did not have the intended effect. Gandhi had his own scheme of "Imperial brotherhood" which, of course, General Smuts couldn't understand, either. Two devious racial game plans spread their roots underneath and their two architects were trying to out-maneuver each other. The Satyagraha had too many racial tentacles to ponder.

The Satyagraha campaign had another spectacle. Gandhi surrounded himself with an entourage of whites. The literature lists the following: Albert West, Henry S. L. Polak, Herbert Kitchin, L. W. Ritch, Herman Kallenbach, Miss Sonja Schlesin, William Hosken, Rev. Joseph J. Doke, Rev. Charles Phillips, Thomas Perry, Rev. John Howard, Dr. N. Audley Ross, David Pollock, Albert Cartwright, Vere Stent, Dewdney Drew, Miss Emily Hobhouse, Miss Molteno, Mrs. Olive Schreiner, and Miss Florence Winterbottom. Gandhi worked closely with this group, and a few acted as his most trusted lieutenants. This situation created a problem within the Indian community. One of the Natal Indian Congress' secretaries asked why Gandhi chose white lieutenants over educated Natal-born Indians like K. R. Nayanah, S. R. Pather, and Bernard Gabriel. Gandhi's reply that Nayanah, Pather, and Gabriel could not be compared with Polak (one of the whites), in terms of "ability, talent, purity, and ideals." This comment provoked a prolonged attack on Gandhi's abilities and state of mind.[7]

A famous Gandhian scholar, Mr. Raghavan Iyer, in his *The Moral and Political Thought of Mahatma Gandhi* has quoted Gandhi, who claimed that Satyagraha in its *pure form* was practiced only in South Africa.[8] So, after leaving South Africa for India and with three decades more of Satyagraha evolution, Gandhi thought that Satyagraha's "pure form" had been left behind in South Africa. Maureen Swan has clearly established in her research that in South Africa, "Passive resistance, in theory at least, was therefore eminently suited to elite ideology."[9] The Satyagraha was hatched in Gandhi's brain, nourished by him, propelled by him, religiously veneered by him, propagandized by him, and financed by his elite group for the elite's vested interests for a very narrow purpose. To be more blunt, Satyagraha had its roots in the protection of money interests and in the hatred of those populations that didn't fit in Gandhi's racial ideology. The evidence is to be found in the midst of the Satyagraha campaign when Gandhi went to prison.

NOTES

1. Pyarelal, *Mahatma Gandhi: The Birth of Satygraha—From Petitioning to Passive Resistance* (Ahmedabad: Navajivan Publishing House, 1986), vol. 3, p. 497.

2. Ibid.

3. Ibid.

4. Mohandas K. Gandhi, *Satyagraha in South Africa* (Ahmedabad: Navajivan Publishing House, 1972), chap. 12, pp. 97–100.

5. James D. Hunt, "Gandhi and the black People of South Africa," *Gandhi Marg* 11, no. 1 (April–June 1989): 17.

6. Ibid., pp. 10–11.

7. Maureen Swan, *Gandhi: The South African Experience* (Johnannesburg: Raven Press, 1985), p. 245.

8. Raghavan Iyer, *The Moral and Political Thought of Mahatma Gandhi* (New York: Oxford University Press, 1973), p. 326.

9. Swan, *Gandhi*, p. 123.

15

Mankind is one, seeing that all are equally subject to the moral law. All men are equal in God's eyes. There are, of course, differences of race and status and the like, but the higher the status of a man, the greater is his responsibility.

—Mahatma Gandhi
Ethical Religion, 1930

Finally, the Transvaal government's patience with Gandhi and his Satyagraha tactics ran out. The authorities took a hard stand that led to his various arrests and convictions. One can and should read the details recorded elsewhere in the Gandhi literature. Gandhi's remaining time in South Africa (1908 to 1914) and his trouble with the law there are summarized below:

January 10, 1908: He was arrested in Transvaal and was sentenced to two months' simple imprisonment. He had a talk with General Smuts on January 30 and he was released following a compromise.

October 7, 1908: While returning from Natal, he was arrested at Volksrust, along with fifteen other Indians, for entering Transvaal without registration certificates. He was sentenced to two months imprisonment and released on December 12, 1908, from the Volksrust jail.

February 25, 1909: After having left Phoenix Settlement for Johannesburg,

157

Gandhi was arrested at Volksrust and sentenced to three months' imprisonment or a fifty-pound fine for failure to produce a registration certificate. On March 2, he was transferred from Volksrust to the Pretoria jail. He was released on May 24, 1909.

November 6, 1913: At 6.30 A.M., Gandhi led a "great march," consisting of 2,037 men, 127 women, and 57 children, from Charlestown; he addressed the marchers halfway between Charlestown and Volksrust. At the Volksrust border, the police superintendent and an immigration officer interviewed Gandhi and his rich white associate, Kallenbach. The marchers broke through a police cordon and crossed the border. Gandhi was arrested at 8.30 P.M. at the Palm-Ford railway station.

November 7, 1913: Gandhi appeared in a Volksrust court; he was released on fifty pounds' bail, furnished by Kallenbach. His case was remanded till November 14; he rejoined the marchers.

November 8, 1913: Gandhi arrived at Standerton; he was again arrested and released on bail; his case was remanded till November 21 and the march continued.

November 9, 1913: While traveling toward Transvaal, Gandhi was arrested at Teakworth near Greylingstaad on a Dundee warrant and charged with inducing a strike. He was secretly taken to Balfour for the night. The next day, the magistrate refused permission for Gandhi to join the marchers.

November 11, 1913: A Dundee magistrate sentenced Gandhi to a sixty-pound fine or nine months imprisonment with hard labor. He chose the latter. On November 13, Gandhi was removed to the Volksrust jail. The next day he made a statement before the Volksrust court; he was convicted on his own evidence and sentenced to an additional three months.

November 18, 1913: Gandhi was transferred to the Bloemfontein jail.

December 18, 1913: Gandhi, Polak, and Kallenbach were released at Pretoria on the Solomon Commission's recommendation. The commission was constituted to look into Indian grievances.

He was arrested, convicted, and incarcerated four times. He actually served a total of seven months and ten days of those sentences. We have evidence about what took place in the prison on the first three occasions. However, what happened during the fourth incarceration is anyone's guess. Before we get into the details, it is perhaps not out of place to look at what Gandhi said about these prison incidents years later:

M. K. Gandhi: An Indian Patriot in South Africa (1909) by Reverend Doke, was written not too long after Gandhi's first encounters with blacks in prison. Here, the Zulu war adventures and the experiences with blacks in the prisons are essentially lumped together.

> It was no trifle for such men to become voluntary nurses to men not yet emerged from the most degraded state. But distinctions of this kind are rarely appreciated in South Africa. Indians are coloured, and are accordingly classed with aboriginal natives. In the Transvaal, they are not allowed to ride in the trams, and there are special compartments for them in the trains. In our prisons "N" is stitched to their collars, to denote the people with whom they are classed, and in food—though the food is wholly unsuitable—in clothing, in work, in the cells, to all intents and purposes they are "natives" . . . There is no perception of the immense distance which separates the Indian from the Kaffir in the scale of civilization. To the average Colonial, they are all "niggers" alike. But to those who think, this Ambulance Corps, tenderly ministering to the wounded or cruelly-lashed Zulus—with the son of an Indian Prime Minister at their head—is worthy of an artist's brush. Some day, perhaps, it will have its need.[1]

In *Satyagraha in South Africa*, Gandhi describes his adventures, with some fine points relating to his first internment in January 1908:

> The next morning we found that prisoners without hard labour had the right to keep on their own private clothing, and if they would not exercise this right, they were given special jail clothing assigned to that class of prisoners. We decided that it was not right to put on our own clothing and that it was appropriate to take the jail uniform, and we informed the authorities accordingly. We were therefore given the clothes assigned to Negro convicts not punished with hard labour. But Negro prisoners sentenced to simple imprisonment are never numerous, and hence there was a shortage of simple imprisonment prisoners' clothing as soon as other Indians sentenced to simple imprisonment began to arrive. As the Indians did not wish to stand upon ceremony in this matter, they readily accepted clothing assigned to hard labour prisoners. Some of those who came in later preferred to keep on their own clothing rather than put on the uniform of the hard labour convicts. I thought this improper, but did not care to insist upon their following the correct procedure in the matter.[2]

In *Autobiography*, one learns nothing concerning blacks while Gandhi was in prison. He gives a clear impression that going to prison was a healthy experience as far as his learning to control dietary habits.[3] Also in the *Gandhi* movie, quite early on, there are scenes of Gandhi in prison uniform in conversation with another Indian named "Khan," but one learns almost nothing considering the matter on a historical basis.

It is clear, from the 1909 biography, that the letter "N" stitched to the collars of these Indian prisoners (including Gandhi) is offensive and degrading, that Gandhi felt a contrast between India's "higher civilized" people and the "niggers" of South Africa. In *Satyagraha*, the story has changed. Gandhi gives the impression that he had no problems whatsoever with the prison uniform designed for blacks. Rather, on a positive note, the implication is that he gladly accepted such clothing and felt that other, unwilling Indians should accept it also. Again we are confronted with an inconsistent Gandhi. What is the truth? Let us now turn our attention to what Gandhi wrote, as it appeared in *Indian Opinion* columns.

Prior to encountering blacks while in prison, the only other time Gandhi had faced them was at the time of the Zulu War. We have already discussed his war experience in detail in part 2. In his autobiographical accounts, Gandhi says that his corps provided medical care to those blacks whose backs were flogged. One would suppose, then, that the close encounter with the injured blacks had offered him the opportunity to get close to them, perhaps, to know them, their habits, their culture, their weaknesses, their strengths, and so on. Did he avail himself of that opportunity? The evidence shows that he did not. Now, in 1908, the circumstances had taken a turn and again brought Gandhi into close proximity with the blacks—facing them in the closed environment of the prison. This was very different from the scenario he had faced in 1906.

FIRST INCARCERATION

On January 10, 1908, Gandhi, his close associates, and two Chinese were sentenced to two months without hard labor for violating the registration requirements under the Asiatic Registration Act. In accordance with prison protocol, Gandhi and the others were weighed, undressed, fingerprinted, and given new prison clothes before being taken to their cells. Gandhi was released on January 30, 1908. Marching into the prison was a jolt and all hell broke loose. Only five weeks after his release, the following columns, written by Gandhi himself, were published by *Indian Opinion*.

Indian Opinion, *March 7, 1908,*
"Classification of Asiatics with Natives"

> The cell was situated in the Native quarters and we were housed in one that was labelled "For Coloured Debtors". It was this experience for which we were perhaps all unprepared. We had fondly imagined that we would have suitable quarters apart from the Natives. As it was, perhaps, it was well that we were classed with the Natives. We would now be able to study the life of Native prisoners,

their customs and manners. I felt, too, that passive resistance had not been undertaken too soon by the Indian community. Degradation underlay the classing of Indians with Natives. The Asiatic Act seemed to me to be the summit of our degradation. It did appear to me, as I think it would appear to any unprejudiced reader, that it would have been simple humanity if we were given special quarters. The fault did not lie with the gaol authorities. It was the fault of the law that has made no provision for the special treatment of Asiatic prisoners. Indeed, the Governor of the gaol tried to make us as comfortable as he could within the regulations. The chief warder, as also the head warder, who was in immediate charge of us, completely fell in with the spirit that actuated the Governor. But he was powerless to accommodate us beyond the horrible din and the yells of the Native prisoners throughout the day and partly at night also. Many of the Native prisoners are only one degree removed from the animal and often created rows and fought among themselves in their cells. The Governor could not separate the very few Indian prisoners (It speaks volumes for Indians that among several hundred there were hardly half a dozen Indian prisoners) from the cells occupied by the Native prisoners. And yet it is quite clear that separation is a physical necessity. So much was the classification of Indians and other Asiatics with the Natives insisted upon that our jumpers, which being new were not fully marked, had to be labelled "N", meaning Natives. How this thoughtless classification has resulted in the Indians being partly starved will be clearer when we come to consider the question of food. (CWMG 8, #56, p. 120)

Gandhi makes it quite clear that his degradation lay in the classification system, which equated him and his fellow Indians with blacks. Yes, he was prepared for hardships, but Gandhi said that being housed with the blacks was too much to "suffer." The black prisoners are portrayed as people who are only a degree removed from the animals. He is somewhat sorry for having not started the passive resistance earlier. In other words, had he known that he was going to be lodged alongside blacks he would have started his passive resistance (Satyagraha) earlier! So much for the truth striving! Apart from having to put up with blacks, he is highly concerned about his meals. He does not like the food that blacks eat, "For the first few days, for most of us, it meant practically starvation. Even when we got over the natural repugnance, it was a diet that constipated some of us and gave diarrhoea to the others; but we were determined to go through it and not to ask for any favours or concessions" (CWMG 8, #56, p. 121). "It is thus clear that both Kaffirs and Europeans get food suited to their tastes." Gandhi pities "The poor Indians—nobody bothers about them! They cannot get the food they want. If they are given European diet, the whites will feel insulted" (CWMG 8, #72, p. 154). Gandhi, to his credit, gives an impression that due to his special situation, he is in a position to study the customs and manners of blacks. But did he?

Indian Opinion, *March 7, 1908,*
"Indians on Par with Kaffirs"
Translated from Gujarati

> There, our garments were stamped with the letter "N", which meant that we
> were being classed with the Natives. We were all prepared for hardships, but not
> quite for this experience. We could understand not being classed with the
> whites, but to be placed on the same level with the Natives seemed too much to
> put up with. I then felt that Indians had not launched on passive resistance too
> soon. Here was further proof that the obnoxious law was intended to emascu-
> late the Indians.
>
> It was, however, as well that we were classed with the Natives. It was a wel-
> come opportunity to study the treatment meted out to Natives, their conditions [of
> life in gaol] and their habits. Looked at from another point of view, it did not seem
> right to feel bad about being bracketed with them. At the same time, it is indu-
> bitably right that Indians should have separate cells. The cells for Kaffirs were
> adjacent to ours. They used to make a frightful din in their cells as also in the
> adjoining yard. We were given a separate ward because we were sentenced to
> simple imprisonment; otherwise we would have been in the same ward [with the
> Kaffirs]. Indians sentenced to hard labour are in fact kept with the Kaffirs.
>
> Apart from whether or not this implies degradation, I must say it is rather
> dangerous. Kaffirs are as a rule uncivilized—the convicts even more so. They are
> troublesome, very dirty and live almost like animals. Each ward contains nearly
> 50 to 60 of them. They often started rows and fought among themselves. The
> reader can easily imagine the plight of the poor Indian thrown into such company!
>
> Apart from us, there were hardly three or four Indian prisoners in the whole
> gaol. They were locked up with the Kaffirs and, to that extent, they were worse
> off than we. . . . (CWMG 8, #61, pp. 135–36)

In this letter, he has pursued the same line of thought. He makes a plea for
cells away from blacks, while acknowledging that they were housed in separate
cells. He still sees the opportunity to study blacks; he evidently didn't have to be
that close to accomplish this. Now, he is as concerned about safety as he is about
degradation. Not only are black convicts uncivilized and dangerous, Gandhi cautions us, it is blacks *as a whole* who are uncivilized. Indians who are locked up
in the same cells with blacks are automatically presumed to be worse off than
Gandhi and his like. Why would Gandhi assume that? Perhaps it reflects the toll
the caste system had taken on him.

SECOND INCARCERATION

This incarceration was probably Gandhi's worst experience of being exposed to
the blacks. While returning from Durban, Natal, he was arrested at Volksrust Sta-

tion on October 7, 1908, along with fifteen other Indians, for entering Transvaal without registration certificates and refusing to give finger impressions. He was sentenced to two months' imprisonment. To Gandhi's delight, at Volksrust jail, Indians and blacks were always lodged separately. Also, the warden made provisions to house Indians with the whites. Therefore, at this prison, Gandhi seems to have no problems with his prison uniform. Also, he seems to be at ease with the food, much of which was prepared and cooked by the Indians themselves.

On October 25, 1908, Gandhi had to be taken to Johannesburg for his testimony in a court case. While in Johannesburg, he was lodged in the local prison, along with blacks. He was released on December 12, 1908, from the Volksrust jail.

Indian Opinion, *January 16, 1909,* *"My Second Experience in Gaol [—III]"* Translated from Gujarati

[A]fter arriving at Johannesburg, I had [again] to reach the gaol on foot, carrying the luggage myself. The incident provoked strong comments in newspapers. Questions were asked in the British Parliament. Many persons felt hurt. Everyone thought that, being a political prisoner, I should not have been made to walk the distance, dressed in gaol uniform and carrying a load. . . .

It was evening when we reached Johannesburg, so that I was not taken where I could be among other Indians. I was given a bed in a cell of the prison where there were mostly Kaffir prisoners who had been lying ill. I spent the night in this cell in great misery and fear. I did not know that the very next day I would be taken among our own people, and, thinking that I would be kept in this place all the time, I became quite nervous. I felt extremely uneasy, but I resolved in my mind that my duty required me to bear every suffering. I read the *Bhagavad Gita* which I had carried with me. I read the verses which had a bearing on my situation and, meditating on them, managed to compose myself.

The reason why I felt so uneasy was that the Kaffir and Chinese prisoners appeared to be wild, murderous and given to immoral ways. I did not know their language. A Kaffir started putting questions to me. I felt a hint of mockery even in this. I did not understand what it was. I returned no reply. He asked me in broken English why I had been brought there in that fashion. I gave a brief reply, and then I lapsed into silence. Then came a Chinese. He appeared to be worse. He came near the bed and looked closely at me. I kept still. Then he went to a Kaffir lying in bed. The two exchanged obscene jokes, uncovering each other's genitals. Both these prisoners had charges of murder and larceny against them. Knowing this, how could I possibly sleep? Thinking that I would bring this to the notice of the Governor the next day, I fell asleep for a while late in the night.

Real suffering lies in this. Carrying luggage and such other troubles are nothing very serious. Realizing that the experience I have had must also sometimes be that of other Indians, and that they too would feel the fear that I did, I was happy that I had suffered in the same way as others. The experience, I thought, would impel me to agitate against the Government all the more tenaciously, and I hoped that I might succeed in inducing prison reforms in regard to these matters. All these are indirect benefits of satyagraha.

As soon as we rose the following day, I was taken to where the other prisoners were lodged, so that I had no chance to complain to the Governor about what had happened. I have, though, resolved in my mind on an agitation to ensure that Indian prisoners are not lodged with Kaffirs or others. When I arrived at the place, there were about 15 Indian prisoners. Except for three, all of them were satyagrahis. The three were charged with other offences. These prisoners were generally lodged with Kaffirs. When I reached there, the chief warder issued an order that all of us should be lodged in a separate room. I observed with regret that some Indians were happy to sleep in the same room as the Kaffirs, the reason being that they hoped there for a secret supply of tobacco, etc. This is a matter of shame to us. We may entertain no aversion to Kaffirs, but we cannot ignore the fact that there is no common ground between them and us in the daily affairs of life. Moreover, those who wish to sleep in the same room with them have ulterior motives for doing so. Obviously, we ought to abandon such notions if we want to make progress. (CWMG 9, #93, pp. 148–49)

Circumstances beyond his control brought Gandhi in close proximity to the blacks. He noticed that they were lying ill. This was the second time that he was sequestered with blacks who were either ill or injured. Remembering the first one, at the war front in 1906, he told us more so in his autobiography; blacks were injured because of the lashes on their backs. Now in 1908, he noticed black prisoners are ill. What was his reaction? He is repulsed at their sight and because they are black, he gets nervous and uneasy, but resolves to bear the suffering! Suffering, a term he has employed many times, is now being used to denote the sensations of a clean, civilized Indian like himself placed next to the unclean, uncivilized blacks. Forget any humanitarian work! Forget any consideration toward black people! You are witnessing the real Gandhi. What did he do? He takes out his Hindu religious text, the *Bhagavad Gita*, and reads and meditates on the appropriate verses. Exactly which verses he meditated on, he never mentioned. Then he narrates the vulgarity of one particular black and one particular Chinese prisoner. When they asked him a question, he sees a mockery in that, though, he acknowledges, he does not know their language. Here he gets a new idea: the starting of a Satyagraha for prison reform—meaning to ensure the complete segregation of Indians from blacks or other people of color.

At this Johannesburg prison, something shocked him: he saw to his regret that some Indians were happy to sleep in the same room as blacks. He thinks that the reason they are willing to stoop so low is because blacks have a "secret supply of tobacco"—cigarettes. To Gandhi, this is a shameful matter. He is very clear in his enunciation that, in the daily affairs of life, there is absolutely nothing in common between blacks and his fellow Indians. He appears to be pure segregationist. This is not something I made up. Gandhi convicts himself with his own words. He also says that the only way for Indians to make further progress in South Africa is if they abandon their contacts (meager as they are) with black people. He doesn't want Indians to come close to blacks, whether in their civic life or during incarceration. Even though one Chinese prisoner was repulsive to him, Gandhi never advised his comrades in such strong terms against the Chinese people. But, toward blacks, the evidence is conclusive—he is a full-fledged racist. You may recall that on June 24, 1906, at Thring's Post (see chapter 10), some Indian soldiers, in association with the whites, looted a shop and got away with items, including cigarettes. It seemed then that Gandhi had no qualms about cigarettes. Even earlier, he encouraged a drive to collect money to buy merchandise such as cigarettes for both Indian and white soldiers—without any reservations. But in prison, Gandhi disapproves of cigarettes as much as Indians being in company with blacks.

Gandhi admits that black prisoners were lying ill. And from his narrative we can draw a reasonable conclusion that he did nothing to relieve their suffering, nor did he seek any help by alerting the prison authorities. Only about two years before, at the Zulu War front in Mapumulo, Natal, do we hear about the Sergeant Major having provided medical care to blacks. If you think he did not, then you are in agreement with me. A few of his Indian corpsmen did render first aid care to blacks in custody, but Gandhi did not. He was too prejudiced.

Indian Opinion, *January 23, 1909,* *"My Second Experience in Gaol [—IV]"* Translated from Gujarati

> I had one further unpleasant experience in the Johannesburg Gaol. In this gaol, there are two different kinds of wards. One ward is for Kaffir and Indian prisoners sentenced to hard labour. The other is for prisoners who are called as witnesses and those who have been sentenced to imprisonment in civil proceedings. Prisoners sentenced to hard labour have no right to go into this second ward. We slept in it, but we could not use its lavatory as of right. In the first ward, the number of prisoners wanting the use of the lavatory is so large that a visit to it is a great nuisance. Some Indians find this a source of great inconvenience. I was one of them. I was told by the warder that there would be no harm in my using a lavatory in the second ward. I therefore went to one of the lavatories in this ward. At these lavatories, too, there is usually a crowd. Moreover, the lavatories have open access. There are no doors. As soon as I had occupied one of them, there came along a strong, heavily-built, fearful looking Kaffir. He asked me to get out and started abusing me. I said I would leave very soon. Instantly he lifted me up in his arms and threw me out. Fortunately, I caught hold of the door-frame, and saved myself from a fall. I was not in the least frightened by this. I smiled and walked away; but one or two Indian prisoners who saw what had happened started weeping. Since they could not offer any help in gaol, they felt helpless and miserable. I heard later that other Indians also had to go through similar tribulations. I acquainted the Governor with what had happened and told him there was urgent need for separate lavatories for Indians.

I also told him that Indian prisoners should never be lodged with Kaffirs. The Governor immediately issued an order for a lavatory for Indians to be sent on from the Central Gaol. Thus, from the next day the difficulty about lavatories disappeared. As for myself, I had no motions for four days, and hence I suffered in health somewhat. (CWMG 9, #102, p. 161)

To a practicing Hindu, going to the toilet is a time of special spiritual contemplation. And to Gandhi it was no different. Rather, his infatuation with the toilet and the bowel movement as a spiritual wonder was indeed a strong one. The details are wonderful to read and are not produced here. At the least, a Hindu likes to take his time on the toilet. When the bowel movement is complete, the ritual is generally described as "enjoyable." In prison, depending upon the situation, one can "enjoy" or not. Apparently, at the Johannesburg jail, Gandhi had a difficult time in his ward toilets because of the sheer number of prisoners. So he went to the toilet area at the next ward. To his surprise, this place is also crowded and the toilets have no doors. The implication was clear that these toilets were not suitable for the "enjoyable experience," since they lacked privacy. What happened to him while he was sitting on the toilet, at the hands of a "fearful-looking" black, only reinforces his plea for a total segregation from blacks. Strangely, his experience with this black does not frighten Gandhi. However, for four full days he couldn't experience his bowel functions. His earlier encounter with blacks who were lying ill, though they never laid a hand on him, caused him to be in great fear! Later on in his narrative, Gandhi tells of another habit that causes the Indians to suffer: "Blankets are constantly interchanged. A blanket that has been used by the dirtiest of Kaffirs may later fall to an Indian's lot. Frequently, the blankets are found to be full of lice. They have a nasty smell" (CWMG 9, #102, p. 165).

Indian Opinion, *January 30, 1909,*
"My Second Experience in Gaol [—V]: Two Attitudes"
Translated from Gujarati

We can take two different attitudes to what I have written above. First, why should we bear such hardships, submit ourselves, for instance, to the restrictions of gaol life, wear coarse and ungainly dress, eat food which is hardly food, starve ourselves, suffer being kicked by the warder; live among the Kaffirs, do every kind of work, whether we like it or not, obey a warder who is only good enough to be our servant, be unable to receive any friends or write letters, go without things that we may need, and sleep in company with robbers and thieves? Better die than suffer this. Better pay the fine than go to gaol. Let no one be punished with gaol. Such an attitude will make a man quite weak and afraid of imprisonment, and he will achieve nothing good by being in gaol.

Alternatively, one may consider oneself fortunate to be in gaol in the cause of the motherland, in defence of one's honour and one's religion. Gaol life, one may think, involves no [real] suffering. Out-side, one has to carry out the will

of many, whereas one has only the warder to reckon with in gaol. One has no
anxieties in gaol, no problem of earning one's livelihood, no worry about getting one's bread, for that is provided regularly by others. One's person is pro-
tected by the Government. None of these things has to be paid for. By way of
exercise, one gets ample work to do and, without any effort on one's part, all of
one's bad habits fall away. The mind enjoys a sense of freedom. One has ready
to hand the benefit of being absorbed in devotions to God. The body is held in
bondage, but the soul grows more free. One is in full enjoyment of the use of
one's limbs. The body is looked after by those who hold it in bondage. Thus,
from every point of view, one is free. One might, perhaps, be in difficulties, be
manhandled by a wicked warder, but then one learns to be patient. One feels
glad to have an opportunity of dissuading [him] from such behaviour. It is up to
us to adopt such an attitude and think of gaol as a holy and happy place and to
make it such. In short, happiness and misery are states of the mind.

    I hope that the reader, after reading this account of my second experience [in
gaol], will resolve in his mind that his only happiness will be in going to gaol for
the sake of the motherland or his religion, in submitting himself to the suffering
involved in it, or bearing hardships in other ways. (CWMG 9, #114, p. 182)

There are now doubts among the Indians as to the wisdom of breaking laws
and seeking prison terms. The news has now leaked out that imprisoned Indians
must cohabit with blacks. That's not good news for the Satyagraha. The very success of the Satyagraha rests on going to prison. Gandhi has to come up with new
tactics to keep his movement going. From his magic bag he plucked the same
bluff, the one that worked during the time of the Zulu War. Yes, we bear hardships. Submit to the restrictions of prison life. Wear coarse and ungainly dress.
Eat food that is hardly food. Starve. Suffer the warder's kicking. *Live among the
Kaffirs.* Obey a warder who is only good enough to be our servant. Be unable to
receive friends or write letters. Sleep in company with robbers and thieves.

    After stating the above "facts," Gandhi begins to address those vulnerable
Indians who would rather imagine "Better die than suffer this. Better pay the fine
than go to gaol. Let no one be punished with gaol. Such an attitude will make a
man quite weak and afraid of imprisonment, and he will achieve nothing good
by being in gaol." Gandhi wants no part of such thinking and powerfully resorts
to a series of bluff tactics that he once employed against the Indians during the
Zulu conflict. Consider yourself fortunate to be in jail in the cause of the motherland, for your honor and religion. Prison life involves no real suffering. While
in jail there is only the warden to reckon with whereas outside there are many.
No anxieties in prison. No problem of earning a livelihood. No worry about getting bread; it is provided. Protection by the government. Everything is free.
Enough exercise without any efforts. Bad habits fall away. The mind enjoys
freedom and the benefit of being absorbed in devotions to God. The body is held
in bondage, the soul grows free. One learns to be patient when provoked. Think
of prison as a holy and happy place. Happiness and misery are states of mind.

This is the first time he acknowledged to his readers that imprisoned Indians had to live among blacks. He asked them to bear this negative side of the Satyagraha campaign because there was so much other good that came out of prison life. In other words, he suggested to his readers that they should learn to "enjoy" this holy place and make the best out of it. That's not really asking for much, considering that Hindus have also been conditioned to "enjoy" the visit to the toilet as a holy place! After all, Gandhi is putting up a smoke screen, but within the Hindu tradition he is not too far off to be reprimanded or shunned. When he refers to "obey a warden who is only good enough to be our servant," Gandhi is referring to the black warden. And there was no actual "warden's kicking."

On November 4, Gandhi returned to the Volksrust jail. His brand of nonviolence never excluded social and psychological violence, whose objects were moral coercion and, if feasible, to extract money:

> The white nations taunt us with being brave enough to start with, but betraying lack of purpose at the critical moment. We want to prove that we are nothing of the kind. The all-too-powerful Government of the Transvaal will not succeed in proving that we are [pliable] like wax.
>
> True religion consists in learning all this, and hence we are prepared to sacrifice our lives in this righteous war. To show that we are so prepared is one of the objects of the struggle; in fact, that is the main object. As for other things, they will follow as a matter of course.
>
> Success in such a big task will require an equally big effort. In what way? Businessmen are the most important Indians in the Transvaal. They must prove their worth and be prepared to embrace poverty in the process. It is only by embracing poverty that they can serve their own interests as well as those of the community. In a tyrannical state, only those who subserve its purposes can be happy or grow prosperous. In such a state, it is not straightforward men who can amass wealth. They can live in such a state only if they are prepared to suffer. That is the position of the Transvaal Indians. The Transvaal Government wants to rob the Indians of their honour and wealth. Why should they allow that? In former times, when in any part of the world the subjects rebelled against their oppressive rulers, before joining battle they would first kill their womenfolk in order to save them from dishonour. At the present moment, the Transvaal Indians are engaged in the battle of satyagraha. They will have to sacrifice their money, as women were sacrificed [in the olden days]. If not, they will be dishonoured and find their money as bitter as poison. No religion believes it possible to worship God and Mammon at the same time. Every religion teaches that if one wants to devote oneself to God, one must forsake wealth. Since we started this struggle with faith in God and with prayerful hearts, we must be prepared to renounce wealth. When we stand in need of wealth, that same God will see that we get it.
>
> In Italy, 300,000 men were buried together with their possessions—such is divine Providence. Keeping that in view, let us always be mindful of our honour. To preserve our honour is in our hands. It is not so with regard to wealth. We hope that the Indians will sacrifice wealth and preserve their honour.[4]

THIRD INCARCERATION

On February 25, 1909, Gandhi was sentenced to three months' imprisonment with hard labor for refusing to produce a certificate of registration and give fingerprints. Fortunately for him, the prison was at Volksrust where there was separate housing for Indians away from the blacks. Also, at this prison the Indians could cook their own food. At this particular time, Indians even had the pleasure of sleeping in their own tent located in the prison compound. The work that Gandhi performed (e.g., cleaning floors and the like) while incarcerated was to his liking and improved his health. However, the good days were numbered. On March 2 he was transferred from Volksrust to Pretoria Gaol, where he was lodged in a small cell, with minimal opportunity for interaction with other Indians. He was kept under close scrutiny, even while on the commode! One of Gandhi's jobs was polishing the floor and the door, a task that brought him in close proximity to blacks.

Indian Opinion, *May 29, 1909,* *"My Third Experience in Gaol [—I]"*
Translated from Gujarati

[T]here were some Kaffirs working with me. They would sometimes talk in broken English of how they had come to be imprisoned, and ask me questions about my imprisonment. One asked me whether I had committed theft, and another whether I had been imprisoned for selling liquor. When I explained the correct position to one of the intelligent Kaffirs, he exclaimed, "Quite right." "Amlungu bad" (The whites are bad). "Don't pay fine." My cell bore the description "isolated". I saw five other cells adjoining mine bearing the same description. My neighbour was a Kaffir who had been serving a term of imprisonment for attempted murder. The three next to him were convicted of sodomy. It was in the company of such men and in such surroundings that I commenced my experience in Pretoria Gaol. (CWMG 9, #148, p. 231)

I am not sure if it ever dawned on Gandhi that he had met a true Satyagrahi in this prison, whom he described as "one of the intelligent Kaffirs." Apparently, Gandhi had met more than one Kaffir who was an intellectual. But we don't hear about them in his descriptions. He minces no words in letting his readers know about the character of his neighbors by bringing up their crimes of "attempted murder" and "sodomy." The question I have is what brought the "intelligent blacks" in the prison in the first place? Gandhi was released from Pretoria Central Jail on May 24, 1909.

FOURTH INCARCERATION

Gandhi stayed at Dundee Jail, Volksrust Jail, Bloemfontein Jail, and then was transferred to Pretoria where he was released. From a letter addressed from Dundee Jail, it seems Gandhi had some leisure time at his disposal. It also appears as if he had no worries about the blacks here. Perhaps, at Dundee Jail, he was lodged in the white section of the prison, similar to that at Volksrust prison. At Bloemfontein prison, located in Orange Free State, he was the single Indian prisoner among whites and blacks. Since he didn't complain about this prison, I presume he was lodged in the whites' section. If Gandhi had any run-ins with blacks during this period of incarceration, we will never know about it. (CWMG 12, #s 191, 193–96, pp. 263–72)

As I mentioned earlier, the Gandhi literature is extensive. But nowhere have I read anyone who addressed Gandhi's behavior toward blacks while in confinement. However, something came across my desk recently that left me puzzled. The material is authored by Nelson Mandela, former president of the Republic of South Africa, who is known for his extensive years of imprisonment for fighting against apartheid. The material I received was a chapter comprising fifty-six pages; much of it was a verbatim copy of Gandhi's accounts from the *Collected Works* and detailing his first three incarcerations. The trouble here is that Mr. Mandela presented the information in an abridged form and expunged some of the derogatory material that Gandhi had written about blacks during his first incarceration. In this chapter, in the first eight pages, former President Mandela provides a summary of Gandhi's experiences in jail, including three small paragraphs on blacks under the subtitle "African Prisoners":

> During his imprisonment in Pretoria, all his fellow prisoners were Africans (Natives as they were then referred to, even by ourselves), and they, seeing him so different from them, were curious to know what he was doing in prison. Had he stolen, or dealt in liquor?
>
> He explained that he had refused to carry a pass. They understood that perfectly well. "Quite right," they said to him, "the white people are bad." Gandhi had been initially shocked that Indians were classified with Natives in prison; his prejudices were quite obvious, but he was reacting not to "Natives", but criminalised Natives.
>
> He believed that the Indians should have been kept separately. However, there was an ambivalence in his attitude for he stated, "*It was, however, as well that we were classed with the Natives. It was a welcome opportunity to see the treatment meted out to Natives, their conditions (of life in gaol), and their habits.*" All in all, Gandhi must be forgiven those prejudices and judged in the context of the time and the circumstances. We are looking here at the young Gandhi, still to become Mahatma, when he was without any human prejudice, save that in favour of truth and justice.[5]

It seems President Mandela has forfeited his critical thought process. He has quoted the narrative somewhat incorrectly. While acknowledging Gandhi's prejudices against blacks, former President Mandela loses his focus when he says that Gandhi's prejudices were directed *only* toward "criminalized Natives." Mr. Mandela needs to reread Gandhi's account in its entirety as published in *Collected Works*. "Young Gandhi" was forty years old, with fully developed faculties. Mr. Mandela seems to think that the post–South African Gandhi was somehow a different, nonracist type. I think he would benefit immensely from reading this book further. Also, under the subtitle "Confrontation with Criminals" he wrote:

> Political prisoners are prisoners of conscience, and as such, very different from other prisoners. The two are bound to meet and mix and the experience can have unpleasant consequences. Gandhi had such experiences, so did I. After my first conviction, I was transported to Pretoria prison in a closed van with a member of the notorious Msomi Gang and as the van reeled and lurched, I was swung against him. I could not trust the man for I feared he was a police plant.
>
> Gandhi writes about a night in Johannesburg prison in 1909. His fellow prisoners appeared to be wild and murderous and given to "unnatural ways". *"Two of them tried to engage him in conversation. When he couldn't understand them, they jeered and laughed at him. Then the one retreated to a bed where another prisoner was lying. The two exchanged obscene jokes, uncovering each other's genitals."* (*Indian Opinion*, 1909)
>
> On another occasion, he was assaulted by a prisoner in a lavatory. *"The lavatories have open access. There are no doors. As soon as I had occupied one of them, there came along a strong, heavily-built, fearful looking Native. He asked me to get out and started abusing me. I said I would leave very soon. Instantly, he lifted me up in his arms and threw me out. Fortunately, I caught hold of the door-frame and saved myself from a fall."* (*Indian Opinion*, 1909) Gandhi and I shared one great good fortune—we were very much in the public eye and once it got out that some undue suffering or indignity was heaped on us, there was public reaction. The assault on Gandhi became an issue of protest in India and the British parliament and from some liberal white quarters in South Africa.[6]

Mr. Mandela has quoted Gandhi incorrectly. It is disappointing to see him let his grip on reality slip away by comparing his years of struggle against apartheid to racist Sergeant-Major Gandhi.

Another Gandhian scholar, E. S. Reddy, is worthy of some comment here. He is the former Assistant Secretary-General of the United Nations and Director of its Center against Apartheid for over twenty years. He seems to be familiar with the Gandhi literature that details his prison encounters but cites only the following of Gandhi's scathing remarks: "Many of the Native prisoners are only one degree removed from the animal and often created rows and fought among themselves in their cells."[7] It seems that the author simply ran out of words to provide a cover for Gandhi's actions and resorted to tactics of engaging black inmates as a sole cause for Gandhi's troubled experiences!

A few final words on the Satyagraha: Gandhi instigated quite a commotion on the nature of the ordinance and later the law. He led himself, his family (especially his eldest son), and many other Indians into a series of unending troubles for refusing to abide by the dictates of the law. Yet, going to prison, filing the prison papers and other examples of humiliation were okay for him. In such actions lay Gandhi's legacy and his tragedy: pick up any cause, channel the propaganda machine on it, make a mountain out of it, rally vulnerable people behind himself, rob them of their savings, lure them into trouble with the law, cajole them through often unnecessary sufferings, and then declare a bogus victory! After one cycle of Satyagraha, take some time off, recuperate, and start all over again! In these destructive chaotic social and political habits of his is buried the genesis of an environment conducive to his assassination, which I discuss in the conclusion to this volume.

The passive-resistance campaign was carried to almost the last days of Gandhi's stay in South Africa and had some interesting finishing touches. At Ladysmith, there was an outbreak of violence, quelled by the armed police. Many of Gandhi's early rich followers left him one by one. The Natal Indian Congress (NIC) formally split. Many NIC (more on that in part 4) members recognized the dangerous course onto which Gandhi was capable of directing his unthinking followers, and the consequences. To its credit, the black press in South Africa smelled the rat quite early on. They virtually ignored Gandhi's passive-resistance movement.[8] In the end Gandhi's Satyagraha was a failure, only to be resurrected again in India with teeming millions under its spell, and leading to much bigger disasters.

NOTES

1. Joseph J. Doke, *M. K. Gandhi: An Indian Patriot in South Africa* (London: Indian Chronicle, 1909), chap. 17, pp. 114–17. This book's "postscript" portion briefly mentions Gandhi's locking up in October 1908, the narrative *spiritualized* somewhat with yoga.

2. Mohandas K. Gandhi, *Satyagraha in South Africa* (1928; reprint, Ahmedabad: Navajivan Publishing House, 1972), pp. 139–40.

3. Mohandas K. Gandhi, *An Autobiography, or The Story of My Experiments with Truth* (Boston: Beacon Press, 1957), pp. 325–28.

4. CWMG 9, #101, p. 160. Translated from Gujarati. From *Indian Opinion*, January 23, 1909.

5. Fatima Meer, ed., *The South African Gandhi: An Abstract of the Speeches and Writings of M. K. Gandhi* (Durban: Madiba Publishers, 1996), chap. 18 titled "The Prisoner," beginning with page 568. The first introductory eight pages by Mr. Mandela were republished under the title "Gandhi, the Prisoner: A Comparison" by the Indian govern-

ment while celebrating Gandhi's 125th birth anniversary. P. J. Mehta's *M. K. Gandhi and the South African Indian Problem* (Madras, India: G. A. Natesan and Co., 1912?) mentioned briefly Gandhi's antiblack remarks. Another article, written by Professor J. H. Stone II, under the title, "M. K. Gandhi: Some Experiments with Truth" is worth reading. *Journal of Southern African Studies* 16, no. 4 (December 1990), pp. 721–40.

6. Meer, *The South African Gandhi*, p. 569.

7. E. S. Reddy, *Gandhiji's Visions of a Free South Africa* (New Delhi: Sanchar Publishing House, 1995), pp. 41–42.

8. Les Switzer, "Gandhi in South Africa: The Ambiguities of Satyagraha," *Journal of Ethnic Studies* 14, no. 1 (Spring 1986): 126.

PART 4

GANDHI and the
RACE IMBROGLIO

I see neither contradiction nor insanity in my life. It is true that as a man cannot see his back, so can he not see his errors or insanity. But the sages have often likened a man of religion to a lunatic. I therefore hug the belief that I may not be insane and may be truly religious. Which of the two I am in truth can only be decided after my death.

—Mahatma Gandhi
Young India, August 14, 1924

16

Africa is one of the biggest continents in the world. India is said to be not a country but a continent, . . . I have moved about over all parts of South Africa with open eyes, I do not remember to have seen a single emancipated cow or bull.

—Mahatma Gandhi
Satyagraha in South Africa

In the foregoing chapters, we have witnessed the inadequacy of Mr. Gandhi's many biographies, the poverty of Gandhi movies, and the role of the government of India in propagating the sanitized image of historical Gandhi. We have also analyzed what the real Gandhi did to the blacks of South Africa, preceding, during, and right after the war. Also, we have thoroughly analyzed the true nature of the Gandhi gospels and the racism imbedded in Gandhi's much-touted Satyagraha, the soul-force. In other words, we have discussed the story of Gandhi's racism covering an eight-year period from 1906 to 1914; thereupon he left South Africa for good. Now, let's take a journey into his racist ideology from the time he set foot in South Africa in 1893 to the time just before the start of the Zulu War in 1906. Before we delve into Gandhi and his activities during this period, it is important to keep in mind the political set-up of South Africa in 1893, especially of those geographic places under the British.

In South Africa, there were four separate colonies—Natal, Cape Colony, Transvaal, and the Orange Free State. Both the Dutch (Boers) and the British were out to grab what really belonged to black people. One by one, the Dutch

177

lost their territories to the British. The final blow occurred during the Boer War (1899–1902), in which Gandhi had participated. South Africa became a part of the British Empire. These four Colonies were independent of each other in the sense that they had their own governments in place. Each had separate laws to deal with the Indians and Asians residing in their respective colonies. Similarly, they also had enacted laws dealing with the original inhabitants, the blacks. For our discussion, we will concentrate briefly here on two of these colonies, Natal and Transvaal. In Natal, the Indian community had its origin in an indentured workforce that was imported beginning in 1860 and continuing till 1911. Each Indian worker had a five-year term of indenture. After five years, a free return passage to India was available along with five years' free labor. Until 1890 an ex-indentured worker had a choice of exchanging his return passage for a plot of land. Many of these migrant workers stayed on in the colony after their contracts had expired. As a result, there arose a permanent group of ex-indentured laborers and their descendents, referred to as "colonial-born," or "colonials." Many of them migrated to Transvaal Republic before the Boer War in search of better wages and then settled there.

With the passage of time, Natal's growing Indian population began to attract Indian merchant immigrants. These new immigrants had paid their own passage and therefore were referred to as "passengers." Once this merchant group settled in Durban, Natal, it was only a short time until members of this group proliferated and established themselves in various businesses and at various other places, including Transvaal. The majority of these merchants were Gujarati Moslems. The whites referred to them sometimes as "Arabs." Once established, these Natal-based and Transvaal-based businessmen took every opportunity to assert their elite status in comparison to the vast majority of the Indians who were either indentured, ex-indentured, or colonial-born, referred to here as underclasses. Moreover, the factor of caste also came into play. The merchant community represented elements from the upper Hindu castes, whereas many of the others were of low caste and Tamil in origin. In other words, a replica of caste-based India emerged in South Africa. The higher castes made a concerted effort to regain a privileged position, similar to that in India. Moslem Gujaratis and their Hindu counterparts were, for all practical purposes, similar in their caste ideology, even though their religions were different. Also, this elite group acquired Western education at quite a rapid pace. Many merchants conducted business in South Africa for some years and then went back to India, leaving a member of the family in charge of the business. But this was not the case with the ex-indentured Indians and their colonial-born children. To them, South Africa was home.

With education came the will to create various religious and nonreligious associations, especially to deal with merchant politics. Understandably, this was important to the group to safeguard their interests. Earlier, they had been expelled from the Orange Free State, and their business interests were under legal threat in Transvaal. They feared the same would soon happen in Natal. In January 1891, merchant politics, led by Haji Mohamed, Haji Dada, and Dada Abdullah, took on a more organized structure, not only to salvage what they could from the Orange Free State, but also to prevent further deterioration of the situation in Transvaal, and more particularly in the home base, Natal. Expectedly, the underclasses lagged behind in every sphere except for their vast population. The merchant elite could no longer rely on their old tactics for success: legal counsel and an occasional petition of protest to a colonial or imperial official. It was clear they needed something else. Because of this concern, the Durban Indian Committee was instituted, which aggressively propagated and extended their base in order to protect the financial interests of this group. Soon the realization of the immensity of the political tasks at hand dawned on them. On top of that, Dada Abdullah was entangled in a 40,000-pound lawsuit against an Indian merchant in Transvaal. They needed a full-time lawyer, fluent in both English and Gujarati. That brought Gandhi into the picture. Early in 1893, the India-based branch of Dada Abdullah's firm hired Gandhi to assist in the above-mentioned lawsuit. According to Gandhi's autobiography, he was offered a first-class return fare to South Africa and a fee of 105 pounds for a job that would take no more than a year to complete.

In 1893, Natal was granted the status of Responsible Government, which gave local government more power to enact laws. As a result, the passage of the Franchise Amendment Bill became a real possibility and potential threat to Indian's enterprises in Natal. These were the circumstances under which Mr. Gandhi entered the politics of the commercial elite. Having said so, I must confess that the events surrounding Gandhi's actual entry into politics are unclear. What Gandhi wrote in his *Autobiography* may not be truthful in its entirety, even though his version has generally been accepted. Fortunately, there was a diverse, readymade Indian constituency for him to tap into and which was spread all over South Africa. The racial makeup of South Africa was complex. There were the minority of whites, the rulers, on one end and the large majority of blacks, about 70 percent of the population, on the other end. In between lay an interesting cluster of Asians, mainly Chinese and Indian. There was also relatively a large group lumped together under the term "colored community." This was a mixed-race group of various combinations of Indians, Malays, Khoi, San, whites, and black slaves of the early Cape Town settlement. Among the Indians there were that majority of the underclasses and a small elite, to which Gandhi belonged. On a hierarchical level, the Indian elite members considered themselves just below whites, followed by others, including the colored community, and then finally the blacks occupied the lowest place. Undoubtedly, Gandhi considered Indians more advanced racially than the "colored community." Judging from the literature, it seems that Gandhi also considered the Indian underclasses better than the "colored community."

17

*My mind is narrow. I have not read much literature. I have
not seen much of the world. I have concentrated upon certain
things in life and beyond that I have no other interest.*

—Mahatma Gandhi
September 28, 1944

From the literature, I have gathered essentially three parallel underlying trends
in Gandhi's political activities: (1) his unflinching loyalty to the British Empire, using the race card, (2) his apathy toward the Indian underclasses, using the caste card, and (3) his virulent antiblack racism using, once again, the race card.

The Natal Indian Congress (NIC) was founded on 22 August 1894 (CWMG
1, #37, pp. 130–35). Its origins are unclear. Most probably, Gandhi provided the initiative for this political organization with a president, Abdoola Hajee Adam, twenty-three vice presidents, and an honorary secretary, M. K. Gandhi. The objectives of the Natal Indian Congress were:

1. *To promote concord and harmony among the Indians and Europeans residing in the colony* [my italics].
2. To inform the people in India by writing to the newspapers, publishing pamphlets, and delivering lectures.
3. To induce Hindustanis—particularly colonial-born Indians—to study the Indian history and literature.
4. To inquire into the conditions of the Indians and to take proper steps to remove their hardships.

5. To inquire into the conditions of the indentured Indians and to take proper steps to alleviate their sufferings.
6. To help the poor and helpless [Indians] in every reasonable way.
7. To do such work as would tend to improve the moral, social, and political conditions of the Indians (CWMG 1, #37, pp. 131–32).

As the first objective makes clear, to promote concord and harmony meant between the Indians and whites, implying that there was no place for blacks, the "colored community," or any of the other Asians in Natal. Though the NIC professed to be inclusive of all Indians, in practice it operated just like a private club. Sir John Robinson, then the prime minister of Natal, referred to the NIC as a "secret body." The NIC's leadership was predominantly a Gujarati Moslem with a functioning young Hindu Gujarati lawyer. Supposedly, the president and vice presidents were elected. However, the vice presidents played no significant roles. In reality, the president held the post on the basis of his financial standing in the community, and the secretary was chosen for his command of the English language. Although in theory the NIC was an open organization, the annual dues of three pounds made it an exclusive club, barring the Indian underclasses. Many NIC objectives claim to provide welfare for the underclasses, but the realities were quite different. It is not that the NIC was hostile to the interests of the underclasses, but the interests of the elite group were paramount. The purpose of the NIC was to serve the upper-caste Hindu business community mentality. Gandhi was their point man to promote the cause and he went about doing the best he could. His tactics were simple: petitions, memorials and delegations to government officials, letters to the press and to prominent public figures, editorials in *Indian Opinion* (once operational), court cases, and official notification to the government of resolutions passed at the party meetings.

A year after its founding, in August 1895, the NIC reported its accomplishments. In this report, Gandhi admitted the "secret" nature of the organization. Though several items are reported, the fact is that there was only one true achievement, and that was the solution to the problem of the Durban Post Office (CWMG 1, #57, p. 236). This post office had two entrances, one for whites and the other for blacks. The Indians had to use the same entrance as blacks, and that was unacceptable to them. Gandhi petitioned Natal authorities and got permission to open a third entrance into the post office. Of course, it would have been better to share the entrance reserved for whites. Why would Gandhi want to segregate himself and other Indians from blacks? Was it insulting to him to walk into the post office through the same entrance that blacks used? If so, why? Unfortunately, we don't possess firsthand information. Rather, we must rely on other petitions to shed light on the question. Some of the other writings of Gandhi may give some insight into his racism.

That brings us to a bold document, titled "Open Letter" and dated December 1894, written by Gandhi and addressed to the members of Natal's Legislative

Assembly and the Legislative Council (CWMG 1, #42, pp. 142–63). This is a *Mahabharata*-sized (a very significant) letter that every admirer of Gandhi should read. Its purpose is to convince white authorities that "both the English and the Indians spring from a common stock, called the Indo-Aryan" (CWMG 1, #42, p. 149) and that "Providence has put the English and the Indians together, and has placed in the hands of the former the destinies of the latter . . ." (CWMG 1, #42, p. 162). Gandhi elaborates the fine points of distinction between Indians: In sharp contrast to the trading community (meaning upper castes), he admits that the indentured Indians (meaning lower castes) are dirty, poor, and lack personal cleanliness. According to Gandhi, these lowly people are absolutely "without any moral or religious instruction," "yield to the slightest temptation to tell a lie," "lying with them becomes a habit and a disease," "their moral faculties have completely collapsed" (CWMG 1, #42, pp. 157–58). On the other hand, Gandhi portrays a high status of the elite: they are "compelled by their religion to bathe once a week at least," "have to perform ablutions," and "offer prayers" (CWMG 1, #42, p. 148). The low castes fared better than the blacks in Gandhi's eyes: they have "helped to make this the Garden Colony of South Africa" (CWMG 1, #42, p. 145).

Gandhi was a superb manipulator. He excelled in the art of inducing guilt in his intended readers and then exploiting that guilt to attain his objective. How did he make the white readers of this Open Letter feel guilty? He told them, "A general belief seems to prevail in the Colony that the Indians are little better, if at all, than savages or the natives of Africa. Even the children are taught to believe in that manner, with the result that the Indian is being dragged down to the position of a raw Kaffir" (CWMG 1, #42, p. 150). Rest assured, "India," to Gandhi "is not Africa, and that it is a civilized country in the truest sense of the term *civilization*" (CWMG 1, #42, p. 157). In "Open Letter," Gandhi opens up his civilization issue largely to convince whites how similar the upper-caste Indians and Europeans are with respect to their race, philosophy, moral laws, architecture, drama, poetry, family relations, physical science, medical science, mythology, and art of war. What better way than to address the issues with quotes from European authors? I will concentrate on only the issues of race and the Hindu laws since they are relevant to this book. Gandhi quoted about race from Sir W. W. Hunter's *Indian Empire*:

> This nobler race (meaning the early Aryans) belonged to the Aryan or Indo-Germanic stock, from which the Brahman, the Rajput, and the Englishman alike descend. Its earliest home visible to history was in Central Asia. From that common camping ground certain branches of the race started for the East, others for the West. One of the Western offshoots founded the Persian Kingdom; another built Athens and Lacedaemon, and became the Hellenic nation; a third went on to Italy and reared the city on the seven hills, which grew into Imperial Rome. A distant colony of the same race excavated the silver ores of prehistoric Spain; and when we first catch a sight of ancient England, we see an Aryan settlement, fishing in wattle canoes and working the tin mines of Cornwall.

The forefathers of the Greek and the Roman, of the Englishman and the Hindoo, dwelt together in Asia, spoke the same tongue, and worshipped the same gods. The ancient religions of Europe and India had a similar origin. (CWMG 1, #42, pp. 149–50)

Continuing to cite from Hunter's *Indian Empire*, we hear about a famous Hindu figure, Manu, the Hindu lawgiver:

The Greek ambassador (Magasthenes) observed with admiration the absence of slavery in India, and the chastity of the women and the courage of the men. In valor they excelled all other Asiatics; they required no locks to their doors; above all, no Indian was ever known to tell a lie. Sober and industrious, good farmers and skillful artisans, they scarcely ever had recourse to a lawsuit, and lived peaceably under their native chiefs. The kingly government is portrayed almost as described in Manu, with its hereditary castes of councillors and soldiers. . . . The village system is well described, each little rural unit *seeming to the Greek an independent republic.* (CWMG 1, #42, pp. 154–55 [italics are Gandhi's])

We hear a bit more about "Aryan," a term that provokes racist images in our minds, as Gandhi quotes from Sir H. S. Maine's *Village-Communities*:

India has given to the world Comparative Philology and Comparative Mythology; it may yet give us a new science not less valuable than the sciences of language and of folk-lore. I hesitate to call it Comparative Jurisprudence because, if it ever exists, its area will be so much wider than the field of law. For India not only contains (or to speak more accurately, did contain) an *Aryan language* older than any other descendant of the common mother-language, and a variety of names of natural objects less perfectly crystallized than elsewhere into fabulous personages, but it includes a whole world of *Aryan institutions, Aryan customs, Aryan* laws, *Aryan ideas, Aryan beliefs*, in a far earlier stage of growth and development than any which survive beyond its borders. (CWMG 1, #42, p. 152 [my italics])

As a punch line, Gandhi quoted the famous German scholar Max Muller:

If I were asked under what sky the human mind has most fully developed some of its choicest gifts, has most deeply pondered on the greatest problem of life, and has found solutions of some of them which well deserve the attention even of those who have studied Plato and Kant—I should point to India; and if I were to ask myself from what literature we here in Europe, we who have been nurtured almost exclusively on the thoughts of Greeks and Romans, and of one Semitic race, the Jewish, may draw that corrective which is most wanted in order to make our inner life more perfect, more comprehensive, more universal, in fact more truly human—a life not for this life only, but a transfigured and eternal life—again I should point to India. (CWMG 1, #42, p. 151)

Finally, Gandhi reminds the Christian legislators of Natal Colony of his firm belief that from "the following copious extracts, . . . the Indians were, and are in no way inferior to their Anglo-Saxon brethren . . ." (CWMG 1, #42, p. 150). The effect, if any, of "Open Letter" on the legislators is not known. Then, in May 1895, Mr. Gandhi addressed another long petition. This one, to Lord Ripon, secretary of state for the colonies, particularly stressed the point that the Indian was being degraded to the lower levels of the blacks (CWMG 1, #52, pp. 187–208). And Gandhi concluded with a mind-boggling prediction of the fate of upper-caste Indians when subjected to racial pressure from whites: "By persistent ill-treatment they cannot but degenerate, so much so, that from their civilized habits, they would be degraded to the habits of the aboriginal Natives, and a generation hence, between the progeny of the Indians thus in course of degeneration, and the Natives, there will be very little difference in habits, and customs, and thought. The very object of immigration will be frustrated, and a large portion of Her Majesty's subjects, instead of being raised in the scale of civilization, will be actually lowered. . . . All Indian enterprise will be stifled" (CWMG 1, #52, p. 202).

In June 1896, Gandhi returned to India to fetch his wife and children, his expenses paid by the NIC. He stayed there for five months and had ample time to mobilize support among the Indian elite for the Indian elite in South Africa. He traveled extensively and presented the situation of South Africa to countrymen of his caste. From his home state of Gujarat, he published a large document, "The Grievances of the British Indians in South Africa: An Appeal to the Indian Public" (also called the "Green Pamphlet") (CWMG 2, #1, pp. 1–52). In this document, Gandhi brings to the attention of his readers that, "We are classed with the natives of South Africa—Kaffir races." Addressing a bylaw in Durban which requires the registration of black servants and "others belonging to the uncivilized races of Asia," Gandhi takes a stand against the presupposition that this includes Indians because, "There is a very good reason for requiring registration of a native [black] in that he is yet being taught the dignity and necessity of labour. The Indian knows it" (CWMG 2, #1, p. 12). He also brings to their notice his post-office victory:

> I may further illustrate the proposition that the Indian is put on the same level with the native in many other ways also. Lavatories are marked "native and Asiatics" at the railway stations. In the Durban Post and Telegraph Offices, there were separate entrances for natives and Asiatics and Europeans. We felt the indignity too much and many respectable Indians were insulted and called all sorts of names by the clerks at the counter. We petitioned the authorities to do away with the invidious distinction and they have now provided three separate entrances for natives, Asiatics, and Europeans. (CWMG 2, #1, p. 13)

Railway stations and trains were important to the merchant community. Not only did they have to share the same restroom with the natives, Gandhi tells the readers that, in Transvaal, "there is a tin compartment reserved for natives and other coloured people in which we are literally packed like sheep, without regard to our dress, our behaviour, or our position" (CWMG 2, #1, p. 30). This, of course, is unacceptable because, "These regulations seriously interfere with our carrying on our trade also" (CWMG 2, #1, p. 30).

Gandhi also published brief notes on grievances, detailing, for example, his four grievances in Natal with laws ranging from franchise rights to travel passes. The franchise law, to Gandhi, was obnoxious because: "The real reason for passing such an Act was to lower the status of the Indian and gradually to bring him down to the level of the South African Natives so that, in time to come, the respectable Indian may become an impossibility" (CWMG 2, #2, p. 56). Whereas on the railway, Gandhi clearly states, "The most respectable Indian, spotlessly dressed, cannot, as of right, travel first or second class on the Transvaal Railways. He is huddled together with the natives of all sorts and conditions in a third-class compartment. This is a cause of very great inconvenience to the Indian community in the Transvaal" (CWMG 2, #2, p. 67).

On September 26, 1896, Gandhi delivered an address at a public meeting at the Framji Cowasji Institute in Bombay, held under the auspices of the Bombay Presidency Association. He described the discriminations meted out to the Indians by the Europeans in South Africa in spite of the fact that "as a matter of fact, there is hardly one Indian in South Africa belonging to the aboriginal stock" (CWMG 2, #3, p. 72). Of the races inhabiting India, he knows at least one example that would equate with blacks: he tells the listeners, "The Santhals of Assam will be as useless in South Africa as the natives of that country" (CWMG 2, #3, p. 72). Gandhi, in no uncertain terms, laid out the challenge that Indians face in faraway South Africa: "Ours is one continual struggle against a degradation sought to be inflicted upon us by the Europeans, who desire to degrade us to the level of the raw Kaffir whose occupation is hunting, and whose sole ambition is to collect a certain number of cattle to buy a wife with and, then, pass his life in indolence and nakedness. . . . There, the deliberately expressed object is not to allow the Indian to rise higher in the scale of civilization but to lower him to the position of the Kaffir" (CWMG 2, #3, p. 74). The low castes fared a bit better than blacks. In a letter to the editor of the *Times of India* dated October 17, 1896, he wrote: "At the most, it can prove that the lot of the indentured Indian cannot be very unhappy; and that Natal is a very good place for such Indians to earn their livelihood. I am prepared to admit both. . . . Moreover, it should be remembered that the return passage story has nothing to do with the trading class, who go to Natal on their own account, and who feel the hardships the most" (CWMG 2, #5, pp. 87–88). To Gandhi, it was the merchants who were experiencing hardship. And he repeatedly expressed this idea. It was the merchants who had the money that mattered the most to Gandhi.

On October 26, 1896, in Madras, Gandhi visited the Hindu Theological High School and entered his remarks in the visitor's book, "I had the honour to visit this excellent institution. I was highly delighted with it. Being a Gujarati Hindu myself, I feel proud to know that this institution was started by Gujarati gentlemen. I wish the institution a brilliant future which I am sure it deserves. I only wish that such institutions will crop up all over India and be the means of preserving the *Aryan religion in its purity*" (CWMG 2, #8, p. 93 [my italics]). It should be clear that in Gandhi's terminology "Aryan religion" is synonymous with what we call today "Hinduism." More on that is discussed in a later chapter. That same day in Madras, Gandhi delivered a speech at Pachaiyappa's Hall, held under the auspices of the Mahajan Sabha. He repeated, essentially, what he had said in Bombay. He mentioned the example of a Durban bylaw which "requires registration of coloured servants." Gandhi was adamantly opposed to this bylaw because, "This rule may be, and perhaps is, necessary for the Kaffirs who would not work, but absolutely useless with regard to the Indians. But the policy is to class the Indian with the Kaffir whenever possible" (CWMG 2, #9, p. 105).

A reporter from the *Statesman* of Calcutta published an interview with Gandhi on November 10, 1896.

"Then, are we to understand," the interviewer asked, "that the Indians in Natal—the great bulk of whom are coolies, who would never have aspired to free institutions in their own country—are desirous of wielding political power in Natal?"

"By no means," Mr. Gandhi replied. "We are most careful to put out, in all our representations to the Government and the public, that the object of our agitation is merely the removal of vexatious disabilities devised, as we believe, to degrade us as compared to the European population." (CWMG 2, #12, p. 126)

With more speeches to his credit in other parts of India, Gandhi returned to South Africa by the year's end. It is not too hard to imagine that in the three and one-half years of Gandhi's presence in South Africa, there is not a single instance when he taken any time to go and meet blacks. The evidence shows beyond doubt that his scathing racist remarks about blacks were deep-rooted and he did not question them in any fashion. His association with the upper-caste Indians in South Africa further reinforced his prejudices against blacks. His perpetual habit of "looking up the civilization scale" toward the whites as a model only generated more condemnation for those relegated to the bottom of the scale, namely blacks. His loyalty to British imperialism was not questioned. In the midst of the Boer War, all he could utter was, "It was the Indians' proudest boast that they were British subjects. If they were not, they would not have had a footing in South Africa" (CWMG 3, #76, p. 136). Gandhi seemed to harbor a vision of upper-caste Indians joining hands with whites to rule the colony of South Africa. It is not hard to imagine the consequences to blacks under the domination of not one, but two, masters. The low-caste Indians perhaps might fare a degree better than blacks, but they too had a dear price to pay in order to travel higher up the civilization scale.

18

I have not the shadow of a doubt that any man or woman can achieve what I have, if he or she would make the same effort and cultivate the same hope and faith.

—Mahatma Gandhi
Harijan, October 3, 1936

Emboldened with the approval of resolutions by his Indian listeners in Bombay and Madras, Gandhi returned to South Africa more determined than ever. This was to steer unidirectional white racist South Africa into a new biracist society with both elite Indian and whites commonly sharing the benefits of that society, except for the power structure. In Calcutta, in an interview with *The Englishman*, he stated, "Political power is not our ambition, but to be let alone to carry on our trading, for which we are eminently suited as a nation, is all we ask. This is, we think, a reasonable demand" (CWMG 2, #14, p. 135). This time, he focused more on the underclasses than before. On reaching the shores of South Africa from India, on January 13, 1897, Gandhi gave an interview to the *Natal Advertiser*. The reporter asked: "In your Indian campaign what attitude did you adopt towards the indentured Indian question?" Gandhi answered, "I have said most emphatically, in the pamphlets and elsewhere, that the treatment of the indentured Indians is no worse or better in Natal than they receive in any other parts of the world. I have never endeavoured to show that the indentured Indians have been receiving cruel treatment" (CWMG 2, #19, p. 160).

On October 15, 1901, on the eve of his second departure to India, he discussed

the NIC's progress, especially dealing with its stated objective of a better understanding between the Europeans and the Indians. While confessing the progress on
that front had been scant, he was looking forward to a day of "Imperial brotherhood"—meaning the British colonists would accept the upper-caste elements as
their equals to run the colonies in South Africa and India under the cloak of "Imperial brotherhood" (CWMG 3, #157, p. 206). More than a year after having served
in the Boer War, in October 1901, Gandhi left South Africa for India and returned
in December 1902, after attempting unsuccessfully to build a law practice.

This time he settled in Johannesburg, Transvaal. Early in 1903, he established the British Indian Association (BIA)—a political party to safeguard the
commercial elite's vested interests. In many ways, the BIA paralleled the NIC,
because it was dominated by Gujarati merchants and, of course, adhered to the
same upper-caste ideology. However, in contrast to the NIC, the BIA lacked a
written constitution, leaving more leeway for Gandhi to maneuver. He was the
BIA's secretary, chief strategist, and the sole tactician.[1]

To understand in depth Gandhi's role, it is imperative to take a close look at
the working conditions of the underclasses in South Africa. Before we get into
that, a few words are essential to describe the ground realities. A new set of circumstances came into existence following the abolition of slavery in 1834. With
the European colonial expansion, it became possible for the colonial powers to
take over southern Africa. After having established its economic infrastructure
and the necessary protection of its lucrative trade, it also established the cultivation of those products in their newly acquired tropical colonies. They instituted
a new method of agriculture called plantation—a method of production on a
large scale, consistent with modern industrial organizations with division of
labor and financial arrangements intact, which were typical of industry rather
than agriculture. With slavery abolished, the planters faced serious shortages of
cheap labor, and they turned to the impoverished India within the British Empire
to supply them the cheap labor to fill that acute need. This ingenious method was
essentially slavery in all aspects but name. Fazlul Huq, a practicing lawyer in
London, succinctly described the underclasses' pathetic situation:

> Indentured labours . . . were strictly confined to the limits of their employers'
> estates. . . . Even when the period of indenture was completed, . . . Indians were
> required to carry passes. Absence from the estate without a pass was an offence
> punishable by a fine or imprisonment, while prolonged absence was treated like
> desertion . . . failure to appear at the correct time for work, refusal to carry out
> an order or instruction, . . . on the part of the labourer, were punishable offences.
> Beating and flogging were regular day-to-day occurrences. . . . While workers
> in industrialised societies faced the penalty of losing their wages if they with-
> held their labour, indentured Indians foreited their pay and . . . condemned and
> prosecuted as criminals. . . . The labourers were kept two to three months,
> sometimes for a year . . . without wages. . . . Another device to defraud [them]

was the system of stoppages operated according to the rules. . . . The main excuse for cuts was an unfinished task: an indentured Indian would receive only one day's pay for two day's work because the first day, with the task unfinished, was booked as a blank. . . . In addition, the most imaginative device invented . . . to defraud [them] was the system of double cuts. If an indentured Indian missed one day's work, due to illness or any other reason, he not only lost that day's wages but was also fined two days' wages. So if he could not work for a month, he had to work for two months without wages to pay off the fine. . . . In addition to double cuts, there was the widespread practice of adding one day to the total period of indenture for every day's absence from work. The Natal Law of 1891 included a provision whereby an indentured Indian, who was absent for more than 25 days in one year, had double-time added to his indenture.[2]

Continuing further, Fazlul Huq cited the comments of Edward Bateson, an ex-magistrate, who said:

The position of indentured coolies when charged in the courts is hopeless—justice they get only by accident—they are deterred from giving evidence themselves and . . . unable to procure evidence. . . . The coolie is absolutely defenseless. . . . I was a machine for sending men to prison for the convenience of the employers.

Their plight is equally unhappy when they bring a charge for assault; witnesses from the estates will not come forward, from fear; indeed it is practically impossible to substantiate a charge against an employer—the hand of every man is against the complainant and the police are quite as corrupt as in India. What stand can a poor, nervous, illiterate, ill-bred, ill-clad, ill-treated and timid Indian make before the courts of a European colony, where the magistrates and lawyers are as a rule cousins, nephews, brothers or sons of planters and, therefore, incapable, being only human beings, of doing or obtaining justice to or for a homeless and defenseless stranger, who neither understands the language, nor the procedure of the courts before which he may stand charged or prefer a complaint?[3]

During this early phase in Transvaal, Mr. Gandhi was involved in trying to stop the new anti-Indian laws or the reactionary amendments to existing laws. These laws affected traders' licenses, immigration, locations and bazaars, indentured labor, permits, and franchise. Just like in Natal, his strategy and tactics here in Transvaal were predictable: he made petitions to such authorities as the town councils, the Permit Office, the Immigration Department, the Asiatic Department, the local legislatures, the governor, the High Commissioner, and the Colonial Office, etc. Also, Gandhi started a weekly newspaper in June 1903 at Durban called *Indian Opinion*. The paper started with a few stated objectives, including: to bring the European and Indian subjects of King Edward closer together. What was the harm in making an effort to bring understanding among all people, irrespective of color, creed, or religion? Gandhi knew that a huge population of blacks and other colored lived in South Africa. They were simply not in his equation, anywhere. Below, I have provided a few good examples of Gandhi's racism.

In response to the White League's fear of the possible consequence of Asian mass immigration into Transvaal, Gandhi declared in the September 24, 1903 *Indian Opinion*: "We believe as much in the purity of race as we think they do, only we believe that they would best serve the interest, which is as dear to us as to them, by advocating the purity of all races, and not one alone. We believe also that the white race in South Africa should be the predominating race . . ." (CWMG 3, #342, p. 453).

In the December 24, 1903, *Indian Opinion*, in response to similar fears voiced by the all-white Transvaal Chamber of Commerce Conference, Gandhi cited to his earlier petition, "The petition dwells upon 'the commingling of the Coloured and white races.' May we inform the members of the Conference that, so far as the British Indians are concerned, such a thing is practically unknown? If there is one thing which the Indian cherishes more than any other, it is the purity of type" (CWMG 4, #70, p. 89). The Indian underclasses evidently did not share Gandhi's distaste for "commingling" the races.

In Ferreiras Township, a working-class suburb of Johannesburg, the population breakdown in late 1904 was listed as 288 Indians, 58 Syrians, 165 Chinese, 295 Cape Coloureds, 75 blacks, and 929 whites. Gandhi could do nothing about a place like the Ferreiras Township, but he claimed the right to speak on the racial composition of Indian locations. In February 1904, he informed the Johannesburg Medical Officer of Health, Dr. C. Porter that, "Why, of all places in Johannesburg, the Indian Location should be chosen for dumping down all the Kaffirs of the town passes my comprehension. . . . Of course, under my suggestion, the Town Council must withdraw the Kaffirs from the Location. About this mixing of the Kaffirs with the Indians, I must confess, I feel most strongly. I think it is very unfair to the Indian population, and it is an undue tax on even the proverbial patience of my countrymen."[4]

Ironically, the BIA backed away from its persistent demands about blacks from being removed from the locations, because many merchants profited from the black rental income; Gandhi had to follow suit. Similarly, in March 1906, in a clear contradiction of his previously stated principles, and on behalf of the BIA, Gandhi protested the proposed removal of blacks from the Pretoria location on the grounds that was harmful to merchant interests. He went out of his way to shield his vested interests from any encroachment. Maureen Swan aptly states:

> He [Gandhi] strenuously protested against the proposal to import indentured Indians into the Transvaal, particularly if their contracts included a repatriation clause. He referred to the proposed scheme as slave labour. But his major concern was evidently the belief that the Indian "problem is complicated enough without their presence," and that hostility to Indian traders would be fed by a vast influx of Indian workers. That his concern was for the future of the merchants, and not the "slave-labourers" per se, is obvious in that he offered sincere congratulations on the decision to import Chinese instead of Indian workers. In

Sergeant-Major Gandhi. *(Courtesy of Navajivan Trust)*

Map of the area in South Africa covered by the Zulu Rebellion, 1906. *(From Walter Bosman,* The Natal Rebellion of 1906, *London, 1907)*

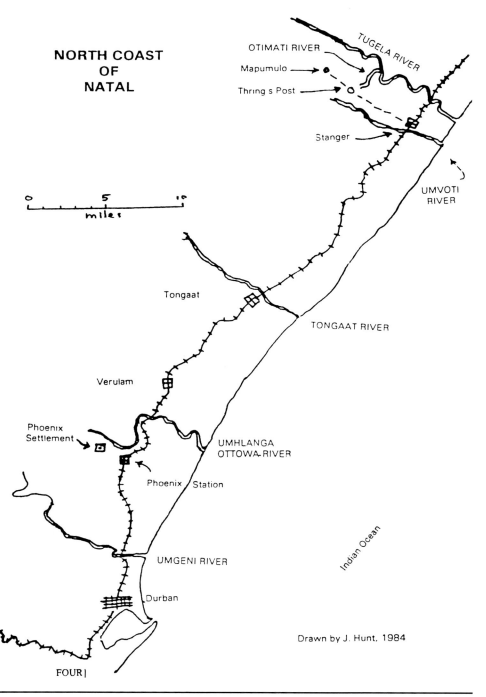

NORTH COAST
OF
NATAL

TUGELA RIVER

OTIMATI RIVER

Mapumulo

Thring s Post

Stanger

UMVOTI
RIVER

0   5   10
miles

Tongaat

TONGAAT RIVER

Verulam

Phoenix
Settlement

UMHLANGA
OTTOWA RIVER

Phoenix Station

Indian Ocean

UMGENI RIVER

Durban

Drawn by J. Hunt, 1984

FOUR I

Sketch of the north coast of Natal. North is at top. *(Courtesy of James D. Hunt)*

Indian Stretcher-Bearer Corps. Gandhi is seated in the center of the middle row. (*Courtesy of Publications Division, Government of India*)

Gandhi during the First World War, as organizer of the Indian Volunteer Corps, London, 1914. Gandhi is standing at center. (*Courtesy of Publications Division, Government of India*)

Dawn of the new Gandhi. Ganesh, an elephant-headed Hindu god, crowns Gandhi, a ritual act signifying Gandhi's break with his British past and establishing bonds with Hindu causes. *(Copyright ©Popperfoto/Retrofile.com)*

The Hindu face of Gandhi the Avatar. *(Dust jacket illustration from* The Mask of the Mahatma, *by kind permission of Tom Sawyer and Constable & Robinson Ltd)*

ὁ ἅγιος

ΜΟ
ΓΑΝ
ΔΑС
ὁ ΓΑΝΔΙ

MOHANDAS GANDHI of INDIA

The Christian face of Saint Gandhi. *(Copyright © Robert Lentz; image courtesy of Natural Bridges, www.natural-bridges.com)*

1906 he actually recommended to the Colonial Secretary that Natal merchants be allowed to bypass the Immigration Restriction Act and import Indian clerks and domestics on the understanding that they must leave the colony at the end of the service with their masters. This was an attempt to break what was described as the "monopoly" created by local Indian clerks and domestics, and cannot be described in any other way than an indenture scheme complete with below market wage rates and a repatriation clause.[5]

His views on Indian immigration were also exacerbated by another bizarre concern of his paranoid prejudice against black people, "Let us have a few of our best men to teach us, to bring the highest ideals with them, to advise and shepherd us, and to minister to our spiritual needs, that we may not sink to the level of the aboriginal natives, but rise to be, in every sense, worthy citizens of the Empire."[6] Regarding work ethics, Gandhi held a low opinion of blacks, and even with time he never wavered on this issue, "It is one thing to register Natives who would not work, and whom it is very difficult to find out if they absent themselves, but it is another thing and most insulting to expect decent, hard-working, and respectable Indians, whose only fault is that they work too much, to have themselves registered and carry with them registration badges" (CWMG 4, #152, p. 193). Commenting in an editorial on the Natal Municipal Corporation Bill, in the March 18, 1905, *Indian Opinion* Gandhi was not enthused with the term "uncivilized races" being used to denote not just blacks but also the Indians. Gandhi was vehemently against including Indians (even underclasses) with blacks: "Clause 200 makes provision for registration of persons belonging to uncivilized races (*meaning the local blacks*), resident and employed within the borough. One can understand the necessity for registration of Kaffirs who will not work; but why should registration be required for indentured Indians who have become free, and for their descendants about whom the general complaint is that they work too much?" (CWMG 4, #319, pp. 379–81 [my italics]).

Continuing on the theme of work ethics, Gandhi once referred to a speech made by John L. Dube. He was a most accomplished African, who said that an African had the capacity for improvement only if the colonial masters would look upon him as better than dirt and give him a chance to develop self-respect. Gandhi suggested that "A little judicious extra taxation would do no harm; in the majority of cases it compels the native to work for at least a few days a year." Then he added: "Now let us turn our attention to another and entirely unrepresented community—the Indian. He is in striking contrast with the native. While the native has been of little benefit to the State, it owes its prosperity largely to the Indians. While native loafers abound on every side, that species of humanity is almost unknown among Indians here."[7]

Living and practicing law in Johannesburg in 1905 also opened more vistas for Gandhi; one was in the field of religious "Hinduism." Under the auspices of the Johannesburg Theosophical Lodge, Gandhi delivered sermons at the Masonic

Temple on Hinduism, with a flavor of *Oceanic Hinduism*. He liberally quoted the Hindu sacred books to make his points. Another point that stands out is his reference to Hindu sacred texts referred to as the Aryan sacred books. After all, Aryan religion comes with a full package of Aryan sacred books![8]

In the February 28, 1905, *Government Gazette* of Natal a bill was published regulating the use of firearms by natives and Asiatics. Commenting on the bill in the March 25, 1905, *Indian Opinion*, Gandhi stated: "In this instance of the fire-arms, the Asiatic has been most improperly bracketed with the Native. The British Indian does not need any such restrictions as are imposed by the Bill on the Native regarding the carrying of fire-arms. The predominant race can remain so by preventing the Native from arming himself. Is there the slightest vestige of justification for so preventing the British Indian?" (CWMG 4, #324, p. 386). Here is a perfect example of our Mahatma pouring out words of wisdom to white South African racists about how they can perpetuate their domination over the vast majority of Africans.

Gandhi's Phoenix Settlement was within the heartland of the sugar plantations, where a large number of indentured Indians were employed. He knew very well what kind of hell those poor creatures lived in. Already many organizations, individuals, and commissions of inquiry had exposed the barbarity of the system. Scandals broke out in India and reports of their scandalous treatment in the colonies were published in the Indian press. It is well known that Gandhi knew about the treatment meted out to these unfortunate people at the hands of their employers; it was so inhumane that it drove many to suicide. But the sufferings of the poor did not stir his cold heart. Gandhi never involved himself in inquiring into their condition or organizing and acting to make their lives more tolerable. Sometimes he reproduced reports published in the colonial press, owned by the planters and mine owners. In *Indian Opinion*, he focused attention on injustice to the merchants, who kept him in comfort and style. Sometimes he casually mentioned the indentured laborers: a few from court cases or reports reproduced from white newspapers. He never had the time, energy, or inclination to launch a campaign for the abolition of flogging, wage deduction, stoppages, or the absurd law that required permission from employers to lodge complaints against them. On the contrary, to please the big money lords, Gandhi certified that indentured laborers were treated well.[9] A few more examples should suffice.

On November 24, 1904, the *Natal Witness* reported that some Indians were wandering without passes, which was a criminal offence. They had "deserted" because of ill treatment. In the December 17, 1904, issue of *Indian Opinion*, Gandhi wrote:

> We print elsewhere a report from the *Witness* representative on the condition of the indentured labour in the coal-mines in Natal. If the allegations are true, they reveal a shocking state of things. Our contemporary demands an inquiry. We join in the request. It should be welcomed by the mine-owners. But if an inves-

tigation is held, we trust that it will be open, public and absolutely impartial. The commission, in order to command confidence, should be preponderatingly non-official; and, if we may venture to say so, should include an Indian gentleman of standing. The general condition of the indentured labourer in the Colony is satisfactory; and it can only enhance its reputation if causes even of suspicion are removed. (CWMG 4, #269, p. 315)

After living in Natal for a decade or so and seeing from very close quarters how badly they suffered, Mr. Gandhi did not hesitate to proclaim that the general condition of indentured laborers in the colony was "satisfactory."

L. W. Ritch, the secretary of the South African British Indian Committee (BIC) had earlier warned of the high suicide rates among indentured Indians. Interviewed on the working of the system, he said: "Does anyone in England know that these Indians are bought and sold as part of the estate to which they are allocated? That they pass, as farm fixtures, from purchaser to purchaser?" In the editorial column of *Indian Opinion* on November 18, 1905, Gandhi first discussed how much indentured laborers were in demand in the colony, and then wrote: "Whilst we are not prepared to subscribe to any general charge of ill-treatment, we have no hesitation in saying that, in the majority of cases, Indian labour is used regardless of any fellow feeling for indentured Indians."[10] He added: "We feel therefore that now is the time for pressing the truth home to the Colonists. If they must continue to draw upon India for the cheap source of prosperity of the Colony, they must also be prepared to share the inconvenience, if it be an inconvenience, of having to give fair treatment to the free Indian population; and if this were done, it would be purely a matter of a reasonable bargain."[11]

The most hated among the apartheid laws was perhaps the Pass Law. Here also Gandhi's attitude toward indentured Indians, not to mention Africans, was very clear, "We recognise that so long as there is indentured Indian population in the Colony, some Pass law is necessary, and the remedy probably lies in the judicious administration thereof. Respectable people, men and women, were only lately arrested under the suspicion that they were indentured Indians; one man was out in search for a doctor for his wife who was in labour" (CWMG 3, #209, pp. 267–68).

Gandhi made it clear from the very beginning that he did not want franchise rights for the Indians. He knew that the demand for franchise rights would bring him in direct conflict with the long-term strategy of his imperial masters to create a white-dominated South Africa, based upon the doctrine of race superiority. He said:

Having said so much, I venture to say on behalf of my fellow-brothers that they would not think of objecting to any measure, with regard to the franchise, which may be devised in order to keep the Voters' Role clear of objectionable men, or to provide against a preponderance of the Indian vote in future. I am confident that the Indians have no wish to see ignorant Indians who cannot possibly be expected to understand the value of a vote being placed on the Voters' List. They submit that all are not such, and that such are to be found, more or less, in all communities. The object of every right-minded Indian is to fall in with the wishes of the European Colonists as far as possible. They would rather forgo a crumb from the loaf than have the whole in opposition to the European Colonists and from England. (CWMG 1, #67, pp. 273–74)

It never dawned on Gandhi, or if it did he didn't care, that for the ex-indentured Indians and their colonial-born children the question of franchise was vital. What mattered most was the money their labor helped create, as he expressed very early on: "Leave them [the elite class] to follow their legitimate [commercial] pursuits, . . . [and] there would be no franchise question . . ." (CWMG 1, #67, p. 271).

Many authors, including Gandhi's apologists, made out that Gandhi fought for and achieved the abolition of the three-pound tax on ex-indentured Indians. The credit really goes to Mr. P. S. Aiyar, who started and continued the campaign for abolition of the three-pound tax for some years. Gandhi refused to cooperate with that campaign, but included the removal of a three-pound tax in his list of demands at the tail end of his stay in South Africa. At that time he was alienated from the merchants, became completely dependent upon the support of colonial-born and ex-indentured Indians, a strange fate for such a crafty lawyer.[12]

Gandhi advised Indians not to align with other political groups of either colored or African communities. The colored community labored to gain the franchise as a means to introducing representative institutions. Its petitions attest to this fact. Commenting on the petition in the March 24, 1906, *Indian Opinion*, Gandhi declared, "British Indians have, in order that they may never be misunderstood, made it clear that they do not aspire to any political power" (CWMG 5, #258, p. 243). He further added:

It seems that the petition is being widely circulated, and signatures are being taken of all the Coloured people in the three Colonies named. The petition is non-Indian in character, although British Indians, being Coloured people, are very largely affected by it. We consider that it was a wise policy, on the part of the British Indians throughout South Africa, to have kept themselves apart and distinct from the other Coloured communities in this country. (CWMG 5, #258, pp. 241–42)

In a statement made on May 29, 1906, to the Constitution Committee, the British Indian Association, led by Gandhi, said: "The British Indian Association has always admitted the principle of white predominance and has, therefore, no desire, to press, on behalf of the community it represents, for any political rights just for the sake of them" (CWMG 5, #364, p. 335).

Commenting on a court case, the June 2, 1906, *Indian Opinion*'s Gujarati section stated:

You say that the Magistrate's decision is unsatisfactory, because it would enable a person, however unclean, to travel by a tram, and that even the Kaffirs would be able to do so. But the Magistrate's decision is quite different. The Court has declared that the Kaffirs have no legal right to travel by trams. And, according to tram regulations, those in an unclean dress or in a drunken state are prohibited from boarding a tram. Thanks to the Court's decision, only clean Indians [*meaning upper-caste Indians*] or Coloured people other than Kaffirs can now travel by the trams. (CWMG 5, #362, p. 333, my italics)

In the September 2, 1905, *Indian Opinion*, Gandhi reported that "some members of the British Association in England," which included scientists, were visiting Natal, among other places. Gandhi told his Gujarati-speaking readers how the Honorable Mr. Marshall Campbell took the visiting guests to his residence at Mount Edgecombe where they were shown—in Gandhi's own words, "what the savage Negroes were like, and also their dances, etc" (CWMG 5, #74, p. 55). Keep in mind that Gandhi's use of the phrase "savage Negroes" was just about two months before his active preparation to participate against blacks in the Zulu war.

In 1904, Gandhi founded the Phoenix Settlement, a bold experiment in communal living away from crowds. Here a gathering of Indians and a few Europeans lived and experimented with a way of life that can only be described today as "spiritualist." No black was a member, although four "hefty Zulu" girls were employed on a part-time basis for a few hours on the printing day for *Indian Opinion*. Millie Polak recalled this incident at the Phoenix Settlement:

Money was always too scarce to enable the well to be dug, and so the problem of giving to the thirsty Zulu wayfarer a cup of water had to be dealt with by each householder, and much heart-searching and real unhappiness was caused by the necessity of refusing the simple request.[13]

It seems Mrs. Polak could not forget this and she anguished over it. Was Gandhi involved? Most probably, yes. It is amazing to see that this "spiritualist" group refused to give a cup of water to a black wanderer. Bringing water should have been no problem for a man such as Gandhi, who was traveling to and from the Phoenix Settlement regularly, not to mention others living there.

In his farewell speech at a meeting held in Cape Town on June 27, 1914, which was reported in the June 29, 1914, *Natal Mercury*, Gandhi said:

We do not aspire to social equality, and I dare say our social evolution lies along different lines. We have stated so repeatedly—that we shall not at present ask for the whole franchise. . . . The Indians knew perfectly well which was the dominant and governing race. They aspired to no social equality with Europeans. They felt that the path of their development was separate. They did not even aspire to the franchise, or, if the aspiration existed, it was with no idea of its having a present effect. (CWMG 12, #342, pp. 437–38)

The time came to say good-bye to South Africa. He bid farewell to the Indians and to the whites, but nowhere did Gandhi remotely mention blacks. At a few going-away parties in his honor, he recalled his past twenty-one years of struggle in South Africa. Proudly he mentioned his heroism during the Boer War, but not a single word crossed his lips about the war against blacks. There was no soul searching, no turmoil inside, and no tough questions asked. All we hear is that he is ceaselessly trying to cement future generations of Indians and whites: "Rightly or wrongly, for good or for evil, Englishmen and Indians have been knit together, and it behooves both races so to mould themselves as to leave a splendid legacy to the generations yet to be born, and to show that though Empires have gone and fallen, this Empire perhaps may be an exception and that this is an Empire not founded on material but on spiritual foundations" (CWMG 12, #377, p. 505).

Anyone can see that the black people of South Africa were in a precarious predicament. They faced not one, but two, masters: (1) the formal ones—whites, who slowly and steadily took over the land and turned blacks into serfs; and (2) Gandhi-style Indians who came to South Africa, piggybacking on whites, and later extolled themselves as one-half partners of an "Imperial brotherhood" whose inner workings were, disgusting to say, conceived on "spiritual foundations." My readers, this is your Gandhi!

NOTES

1. Maureen Swan, *Gandhi: The South African Experience* (Johannesburg: Raven Press, 1985), p, 104.

2. Fazlul Huq, *Gandhi: Saint or Sinner?* (Bangalore: Dalit Sahitya Akademy, 1992), pp. 13–15.

3. Ibid.

4. CWMG 4, #202, pp. 244–45. From *Indian Opinion*, September 3, 1904.

5. Swan, *Gandhi*, pp. 113–14.

6. Joseph J. Doke, *M. K. Gandhi: An Indian Patriot in South Africa* (London: Indian Chronicle, 1909), p. 97.

7. Huq, *Gandhi*, pp. 23–24.

8. CWMG 4, # 331, p. 394. From *Indian Opinion*, April 1, 1905.

9. Huq, *Gandhi*, p. 19.

10. Swan, *Gandhi*, p. 133. The quote is cited in "*Indian Opinion*, 18, November 1905.

11. Huq, *Gandhi*, p. 20.

12. Ibid., p. 21.

13. Millie G. Polak, *Mr. Gandhi: The Man* (London: George Allen & Unwin, 1931), p. 43.

19

I fancy I know the art of living and dying nonviolently. But I have yet to demonstrate it by one perfect act.

—Mahatma Gandhi
September 1947

The literature is inadequate with respect to scholars who have studied Gandhi and found his relationship toward black people disturbing and unsatisfactory. The list comprises only the following seven, as far as I know.

D. B. Mathur, an Indian scholar, has noted: "Gandhi did not raise protest against White racists' defiance of justice and rights of the black natives. . . . Gandhi made no efforts to send feelers to probe preparedness or willingness of the black natives to unite and organize for a movement in defence of their rights."[1] Ironically, in his next book, Mathur made a U-turn and followed the traditional story line: "Gandhi accepted the challenge of apartheid . . . in South Africa."[2]

An English scholar, Geoffrey Ashe, whose biography of Gandhi was mentioned in earlier chapters, has observed:

> By confining his attack to a narrow front, on Satyagrahi principles, the "saint" had broken through to his objectives. But he had also excluded the only kind of campaign that might have made a difference to South Africa. Apart from his joint action with a few Chinese, he had never attempted to enlist a non-Indian people. Therefore, he had never directly challenged white racist supremacy as such. Myriads of Negroes were all around him; he liked them, he knew them to be oppressed; yet he never made them his allies, because the particular laws he

199

was combating did not apply to them. Saytagraha in South Africa was purely a minority movement, and the end left a question mark overhanging its claims. Several discriminatory laws still stood, and afterwards, when the Indians had to rely on second-rate leadership, most of the ground gained was lost. Smut's son even claimed that they had been beaten.[3]

Les Switzer, at the time an expatriate South African residing in the United States, wrote:

> There is no record in the Mahatma's published remembrances or in the pages of *Indian Opinion* during this period to suggest that Gandhi saw passive resistance as anything other than an instrument of protest on behalf of the Indians in South Africa. . . . Men of the moral and intellectual stature of Solomon Plaatje, John Dube, John Tengo Jabavu, Walter Rubusana and Abdul Abdurrahman, to name but a few, exercised, if anything, a more profound influence in the history of resistance in this period than did Gandhi. Did the Mahatma have links with any of these black leaders or with any of the political, economic and cultural organizations being developed by blacks during this period? The record suggests that he did not.[4]

Switzer's critical comments are accurate except for a minor error: Gandhi had met Dr. Abdurrahman and knew the African Political Organization, but didn't care for any close alliance. Gandhi referred to Tengo Jabavu in relation to his efforts to establish an interstate college for blacks. He had also met John L. Dube, the editor of *Ilanga lase Natal*, who founded a commune not far from the Phoenix Settlement. Gandhi may have followed his example in setting up the Phoenix Settlement.

Dr. Surendra Bhana, another South African scholar of Indian descent and now a professor at the University of Kansas, has commented: "Gandhi's thoughts on the Africans were racially inspired; he felt a great distance between them and the Indians."[5] He also said, "Gandhi, in common with the Indian leaders generally, not only harboured racial prejudice against Africans, but considered them inferior."[6]

Maureen Swan, in her well-researched book, couldn't have expressed the issue more perceptively:

> The defects in Gandhi's political insight are of dual significance. On one hand they were, as suggested, an important part of the reason for the failure of merchant politics in Natal and the Transvaal during the immediate post-war years. In this respect it is important to remember that in choosing not to attempt to ally with the articulate politicized elements in either the coloured or African communities, Gandhi facilitated the implementation of the divisive segregationalist policies which helped ease the task of white minority rule in South Africa. Indeed, where the Transvaal whites insisted on separate facilities for themselves, Gandhi demanded further subdivision to separate Indians from other blacks. In fact, in his eagerness to compromise, to conciliate, to ensure the white South Africans their predominant position, he was sometimes even ahead of

them in advocating separate facilities for whites and others. . . . Gandhi was a racial purist, and proud of it.[7]

Born and raised in the Bengal region of British India, barrister Fazlul Huq of London turned activist in the anti-apartheid movement, and he later investigated misappropriation of funds going to his native home of Bangladesh. He is of the opinion that irrespective of what the Gandhi propaganda machine proclaims, Gandhi never fought against apartheid and he favored the white domination and oppression of the blacks. Huq believes that Gandhi was no less of a racist than the white racists of South Africa. As Huq put it, the reason for Gandhi's behavior was:

> Gandhi accepted racial segregation, not only because it was politically expedient as his Imperial masters had already drawn such a blueprint, it also conformed with his own attitude to the caste system. *In his own mind he fitted Apartheid into the caste system: whites in the position of Brahmins, Indian merchants and professionals as Sudras, and all other non-whites as Untouchables. . . .*[8]

I should add, or perhaps clarify, that in my reading of Gandhi, he considered the Negro race of South Africa below that of India's untouchables in the overall stratum of the races.

Professor James D. Hunt, who has worked more on this issue than anybody I know, has taken an apologetic stand, or perhaps, even a forgiving attitude toward Gandhi and his activities in South Africa:

> We should not take Gandhi's personal sense of distance from the blacks as a sufficient explanation for his lack of cooperation with them. He had the capacity to grow beyond his limitations and also to recognize errors and learn from them. . . . He shared the prejudices of his class concerning black people, and his lifestyle and work kept him isolated from them. . . . He did fail to accomplish very much for the oppressed races in South Africa, but in so doing he learned a great deal, and grew in personal stature.[9]

What Professor Hunt has implied here is that the "failed Gandhi" that we know from his twenty-one years in South Africa somehow mended his ways after learning from his racially indoctrinated aberrations. After this transformation, he jumped into the arena again—this time in British India—for the benefit of all Indians and their freedom from British colonialism. Dr. Hunt seems to imply that once Gandhi left for India in 1914, he did an about-face. No more race wars! No more caste wars! No more championing elites' causes! Is this true? Well, the only way to find the truth is to look for it. Subsequent chapters will bear testimony to that effort.

NOTES

1. D. B. Mathur, *Gandhi, Congress, and Apartheid* (Jaipur, India: Aalekh Publishers, 1986), p. 213.

2. D. B. Mathur, *Prefacing Gandhi* (Jaipur, India: RBSA Publishers, 1988), p. 109.

3. Geoffrey Ashe, *Gandhi* (New York: Stein and Day, 1968), p. 125.

4. Les Switzer, "Gandhi in South Africa: The Ambiguities of Satyagraha," *Journal of Ethnic Studies* 14, no. 1 (Spring 1986): 125–26.

5. James D. Hunt, quoting Surendra Bhana in "Gandhi and the black People of South Africa," *Gandhi Marg* 11, no. 1 (April–June 1989): 20.

6. Surendra Bhana, *Gandhi's Legacy: The Natal Indian Congress 1894–1994* (Pietermaritzburg, South Africa: University of Natal Press, 1997), p. 22.

7. Maureen Swan, *Gandhi: The South African Experience* (Johannesburg: Raven Press, 1985), p. 112.

8. Fazlul Huq, *Gandhi: Saint or Sinner?* (Bangalore: Dalit Sahitya Akademy, 1992), p. 25.

9. Hunt, "Gandhi and the black People," pp. 11, 20, 21.

Special note: The author wishes to acknowledge utilizing Dr. Maureen Swan and Fazlul Huq's research in preparing for part 4. Robert A Huttenback, in his chapter titled "Was Gandhi's South African Struggle Inspired by Race, Class, or Nation?" reported that Gandhi was no racist while acknowledging at least some of Gandhi's antiblack activities. According to Huttenback, as he put it, "The fight that Gandhi led in South Africa was not a race or class struggle (nor even an indivdual or personal struggle) but a national struggle—a struggle on behalf of the truth, God and India." This chapter can be read in Jay Naidoo, *Tracking Down Historical Myths: Eight South African Cases* (Johannesburg: A. D. Donker Publisher, 1989). Yet in contrast to Huttenback, V. S. Naipaul, after reading Gandhi's autobiography, sensed Gandhi to be a racial leader committed to fighting racial battles while camoflaging his identity with an overlay of religious overtures. See V. S. Naipaul, *India: A Wounded Civilization*, pp. 168–69.

PART 5

Gandhiji was a genius. It is dangerous to copy a genius, or try to think what he would have done in particular situations. He was always changing his methods. Sometimes he was impatient and sometimes very patient; he could go underground for years. Genius is self-regulating and often breaks its own laws. You cannot imitate him; you must learn to deal with your situations in your own way.

—Acharya J. B. Kripalani
Search after Sunrise

20

Yes, I know my husband. He [is] always mischief.

—Kasturba Gandhi
The Life and Death of Mahatma Gandhi

In the preceding chapters we have exposed Gandhi. When we see past the propaganda blitz, Gandhi does not look so good. Only a very few people are aware of Gandhi's long stay in South Africa. Of those, only a handful are knowledgeable of Gandhi's racist activities. Up until his last days in South Africa, Gandhi never apologized to the blacks. Obviously then, a question arises: Did he apologize to the blacks while in India? When confronted with Gandhi's antiblack actions, many of his admirers still defend him: "Nobody's perfect, everybody is entitled to some mistakes . . . with time Gandhi changed . . . and became a great leader." Some have the audacity to cite George Wallace, the former Governor of Alabama, who apologized for his racist past. One is tempted to assume that Gandhi likewise also experienced a transformation. Did Gandhi change? If so, when, where, and why? This chapter will explore these questions, concentrating on what Gandhi said from 1915 to 1948 about his African activities after he had returned to India. Keep in mind that, according to Gandhi's autobiography, he had an awakening during the war against blacks in 1906. But did he?

From South Africa, Gandhi made his way to England. By that time, World War I had already started. There is a world of a difference between small conflicts such as the Boer and Zulu wars and a war that engulfed the globe. To Gandhi, this was a window of opportunity to add to his credentials. Based upon his past experience, he organized the local Indians (who were students) to form an Indian vol-

205

unteer corps to aid the British. However, things didn't work out according to his plan—he became incapacitated by pleurisy. Nevertheless, for a short time he embroiled himself in a strange controversy which he labeled "miniature satyagraha." The issue was a simple one: As per military rules, the commanding officer (Colonel Baker) officially allocated to the corps a retired member of the Indian Medical Service. This person refused to deal with or through Gandhi as the unofficial leader or representative of the corps. This did not please the egotistic Gandhi and he resorted to "satyagraha," as he called it. In a letter to C. Roberts, Gandhi made it clear, "We appointed our own leaders and others. As it so happened, all orders ultimately passed through my hands. Similarly, at the time of the Zulu rebellion in Natal, we were under Col. Sparks' command. Col. Sparks never appointed officers of our Corps" (CWMG 12, #400, p. 541).

Here is a precedent for any member of the armed forces to resort to a "satyagraha" if one is disappointed with the appointment of someone in the higher-chain-of-command structure. Gandhi was perfectly right when he referred to the Zulu rebellion in which he had hand-appointed three sergeants and a corporal to intermediate leadership positions.

He returned to India after a mere five months in England, hoping to return one day to continue the war effort. Upon his arrival in Bombay, he received the Gold *Kaisar-i-Hind* medal, presumably for his African war services.

In 1918 the British were in dire need of more soldiers for the European theater. What better way for Gandhi, already a seasoned veteran, to fulfill one of his dreams by being a recruiting sergeant? I suppose, under the British-Indian colonial system, one would have to earn the designation. But Gandhi was not about to waste time trying to earn the title he coveted. Before attending the war conference in Delhi, he shifted himself into overdrive to accomplish this mission. In a speech at Nadiad on April 12, 1918, to enlist the new recruits, Gandhi couldn't have been more lucid in mixing religious phraseology to rally his listeners for the war effort:

> To lose one's land in the fight is nothing very great. It is a householder, not a sannyasi, who is in a position to sacrifice land. They are not sannyasis in Europe who are shedding rivers of blood; they are but householders. Mr. Lloyd George, running all over the place, himself and his possessions at the disposal of the country, is he a sannyasi? Is the war which England is fighting one for land? Surely not. Why, she felt, should Germany be allowed to have her way? Germany, too, on her part, is fighting for her self-respect. She wants to vindicate herself. We have been assured by some others that we shall not starve. The only assurance the people of Europe have is the strength of their arms. They see so many of their sons dying every second, but they don't shed tears over them. You will have your lands back with honour in this struggle. If you put up with the loss of your lands, sacrificing your very souls in doing so, you will earn a name for yourselves not only in Kheda district but in the whole of India.
>
> Finally, I have only this to tell you: whatever the cost, honour the pledge you have taken with God as witness and with full knowledge and understanding. And

have faith, not in me, but in God. What does it matter even if you lose your lands? We shall earn greater respect and fame by doing so. The Government will also take pride in ruling over such a brave people. (CWMG 14, #230, p. 337)

A day after the war conference, Gandhi emphatically stated to the viceroy: "I would make India offer all her able-bodied sons as a sacrifice to the Empire at its critical moment; and I know that India by this very act would become the most favoured partner in the Empire and racial distinctions would become a thing of the past" (CWMG 14, #257, p. 378). Gandhi knew well in advance that the official who had the power to add muscle to his resume was Mr. John L. Maffey (1877–1969). He was a veteran British official, who at the time of World War I held an important assignment as private secretary to the viceroy of India, Lord Chelmsford. In one letter to him, Gandhi pleaded: "I have an idea that, if I became your recruiting agent-in-chief, I might rain men on you" (CWMG 14, #259, p. 382). Recruiting agent-in-chief is not something you can secure with a snap of your fingers. Gandhi probably thought it wouldn't be a bad idea to acquaint Mr. Maffey with his own past experiences and honors:

I suppose I must give you something of my past record. I was in charge of the Indian Ambulance Corps consisting of 1,100 men during the Boer Campaign and was present at the battles of Colenso, Spionkop and Vaalkranz. I was specially mentioned in General Buller's despatches. I was in charge of a similar Corps of 90 Indians at the time of the Zulu Campaign in 1906, and I was specially thanked by the then Government of Natal. Lastly, I raised the Ambulance Corps in London consisting of nearly 100 students on the outbreak of the present war, and I returned to India in 1915 only because I was suffering from a bad attack of pleurisy brought about while I was undergoing the necessary training. On my being restored to health, I offered my services to Lord Hardinge, and it was then felt that I should not be sent out to Mesopotamia or France, but that I should remain in India. I omit reference to renewals of my offer to Provincial authorities. (CWMG 14, #258, p. 381)

Ninety Indians at the time of the Zulu campaign in 1906! Gandhi has certainly embellished his record. Here is one confirmation that Gandhi had no soul-searching experience during or after the 1906 Zulu War. Continuing in the same letter, Gandhi states: "In pursuance of my declaration at the Conference yesterday, I wish respectfully to state that I place my services at the disposal of the authorities to be utilized by them in any manner they choose, save that I personally will not kill or injure anybody, friend or foe" (CWMG 14, #258, p. 380). Yet the contrast is striking. For example, during 1917–18, Mr. and Mrs. Polak were on a visit to India and met their old "friend" from South Africa. Mrs. Polak wrote of Gandhi, "Indeed, it was with great difficulty that some of his friends, including my husband, prevailed upon him not to offer himself as a combatant soldier, as an example to others."[1]

There is every reason to believe that, in pursuing the role of a recruiting agent-in-chief for the war, Gandhi was in Satyagraha's tactical mode. In his speech at Khandhali, the crowd listened to a beautiful sermon where Gandhi blended Satyagraha with his plea for military enlistment, "If our Government will not fight with the Germans as it does now, if our soldiers go and stand before them weaponless and will not use explosives and say, 'We will die of your blows,' then, I am sure our Government will win the war at once. But such an action requires *samskar* and India possesses most of it. . . . It is real satyagraha" (CWMG 14, #283, pp. 407–408). Gandhi harbored a fantasy as shown here when he made an appeal for enlistment in the Kheda district (equivalent to a county in the United States):

> To sacrifice sons in the war ought to be a cause not of pain but of pleasure to brave men. Sacrifice of sons at this hour will be a sacrifice for swaraj. . . . There are 600 villages in Kheda district. Every village has on an average a population of over 1,000. If every village gave at least twenty men, Kheda district would be able to raise an army of 12,000 men. The population of the whole district is seven lakhs and this number will then work out at 1.7 per cent, a rate which is lower than the death rate. If we are not prepared to make even this sacrifice for the Empire, for the sake of swaraj, no wonder that we should be regarded unworthy of it. If every village gives at least twenty men, on their return from the war they will be the living bulwarks of their village. If they fall on the battlefield, they will immortalize themselves, their village and their country, and twenty fresh men will follow their example and offer themselves for national defence. (CWMG 14, #304, p. 443)

People of Gujarat, India, (Gandhi's native state) had a knack for knowing Gandhi in a true sense and his war-crazed Satyagraha. They ignored him even after being bombarded with propaganda such as:

> Swaraj means—complete independence in association with Britain. If we can help in this war, instead of her ruling over us we shall have the upper hand. It is essential for us to get military training. I have come across none in India who adheres to non-violence so scrupulously as I do. I am overful of love. . . . To him who wants to learn the art of fighting, who would know how to kill, I would even teach the use of force. . . . He who does not know how to lay down his life without killing others may learn how to die killing. (CWMG 14, #326, p. 469)

Some words of wisdom!

NOTE

1. Millie G. Polak, *Mr. Gandhi: The Man* (London: George Allen & Unwin, 1931), chap. 17.

21

It is a very strange thing that almost all the professors of great religions of the world claim me as their own. The Jains mistake me for a Jain. Scores of Buddhist friends have taken me for a Buddhist. Hundreds of Christian friends still consider that I am a Christian. . . . Many of my Mussalman [Moslem] friends consider that, although I do not call myself a Mussalman, to all intents and purposes, I am one of them . . . still something within me tells me that, for all that deep veneration I show to these several religions, I am all the more a Hindu, none the less for it.

—Mahatma Gandhi
Gandhi's Significance for Today

Macho Gandhi took a somersault and his collaboration with the government came to a sudden halt. From very early in 1919 he was highly opposed to the Rowlatt bills, which were designed to curb terrorist activities and which brought about the campaign of Satyagraha. The political situation deteriorated further with the massacre at the mass meeting held in Amritsar, after which Gandhi incorporated the "Khilafat Movement," whereby the subcontinent Moslems were assimilated into his hydra-headed Satyagraha. By the time Gandhi was arrested on March 10, 1922, he had already conducted two nationwide Satyagrahas. The first Satyagraha ended in a disaster when Gandhi suspended the

209

action and confessed to having committed a "Himalayan blunder." His second nationwide effort was dubbed as the "non-violent non-cooperation movement" of 1921–22. This led to riots and massacres, just like the first one; Gandhi suspended the campaign and went on a fast, just as he did during the first Satyagraha. Here are the highlights that the new Gandhi followed through with his uncooperative stance toward the British:

Writing from the city of Bombay on August 1, 1920, Gandhi addressed a letter to the Viceroy:

> It is not without a pang that I return the Kaiser-i-Hind gold medal, granted to me by your predecessor for my humanitarian work in South Africa, the Zulu War medal granted in South Africa for my war services as officer in charge of the Indian Volunteers Service Corps in 1906 and the Boer War medal for my services as Assistant Superintendent of the Indian Volunteer Stretcher-Bearer Corps during the Boer War of 1899. I venture to return these medals in pursuance of the scheme of non-co-operation, inaugurated today in connection with the Khilafat movement. Valuable as these honours have been to me, I cannot wear them with an easy conscience so long as my Mussulman [Moslem] countrymen have to labour a wrong done to their religious sentiments.[1]

In 1920 Gandhi wrote two separate "The Doctrine of the Sword" papers that are of interest to us. The first one expounds:

> I do believe that where there is only a choice between cowardice and violence I would advise violence. Thus when my eldest son asked me what he should have done, had he been present when I was almost fatally assaulted in 1908, whether he should have run away and seen me killed or whether he should have used his physical force which he could and wanted to use, and defended me, I told him that it was his duty to defend me even by using violence. Hence it was that I took part in the Boer War, the so-called Zulu rebellion and the late War. Hence also do I advocate training in arms for those who believe in the method of violence. I would rather have India resort to arms in order to defend her honour than that she should in a cowardly manner become or remain a helpless witness to her own dishonour. . . . Let me not be misunderstood. Strength does not come from physical capacity. It comes from an indomitable will. An average Zulu is any way more than a match for an average Englishman in bodily capacity. But he flees from an English boy, because he fears the boy's revolver or those who will use it for him. He fears death and is nerveless in spite of his burly figure. (CWMG 18, #91, p. 132)

The new Gandhi tells us that his reason for participating in the Zulu rebellion was his "duty," just as his eldest son's duty was to defend his father even if it meant using the violence! What logic! The implication is clear that if Gandhi had not participated in the war it would have amounted to cowardice! And although he pulled no trigger, his heart was aligned with those doing so. Thus it was of less significance that he served in a "humanitarian" capacity, because he would have used violence, had it been required of him.

In another commentary under the same title, Gandhi made use of the example of a Pathan, the same individual in the above narrative that had once assaulted Gandhi. Continuing to explain his doctrine:

> It is any day better to use brute force than to betray cowardice. . . . It is better that India should arm itself and take the risk than that it should refuse to take up arms out of fear. It was for this reason that I had joined the Boer War and did my bit in helping the Government during the Zulu rebellion. It was for this same reason that, during the last War, I gave help in England and in India, too. I engaged myself in recruiting work. Forgiveness is the virtue of the brave. He alone who is strong to avenge a wrong knows how to love [and forgive]. He alone who is capable of enjoying pleasures can qualify to be a brahmachari by restraining his desires. There is no question of the mouse forgiving the cat. It will be evidence of India's soul-force only if it refuses to fight when it has the strength to do so. It is necessary to understand what the phrase, "strength to fight" means in this context. It does not mean only physical strength. Everyone who has courage in him can have the strength to fight, and everyone who has given up fear of death has such strength. I have seen sturdy Negroes cowering before white boys, because they were afraid of white man's revolver. . . . (CWMG 18, #96, pp. 156–57)

Here, rather than "duty" as a justification, now he raises a baffling statement to tortuously justify his participation in the Zulu rebellion. If I understand it correctly, Gandhi seems to be saying that he armed himself and willingly and fearlessly took the risk. Again, what logic! Gandhi has clearly stated that he was *helping the government* in the Zulu War. It should not be a surprise in the present-day nuclear India that its hawks take strength from Gandhi's logic by citing these two "The Doctrine of the Sword" papers.

The year is 1921. A certain correspondent in search of an answer to the riddle of Gandhi's behavior asked:

> When the Zulus broke out for liberty against the British usurpers, you helped the British in suppressing the so-called rebellion. Is it a rebellion to try to shake off the foreign yoke? Was Joan of Arc a rebel? Was George Washington a rebel? Is De Valera one? You may say that the Zulus had recourse to violence. I then ask, was the end bad or the means? The latter may have been so but certainly not the former. . . .
>
> In the last War, when the gallant Germans and Austrians were fighting so bravely against a world combination, you raised recruits for the British to fight against the nations that had done India no harm. Whenever there is a war between two races, one has to hear both parties before coming to a decision, either for or against any of them. . . .
>
> You have all along been an advocate of passive resistance and non-vio-

lence. Why then did you induce people to take part in a war the merits of which they knew not, and for the aggrandizement of a race so miserably wallowing in the mire of imperialism? (CWMG 21, #190, p. 437)

In response, Gandhi stated:

Not only did I offer my services at the time of the Zulu revolt but before that at the time of the Boer War, and not only did I raise recruits in India during the late War, but I raised an ambulance corps in 1914 in London. If therefore I have sinned, the cup of my sins is full to the brim. I lost no occasion of serving the Government at all times. Two questions presented themselves to me during all those crises. What was my duty as a citizen of the empire as I then believed myself to be, and what was my duty as an out and out believer in the religion of ahimsa—non-violence?

I know now, that I was wrong in thinking that I was a citizen of the empire. But on those four occasions I did honestly believe that in spite of the many disabilities that my country was labouring under, it was making its way towards freedom, and that on the whole the Government from the popular standpoint was not wholly bad and that the British administrators were honest though insular and dense. Holding that view, I set about doing what an ordinary Englishman would do in the circumstances. I was not wise or important enough to take independent action. I had no business to judge or scrutinize ministerial decisions with the solemnity of a tribunal. I did not impute malice to the ministers either at the time of the Boer War, the Zulu revolt or the late War. I did not consider Englishmen nor do I now consider them as particularly bad or worse than other human beings. I considered and still consider them to be as capable of high motives and actions as any other body of men and equally capable of making mistakes. I therefore felt, that I sufficiently discharged my duty as a man and a citizen by offering my humble services to the empire in the hour of its need whether local or general. That is how I would expect every Indian to act by his country under swaraj. I would be deeply distressed, if on every conceivable occasion every one of us were to be a law unto oneself and to scrutinize in golden scales every action of our future national assembly. I would surrender my judgment in most matters to national representatives, taking particular care in making my choice of such representatives. I know that in no other manner would a democratic government be possible for one single day.

The whole situation is now changed for me. My eyes, I fancy, are opened. Experience has made me wiser. I consider the existing system of Government to be wholly bad and requiring special national effort to end or mend it. It does not possess within itself any capacity for self-improvement. . . . (CWMG 21, #190, p. 438)

Here we learn another new justification why Gandhi participated in the Zulu rebellion: He considered himself "a citizen of the empire" and he discharged his duty as a man and as a citizen by offering his humble services to the empire in the hour of its need. He says he copied the ordinary British—what "an ordinary

Englishman would do in the circumstances." Here in this reply, Gandhi did not apologize, nor did he tell the correspondent what his job was during those wars.

Gandhi was arrested, charged, detained, and convicted of sedition on March 18, 1922. In his long statement delivered in the courtroom, Gandhi mentioned his war services: "Similarly, in 1906, at the time of the Zulu revolt, I raised a stretcher-bearer party and served till the end of the rebellion" (CWMG 23, #57, p. 115). Again, the statement was neither an apology nor remorse of his past actions.

While in prison but before his trial, Gandhi agreed to an interview with the British newspaper the *Manchester Guardian*. This interview is worth reading, especially that portion with reference to South Africa:

> Question: What is your definition of this commonwealth to which India shall belong, what is to be its structure?
>
> Answer (by Gandhi): It is to be a fellowship of free nations joined together by "silver cords of love." Such a fellowship already exists for many parts of the Empire. Look at South Africa, what fine fellows they are there! Australia—fine fellows! And New Zealand—splendid land and fine people! I would have India enter freely into such a fellowship and with the same rights of equality for Indians as for other members of the commonwealth. (CWMG 23, #55, p. 106)

One can forgive Gandhi for not having seen Australia or New Zealand. But what about South Africa? Fine fellows! What about black people? Seven years had passed since Gandhi had landed in India and now behind the prison walls he still shows no concern for blacks whatsoever. Rather, their apartheid persecutors (the white ruling minority) are portrayed as "fine fellows."

After serving only two years of his six-year sentence, Gandhi was released in February 1924 on the grounds of poor health. In March 1924, *Stead's Review* interviewed him on a number of issues. To one particular question, Gandhi answered: "But our greatest grievance against the English is that they have steadily impoverished India. If Englishmen living in India became loyal, useful citizens of this country, as they became in Australia or South Africa, I should welcome them as my brothers" (CWMG 23, £144, pp. 240–41). Again, there is no reference to the plight of black people in South Africa. blacks are simply not part of the equation! Although Gandhi continues to represent himself as an ardent supporter of the "Imperial brotherhood" belief, in reality, there have already been perceptible changes in him. His support for "Imperial brotherhood" has given way to a dangerous new doctrine—"Hindu Imperialism."

Something else also came to pass while Gandhi was in prison. He decided to write an autobiographical account of his life in two volumes: *Satyagraha in South Africa*, and *An Autobiography, or The Story of My Experiments with Truth*. At this stage of the game, what was the urgency for two autobiographical accounts? I have already shown in preceding chapters how inadequate these accounts are;

they are essentially deceptive in character and should be called more appropriately the "pseudohistorical accounts of Gandhi." What purpose did this pseudohistory serve for Gandhi? We know that pseudohistory—rewriting the past for present personal or political purposes—takes many forms. There were many compelling factors for him: (1) His name was being associated with Jesus Christ and gaining ground; (2) The pacifists in the West were beginning to take serious note of him; (3) He was the Hindu avatar at home; (4) He was fighting a remarkable war— "nonviolently"—against the British Empire to bring freedom to his people and his country; and (5) his public-spirited ventures. The immense publicity and popularity that Gandhi enjoyed could all come to a halt if his past activities in South Africa ever surfaced. For Gandhi, the only safeguard was to rewrite his past to fit present and, hopefully, future needs. His prestige, his holiness, his aspirations, and his leadership made it possible for him to reconstruct his past. It took a few painstaking years to accomplish this feat but no one suspected.

The gamble paid off. Why? It is a common characteristic of human nature to have a fascination with the strange and the fantastic. And Gandhi's autobiography was certainly that. When it came to the Zulu rebellion of 1906, Gandhi provided a fantastic and strange motive—*he joined the army in South Africa for humanitarian reasons, to aid the black casualties belonging to the enemy side!* An example of his strange bent is the fact that Gandhi candidly explored his sexual life and other private matters for the readers. Amazingly, the autobiography had quite an effect in both the East and the West, as if a holy doctor had filled a soothing prescription for his followers' spiritual emptiness. Once the autobiographical accounts hit the market, the cover-up was in place and well-orchestrated, relentless propaganda ensured its permanent success. From here on, Gandhi no longer had to justify his war efforts against blacks or his other racist activities. Now there was a straight, beautiful answer—humanitarian purposes. Gandhi apologists and scholars tiptoed themselves into highlighting the "humanitarian" mirage-inspired publicity. Arun Gandhi, Mahatma Gandhi's grandson, embellished the new story: "At home one night, when the dinner table talk turned to a discussion of the Zulu hostilities, Mohandas spoke of his concern about political implications, his misgivings about the military tactics. Listening to her husband, Kasturba did not fully comprehend all the issues involved. But she quickly discerned the nature of his quandary. 'I think you should go and help with the wounded' she said. Mohandas was surprised because Kasturba had expressed the thoughts as if she knew what he was about to say."[2] Mrs. Gandhi becomes an affiliate to the "humanitarian cause." The new Gandhi was comfortably seated and no one could dislodge him.

Now, with the umbrella of pseudohistory and the new image in place, we need to revisit our original question: Did Gandhi apologize to blacks? The question is no longer valid. How do you apologize to someone for having provided humanitarian aid? Gandhi had done nothing to apologize for! From this period forward, all hopes for an apology were forever dashed.

Before March 1, 1929, Gandhi allowed an interview with three unnamed foreign visitors described only as a "fair female British Labour Imperialist," a "fair American female" and a "male highly educated Negro from South Africa." The individual from South Africa related to Gandhi his pain at the apathy of educated Negroes toward their own race, an all-too-familiar dilemma that blacks still face in our society. "They become altogether like aliens, they are lost to the race. . . . We are crushed, trampled upon and oppressed. We do not know which way to turn. The bulk of us are ignorant. The daughter of ignorance is poverty. The two processes go hand in hand and move in a vicious circle. Then there is the outside force, pitiless and unrelenting like a blind force of Nature without any possibility of reprieve or appeal. We feel stricken and overwhelmed. Instinctively we turn to India for a message of hope and deliverance, for we believe that India has a mission to fulfil with regard to all the oppressed races of the world" (CWMG 40, #62, p. 63). Since he needed a "message of hope and deliverance," I am not sure that he was satisfied with Gandhi's "wisdom of hope" answer:

I had occasion to discuss this subject with the natives [Negroes] while I was in South Africa. I told them that they had got to help themselves and always to work in the hope that help would come to them from somewhere when the hour for it arrived. In the meantime they had to prepare themselves for it by a process of self-purification. (CWMG 40, #62, p. 63)

This statement seems somewhat mysterious. It sounds almost religious, somewhat difficult to interpret without more information. I have not been able to locate any evidence that Gandhi discussed "this subject" with blacks while he lived in South Africa. It was well known that Gandhi would say whatever that suited his purpose. He used lies in a matter-of-fact manner, never expecting to be held accountable. So we should not be surprised when these falsehoods are brought to light. It was his style of doing business. The new Gandhi image gave birth to another phenomenon I call the "True Believer Syndrome," described here by the famous skeptic James Randi:

A man with a conviction is a hard man to change. Tell him you disagree and he turns away. Show him facts or figures and he questions your sources. Appeal to logic and he fails to see your point. We have all experienced the futility of trying to change a strong conviction, especially if the convinced person has some investment in his belief. We are familiar with the variety of ingenious defenses with which people protect their convictions, managing to keep them unscathed through the most devastating attacks. But man's resourcefulness goes beyond simply protecting a belief. Suppose an individual believes something with his whole heart; suppose further that he has a commitment to this belief, that he has taken irrevocable actions because of it; finally, suppose that he is presented with evidence, unequivocal and undeniable evidence, that his belief is wrong: what will happen? The individual will frequently emerge, not only unshaken, but even more convinced of the truth of his beliefs than ever before. Indeed, he may even show a new fervor about convincing and converting other people to his view.[3]

Reverend Holmes suffered from the "True Believer Syndrome" in regard to Gandhi. A large number of influential and popular American blacks were attracted and then converted through his appeals and propaganda. "Gandhi witnessing" spread like wildfire. Someone's dream was being realized. Whether it was Rev. Holmes's, or Gandhi's, or both, it isn't hard to pinpoint. The fervor of conversion intensified with each new convert, and each one revalidated the new image, adding to its credibility. However, sincerity in following Gandhi was never a substitute for the truth.

NOTES

1. K. Gopalaswami, *Gandhi and Bombay* (Bombay: Bharatiya Vidya Bhavan, 1969), p. 107.
2. Arun & Sunanda Gandhi, *The Forgotten Woman: The Untold Story of Kasturba Gandhi, Wife of Mahatma Gandhi* (Huntsville, Ark.: Ozark Mountain Publishers, 1998), p. 134.
3. James Randi, *The Mask of Nostradamus* (New York: Charles Scribner's Sons, 1990), pp. 97–98.
Special Note: In 1932, as recorded in CWMG 50, #315, p. 326, Gandhi provides another new "sense of justification" when he says that on the battlefield in 1906 his "inner voice"—which he equated with God—spoke to him and that event transformed him.

22

These Negroes [of South Africa] are supposed to have been the descendants of some of the slaves in America who managed to escape from their cruel bondage and migrated to Africa.

—Mahatma Gandhi
Satyagraha in South Africa

Well, if it comes true it may be through the Negroes that the unadulterated message of non-violence will be delivered to the world.

—Mahatma Gandhi
Harijan (March 14, 1936)

The macho Gandhi was dead; the new Gandhi was alive and well. This new image generated support for him in the West and at home. In spite of the fact that two Satyagrahas had been tried and failed miserably, subsequently leading to his conviction, his popularity grew in the West, especially among churchgoers. The two autobiographical accounts were already published, and there was another large and vulnerable audience—the blacks of America—who needed to be courted, not by Gandhi himself but by his white American followers. The stage was set for the following African American church leaders, many with a Howard University connection to visit India at different times to meet Gandhi in person: Dr. Howard Thurman, Sue Bailey Thurman, Reverend Edward Carroll, Benjamin

E. Mays, Channing H. Tobias, and William Stuart Nelson. None of these leaders had a deep understanding of Hinduism, British India, or the complexities of Gandhi's convoluted, multilayered Hindu mind. To be more exact, these leaders had not achieved parity with Gandhi. That may not have even mattered to them. For purposes of analysis, we will discuss first Howard Thurman, Channing Tobias, and Benjamin Mays before moving on to William Stuart Nelson.

To understand how and why these black leaders got caught up in the Gandhi euphoria, it is imperative that we briefly review a rapid succession of events, which in my opinion had a significant impact on these black leaders. I have no doubt that they accepted Gandhi without doing their homework, just like their white counterparts. The following events, in addition to the published news reports (mostly outright disinformation) under the watchful eye of W. E. B. Du Bois in the *Crisis* from the early 1920s, were instrumental for the African American acceptance of the new Gandhi:

In the interview with three unnamed foreign visitors (see p. 287), Gandhi was asked: "[I]s the plight of the untouchable as hard as that of the Negro in America?" Gandhi responded with a bluff:

> There can be no true comparison between the two. They are dissimilar. Depressed and oppressed as the untouchable is in his own land there is no legal discrimination in force against him as it is in the case of the Negro in America. Then, though our orthodoxy sometimes betrays a hardness of heart that cannot but cause deep anguish to a humanitarian, the superstitious prejudice against the untouchable never breaks out into such savage fury as it does sometimes in America against the Negro. The lynching of the Negro is not an uncommon occurrence in America. But in India such things are impossible because of our tradition of non-violence. Not only that, the humanitarian sentiment in India has so far prevailed against caste prejudice as to result even in the canonization of individual untouchables. We have several untouchable saints. I wonder whether you have any Negro saints among you. The prejudice against untouchability is fast wearing out. I wish somebody could assure me that the tide of colour prejudice had spent itself in America. (CWMG 40, #62, pp. 62–63)

C. F. Andrews, a well-known white disciple of Gandhi's, landed in the United States in January 1929 after a long journey. In late February, he visited Booker T. Washington's great institute of Negro education at Tuskegee in Alabama, where he spent ten days. While there, he apprised the students and faculty of the wisdom of the East as represented by the Hindu prophets, including Mahatma Gandhi. The *Tuskegee Messenger*, on March 9, 1929, reported a brief account of the visit:

> Tuskegee has had a messenger from the East. His spirit was a spirit of simplicity, of repose, of reflection and peace. He had a message, a plain unadorned story of the two greatest spirits in the world today, Tagore and Gandhi. Always

there was the note of India's aspiration, of the self-denial of its leaders, and of the unity of their cause with the upward striving of all suppressed groups. He desired to establish bonds between Tuskegee in America and Santiniketan in India, which are dedicated in the same spirit to the same cause of emancipation.

He was no recluse. He did not seem of another world; he was curiously practical. But as he lingered among us his face continuously reflected the joy of his inward spirit. One of the boys said it was just like Jesus himself talking to us.[1]

Andrews's letter to Gandhi dated March 8, 1929, was penetrating and timed well for the occasion: "The hearts of those Negroes there in Tuskegee are with you in every way that is indescribably real and deep. . . . It is a real ashram, both of prayer and work."[2]

The *Crisis*, the official publication of the National Association for the Advancement of Colored People (NAACP), published in the July 1929 issue a typewritten note, dated May 1 and supposedly from Gandhi. It bore the heading, "To the American Negro: A Message from Mahatma Gandhi."

> Let not the 12 million Negroes be ashamed of the fact that they are the grand children of the slaves. There is no dishonour in being slaves. There is dishonour in being slave-owners. But let us not think of honour or dishonour in connection with the past. Let us realise that the future is with those who would be truthful, pure and loving. For, as the old wise men have said, truth ever is, untruth never was. Love alone binds and truth and love accrue only to the truly humble.[3]

Mrs. Sarojini Naidu, one of Gandhi's principal lieutenants, arrived in New York in October 1928. By the time she returned to India in July 1929, she had traveled the length and breadth of America. In one of her letters to Gandhi, she mentioned she had planned to visit Howard University in Washington, D.C. At least one report says she did and met black students and professors.[4] With her known eloquence, it is logical and reasonable to assume that she impressed them talking about her holy master, Gandhi.

Beginning in March 1930, Gandhi began his third and the last nationwide Satyagraha campaign, often known as the Salt March to the seaport of Dandi to symbolically break the salt tax law. This march evoked images of Jesus among Gandhi's followers, including the ones in the West, blacks not excluded. Thanks to the propaganda machine, this Satyagraha was hailed as a great success. It seemed nobody read the April 9, 1930, *New York Times*, which printed Gandhi's final culmination of Satyagraha's "non-violent" rhetoric:

> Resist the confiscation of the salt from your grasp with all your might until blood is spilled. All women and children should also resist interference. Let us see whether the police dare to touch our women. If they do, and if the sons and daughters of India are not so emasculated as to take such an insult lying down, the whole country will be ablaze.[5]

If Gandhi lovers in the West (American blacks included) could read this without a sense of alarm, they were afflicted with "True Believer Syndrome." By all available accounts, this third Satyagraha was as much a failure as the first and second. The British out-maneuvered Gandhi and the Indian masses were not interested—they had had enough of him. This was too much for Gandhi to bear and he resorted to another brainchild of Satyagraha: "wife-beating syndrome." Following an interview Gandhi had with Negley Farson of the *Chicago Daily News*, the correspondent reported:

> Gandhi had his eye on the British House of Commons, and on the face of American public opinion; both of which he was trying to horrify. That was where he thought he might win his fight. He longed to hold the British up as wife-beaters before a shocked world. The spirituality of his civil disobedience movement rested upon a masochistic base.[6]

Gandhi could control the emotional excitement of a few thousand people and dextrously impel them to tear down the law (salt tax law, for example) while maintaining order. In this case, the innocent, emotionally driven Indians turned themselves into Gandhi puppets, provoking law enforcement to beat them, just as if a husband was mercilessly beating his virtuous wife. Besides playing such diabolical games, there is evidence that Gandhi exploited the horror of this spectacle among his audience in the West. So, when Gandhi lovers talked about how mean the British were to the peaceful protestors, they didn't realize that the roots of "satyagraha success," as envisioned in their minds in the West, were somehow controlled thousands of miles away in India under Gandhi's influence.

Time magazine carried Gandhi's white-robed portrait on the cover of its first issue in 1931 as its choice for Man of the Year. *Time*'s choice fell on Gandhi "for Mr. Gandhi, for the Mahatma, for St. Gandhi, for jailbird Gandhi's . . . 1930 mark on world history will understandably loom longest of all."[7]

In a well-publicized and emotionally charged atmosphere, Reverend John H. Holmes, in 1932, presented to Mahatma Gandhi, in absentia, the prestigious Community Church Medal, in recognition of his "distinguished religious service." This medal had a biblical declaration inscribed on one side: "They that turn many to righteousness shall shine as the stars for ever and ever," while its other side was inscribed, "Religion is conscience in action."[8]

The *Christian Century* recommended that the 1933 Nobel Peace Prize be awarded to Mahatma in keeping with the founder's aim of honoring "bold dreamers and prophetic spirits whose ideas are too far ahead of their time. . . ."[9]

Madeleine Slade (1892–1982), Gandhi's close disciple, visited Howard University in Washington, D.C., in October 1934. She addressed the faculty and student body and had a profound spiritual impact. No doubt she made Gandhi look good. The audience felt her presentation must be true because she was a white woman, the daughter of a distinguished British admiral, and a member of the

British ruling class. She had embraced Gandhi (spiritually speaking) after reading Romain Rolland's *Mahatma Gandhi*. Rolland himself had envisioned Gandhi as "another *Christ*." Another one of Gandhi's adherents in all likelihood had an impact on Reverend Howard Thurman. Murial Lester was a white British member of the pacifist International Fellowship of Reconciliation. He met her on the West Coast of the United States. Apparently, she had lived at Gandhi's ashram for a month in 1926 and thereafter promoted herself as his faithful spokesperson in the West. Howard University in the 1930s was an excellent place for Gandhi propaganda to take root among black people. Mordecai Johnson, the university's dynamic preacher-president, declared in March 1930: "Gandhi is conducting today the most significant religious movement in the world, in his endeavor to inject religion into questions of economics and politics."[10]

It's easy to see the dynamics of these events, some behind the scenes, that finally convinced black leaders to visit India. Keep in mind that blacks at that time lived in a segregated America and, to them, Gandhi was a "symbol of hope." Also, they were being bombarded with another of Gandhi's bold and compassionate campaigns, fighting for the welfare of India's Untouchables—a group of people treated as social lepers within Hindu society. The blacks had no means to evaluate the Gandhi story. They simply accepted what they heard, which sounded good to those who were discriminated against. There was another motivating factor for some of these black preacher-leaders: they harbored a vision of evangelizing India. The primary objective for them to go to India was not to meet Gandhi per se but to explore various avenues for evangelism. In all likelihood, Christianizing "Saint Gandhi" was part of their purpose. Yet this was not to the exclusion of the blacks' hope of fighting racial discrimination in America.

Now the stage was set, so to speak. In September 1935, the African American delegation, comprising Reverend Howard Thurman, Mrs. Sue Bailey Thurman, Reverend Edward G. Carroll, and Mrs. Phenola Carroll, sailed on a "pilgrimage of friendship" as guests of the Student Christian Movement of India, Burma, and Ceylon. On February 21, 1936, the delegation, without Phenola Carroll, met Gandhi in person. The narrative from here on deals only with what transpired between Reverend Thurman and Gandhi in relation to the questions we raised earlier. In his autobiography, Rev. Thurman pointed out something that baffled Gandhi:

> One of things that puzzled him was why the slaves did not become Moslems. "Because," said he, "the Moslem religion is the only religion in the world in which no lines are drawn from within the religious fellowship. Once you are in, you are all the way in. This is not true in Christianity, it isn't true in Buddhism or Hinduism. If you had become Moslem, then even though you were a slave, in the faith you would be equal to your master."[11]

It seems Gandhi would have been satisfied if the American Negroes, while in slavery, had converted to Islam. Moreover, one can draw another relevant implication: Gandhi would advise American blacks to adopt Islam in the post-slavery segregated America. In that case, there is a change in Gandhi. In South Africa, he offered a different recommendation for blacks, which he then related to Bishop Joseph J. Doke in 1909: "When the native [black] peoples have risen sufficiently high in the scale of civilisation to give up savage warfare and use the Christian method of settling dispute, they will be fit to exercise the right to vote in political affairs."[12]

Again, it is quite clear what Gandhi was recommending to the South African blacks: adopt Christian habits, or, in other words, become Christian. Reverend Howard Thurman, however, was no skeptic, did not possess critical knowledge, and had no desire to dig into Gandhi's past. As I have said earlier, Rev. Thurman was more interested in spreading Jesus. So he asked Gandhi, "What do you think is the greatest handicap to Jesus Christ in India?" Gandhi answered: "Christianity as it is practiced, as it has been identified with Western culture, with Western civilization and colonialism. This is the greatest enemy that Jesus Christ has in my country—not Hinduism, or Buddhism, or any of the indigenous religions—but Christianity itself."[13] If I am reading this correctly, Gandhi is saying that Christianity itself is the greatest enemy of Jesus Christ! Whether this provoked any outburst from Rev. Thurman, the literature does not say. Why didn't Gandhi recommend Hinduism for Negroes? After all, his love for Hinduism knew no bounds. We learn from Thurman's autobiography that he was well aware of at least one element of Gandhi's past: "Of course, because of his experience in South Africa, Gandhi was acquainted with African people, but he had no opportunity to know African-Americans firsthand."[14] Of all the black leaders who had met Gandhi in person, it seems that Rev. Thurman was the only one privy to Gandhi's past, and regrettably, all too little of it. Here was a once-in-a-lifetime opportunity for him to question Gandhi face to face, to learn of his past association (or nonassociation) with blacks in South Africa. His silence on this subject is conspicuous.

However, in *Collected Works*, Gandhi's secretary recorded that Thurman did ask this question:

Dr. Thurman: But there has been a lot of intermixture of races as for 300 years or more the Negro woman had no control over her body. . . . *Did the South African Negro take any part in your movement?*

Gandhi: No, I purposely did not invite them. It would have endangered their cause. They would not have understood the technique of our struggle nor could they have seen the purpose or utility of non-violence. (CWMG 62, #247, p. 199 [my italics])

This answer is both evasive and untruthful, but Dr. Thurman had no way of knowing it. Let us dig a little deeper to analyze Gandhi's answer.

Gandhi said that he purposely did not invite blacks. This is in his reference to the Satyagraha movement (1906–1913) in South Africa. He never divulged to Rev. Thurman his role against blacks during the Zulu rebellion. Here was an opportunity and perhaps an occasion to apologize and clear his conscience. Then Gandhi lays out the rationale for not inviting blacks: The blacks' cause would have been endangered! What cause? It would have been commendable if Gandhi had said: "My cause would have been endangered!" Had he put aside his racial prejudices against blacks and included them in his Satyagraha movement, the blacks' cause would not have been endangered. Of this I am certain; rather it would have been helped.

Gandhi said that the blacks of South Africa would not have understood his technique, referring to the "technique of non-violence." Also, that blacks had not seen the "purpose or utility of non-violence." Gandhi paints a picture of South African blacks as simple dumb folks. How did Gandhi know that blacks could not understand the technique of non-violence? How dare Gandhi say blacks would not have seen the purpose or utility of non-violence? Let's travel back and let the record speak for itself:

In the chapter "Getting Ready for Satyagraha," Gandhi gave a speech on September 9, 1906, at the Hamidiya Islamic Society in Johannesburg, in which he mentioned the half-castes and the Kaffirs (see page 190). Gandhi was clearly giving the impression to the caste-minded Indians that these "less advanced" people were already practicing Satyagraha. And they were effective! Or, Gandhi was saying that if these "less advanced blacks" can practice Satyagraha, then why not the caste Indians!

Shula Marks, in *Reluctant Rebellion: The 1906–8 Disturbances in Natal,* has examined the subject matter and classified the black struggle in question in three phases: Phase 1: Passive Resistance and Martial Law; Phase 2: With Bambatha in Nkandla; and Phase 3: The Uprising in Mapumulo. It is clearly shown that during Phase 1 the black people were well ahead of Gandhi in their own Satyagraha campaign.[15]

In November 1936, another African American delegation, which included Reverend Benjamin E. Mays and Dr. Channing H. Tobias, sailed to India to attend the World Conference of the Young Men's Christian Association (YMCA). In January 1937, they met with Gandhi for a total of ninety minutes. The narrative of this visit deals first with what transpired between Reverend Mays and Gandhi and then with Dr. Tobias. In reference to the questions we had raised in the beginning of part 5, we learn almost nothing. However, Dr. Mays, to his credit, questioned Gandhi about his publicly stated position of approving the caste system while at the same time attacking the practice of Untouchability. Based upon Gandhi's answers, Dr. Mays noted in his autobiography:

Mahatma Gandhi made it clear to me that he was not fundamentally against caste. He believed in caste. He described it as an economic necessity. To him there was no "lower" caste. Caste was a division of labor. Society must have priests and teachers, politicians, warriors, merchants, and farmers. Someone must do the ordinary work. For the most part, it is a good thing for sons to follow in the footsteps of their fathers, for there are no inferior and no superior castes. He said he condemned caste as it was practiced and that he himself recognized no caste in his evaluation of people. Certainly Gandhi condemned the hard, rigid lines that had developed among the various castes in India, whereby one caste had no social concern for anyone outside its own group. Essentially, however, Mahatma Gandhi thought that caste was not an evil in itself. Caste does give status, he believed, but the untouchable had no status and no rights which any caste man was bound to respect. All caste men could with impunity step on and spit upon the untouchable. So Gandhi had cast his lot with the man farthest down, the untouchable.[16]

As far as what transpired between Dr. Channing H. Tobias and Gandhi, the only description available is in *Collected Works*, which is as follows:

Dr. Tobias: Your doctrine of non-violence has profoundly influenced my life. Do you believe in it as strongly as ever?

Gandhi: I do indeed. My faith in it is growing.

Tobias: Negroes in the U.S.A.—12 million—are struggling to obtain such fundamental rights as freedom from mob violence, unrestricted use of the ballot, freedom from segregation, etc. Have you, out of your struggle in India, a word of advice and encouragement to give us?

Gandhi: I had to contend against some such thing, though on a smaller scale, in South Africa. The difficulties are not yet over. All I can say is that there is no other way than the way of non-violence, a way, however, not of the weak and ignorant but of the strong and wise. (CWMG 64, #254, pp. 229–30)

Gandhi completely sidestepped the question. Gandhi did not address at all the race issues of freedom from mob violence, the right to vote, and freedom from segregation. He merely acknowledged the issue—a nonanswer. It was unfortunate that Dr. Tobias had no way of knowing the truth of Gandhi's activities in South Africa against blacks. From India, Tobias sent a brief account to the black-owned paper *Chicago Defender*, which published the report on March 6, 1937:

Mahatma Gandhi is still the proponent of the philosophy of non-violence, believing that if caste and religious lines are modified to the extent that political unity is realized, and the masses are taught to develop simple home industries for sustenance, political freedom can be won without bloodshed. . . . Regardless of the fact that he has for the past two years taken no active part in politics, Gandhi is still the idol of the masses of India. He is now living in an ashram or hut in a village of outcasts in order to set the example for high caste Indians to abolish caste.[17]

Here is an interesting contradiction: Dr. Benjamin E. Mays had reported that Gandhi "believed in caste," and Dr. Tobias reported that Gandhi wanted to "abolish caste." This discrepancy is all the more puzzling, considering that these African American leaders met Gandhi together! Perhaps it shows that comprehending the elusive Gandhi was no easy task. However, a more troubling question is: Why, of all the black leaders who traveled to India to meet Gandhi in person, did not a single one care enough to meet Dr. B. R. Ambedkar, who at the time was the undisputed leader of India's Untouchables. He was a well-known figure and was reported about in the print media, including the publication *Crisis*. Perhaps the Christian channels had charted out their itinerary. I also believe that by this point they were afflicted with "True Believer Syndrome," and any encounter with Dr. Ambedkar would have caused untold damage to Gandhi's religious and political causes. In addition, the prospect of Gandhi's image being tarnished was not likely to fit in with their future plans for evangelizing India. The situation of Dr. William Stuart Nelson, at the time dean and vice president of Howard University, is hardly encouraging. He, along with three other Quaker members of the American Friends Service Committee (AFSC), met Gandhi in January 1947 under surroundings dictated by an ongoing bloodletting in the Bengal region. In the midst of indescribable bloodshed, Gandhi, in his infinite wisdom, decides to sleep naked with young girls to "fortify his spiritual powers" and in the process, unexpectedly, he creates a scandal. In spite of being an eyewitness and conscious of what obviously was so wrong with Gandhi and the terrible surroundings, Dr. Nelson decided to forgo asking any tough questions. As a result, Gandhi's image as a spiritual guide remained intact, on a high pedestal. In a report that Dr. Nelson submitted to the AFSC in March 1947, he wrote about his meeting:

> [Gandhi] has proved one of my very great moments in India. The two hours in his retreat were packed with an inspiration which will abide with me for a very long time. This, I realize, can be accounted for in part by the fact that I was meeting for the first time one of the very great men of the earth. I am equally convinced that the impression which I bore away from the conference derived from the extraordinary spiritual and intellectual qualities which he revealed even in so short a time. A mere glance at the scene was proof sufficient that Mr. Gandhi has a complete mastery over the material demands upon his life. His pure white homespun garment covered but a portion of his body, the food which he ate as we talked with him was simple and of such secondary concern that neither he nor we were distracted by his eating, and the room could scarcely have been plainer. His mind met our problems most directly and constructively and in the light, I felt, of a total view of life which makes easy his answers to most questions.[18]

Regrettably, the church-based black leaders from Howard University were not up to the task of comprehending Gandhi. Not only did they fall for the smoke and mirrors, the chimera of Gandhi, they also gave him great credibility. They apparently were so overwhelmed by their perception of Gandhi that they saw what they wanted to see, in spite of the truth that surrounded them. Rather than calling Gandhi to account for his inconsistencies, they based their evaluation more on emotion than truth. These learned black gentlemen seem to have abanoned their critical faculties and fallen for what appeared to be a pure and humble man, and they accepted him as being at a higher level than they.

MISCELLANEOUS

Continuing with our search for the "transformed" post–South African Gandhi, I reproduce here more relevant information. This occurred after the American blacks under Rev. Thurman and Rev. Mays's leadership had left India.

On January 1, 1939, a Chinese delegation comprised of Tingfang Lew, Y. T. Wu, and P. C. Hua paid a visit to Gandhi to seek his moral advice. They faced a horrible state of affairs brought on by Japanese aggression. One of these Chinese had read Gandhi's *Autobiography* and had taken the trouble to translate it into Chinese. In response to their appeal, Gandhi mentioned the conflicts in which he had participated, including the Zulu rebellion. Gandhi's emphasis has changed since his 1906 *Indian Opinion* days:

> I have no sense of remorse. . . . The actual work I was called upon to do was purely humanitarian, especially during the Zulu revolt. . . . I and my companions were privileged to nurse the wounded Zulus back to life. It is reasonable to suggest that but for our services some of them would have died. . . . I cite it to show that I came through that experience with greater non-violence and with richer love for the great Zulu race. And I had an insight into what war by white men against coloured races meant. (CWMG 68, #310, p. 269)

If one is not knowledgeable of the facts on Gandhi's past, one might easily believe his humanitarian talk.

On the same day (January 1, 1939) Reverend S. S. Tema, a black belonging to the D. R. Mission in Johannesburg, came to see Gandhi and asked him for his opinion for a possible united Indian-African nonwhite front in South Africa. When Gandhi replied negatively, Rev. Tema asked about Christianity and the salvation of Africa. Gandhi couldn't have been more blunt:

> Christianity, as it is known and practised today, cannot bring salvation to your people. It is my conviction that those who today call themselves Christians do not know the true message of Jesus. I witnessed some of the horrors that were

perpetrated on the Zulus during the Zulu Rebellion. Because one man, Bambatta, their chief, had refused to pay his tax, the whole race was made to suffer. I was in charge of an ambulance corps. I shall never forget the lacerated backs of Zulus who had received stripes and were brought to us for nursing because no white nurse was prepared to look after them. And yet those who perpetrated all those cruelties called themselves Christians. They were "educated," better dressed than the Zulus, but not their moral superiors. (CWMG 68, #311, pp. 273–74)

Sometime after January 21, 1946, Gandhi held a discussion with black soldiers from West Africa. Gandhi made it clear that he considered India the leader in the struggle for emancipation of all suppressed races, often against superior might. He cautioned these soldiers to renounce their evil habits. He told them that many, perhaps most of the "evils that are at the back of the prejudice against Negroes are the result of nominal Christianity imported from America" (CWMG 83, #12, p. 12).

Gandhi also offered them the spinning wheel as an economic protector from the Western exploiters. Not only that, Gandhi articulated that, had he discovered the spinning wheel while living in South Africa, he would have introduced it to the blacks who were his distant neighbors, adjoining the Phoenix Settlement. Before meeting these soldiers from West Africa, Gandhi gave an interview to Denton J. Brooks Jr., *Chicago Defender*'s war correspondent. Brooks reported that Gandhi had "keen sympathy and understanding of the American Negro's problems." Apparently, Frank Bolden of the National Negro Press Association also accompanied Brooks to the interview.[19] Gandhi's message to them was similar to the one he delivered to the West African soldiers, though it appears quite possible that the African Americans were not to benefit from the spinning wheel.

NOTES

1. Benarsidas Chaturvedi and Marjorie Sykes, *Charles Freer Andrews: A Narrative* (Delhi: Publications Division, Ministry of Information and Broadcasting, Government of India, 1982), pp. 269–70. This work was first published in 1949 in Great Britain. Chaturvedi and Sykes provide an abridged version of the *Tuskegee Messenger*'s observations.

2. Sudarshan Kapur, *Raising Up a Prophet: The African-American Encounter with Gandhi* (Boston: Beacon Press, 1992), p. 75.

3. *The Crisis* 36, no. 7 (July 1929): 225. I did not come across this letter anywhere in *Collected Works*.

4. E. S. Reddy, comp., *The Mahatma and the Poetess* (Mumbai: Bharatiya Vidya Bhavan, 1998), p. 164. Another recommended book is *Sarojini Naidu: Selected Letters 1890s to 1940s*, ed. Makarand Paranjape (New Delhi: Kali for Women, 1996).

5. "Die Before Yielding Is Gandhi's Appeal," *New York Times* April 9, 1930.

6. Negley Farson, *The Way of a Transgressor* (New York: Harcourt, Brace and Company, 1936), p. 559. Also recommended is the chapter titled "Indian Hate Lyric" authored by Farson in *We Cover the World*, ed. Eugene Lyons (New York: Harcourt Brace, 1937).

7. "Foreign News," *Time*, January 5, 1931, pp. 14–15.

8. Haridas T. Muzumdar, *Mahatma Gandhi: A Prophetic Voice* (Ahmedabad: Navajivan Publishing House, 1963), p. 164.

9. "We Nominate Gandhi for Nobel Peace Prize," *Christian Century* 51 (March 14, 1934): 350.

10. Quoted in Kapur, *Raising Up a Prophet*, p. 86.

11. Howard Thurman, *With Head and Heart: The Autobiography of Howard Thurman* (New York: Harcourt Brace Jovanovich, 1979), p. 132. The National YMCA and YWCA International Committee, acting on behalf of the World Christian Federation, initiated this "pilgrimage of friendship." In September 1934, Gandhi had a meeting with Dr. Dodd. The details are not discussed in this book because of their irrelevancy. Earlier, Murial Lester had arranged for a meeting between the Negro group headed by Reverend Thurman and Gandhi. It is difficult to assess whether *That Strange Little Brown Man Gandhi*, published in 1932, had any impact. The late Reverend Edward G. Carroll also confirmed Gandhi's advice to blacks converting to Islam, as recorded in George K. Makechnie, *Howard Thurman: His Enduring Dream* (Boston: Boston University Press, 1988), p. 75.

12. Joseph J. Doke, *M. K. Gandhi: An Indian Patriot in South Africa* (London: Indian Chronicle, 1909), chap. 21.

13. Thurman, *With Head and Heart*, p. 135.

14. Ibid., p. 106.

15. Shula Marks, *Reluctant Rebellion: The 1906–8 Disturbances in Natal* (Oxford: Clarendon Press, 1970).

16. Benjamin E. Mays, *Born to Rebel: An Autobiography by Benjamin E. Mays* (New York: Charles Scribner's Sons, 1971), p. 157.

17. "India Wants National Independence, Says Dr. Channing H. Tobias," *Chicago Defender*, March 6, 1937, p. 24. Cited in Kapur, *Raising Up a Prophet*, p. 99.

18. Kapur, *Raising Up a Prophet*, p. 135. Also recommended is *My Days with Gandhi* by Nirmal Kumar Bose (New Delhi: Orient Longman, 1974).

19. Kapur, *Raising Up a Prophet*, p. 125.

23

MEETING the SOUTH AFRICAN INDIAN DELEGATION

The mantra is: "Do or Die."

—Mahatma Gandhi
August 8, 1942.

After leaving South Africa, Gandhi lived in India for roughly thirty-two years. During this time, there had been a number of Indians from South Africa who came to Gandhi for counsel. Presented below is a small sample to show Gandhi in his true colors.

In February 1939, a South African Indian delegation visited Gandhi. He advised them to stick to the method of Satyagraha and not use the constitutional legislative process (CWMG 68, #427, p. 385).

On April 1, 1946, another South African Indian delegation visited Gandhi to seek his council. Gandhi agreed, "I know, I know. The South Africa of today is not far different from the South Africa that I have known." They discussed the nature of Satyagraha in South Africa. Gandhi was abundantly clear that specifically, he was opposed to "sitting in prohibited seats in trains and railway carriages" as a method of Satyagraha (CWMG 83, #415, p. 352–53). I suppose Gandhi would not have approved of Rosa Parks's action, when she refused to vacate her seat for a white person on December 1, 1955. One member of this delegation asked Gandhi if they should associate with the blacks and form a common, antiwhite front. Gandhi replied, yes, but he emphasized what he thought the character of the perceived joint association ought to be:

229

It means you take them [blacks] under your wing when you have developed that power of non-violence. It will be good, if you fire them with the spirit of non-violence. You will be their saviour. But if you allow yourselves to be over-whelmed and swept off your feet, it will be their and your ruin. . . . On India rests the burden of pointing the way to all the exploited races. . . . I have been trying to fit ourselves for that mission by giving a wider bend to our struggle. . . . (CWMG 83, #415, p. 353)

Here is a "positive" change in Gandhi, less than two years before his assassination. Regrettably, even here, the "positive" change has qualifications: Indians must be in the leadership position and blacks under them.

Another member of the delegation sought direction from Gandhi regarding a dilemma that revolved around the fact that Indians in South Africa sent their children to black schools. Indians contributed nothing in return: blacks were responsible for all educational expenses. In addition, Indians didn't like the name "natives"—meaning blacks—applied to them. Eventually the blacks became resentful of this situation. *Collected Works* neglects recording Gandhi's response to this question.

As to the matter of the leadership of the South African Indians, there was a question about who India should send to organize and lead in South Africa. Gandhi had an eye on his second son, Manilal, to train his children for the task. He hoped "they would go back and settle down in South Africa and serve the Indian community" (CWMG 83, #415, p. 354). The blacks and their future are implied again to be subservient to that of the Indians! Two days before his assassination, on January 28, 1948, from Delhi, Gandhi elaborated in a message to the government of South Africa:

Today I would like to tell you something about South Africa. Anybody can come to India and settle here. He can own land in any part of the country. Nobody can deprive him of his right, although it is true that we segregate Harijans [Untouchables]. But in Africa dark or coloured people have no right even to use certain roads, let alone other rights. I have seen it with my own eyes. That is the reason why our countrymen there are fighting for their just rights. There are other ways of fighting, but the Indians domiciled there have given the name of *satyagraha* to their own way of fighting. The Government does not even allow them to migrate from one town to another, for example, Natal, Transvaal, Hill State, Cape Colony, etc. It requires a passport to go from one place to another. This is very unfortunate. Therefore, some people marched from Natal to Transvaal. I must say that the Government there has been reasonable and courteous in that it has not arrested these men so far. Both Hindus and Muslims are taking part in the march. They live and work in harmony. They will keep on marching until they are arrested. Perhaps later we may have occasion to thank them for their courage. If Indians live there with a sense of responsibility, why should the white men look down upon them? We are also free like them. Therefore, I want to tell the Government of Africa from here that whoever wants to reside at a certain place should be allowed to live there, because he regards it as his own place. I have lived for twenty years in South Africa. Therefore, I regard it as my own country like India.[1]

Even up to two days before his death, Gandhi sees South African blacks as being in need of a leader, a master if you will, which he will gladly provide out of compassion and humanitarian interest.

In this part we raised the interesting question of whether Gandhi's attitude toward blacks changed while he was in India from 1915 to 1948. The apparent good news is yes; the bad news is, the change wasn't for good at all. Briefly, we can roughly tally the following changes: He came to be called Mahatma; he turned into a macho Gandhi in support of World War I; when the opportunity came, he transformed himself into the *new Gandhi*; He changed from loyally pro-British to fiercely anti-British; he turned anti-colonial, converting his "Imperial brotherhood" concept to a "Hindu imperialism" ideology; he became opposed to Western civilization; while turning pro-Islamic, he definitely shifted to anti-Christianity; from a shadowy background, he became world famous, referred to as the Hindu avatar and the new Christ. Above all, he never apologized to the blacks. He remained steadfastly antiblack!

Moreover, there is always that nagging issue of the caste system. What was Gandhi's relationship to this entrenched system? Did he instigate any change in that direction? A cursory examination tempts one to say that Gandhi appears to have made a positive change. However, before rendering a final verdict on this matter, it is important to study what caste is, and also the ways Gandhi wanted the modifications to be brought about—a "novel" method of organization based upon not caste but *varna*.

NOTE

1. Manuben Gandhi, *Last Glimpses of Bapu* (Delhi: Shiva Lal Agarwala, 1962), pp. 276–77.

PART 6

GANDHI and the
BLACK PEOPLE of INDIA

Hinduism is not a religion.

—Mahatma Gandhi
A Week with Gandhi

24

CASTE:
HINDUISM'S MOST DANGEROUS MYTH

Untouchabilty is as integral a part of the Hindu faith as anti-Semitism of the Nazi.

—Beverley Nichols
Verdict on India

I remember when Mrs. King and I were in India, we journeyed down one afternoon to the southernmost part of India, the state of Kerala, the city of Trivandrum. That afternoon I was to speak in one of the schools, what we would call high schools in our country, and it was a school attended by and large by students who were the children of former untouchables. . . . The principal introduced me and then as he came to the conclusion of his introduction, he says, "Young people, I would like to present to you a fellow untouchable from the United States of America." And for a moment I was a bit shocked and peeved that I would be referred to as an untouchable. . . . I started thinking about the fact: twenty million of my brothers and sisters were still smothering in an airtight cage of poverty in an affluent society. I started thinking about the fact: these twenty million brothers and sisters were still by and large housed in rat-infested, unendurable slums in the big cities of our nation, still attending inadequate . . . schools faced with improper recreational facilities. And I said to myself, "Yes, I am an untouchable, and every Negro in the United States of America is an untouchable."

—Reverend Martin Luther King Jr.
"Sermon at Ebenezer Baptist Church, July 4, 1965"
The Autobiography of Martin Luther King, Jr.

Hinduism is a vast and complex subject. There are countless ways to approach this topic and yet every explanation falls short. Scholars have devoted innumerable years exploring its corridors and have walked away more flustered than when they started. Take the case of a literary giant, Mark Twain, who, on his visit to India in 1896, took the plunge to learn Hinduism's ABCs. Very soon, recognizing the bottomless pit, he dropped the project. The bafflement Westerners experience in connection with Hinduism springs not just from its tremendous size, but also from concepts that the Western mind has difficulty grasping. Take, for example, Percival Spear's attempt at clarification:

> Hinduism has been likened to a vast sponge, which absorbs all that enters it without ceasing to be itself. The simile is not quite exact, because Hinduism has shown a remarkable power of assimilating as well as absorbing; the water becomes part of the sponge. Like a sponge it has no very clear outline on its borders and no apparent core at its centre. An approach to Hinduism provides a first lesson in the "otherness" of Hindu ideas from those of Europe. The Western love of definition and neat pigeon-holing receives its first shock, and also its first experience of definition by means of negatives. For a while it is not at all clear what Hinduism is, it is clear that it is not many things with which it may be superficially compared.[1]

Definition of Hinduism by means of negatives is striking. No Church! No pope! No bishop! No church council! No one Bible! No history! No beginnings! No ends! Trying to put a score on the number of "Hindu Bibles" is a daunting endeavor. As an example, the field of yoga, which is part of Hinduism, has at least 688 scriptures. Nothing in Hinduism is easy to grasp.

Few scholars have tried to explain the unexplainable by way of its psychic origins pointing the finger to a gross undertaking building a "faith" based on fertile imagination. G. W. F. Hegel, a German scholar, held that "Hindu India had the same characteristics in the spiritual development of man as the mental condition of a man dreaming just before he awakened."[2] Beverley Nichols, a British scholar, pointed out, "Hinduism is almost indefinable, because it is a hotchpotch of almost every fear, dream, and delusion which has ever drifted through the tangled shadowy jungle of man's brains."[3]

Other scholars have used the metaphor of a jungle to explain the mystery of Hinduism. The famous British scholar Sir Charles Eliot said:

> As in the jungle every particle of soil seems to put forth its spirit in vegetable life and plants grown on plants, creepers and parasites on their more stalwart brethren, so in India art, commerce, warfare and crime, every human interest and aspiration seek for a manifestation in religion, and since men and women of all classes and occupations, all stages of education and civilization, have contributed to Hinduism, much of it seems low, foolish and even immoral. The jungle is not a park or garden. Whatever can grow in it, does grow. The Brahmans are not gardeners but forest officers.[4]

A few others have tried to depict Hinduism as a "social disease." One famous scholar went on to express Hinduism as a "contagious disease."[5] Trying to figure out what Hinduism is becomes an endless process. The fact of the matter is, you can overextend your research to "demonstrate" that *it is everything*. Or, you can exhaust yourself and at the end come up with—*it is nothing*. The beauty here is that both are considered accurate. It may drive you insane but to a Hindu it makes sense. A sizable portion of the Hindu "scriptures" is repugnant, only if you set your eyes upon it. My years of scrutinizing Hinduism have convinced me that a profitable angle from which to study and analyze Hinduism is the political angle.

Beverley Nichols experienced a glimpse of this in 1944: "Hinduism in its most extreme and aggressive form is a living and turbulent force. Its voice rises above the roar of the factories and the workshops, it dominates the assemblies of politicians and students."[6] Yet we lack serious, in-depth studies exclusively devoted to Hinduism from a political angle. My intention is not to turn this chapter into such a study, but to furnish you with a taste of the subject's complexity. The New Age movement has grossly and mindlessly oversimplified Hinduism, at the expense of some of the more meaningful components. However, given any approach to Hinduism, there is one thing you will bump into at almost every step: that is, caste—the spinal cord of Hinduism. Just as the vertebrate column holds the human structure straight, similarly the caste provides the fundamental support to the elusive components of Hinduism. Given Hinduism's intangibility, fluidity, and elusiveness, a Hindu can believe in anything or everything. But he must, come what may, believe in the law of caste—the anchor of the Hindu ship. So then, what is caste?

The word "caste," (like "Hindu") is a derivative from a foreign language. It is derived from a Latin term which signifies purity of breed. The Portuguese used this term first. If one is looking for a way to pigeonhole Hindus, caste provides it. The four major caste groupings are: *Brahmins* (or Brahmans)—the scholars and intellectuals, those who pass on ancient wisdom to the next generation; *Kshatriyas*—the warriors, defenders of the realm, kings, and so forth; *Vaisyas*—the merchants, traders, and bankers who keep the wheels of society turning; and *Sudras* or *Shudras*—the serfs who perform the agricultural tasks, and what have you. After centuries of fine-tuning, each caste has sprouted many subcastes. The group relegated to the very bottom of the *Sudra* caste are classified as *Untouchables*—whose sole occupation is to empty lavatories, mend shoes, cremate the dead, etc. The Untouchables are classed as such because, if their shadow crosses your path, you are expected to take off your clothes and throw them away. If they were touched, even accidentally, you must perform more rigorous ablutions to clean yourself. The caste laws are very interesting to say the least, and I recommend the prospective student to read further to acquire the proper caste picture. Even more despised are the totemistic castes—a group of people displaced from the higher castes by long distances. Moreover, castes are hereditary. You are born into your caste and there is no escape. Therefore, the pariahs of Hinduism (the Untouchables) have no choice but to produce more pariahs, contributing their fair share to the Hindu pulullation (its breeding) bank. The original caste designers also laid the foundations to protect the caste hierarchy through the sophisticated mechanism of the caste system. The system in place exhibited the external and the internal pillars designed to cement the myriad of components of Hinduism. The system ensures no revolution from within or without. Today, the Untouchables comprise roughly 20 percent to 25 percent of the total Hindu population and the *Sudra* caste encompasses about 85 percent of that population. In other words, what we have in the Hindu hierarchy is really a system of apartheid.

The next logical question would be: By what mechanism were people separated into their respective castes or subcastes? There should be a simple answer to that question, but there isn't. There have been many theories purporting to explain the phenomenon of caste and Untouchability. The literature abounds with theories such as: religious theory, tribal theory, social theory, occupational theory, division of labor theory, and the crossing theory. The word for caste in the Hindu vocabulary is *varna*, which actually means "color." What is so unique about caste in Hinduism is that it has always been characterized by *whiteness* and *blackness*, and it is the great pride of the highest caste, the Brahmins, that they have preserved their relative whiteness. After a close examination of the Untouchables, it should come as no surprise that they are black or exhibiting more blackness in color. Collectively, and with few regional exceptions, they are the black people of India. By what process did they end up at the bottom of the Hindu scale? The answer is a simple one, even though there had been attempts by caste Hindus (Gandhi included) to revise history. Many scholars believe that the roots of *varna* are buried in the history of conquest when the physically strong, aggressive Aryan nomads poured into the plains of the Indian subcontinent thousands of years ago:

[Aryans] found [India] occupied by *Adi-Dravidians* and *Dravidians*, a dark-skinned people. . . . Their descendants are the oppressed "low caste" Untouchables of today's India. The Aryans quickly subjugated the natives, . . . and built up another civilisation known as . . . Hindu Civilisation. To perpetuate [their] enslavement . . . Hindu intruders created the diabolical caste system, which excluded the dark-skinned Dravidians from their society and made them serfs. . . . Caste originally was a colour bar in India. . . . Gradually over the centuries it became the foundation of a religiously ordained social fabric for the Hindu people. The four original divisions had multiplied like cancer cells into almost 5,000 sub-castes, 1,836 for the Brahmins alone. Every occupation had its caste, splitting society into a myriad of closed guilds in which a man was condemned by his birth to live, work, marry and die.[7]

It is no coincidence to find similarities between Nazi expressions about the purity of the Aryan race and those expressed by Hindus. We have already read in previous chapters that in South Africa, Gandhi proudly used the term Aryan and the Aryan religion synonymously with Hinduism. Vincent Sheean, one of Gandhi's most famous biographers, has described Swami Vivekananda as one of the "forerunners of Gandhi," not unlike what John the Baptist was to Jesus. Swami Vivekananda was Gandhi's hero. To Hindus, both Swami Vivekananda and Gandhi are prophets of modern Hinduism. Swami Vivekananda's analyses of caste couldn't have been more pointed. A speech he delivered on February 2, 1900, in Pasadena, California, sheds some light on the Aryan Hindu's attitude to darker-skinned races and on the breathtaking convolutions of the swami's Hindu mind:

There is something in caste, so far as it means blood: such a thing as heredity there is, certainly. Now try to [understand]—why do you not mix your blood with the Negroes, the American Indians? Nature will not allow you. Nature does not allow you to mix your blood with them. There is the unconscious working that saves the race. That was the Aryan's caste. Mind you, I do not say that they are not equal to us. They must have the same privileges and advantages, and everything; but we know that if certain races mix up, they become degraded. With all the strict caste of the Aryan and non-Aryan, that wall was thrown down to a certain extent, and hordes of these outlandish races came in with all their queer superstitions and manners and customs. Think of this: not decency enough to wear clothes, eating carrion, etc. But behind him came his fetish, his human sacrifice, his superstition, his diabolism. He kept it behind, [he remained] decent for a few years. After that he brought all [these] things out in front. And that was degrading to the whole race. And then the blood mixed; [intermarriages] took place with all sorts of unmixable races. The race fell down. But, in the long run, it proved good. If you mix with Negroes and American Indians, surely this civilisation will fall down. But hundreds and hundreds years after, out of this mixture will come a gigantic race once more, stronger than ever; but, for the time being, you have to suffer. The Hindus believe—that is a peculiar belief, I think; and I do not know, I have nothing to say to the contrary, I have not found anything to the contrary—they believe there was only one civilised race: the Aryan. Until he gives his blood, no other race can be civilised. No teaching will do. The Aryan gives his blood to a race, and then it becomes civilised. Teaching alone will not do. He would be an example in your country: would you give your blood to the Negro race? Then he would get higher culture.[8]

Once analyzed, caste is nothing less than a euphemism for blood or race. In what manner is that different from Hitler's Aryan Nazism, whose victims were not only the Jews but also the Gypsies and others? In volume 4 of the *Trials of War Criminals before the Nuremberg Military Tribunals*, in a section entitled "The Einsatzgruppen Case," there appears a statement by defendant Otto Ohlendorf worth reproducing:

Mr. Heath: On what basis did you kill gypsies, just because they were gypsies? Why were they a threat to the security of the Wehrmacht?

Ohlendorf: It is the same as for the Jews.
Question: Blood?
Answer: I think I can add up from my own knowledge of European history that the Jews actually during wars regularly carried on espionage service on both sides.

Presiding Judge Musmanno: You were asked about gypsies.
Mr. Heath: I was asking you about gypsies, as the Court points out, and not Jews. I would like to ask you now on what basis you determined that every gypsy found in Russia should be executed because of the danger to the German Wehrmacht?
Answer: There was no difference between gypsies and Jews.[9]

Have no doubt, caste is a system of organized slavery, and Hinduism should be looked upon as a system that sanctions racism.

NOTES

1. Quoted in Ronald Inden, *Imagining India* (Oxford: Basil Blackwell Ltd., 1990), p. 85
2. Ibid., p. 96.
3. Beverley Nichols, *Verdict on India* (New York: Harcourt, Brace and Company, 1944), p. 73.
4. Inden, *Imagining India*, p. 86.
5. Francis Yeats-Brown, *Lancer At Large* (New York: Garden City Publishing, 1939), p. 213.
6. Nichols, *Verdict on India*, p. 72.

7. Fazlul Huq, *Gandhi: Saint or Sinner* (Bangalore, India: Dalit Sahitya Akademy, 1992), p. 67.

8. Swami Vivekananda, *The Complete Works of Swami Vivekananda* (Mayavati: Advaita Ashrama, 1954), vol. 3, pp. 533–34. The Swami and the Mahatma held another date in common. One landed in North America and the other in South Africa in 1893, respectively.

9. Patricia C. Rose, "Don't Forget the Gypsies," *Skeptic* 3, no. 2 (1995): 26.

25

If a man with God's name on his tongue and a sword under his armpit deserved the appellation of a Mahatma, then Mohandas Karamchand Gandhi was a Mahatma!

—B. R. Ambedkar
Gandhi and Gandhism

This chapter is a study of the striking contrasts between Gandhi and Dr. Ambedkar. Given what we know of Hinduism with its core caste system, a simple question should be asked: How do you bring into being ready-made, caste-ridden Hindus? Or, even more specifically, how did Gandhi, a Western-educated lawyer, turn into a fundamentalist Hindu? Can we identify those forces in action working above or below the surface that can transform any decent human being into a racist, caste-conscious person? Similarly, what factors can one born and raised a Hindu turn into a partisan of insubordination and revolt? There is a paucity of research literature into the Hindu psyche. Yet, there is enough background information available to answer why and how Gandhi turned to Hinduism and Dr. Ambedkar away from Hinduism. Before we get to that, we must understand the nature of Hinduism and its close association with power, a term used in politics.

The Earl of Ronaldshay, former governor of Bengal in British India, became a student of the new burgeoning discipline of Hindu spirituality and power politics. I must quote him here at length to provide you with a small, nonrepugnant dose of the kinds of things you encounter in the "Hindu scriptures":

243

The ancient literature of India is strewn with examples of the efficacy of self-mortification as a means of acquiring power. A famous figure who appears in the Vedas, in both the great epics, the Mahabharata and the Ramayana, as also in the Puranas is the hero of a story which may, perhaps, be described as the classic example of this practice. The figure is Visvamitra, a king, and the story is that of a fierce and sustained conflict between him and Vasistha, a Brahman. It can be recalled in a few words. The cupidity of Visvamitra was excited by a "cow of plenty" in the possession of Vasishta, which he determined to acquire. Failing to obtain the animal by force, he abandoned his kingdom and retired to the Himalayas, where he lived the life of an ascetic, subjecting himself to the severest austerities. His earliest reward came in the shape of an armoury of celestial weapons presented to him by the great god Mahadeva. With these he hurried back to the conflict with Vasishta, but was again defeated by the powerful priest and returned to the Himalayas and his self-imposed austerities with a view to acquiring further reserves of soul-force. We need not follow him through the thousand-year periods of self-mortification which he indulged in, obtaining with each successive period greater power, and being offered by the gods steadily increasing rewards. In the end the "cow of plenty," which had been the source of all the trouble, pales into insignificance before the prodigious developments arising out of Visvamitra's sustained practice of intense austerities, and it becomes a question of the continued existence of the universe. The supernatural power acquired by him does, indeed, become a menace to gods and men, so much so that the former proceed to Brahma to lay before him the critical state of affairs with which they find themselves confronted. "The great *muni* Visvamitra," they declare, "has been allured and provoked in various ways, but still advances in his sanctity. If his wish is not conceded, he will destroy the three worlds by the force of his austerity. All the regions of the universe are confounded, no light anywhere shines; all the oceans are tossed, and the mountains crumble, the earth quakes and the wind blows confusedly." The heavenly deputation is successful in impressing Brahma with a sense of the urgency of the matter, and, accompanied by the heavenly host he himself approaches the terrible ascetic and, pronouncing a blessing upon him, hails him as *Brahman-rishi*. Visvamitra the king having thus compelled the gods to grant him the supreme rank of Brahmanhood, desists from the course which through successive millenniums he had been following to the danger of the universe.

It will be seen that, viewed in the light of Indian thought, Mr. Gandhi's doctrine of soul-force, which to many Westerners appeared to be a meaningless fad, becomes not only intelligible, but perfectly natural. There are, indeed, striking points of resemblance between the story of King Visvamitra and that of Mr. Gandhi. The original cause of Visvamitra's campaign was a comparatively small thing, namely, Vasishta's "cow of plenty". Similarly, the original cause of Mr. Gandhi's campaign was a comparatively small thing, namely, a legislative enactment known as the Rowlatt Act. And just as in the former case the "cow of plenty" lost all importance in face of the shattering developments to which Visvamitra's action gave rise, so in the latter case did the Rowlatt Act lose all importance in face of the convulsion which Mr. Gandhi's action produced.[1]

Like Lord Ronaldshay, Nirad C. Chaudhuri also provided another penetrating insight into Hinduism: "that the Hindu spirituality which is truly Hindu, that is, when it is a pursuit of power. . . . Hindu spiritual life became pursuit of power through religion." "Pursuit of power," he explains is of two types: the Way of Knowledge—the *Jnana Marga*, and the Way of Action—the *Karma Marga*. The Way of Knowledge gives the devotee the "capacity to rise above the termination of selfhood, and the destruction of all things outside the self. It is partly a quest of power in a passive manner and that power is sought for the inner life of the devotee." Through the Way of Action, the devotee "acquires the capacity to do things beyond what is within the natural physical and mental powers of man—the capacity to see into the future, read the minds of other men, control physiological processes, disregard the laws of gravitation, etc. Power actually gained through this method is a variant of political power." Hindu renunciation, self-mortification, and asceticism "constitute the method of obtaining more and more power over men and nature and so effective among the Hindus that Mahatma Gandhi felt compelled to bring it into politics."[2] In Hindu social and family life, refusing to take food or exposing oneself to cold or heat is a recognized method of psychological coercion, designed to make relatives, neighbors, creditors, or even doctors yield to one's wishes or demands. Generally, it succeeds. In Gandhi's mind, the distinction between religion and politics was so blurred that he looked at both as a "religious battle."

The Hindu literature is replete with heroes and heroines acquiring Hindu spirituality in pursuit of political power. From that perspective, Gandhi's motives are understandable. We can briefly look at the events in Gandhi's life that turned him into a full-fledged Hindu. His childhood, according to his *Autobiography*, was unremarkable in the sense that he was raised in a typical Hindu fashion. He was born in an orthodox, conservative *Vaisya* caste with *Gandhi* as subcaste following the precept of Vaishnava sect. Early on, the Hinduism seeped in at home, where the Hindu customs were the norm, and outside, through listening and watching various Hindu plays as a part of popular Hinduism. Also, he was exposed to the "Hindu scriptures" of *Ramayana, Bhagavat,* and *Manusmriti.* There is every reason to believe that the Gandhi family believed in and practiced the caste system. One glimpses many years later, in 1921, when Gandhi mentioned a certain Untouchable named Ukha he knew when he was twelve years old—only one time. In England, in 1889, thanks to two Theosophists, Gandhi was introduced to Sir Edwin Arnold's English translation of *"Gita,"* another Hindu text. This was the beginning of intellectual Hinduism for Gandhi. Dressed in Western clothes and with a law degree in hand, Gandhi landed in Durban, South Africa, in 1893. We have already analyzed Gandhi's racist practices against the blacks there. This points to the toll that caste had on his early upbringing. Slowly and steadily Gandhi turned to ascetic Hinduism, while not discarding its other varieties. Keep in mind, he was already practicing political Hinduism, as evidenced by his racial, caste-oriented strategy and tactics. Many people, unaware of Hinduism's intricacies, have a hard time reconciling Gandhi's spiritual life with his multiple war services.

Ascetic Hinduism gave way to commune-style habitat, prayers, fastings, dietary experiments, semen conservations, and other exotic practices. With time, he began to exude Hindu spirituality and it was a predictable progression for him to jump into a bigger political arena. Satyagraha was born. During the Satya-graha years in South Africa, Gandhi experimented with mass conditionings and mass manipulations, using all available avenues at his disposal. His physical out-look mimicked that of a Hindu ascetic. While incarcerated in South Africa, he read more Hindu texts incorporating more databases to intellectual Hinduism. During the last few years of his "South African pilgrimage," his transformation from a Western-trained lawyer to a Hindu *sadhu* was complete. He mastered the art of living off of others. Upon his return to India in 1915, he was bestowed with the title of Mahatma and from then on he was called Mahatma Gandhi.

In India, Gandhi's flip-flopping from religion to politics and vice versa was a norm. He delved further into Hinduism and that brought more changes. He removed his turban, wore a *shikha*, or tuft of hair on top of his head (by which Hindu gods lift all good Hindus to heaven). He began to worship cows, practiced Hindu medicine, and also began an earnest experimentation with bodily waste products. Stories of Gandhi's miracles were widespread and had an impact on the educated and uneducated alike. There was another variety of Hinduism that had been developing for the last century or so, modern Hinduism, and Gandhi was declared one of its prophets. His earlier notion of "imperial brotherhood" was replaced by a new doctrine of "Hindu Imperialism." Naturally, the existing caste system had to be tinkered with to adapt to the newly created Hindu imperialist designs, and the large Untouchable population had to be controlled and outfitted with a "new status and new role." Political novelist Arthur Koestler aptly described Gandhi as a "Yogi and the Commissar"—a perfect blend of Hindu spirituality with power politics.[3]

Dr. B. R. Ambedkar (1891–1956), born and raised as an Untouchable in British India, had an upbringing quite unlike that of Gandhi. He received his early education contrary to the prevailing conditions among the Untouchables. Through the benevolence of a Maharaja, young Ambedkar earned M.A. and Ph.D. degrees from Columbia University. On top of that, he also earned M.Sc. and D.Sc. from the University of London, and Bar-at-Law from Grey's Inn in London before returning to Bombay in 1923. He too, like his community mem-bers, had suffered from caste discriminations. He read the "Hindu scriptures" and was appalled at the contents. In 1927, he publicly burned *Manusmiriti*, one of Hindu's sacred texts, as protest against caste restrictions. But in the early 1920s, he went out of the way to participate in Hindu rituals:

> [Ambedkar] participated in efforts at "Sanskritization" in which Untouchables imitated high caste religious ritual. But he soon found that the performance of

Vedic style weddings, the donning of the sacred thread, and similar efforts to emulate upper caste ritual practice had little effect on the attitudes of others. Such innovations were dropped in the 1930s.[4]

By brainpower and bulldog courage, Dr. Ambedkar lifted himself to the ranks of political eminence and was committed to uplift his Untouchable community and to protect them by all necessary legal means. Early during his public career, he learned the necessity of Untouchables organizing and educating themselves. Ambedkar and Gandhi's political paths crossed in during the late 1920s and 1930s, resulting in a war of words. They both wanted the same turf—leadership status over the Untouchable population. Both were products of Western education, but Gandhi turned toward Hinduism, and Ambedkar opted for the Western ideals of democracy and constitutional safeguards to protect fundamental rights. Though one has been described as the Hindu of Hindus and the other as the Untouchable of Untouchables, the truth of the matter is that their differences truly lay somewhere else. Gandhi and Ambedkar were really like a witch doctor of the worst kind and a well-trained surgeon, respectively. Dr. Ambedkar was well aware of the predicament his Untouchable brethren were in. Apart from being "religiously" ordained, Untouchability is embedded in the Hindu economic order. The results are far worse than any other type of slavery that has existed in human history.

In traditional slavery systems, the owner, as an economic necessity, has the responsibility to feed, clothe, and house slaves and keep them in good condition. But in the Untouchability system, the Hindu takes no responsibility for the Untouchable's maintenance. Moreover, the Hindu economic system permitted unmitigated, uncontrolled exploitation, since there had been no truly independent public opinions and no hindrance from law enforcement officials to counter the Hindus. Beyond economic exploitation, the system perpetuates itself with humiliations of the worst kind, and controlling the Untouchables' social outlook with far-reaching psychological and physical damage. In the villages where they live in large numbers, Dr. Ambedkar addressed a few examples that they face on a daily basis: Hindus will not allow Untouchables to share the water from the village well, to enter schools, to travel in buses or in the same railway compartment, to wear clean clothes or jewelry, to put tiles on the roofs of their houses, to own land or keep cattle, or to sit when a Hindu is standing. For Untouchability to go away, Dr. Ambedkar argued that it required Hindus to change their views completely.

To Ambedkar, Hinduism was a great stumbling block, and all his efforts to reform it from within failed. Before his death, this truly great man formally left Hinduism. He died a free man. It had taken him more than thirty years of active struggle to expunge Hinduism, by no means an easy undertaking. In death, he left the Untouchable community a legacy of not submitting to slave status. Today, a few brave Untouchables are leading that fight in the midst of pervasive human rights violations in Hindu India. In my in-depth studies, I couldn't isolate those factors that ignite a born Hindu to rebel against the system. Each individual has to be assessed separately. Ambedkars come neither readymade nor cloned. Similarly, not every caste Hindu will turn into a Gandhi. There are too many variables, subject to change with time, politics, and geography. Gandhi was a product of a variety of Hinduisms and a few alien cultures.

Because of his position, Dr. Ambedkar had a unique insight into Gandhi, especially into what Gandhi was up to when he started to tinker with the caste system. The next chapter replicates what Dr. Ambedkar wrote in 1945, after many years of closely observing the man. I have made slight changes to his text not to alter any meaning but to clarify for the benefit of today's readers. It is dealt with in the context of new terminology—Gandhism—a prescription that our [economic and political professor] Gandhi had charted out the blueprint for the Untouchables. The words caste and class are used interchangeably.

NOTES

1. Earl of Ronaldshay, *The Heart of Aryavarta: A Study of the Psychology of Indian Unrest* (Boston: Houghton Mifflin Company, 1925), pp. 5–7.

2. Nirad C. Chaudhuri, *Hinduism: A Religion to Live By* (Delhi: Oxford University Press, 1996), pp. 316–25.

3. Arthur Koestler, *The Heel of Achilles: Essays 1968–1973* (New York: Random House, 1974), pp. 233–73.

4. Eleanor Zelliot, "Gandhi and Ambedkar—A Study in Leadership," in *The Untouchables in Contemporary India*, ed. J. Michael Mahar (Tuscon: University of Arizona Press, 1972), p. 76.

26

GANDHI'S CASTE IDEOLOGY

Pretty soon we discovered that these people were the untouchables. This caste system had existed for years. . . . Gandhi looked at this system and couldn't stand it. . . . He looked at his people and said, "Now you have selected me, you've asked me to free you from the political domination and the economic exploitation inflicted upon you by Britain, and here you are, trampling over and exploiting seventy million of your brothers." And he decided that he would not ever adjust to that system, and that he would speak against it and stand up against it the rest of his life.

—Rev. Martin Luther King Jr.
The Autobiography of Martin Luther King, Jr.

Allow me to start with Mr. Gandhi's teachings on the social problem. Mr. Gandhi's views on the caste system—which constitutes the main social problem in India—were fully elaborated by him in 1921–22 in a Gujarati journal called *Navajivan*. The article is written in Gujarati language. I give below an English translation of his views as near as possible in his own words. Says Mr. Gandhi:

This chapter adapted from B. R. Ambedkar, *What Congress and Gandhi Have Done to the Untouchables*, 2d ed. (Bombay: Thacker & Co., Ltd., 1946), pp. 275–97.

249

(1) I believe that if Hindu Society has been able to stand, it is because it is founded on the caste system.

(2) The seeds of *Swaraj* are to be founded in the caste system. Different castes are like different sections of military division. Each division is working for the good of the whole. . . .

(3) A community, which can create the caste system, must be said to possess unique power of organization.

(4) Caste has a ready-made means for spreading primary education. Each caste can take the responsibility for the education of the children of the caste. Caste has a political basis. It can work as an electorate for a representative body. Caste can perform judicial functions by electing persons to act as judges to decide disputes among members of the same caste. With castes it is easy to raise a defense force by requiring each caste to raise a brigade.

(5) I believe that interdining or intermarriage is not necessary for promoting national unity. That dining together creates friendship is contrary to experience. If this were true there would have been no war in Europe. . . . Taking food is as dirty an act as answering the call of nature. The only difference is that after answering call of nature we get peace while after eating food we get discomfort. Just as we perform the act of answering the call of nature in seclusion so also the act of taking food must also be done in seclusion.

(6) In India children of brothers do not intermarry. Do they cease to love because they do not intermarry? Among the *Vaishnavas* many women are so orthodox that they will not eat with members of the family nor will they drink water from a common water pot. Have they no love? The caste system cannot be said to be bad because it does not allow interdining or intermarriage between different castes.

(7) Caste is another name for control. Caste puts a limit on enjoyment. Caste does not allow a person to transgress caste limits in pursuit of his enjoyment. That is the meaning of such caste restrictions as interdining and intermarriage.

(8) To destroy caste system and adopt Western European social system means that Hindus must give up the principle of hereditary occupation, which is the soul of the caste system. Hereditary principle is an eternal

principle. To change it is to create disorder. I have no use for a *Brahmin* if I cannot call him a *Brahmin* for my life. It will be chaos, if every day a *Brahmin* is to be changed into a *Shudra* and a *Shudra* is to be changed into a *Brahmin*.

(9) The caste system is a natural order of society. In India it has been given a religious coating. Other countries not having understood the utility of the caste system, it existed only in a loose condition and consequently those countries have not derived from caste system the same degree of advantage, which India has derived.

These being my views I am opposed to all those who are out to destroy the caste system.

In 1922, Mr. Gandhi was a defender of the caste system. Pursuing the inquiry, one comes across a somewhat critical view of the caste system by Mr. Gandhi in the year 1925. This is what Mr. Gandhi said on February 3, 1925:

I gave support to caste because it stands for restraint. But at present caste does not mean restraint, it means limitations. Restraint is glorious and helps to achieve freedom. But limitation is like chain. It binds. There is nothing commendable in castes as they exist today. They are contrary to the tenets of the *Shastras*. The number of castes is infinite and there is a bar against intermarriage. This is not a condition of elevation. It is a state of fall.

In reply to the question: What is the way out? Mr. Gandhi said:

The best remedy is that small castes should fuse themselves into one big caste. There should be four big castes so that we may reproduce the old system of four *Varnas*.

In short, in 1925 Mr. Gandhi became an upholder of the *Varna* system.

The old *Varna* system prevalent in ancient India had the society divided into four orders: (1) *Brahmins*, whose occupation was learning; (2) *Kshatriyas*, whose occupation was warfare; (3) *Vaishyas*, whose occupation was trade and (4) *Shudras*, whose occupation was service of the other classes. Is Mr. Gandhi's *Varna* system the same as this old *Varna* system of the orthodox Hindus? Mr. Gandhi explained his *Varna* system in the following terms:

(1) I believe that the divisions into Varna are based on birth.

(2) There is nothing in the *Varna* system, which stands in the way of the *Shudra* acquiring learning or studying military art of offense or defense. Contra it is open to a *Kshatriya* to serve. The *Varna* system is no bar to

him. What the *Varna* system enjoins is that a *Shudra* will not make learning a way of earning a living. Nor will a *Kshatriya* adopt service as a way of earning a living. [Similarly a *Brahmin* may learn the art of war or trade. But he must not make them a way of earning his living. Contra a *Vaishya* may acquire learning or may cultivate the art of war. But he must not make them a way of earning his living.]

(3) The *Varna* system is connected with the way of earning a living. There is no harm if a person belonging to one *Varna* acquires the knowledge or science and art specialized in by persons belonging to other *Varnas*. But as far as the way of earning his living is concerned he must follow the occupation of the *Varna* to which he belongs which means he must follow the hereditary profession of his forefathers.

(4) The object of the *Varna* is to prevent competition and class struggle and class war. I believe in the *Varna* system because it fixes the duties and occupations of persons.

(5) *Varna* means the determination of a man's occupation before he is born.

(6) In the *Varna* system no man has any liberty to choose his occupation. His occupation is determined for him by heredity.

The social life of Gandhism is either caste or *Varna*. Though it may be difficult to say which, there can be no doubt that the social ideal of Gandhism is not democracy. For, whether one takes for comparison caste or *Varna*, both are fundamentally opposed to democracy. . . .

That Mr. Gandhi changed over from the caste system to the *Varna* system does not make the slightest difference to the charge that Gandhism is opposed to democracy. In the first place, the idea of *Varna* is the parent of the idea of caste. If the idea of caste is a pernicious idea it is entirely because of the viciousness of the idea of *Varna*. Both *Varna* and caste are evil ideas; it matters very little whether one believes in one or the other.

Turning to the field of economic life, Mr. Gandhi stands for two ideals:

One of these is the opposition to machinery. As early as 1921 Mr. Gandhi gave vent to his dislike for machinery. Writing in the *Young India* of January 19, 1921, Mr. Gandhi said:

Do I want to put back the hand of clock of progress? Do I want to replace the mills by hand-spinning and hand-weaving? Do I want to replace the railway by the country-cart? Do I want to destroy machinery altogether? These questions have been asked by some journalists and public men. My answer is: I would not weep over the disappearance of machinery or consider it a calamity.

His opposition to machinery is well evident by his idolization of *charkha* (the spinning wheel) and by insistence upon hand spinning and hand weaving. His opposition to machinery and his love for *charkha* are not matter of accident. It is a matter of philosophy. This philosophy Mr. Gandhi took special occasion to propound in his presidential address at the Kathiawad Political Conference held on January 8, 1925. This is what Mr. Gandhi said:

> Nations are tired of the worship of lifeless machines multiplied *ad infinitum*. We are destroying the matchless living machines viz., our own bodies by leaving them to rust and trying to substitute lifeless machinery for them. It is a law of God that the body must be fully worked and utilized. We dare not ignore it. The spinning wheel is the auspicious symbol of Sharir Yajna——body labor. He who eats his food without offering this sacrifice steals it. By giving up this sacrifice we become traitors to the country and banged the door in the face of the Goddess of Fortune.

Anyone who has read Mr. Gandhi's booklet on *Hind Swaraj* (Indian Home Rule) will know that Mr. Gandhi is against modern civilization. Writing in 1921, Mr. Gandhi said:

> The booklet is a severe condemnation of 'modern civilization.' It was written in 1909. My conviction is deeper today than ever. I feel that, if India would discard 'Modern civilization' she can only gain by doing so.

In Mr. Gandhi's view: "Western civilization is the creation of satan."

The second ideal of Mr. Gandhi is the elimination of class war and even class struggle in the relationships between employers and employees as well as between landlords and tenants. . . . Mr. Gandhi does not wish to hurt the propertied class. He is even opposed to a campaign against them. He has no passion for economic equality. Referring to the propertied class, Mr. Gandhi said quite recently that he does not wish to destroy the hen that lays the golden egg. His solution for the economic conflicts between the owners and the workers, between the rich and the poor, between the employers and the employees and between the landlords and the tenants is very simple. The owners need not deprive themselves of their property. All they need do is to declare themselves trustees for the poor. Of course, the Trust is to be a voluntary one carrying only a spiritual obligation.

Is there anything new in the Gandhian analysis of economic ills? Are the economics of Gandhism sound? What hope does Gandhism hold out to the common man abandoned at the bottom? Does it promise him a better life, a life of joy and culture, a life of freedom, not merely freedom from want but freedom to rise, to grow to the full stature which his capacities can reach?

There is nothing new in the Gandhian analysis of economic ills, in so far as it attributes them to machinery and the civilization that is built upon it. The arguments that machinery and modern civilization help to concentrate management and control into relatively few hands, and with the aid of banking and credit facilitate the transfer into still fewer hands of all materials and factories and mills in which millions are bled white in order to support huge industries thousands of miles away from their cottages, or that machinery and modern civilization cause deaths, maimings and cripplings far in excess of the corresponding injuries by war, and are responsible for disease and physical deterioration caused directly and indirectly by the development of large cities with their smoke, dirt, noise, foul air, lack of sunshine and outdoor life, slums, prostitution and unnatural living which they bring about, are all old and worn-out arguments. There is nothing new in them. Gandhism is merely repeating the views of Rousseau, Ruskin, Tolstoy and their school.

The ideas that make up Gandhism are just primitive. It is a return to nature, to animal life. The only merit is their simplicity. As there is always large corps of simple people who are attracted by them, such simple ideas do not die, and there is always some simpleton to preach them. There is, however, no doubt that the practical instincts of men—which seldom go wrong—have found them unfruitful. . . .

The economics of Gandhism are hopelessly fallacious. The fact that machinery and modern civilization have produced many evils may be admitted. But these evils are no arguments against them. For the evils are not due to machinery and modern civilization. They are due to wrong social organization, which has made private property and pursuit of personal gain, matters of absolute sanctity. If machinery and civilization have not benefited everybody, the remedy is not to condemn machinery and civilization but to alter the organization of society so that the benefits will not be usurped by the few but will accrue to all.

In Gandhism, the common man has no hope. It treats man as an animal and no more. It is true that man shares the constitution and functions of animals, i.e. nutritive, reproductive, etc. But these are not distinctively human functions. The distinctively human function is reason, the purpose of which is to enable man to observe, meditate, cogitate, study and discover the beauties of the Universe and enrich his life and control the animal elements in his life. Man thus occupies the highest place in the scheme of animate existence. If this is true what is the conclusion that follows? The conclusion that follows is that while the ultimate goal of a brute's life is reached once his physical appetites are satisfied. The ultimate goal of man's existence is not reached unless and until he has fully cultivated his mind. In short, what divides the brute from man is culture. Culture is not possible for the brute, but it is essential for man. Therefore, the aim of human society must be to enable every person to lead a life of culture, which means the cultivation of mind as distinguished from the satisfaction of mere physical wants. How can these happen?

Both for society as well as for the individual, there is always a gulf between merely living and living worthily. In order that one may live worthily one must first live. The time and energy spent upon mere life, upon gaining of subsistences detracts from that available for activities of a distinctively human nature and which go to make up a life of culture. How then can a life of culture be made possible? It is not possible unless there is sufficient leisure. For, it is only when there is leisure that a person is free to devote himself to a life of culture. The problem of all problems, which human society has to face, is how to provide leisure to every individual. What does leisure mean? Leisure means the lessening of the toil and effort necessary for satisfying the physical wants of life. How can leisure be made possible? Leisure is quite impossible unless some means are found whereby the toil required for producing goods necessary to satisfy human needs is lessened. What can lessen such toil? Only when machine takes the place of man. There is no other means of producing leisure. Machinery and modern civilization are thus indispensable for emancipating man from leading the life of a brute, and for providing him with leisure and for making a life of culture possible. The man who condemns machinery and modern civilization simply does not understand their purpose and the ultimate aim which human society must strive to achieve.

Gandhism may be well suited to a society, which does not accept democracy as its ideal. A society, which does not believe in democracy, may be indifferent to machinery and the civilization based upon it. But a democratic society cannot. The former may well content itself with a life of leisure and culture for the few and a life of toil and drudgery for the many. But a democratic society must assure a life of leisure and culture to each one of its citizens. If the above analysis is correct then the slogan of a democratic society must be machinery, and more machinery, civilization and more civilization. Under Gandhism, the common man must keep on toiling ceaselessly for a pittance and remain a brute. In short, Gandhism with its call of back to nature means back to nakedness, back to squalor, back to poverty and back to ignorance for the vast mass of the people.

Gandhism insists upon class structure and regards it as a part of society and also the income structure as sacrosanct with the consequent distinctions of rich and poor, high and low, owners and workers, as permanent parts of social organization. From the viewpoint of social consequences, nothing can be more pernicious. . . . It is not enough to say that Gandhism believes in a class structure. Gandhism stands for more than that. A class structure, which is a faded, jejune, effete thing—a mere sentimentality, a mere skeleton, is not what Gandhism wants. It wants class structure to function as a living faith. In this there is nothing to be surprised at. For class structure in Gandhism is not a mere accident, it is its official doctrine.

The idea of trusteeship, which Gandhism proposes as a panacea and by which the rich classes will hold their properties in trust for the poor, is the most ridiculous part of it. All that one can say about it is that, if anybody else had pro-pounded it, the author would have been laughed at as a silly fool. Gandhi knew well the hard realities of life. He was deceiving the servile classes by telling them that a little dose of moral rearmament to the propertied classes—those that by their insatiable cupidity and indomitable arrogance have made and will always make this world a vale of tears for the toiling millions. Accordingly the rich will recondition them to such an extent that they will be able to withstand the temp-tation to misuse the tremendous powers, which the class structure gives them over servile classes. . . .

Mr. Gandhi sometimes speaks on social and economic subjects as though he was blushing Communist. Those who will study Gandhism will not be deceived by the occasional aberrations of Mr. Gandhi in favor of democracy and against capitalism. For, Gandhism is in no sense a revolutionary creed. It is conservatism in *excelsis*. So far as India is concerned, it is a reactionary creed blazoning on its banner the call of Return to Antiquity. Gandhism aims at the resuscitation and reanimating of India's dreadful, dying past.

Gandhism is a paradox. It stands for freedom from foreign domination, which means the destruction of the existing political structure of the country. At the same time, it seeks to maintain intact a social structure that permits the dom-ination of one class by another on a hereditary basis, which means a perpetual domination of one caste by another.

The first special feature of Gandhism is that its philosophy helps those who want to keep what they have and to prevent those who have not from getting what they are entitled to. No one who examines the Gandhian attitude to strikes, the Gandhian reverence for caste and the Gandhian doctrine of Trusteeship by the rich for the benefit of the poor can deny that this is an upshot of Gandhism. Whether this is the calculated result of a deliberate design or by accident, may be open to argument. But the fact remains that Gandhism is the philosophy of the well to do and the leisure class.

The second special feature of Gandhism is to delude people into accepting their misfortunes by presenting them as best of good fortunes as possible. One or two illustrations will suffice to bring out the truth of this statement.

The Hindu sacred law penalized the *Shudras* (belonging to the fourth caste) from acquiring wealth. It is a law of enforced poverty unknown in any other part of the world. What does Gandhism do? It does not lift the impaled ban and it blesses the *Shudra* for his moral courage to give up property. It is as well worth quoting Mr. Gandhi's own words:

> The *Shudra* who only serves (the higher caste) as a matter of religious duty, and who will never own any property, who indeed has not even the ambition to own anything, is deserving of thousand obeisance. . . . The very Gods will shower flowers on him.

Another illustration is the attitude of Gandhism towards the scavenger. The sacred law of the Hindus lays down that a scavenger's progeny shall live by scavenging. Under Hinduism scavenging was not a matter of choice, it was a matter of force. What does Gandhism do? It seeks to perpetuate this system by praising scavenging as the noblest service to society! As President of a Conference of the Untouchables, according to Mr. Gandhi:

> I do not want to attain *Moksha*. I do not want to be reborn. But if I have to be reborn, I should be born an untouchable, so that I may share their sorrows, sufferings and the affronts levelled at them, in order that I endeavor to free myself and them from that miserable condition. I, therefore prayed that if I should be born again, I should do so not as a *Brahmin, Kshatriya, Vaishya*, or *Shudra*, but as an *Atishudra*. . . . I love scavenging. In my Ashram, an eighteen-years-old Brahmin lad is doing the scavenger's work in order to teach the Ashram scavenger cleanliness. The lad is no reformer. He was born and bred in orthodoxy. . . . But he felt that his accomplishments were incomplete until he had become also a perfect sweeper, and that, if he wanted the Ashram sweeper to do his work well, he must do it himself and set an example. You should realize that you are cleaning Hindu Society.

Can there be a worse example of false propaganda than this attempt of Gandhism to perpetuate evils, which have been deliberately imposed by one caste over another? If Gandhism preached the rule of poverty for all and not merely for the *Shudra* the worst that could be said about it is that it is mistaken idea. But why preach it as good for one caste only? For in India a man is not a scavenger because of his work. He is a scavenger because of his birth irrespective of the question whether he does scavenging or not. If Gandhism preached that scavenging is a noble profession with the object of inducing those who refuse to engage in it, one could understand it. But why appeal to the scavenger's pride and vanity in order to induce him and him only to keep on to scavenging by telling him that scavenging is a noble profession and that he need not be ashamed of it? To preach that poverty is good for the *Shudra* and for none else, to preach that scavenging is good for the Untouchables and for none else and to make them accept these onerous impositions as voluntary purposes of life, by appeal to their failings is an outrage and a cruel joke on the helpless classes which none but Mr. Gandhi can perpetrate with equanimity and impunity.

Criticism apart, this is the technique of Gandhism to make wrongs done appear to the very victim as though they were his privileges. If there is an "ism" which has made full use of religion as opium to lull the people into false beliefs and false security, it is Gandhism. Following Shakespeare, one can well say: Plausibility! Ingenuity! Thy name is Gandhism.

Such is Gandhism. A question is asked: Should Gandhism become the law of the land what would be the destiny of the Untouchables under it? The answers cannot require much scratching of the brain. How would it compare with the lot of the lowest Hindu? Enough has been said to show what would be his lot, should the Gandhian social order come into being. In so far as the lowest Hindu [totemistic caste] and the Untouchable belong to the same disinherited class, the Untouchable's fate cannot be better. If anything it might easily be worse. . . . The Untouchable will therefore continue to suffer the worst future as he does now. . . .

What does Gandhism do to relieve the Untouchables from this fate? Gandhism professes to abolish Untouchability. That is hailed as the greatest virtue of Gandhism. But what does this virtue amount to in actual life? To assess the value of this anti-Untouchability, which is regarded as a very big element in Gandhism, it is necessary to understand fully the scope of Mr. Gandhi's programme for the removal of Untouchability. Does it mean anything more than that the Hindus will not mind touching the Untouchables? Does it mean the removal of the ban on the right of the Untouchables to education? It would be better to take the two questions separately.

Dealing with the first question, Mr. Gandhi does not say that a Hindu should not take a bath after touching the Untouchables. If Mr. Gandhi does not object to it as a purification of pollution then it is difficult to see how Untouchability can be said to vanish by touching the Untouchables. Untouchability centers round the idea of pollution by contact and purification by bath to remove the pollution. Does it mean social assimilation of the Untouchables with the Hindus? Mr. Gandhi has most categorically stated that removal of Untouchability does not mean interdining or intermarriage between the Hindus and the Untouchables. Mr. Gandhi's anti-Untouchability means that the Untouchables will be graded as *Shudras* instead of being classed as *Atishudras* [i.e., "beyond *Shudras*"]. There is nothing more in it. Mr. Gandhi has not considered whether the old *Shudras* will accept the new *Shudras* into their fold. If they don't then the removal of Untouchability is a senseless proposition for it will still keep the Untouchables as a separate social category. Mr. Gandhi probably knows that the abolition of Untouchability will not bring about the assimilation of the Untouchables by the *Shudras*. That seems to be the reason why Mr. Gandhi himself has given a new and a different name to the Untouchables. The new name registers by anticipation what is likely to be the fact. By calling the Untouchables *Harijans*, Mr. Gandhi has killed two birds with one stone. He has shown that assimilation of the Untouchables by the *Shudras* is not possible. He has also by his new name counteracted assimilation and made it impossible.

Regarding the second question, it is true that Gandhism is prepared to remove the old ban placed by the Hindu *Shastras* on the right of the Untouchables to education and permit them to acquire knowledge and learning. Under Gandhism, the Untouchables may study law, they may study medicine, and they may study engineering or anything else they may fancy. So far so good. But will the Untouchables be free to make use of their knowledge and learning? Will they have the right to choose their profession? Can they adopt the career of lawyer, doctor or engineer? To these questions the answer, which Gandhism gives, is an emphatic "no." The Untouchables must follow their hereditary professions. That those occupations are unclean is no excuse. That before the occupation became hereditary it was the result of force and not volition does not matter. The argument of Gandhism is that what is once settled is settled forever even if it was wrongly settled. Under Gandhism, the Untouchables are to be eternal scavengers. There is no doubt that the Untouchables would much prefer the orthodox system of Untouchability. A compulsory state of ignorance imposed upon the Untouchables by the Hindu *Shastras* made scavenging bearable. But Gandhism, which compels an educated Untouchable to do scavenging, is nothing short of cruelty. The grace in Gandhism is a curse in its worst form. The virtue of the anti-Untouchability plank in Gandhism is quite illusory. There is no substance in it.

What else is there in Gandhism that the Untouchables can accept as opening a way for their ultimate salvation? Barring this illusory campaign against Untouchability, Gandhism is simply another form of Sanatanism, which is the ancient name for militant orthodox Hinduism. What is there in Gandhism that is not to be found in orthodox Hinduism? There is caste in Hinduism; there is caste in Gandhism. Hinduism believes in the law of hereditary profession, so does Gandhism. Hinduism enjoins cow-worship. So does Gandhism. Hinduism upholds the law of *karma*, predestination of man's condition in this world, so does Gandhism. Hinduism accepts the authority of the *Shastras*. So does Gandhism. Hinduism believes in idols. So does Gandhism. All that Gandhism has done is to find a philosophic justification for Hinduism and its dogmas. Hinduism is bald in the sense that it is just a set of rules that bear on their face the appearance of a crude and cruel system. Gandhism supplies the philosophy, which buffs its surface and gives it the appearance of decency and respectability and so alters it and embellishes it as to make it even more attractive.

What hope can Gandhism offer to the Untouchables? To the Untouchables, Hinduism is a veritable chamber of horrors. The sanctity and infallibility of the *Vedas*, *Smritis* and *Shastras*, the iron law of caste, the heartless law of *karma* and the senseless law of status by birth are to the Untouchables veritable instruments of torture which Hinduism has forged against the Untouchables. These very instruments that have mutilated, blasted and blighted the life of the Untouchables are to be found intact and untarnished in the bosom of Gandhism. How can the Untouchables say that Gandhism is a heaven and not a chamber of horrors that Hinduism has been? The only reaction and a very natural reaction of the Untouchables would be to runaway from Gandhism.

Gandhists may say that what I have stated applies to the old type of Gandhism. There is a new Gandhism, Gandhism without caste. This has reference to the recent statement of Mr. Gandhi that caste is an anachronism. Reformers were naturally gladdened by this declaration of Mr. Gandhi. And who would not be glad to see that a man like Mr. Gandhi having such terrible influence over the Hindus? This was after having played the most mischievous part of a social reactionary, after having stood out as the protagonist of the caste system, after having beguiled and befooled the unthinking Hindus with arguments which made no distinction between what is fair and foul should have come out with this recantation. But is this really a matter for jubilation? Does it change the nature of Gandhism? Does it make Gandhism a new and better "ism" than it was before? Those who are carried away by this recantation of Mr. Gandhi, neglect two things. In the first place, all that Mr. Gandhi has said is that caste is an anachronism. He does not say it is an evil. He does not say it is anathema. Mr. Gandhi may be taken to be not in favor of caste. But Mr. Gandhi does not say that he is against the *Varna* system. And what is Mr. Gandhi's *Varna* system? It is simply a new name for the caste system and retains all the worst features of the caste system.

The declaration of Mr. Gandhi cannot be taken to mean any fundamental change in Gandhism. It cannot make Gandhism acceptable to the Untouchables. The Untouchables will still have ground to ask with a: "Good God! Is this man Gandhi our Savior?"[1]

NOTE

1. The book from which this chapter was taken was published at the time when Gandhi was alive and, as expected, he should have answered Dr. Ambedkar. Instead, two of Gandhi's disciples wrote the following rebuttals:

a. C. Rajagopalachari, *Ambedkar Refuted* (Bombay: Hind Kitabs, 1946).

b. K. Santhanam, *Ambedkar's Attack, A Critical Examination of Dr. Ambedkar's Book:* What Congress and Gandhi Have Done to the Untouchables (New Delhi: Hindustan Times, 1946).

In both of these refutations, the authors, while trying their best to cast doubts on Dr. Ambedkar and his works, instead end up fortifying his arguments. More recently, another author and a famous Indian journalist (today he is a member of India's cabinet) by the name of Arun Shourie in his book, *Worshipping False Gods: Ambedkar, and the Facts which Have Been Erased* (New Delhi: ASA Publications, 1997), took upon himself the task of demolishing Dr. Ambedkar's scholarship. While charging like a raging bull in his attempt to knock down Ambedkar, he overextended his weak arguments while relying too heavily on questionable references. At times he employed the tactics of character assassination. In the end, his attempts to rescue Gandhi and Hinduism from Ambedkar's incisive commentary failed.

27

One day Mahatma Gandhi stood before his people and said: "You are exploiting these untouchables. Even though we are fighting with all that we have of our bodies and our souls to break loose from the bondage of the British Empire, we are exploiting these people and we are taking from them their selfhood and their self-respect." He said, "I will refuse to eat until the leaders of the caste system will come to me with the leaders of the untouchables and say that there will be an end to untouchability and the Hindu temples of India will open their doors to the untouchables." And he refused to eat, and days passed. Finally when Gandhi was about to breathe his last breath, and his body was all but gone, a group from the untouchables and a group from the Brahmin caste came to him and signed a statement that they would no longer adhere to the caste system. The priest of the temple came to him and said, "Now the temples will be opened to the untouchables." That afternoon, untouchables from all over India went into the temples and all of these thousands and millions of people put their arms around the Brahmins and people of other castes. Hundreds of millions of people who had never

261

*touched each other for two thousand years were now singing
and praising all together. This was a great contribution that
Mahatma Gandhi brought about.*

—Rev. Martin Luther King, Jr.
The Autobiography of Martin Luther King, Jr.

The myth-making enterprise in India and abroad continues to project Gandhi
as a champion of the Untouchables. This paradox has a strange background:
Not only did he wish to keep the caste system intact, Gandhi envisioned perpet-
uating it further, not just in India, but throughout the world. He appealed repeatedly to abolish the practice of Untouchability, but this presents a problem:
Untouchability is part and parcel of the caste system. If you are going to have
caste, then you had better expect Untouchability, or something akin to it. That
much should be clear. If Adolf Hitler had announced a new Nazism without anti-
Semitism, we would have been skeptical. If a leader of the old South Africa had
announced the simultaneous continuation of apartheid and the liberation of black
people, we would have scoffed. But when Gandhi announced the continuance of
the caste system and the emancipation of the Untouchables, many swallowed it,
especially many American black leaders.

The world has heard plenty of Gandhi's anti-Untouchability pronounce-
ments, but the time has come to ponder his actions. Again, we turn to Ambedkar
for help, because he is the only contemporary of Gandhi who left a critical, eyewitness account of what Gandhi did to the black people of India. This is so unique.
Take for example Gandhi's involvement in the Zulu rebellion of 1906. Every
detail of that conflict we have on paper was authored by Gandhi himself, or he
dictated, or his disciples repeated verbatim from Gandhi's own prior written
accounts. In other words, there are no independent versions available. We are left
to rely solely on Gandhi's own multiple versions. Take the case of racial politics
in practice before and after the Boer War. Here also we are relying heavily on
Gandhi's original *Indian Opinion* reliable and valid accounts. Otherwise, it would
have been impossible to assess. It is the same scenario for those seven years of
Satyagraha in South Africa. I wish there were a Negro account of Gandhi's incarceration in South Africa and his encounters there with blacks. No independent
Gandhi contemporary has left for us anything of worthiness except for Millie G.
Polak. Her account is of minor significance to us because of the specificity of the
subject matter, and also because she wrote her book many years later.

In India, the situation would have resembled the South African situation if it
had not been for Ambedkar. Dr. Ambedkar spent his entire adult life confronting
Gandhi over the damage Gandhi was inflicting on the poverty-stricken Untouchables. What he had written is valid, methodical, and verifiable.

Gandhi knew what he was up against and consequently channeled his entire

Hindu propaganda machine to out-maneuver Ambedkar and the Untouchables. He championed deceptive double-game practices against the Untouchables, leading to the sabotage of their human rights crusade. His multipronged attacks were designed to force them into submission. The underlying strategy was simple: never let the Untouchables get organized; never harm the caste-Hindu interests; never let up on his own propaganda line, which depicted his anti-Untouchability campaign as humanitarian. Any serious observer of Gandhi's campaign to eliminate Untouchability will come to the conclusion that it was marked by inconsistencies and contradictions, calling for serious questions about his real goals.

Gandhi entered actively into Indian politics in 1919. Soon thereafter, he captured the Congress Party, overhauled it, and transformed it to fit modern Hinduism ideology, remarkably similar and suited to his own. In 1921, Gandhi collected a whopping 13.5 million rupees (Rs.) for the *Tilak Swaraj* Fund. Gandhi insisted that there was no possibility of winning *swaraj* (freedom) unless Untouchability was removed. But out of this huge collected amount, a paltry Rs. 43,000 was earmarked to the cause of Untouchables. When his attention was drawn to the inadequacy of this, he simply said that he was busy planning a campaign to win *swaraj*, and that he had no time to spare for the cause of Untouchables.

In February 1922, the Congress Working Committee, under Gandhi's direction, drew up the Bardoli Programme of Constructive Work. Rehabilitation of Untouchables was hailed as an important component of it. A great deal of money was collected and a committee was appointed to work out the details. However, the committee never took action. It was dissolved and the upgrading of the lot of Untouchables was dropped from the Bardoli Programme. Only meager sums of Rs. 500 were allotted to the committee for working expenses only to expire peacefully. There were no shortages of funds. When asked, Gandhi answered in his habitual vague terms. Dr. Ambedkar summed it:

> The regrettable part of this tragedy is the realization of the fact how Mr. Gandhi has learned to find unction in illusions. . . . There is no doubt he likes to create illusions in order to use them as arguments to support his cherished proposition. The reason he has given for not taking personal responsibility for the uplift of the Untouchables furnishes the best evidence of this habit of Mr. Gandhi. . . . But to go to the length of assuring oneself that the Hindus are so overwhelmed with a sense of shame for the inhuman treatment they have accorded to the Untouchables that they dare not fail to abolish untouchability and that there is a band of Hindu Reformers pledged to do nothing but remove untouchability is to conjure an illusion to fool the Untouchables and to fool the world at large. It may be sound logic to argue that what benefits the whole also benefits the part and that one need not confine himself to looking after the part. But to assume that a piece, as separate as the Untouchables, is a part of the Hindu whole is to deceive oneself. Few know what tragedies the Untouchables as well as the country have had to go through on account of the illusions of Mr. Gandhi.[1]

To make matters worse, during this Bardoli Programme, Gandhi decided to transfer the "Untouchable uplift" scheme to the hands of *Hindu Mahasabha*—a group known for its fundamentalism. This was similar to asking the Ku Klux Klan to take care of blacks!

In 1929, the Untouchables in the Bombay presidency opened a campaign of Satyagraha against the Hindus in order to establish their civic rights regarding temple entry and taking water from public wells. They hoped to get the blessing of Gandhi, since Satyagraha was Gandhi's own weapon for redressing wrongs. However, Gandhi surprised the Untouchables by issuing a statement condemning their campaign of Satyagraha against the Hindus. The argument urged by Gandhi was very ingenious: he stated that Satyagraha was to be used only against foreigners; it must not be used against one's own kindred or countrymen, and as the Hindus were the kindred and countrymen of the Untouchables, by the rules of Satyagraha, the latter were debarred from using this weapon against the former.

Here is an example of one Satyagraha that occurred in November 1929, reported by Katherine Mayo:

> Other Untouchable unions, more bodily assertive, "offered Satyagraha" before Hindu temples, day after day approaching the precincts, to be beaten back with sticks and stones, or barring the entry to the temple with their own bodies stretched upon the earth so that Hindus coming forth from worship must touch them and be defiled. And when one of these demonstrating masses was stayed in its course to be warned that Gandhi would probably condemn its aggressiveness, its spokesman is thus quoted: "We know Mr. Gandhi is against it. But we don't care. We will resume Satyagraha if Mr. Gandhi or God himself is against it."[2]

It shouldn't surprise us that at one time, post-British Hindu India leaders seriously contemplated declaring Satyagraha unlawful when directed against the government! Also, hardly another surprise, in more recent times, given the unrest and instability, Hindu India is free from Satyagraha.

In order to frame a new constitution of India, the British Government asked various Indian delegates (Gandhi included) to participate in what has been called the Round Table Conference in London in 1931. Untouchables were represented by two members, one of whom was Dr. Ambedkar. The most difficult task rested with the Minorities Committee: to resolve the communal question. To their credit, they finally settled on the pressing issues in what is called the Minorities Pact. This infuriated Gandhi particularly, because the pact recognized Untouchables as a separate political entity. Gandhi sabotaged the pact by using the Moslem card to sidetrack the Untouchables. Dr. Ambedkar wrote:

> During the Round Table Conference he told people, "I shall not raise any objection against the demands presented by the representatives of the depressed classes [the Untouchables]." But, as soon as the representatives of the depressed classes pressed their demands, Gandhi quietly forgot about the assurances given

by him. I call it a betrayal of the people belonging to the depressed classes. He went to the Moslems and told them that he would support their fourteen demands if they in turn opposed the demands placed by the representatives of the depressed classes. Even a scoundrel would not have done this. This is only one instance of Gandhi's treachery.[3]

As a follow-up to the failed settlement, the delegates to the Minorities Committee accepted the proposal of British prime minister Ramsay MacDonald to put in a signed requisition authorizing him to arbitrate and give his decision on the communal issue. Mr. Gandhi, along with the majority of the delegates, signed before returning home.

On August 17, 1932, Prime Minister MacDonald announced his final decisions on the communal question in spite of the fact that Gandhi had earlier resorted to his habitual threats. Gandhi didn't like the communal award because in it the British Government had accepted the Untouchables' claim for special representation. He tried to change the terms of the award and, when that failed, he commenced a "fast unto death" on September 20, as a protest against the grant of separate electorates to the Untouchables. To cut the story short, this fiasco of Gandhi's led to the Poona Pact, which Dr. Ambedkar signed on September 24. Untouchables were worse off under the Poona Pact than under the Prime Minister's award. Ambedkar never pardoned himself for his blunder in submitting to Gandhi's threats.

In a frenetic follow-up to the Poona Pact, Gandhi renamed the Untouchables Harijan, meaning Children of God, and started a weekly paper named *Harijan.* Through this newspaper, Gandhi masterminded a propaganda blitz and published weekly columns of long lists of temples, public wells, and schools thrown open to Untouchables by the Hindus. And then it suddenly ended. As it turned out, the columns were bogus, part of an effort to deceive the world. To comprehend the Poona Pact and its aftereffects, it is better to turn to Beverley Nichols—a famous novelist, musician, playwright, essayist, reporter, and journalist—who on her visit to British India met Dr. Ambedkar, and was not surprised when told by him: "Gandhi is the greatest enemy the untouchables have ever had in India." What did Dr. Ambedkar mean? Ms. Nichols explained it as follows:

> We can best explain it by a parallel. Take Ambedkar's remark, and for the word "untouchable" substitute the word "peace." Now imagine that a great champion of peace, like Lord Cecil, said, "Gandhi is the greatest enemy of peace the world has ever had." What would he mean, using these words of the most spectacular pacifist of modern times? He would mean that passive resistance—which is Gandhi's form of pacifism—could only lead to chaos and the eventual triumph of brute force; that to lie down and let people trample on you (which was Gandhi's recipe for dealing with the Japanese) is a temptation to the aggressor rather than an example to the aggressed; and that in order to have peace you must organize, you must be strong, and that you must be prepared to use force.
>
> *Mutatis mutandis,* that is precisely what Ambedkar meant about the

untouchables. He wanted them to be recognized and he wanted them to be strong. He rightly considered that the best way of gaining his object was by granting them separate electorates; a solid block of 60 million would be in a position to dictate terms to its oppressors.

Gandhi fiercely opposed this scheme. "Give the untouchables separate electorates," he cried, "and you only perpetuate their status for all time." It was a queer argument, and those who were not bemused by the Mahatma's charm considered it a phoney one. They suspected that Gandhi was a little afraid that 60 million untouchables might join up with the 100 million Muslims—(as they nearly did)—and challenge the dictatorship of the 180 million orthodox Hindus. When such irreverent criticisms were made to him, Gandhi resorted to his usual tactics: he began to fast unto death. (As if that altered the situation by a comma or proved anything but his own obstinacy!) There was a frenzy of excitement, ending in a compromise on the seventh day of the fast. The untouchables still vote in the same constituencies as the caste Hindus, but a substantial number of seats are now reserved for them in the provincial legislatures. It is better than nothing, but it is not nearly so good as it would have been if Gandhi had not interfered.

That is what Doctor Ambedkar meant. And I think that he was right.[4]

Another issue that caught the imagination of American black leaders was that of temple entry. Particularly interesting is the case of Guruvayur Temple. Gandhi gave the impression that he would resort to his ultimate weapon, fasting, to gain entry to this temple for the Untouchables. However, nothing happened and he did not carry out his threat to fast. Then in 1932, Gandhi virtually coerced the governor-general to give his sanction to the introduction of the Temple Entry Bill, authored by Ranga Iyer on behalf of the Congress Party in the Central Legislature. The bill was finally introduced in the Assembly on March 24, 1933, and since the bill proceeded at a snail's pace, the assembly dissolved, which caused Iyer to hold strong opinions against the Congress Party. As fresh elections to the Central Legislature were announced, the Congress Party withdrew its support for the bill as it was referred to the select committee, on the grounds that the bill gave offence to Hindus. Gandhi went so far as to justify the conduct of the Congress Party. Dr. Ambedkar's judgment was categorical:

> The Temple Entry, what is one to say of it, except to describe it a strange game of political acrobatics! Mr. Gandhi begins as an opponent of Temple Entry. When the Untouchables put forth a demand for political rights, he changes his position and becomes a supporter of Temple entry. When the Hindus threaten to defeat the Congress in the election, if it pursues the matter to a conclusion, Mr. Gandhi, in order to preserve political power in the hands of the Congress, gives up Temple Entry! Is this sincerity? Does this show conviction? Was the "agony of soul" which Mr. Gandhi spoke of more than a phrase?[5]

In the end, the entire temple entry issue was a sham. On August 17, 1939, B. K. Gaikwad, a low-caste member of the Bombay Legislative Assembly, asked how many temples in the Bombay presidency had been thrown open to the Untouchables since 1932 when Gandhi started his temple-entry movement. According to the figures given out by a Congress Party minister, the total number of temples thrown open was 142. Of these, 121 were ownerless temples, which were under nobody's care in particular and which nobody used as places of worship. Another peculiar fact was that not a single temple had been thrown open to the Untouchables in Gujarat, Gandhi's home state.

As another outcome of the Poona Pact, in 1933 Gandhi established the *Harijan Sevak Sangh*, or the Servants of Untouchables Society, dedicated to the welfare of Harijans and with branches spread all over India. Some people demanded that the institution be handed over to Untouchables and be run by them. Others demanded that Untouchables have representation on the Governing Board. Gandhi flatly refused both on the grounds that the *Harijan Sevak Sangh* was an act of penance on the part of Hindus, so they must do the penance, and contribute money to the cause. From the very outset, the *Sangh* was plagued by an acute lack of funds. The Hindus simply wouldn't give money for Untouchables, though they had showered money on Gandhi for other political purposes. Again, in the words of Dr. Ambedkar:

> What does all this show? Does it not show that the *Harijan Sevak Sangh* is a charitable organization only in name, and that its real aim is to ensnare the Untouchables, to make them the camp-followers of the Hindus and the Congress and to scotch any movement by them the aim and object of which are to free themselves from the social, religious, economic and political domination of the Hindus? Is there any wonder if the Untouchables look upon the *Harijan Sevak Sangh* as an abomination, the object of which was to kill them by kindness?[6]

Dr. Khare was a prime minister in the Congress ministry in the Central Provinces of British India. With a view to forming a new cabinet and in full conformity with constitutional practice, Dr. Khare submitted his resignation, and the governor recalled him to form a new ministry (cabinet), which he did. Dr. Khare's new cabinet was different from the old one in one important respect: namely, it included Agnibhoj, an Untouchable. He was a member of the Congress Party, and the Congress Party assembly, and was in many ways better qualified than some other ministers. On July 26, 1938, the Congress Working Committee met in Wardha and passed a resolution condemning Dr. Khare on the grounds that, in tendering the resignation of colleagues in the old ministry, he was guilty of a grave error of judgment, and that, in forming a new ministry, he was guilty of indiscipline. Dr. Khare openly said that according to Gandhi the act of indiscipline lay in the inclusion of an Untouchable in the ministry. Dr. Khare also said that Gandhi told him it was wrong to raise such aspirations and ambitions in Untouchables, and it was such an act of bad judgment that he [Gandhi] would never forgive him [Dr. Khare]. Dr. Khare repeatedly and publicly made these allegations about Gandhi. Gandhi never responded to them, but Agnibhoj was dropped from the new ministry.

Kavitha is a village in the Ahmedabad district in Gujarat, Gandhi's home state. In 1935, Untouchables of that village demanded that their children be admitted to the common village school along with other Hindu children. The Hindus were enraged and took their revenge by proclaiming a complete social boycott. As a result, the Untouchable boys were thus practically banned from the village school with nobody to help them. This caused despondency among the Untouchables to such an extent that they were thinking of migrating in a body to some other village. A detailed report on this incident was handed to Gandhi in the hope that he would intercede. He read the report and advised Untouchables:

> There is no help like self-help. God helps those who help themselves. If the Harijans concerned will carry out their reported resolve to wipe the dust of Kavitha off their feet, they will not only be happy themselves but they will pave the way for others who may be similarly treated. If people migrate in search of employment, how much more should they do so in search of self-respect? I hope that well-wishers of Harijans will help these poor families to vacate inhospitable Kavitha.[7]

Mr. Gandhi advised the Untouchables to migrate elsewhere.

We have already read, in a previous section, Dr. Ambedkar's views of Gandhi's much-touted new economic theory: trusteeship. Margaret Bourke-White, a *Life* magazine photographer and one of the last persons to interview Gandhi before his assassination, did a good job of analyzing this cruel hoax that Gandhi had inflicted on the poor, including Untouchables. According to the theory, Indian tycoons were to act as the people's trustees. When questioned about this, Gandhi explained,

> A good trustee is one who discharges his trusteeship faithfully to the letter and in spirit. . . . A trustee does not make a single farthing for himself. A trustee is always entitled to his commission. He will take his commission subject to those for whom he is a trustee—the consent of his guardians—no, I do not mean guardians.[8]

Suddenly, he changed the word "guardians" to "wards" and continued to explain: "If the wards say he must not take more than five rupees a month, he must do this, or hand over the trust."[9]

Mr. Gandhi (and Pyarelal) told Ms. Bourke-White that he had had prior conversations about the trusteeship subject with his main financial benefactor, Mr. G. D. Birla, the richest man in India at the time. It was only after she had interviewed Mr. Birla herself that she realized Gandhi and Birla had never discussed the matter in question, or at least not the way Gandhi propaganda had led her to believe. Of all the tycoons on the horizon, Mr. Birla was Gandhi's closest disciple. In the end, Ms. Bourke-White laid to rest the hoax with a rhetorical question:

If in thirty-two years of intimate association Mr. Birla with his genuine affection and veneration for Gandhi had not absorbed sufficient spiritual strength to be a trustee, where outside this close circle could you hope to find the industrialist, the owner of property, the maharaja, the businessman who would have the spiritual strength for trusteeship?[10]

Dr. Ambedkar has been known to refer to Gandhi as: "Number 1 Enemy of the Untouchables" and he said, "Gandhi is the greatest enemy the untouchables have ever had in India." There is ample documentation to conclude that Dr. Ambedkar was right on the mark. With respect to Gandhi's caste ideology, Dr. Ambedkar has called his logic the: "arguments of a cave man" and the "arguments of a madman."

THE PLIGHT OF UNTOUCHABLES TODAY

Writing in 1930, Katherine Mayo recognized the tragedy of the Untouchables:

The Untouchables today are only a vast, unorganized mass of slaves, tragically lacking a Moses to lead them. That, here and there, a group should rebel as they are now doing, is almost a miracle, in view of the mental narcotic with which they have so long been drugged.[11]

Dr. B. R. Ambedkar, their Moses, had come and had gone, leaving the project far from finished. Largely due to his efforts, the Constitution of the Republic of India outlawed Untouchability; however, the caste system remained intact and lawful, making a mockery of the anti-Untouchability clause.

The modern Indian state, with its huge bureaucracy, modern technology and industrialization, and entrenched Hindu ideology, has only strengthened the repression of Untouchables. The rest of the world conveniently thinks of Untouchables as ex-Untouchables, and continues to credit Mahatma Gandhi for this "miracle." But as long as we cherish that false image of Gandhi and his so-called humanitarian association with that of Untouchables, the plight of this group will continue. Human Rights Watch has recently issued a scathing report, *Broken People: Caste Violence against India's "Untouchables,"* that details the scope of the human rights abuses against these *Dalits*, meaning, "the broken."[12]

NOTES

1. B. R. Ambedkar, *What Congress and Gandhi Have Done to the Untouchables*, 2d ed. (Bombay: Thacker & Co., Ltd, 1946), pp. 38–39.
2. Katherine Mayo, "Mahatma Gandhi and India's Untouchables," *Current History* 32 (1930): 870.

3. Fazlul Huq, *Gandhi: Saint or Sinner?* (Bangalore: Dalit Sahitya Akademy, 1992), p. 70.

4. Beverley Nichols, *Verdict on India* (New York: Harcourt Brace, 1944), pp. 37–38.

5. Ambedkar, *What Congress and Gandhi Have Done to the Untouchables*, p. 125.

6. Ibid., p. 145.

7. Ibid., pp. 265–66.

8. Margaret Bourke-White, *Halfway to Freedom* (New York: Simon & Schuster, 1949), pp. 227–28.

9. Ibid., p. 228.

10. Ibid., p. 70.

11. Mayo, "Mahatma Gandhi and India's Untouchables," p. 870.

12. Smita Narula, *Broken People: Caste Violence against India's "Untouchables"* (New York: Human Rights Watch, 1999).

PART 7

GANDHI, WHITES,
and ETHNIC CLEANSING

In Independent India of the non-violent type, there will be crime but no criminals. They will not be punished. Crime is a disease like any other malady and is a product of the prevalent social system. Therefore, all crime, including murder, will be treated as a disease. Whether such an India will ever come into being is another question.

—Mahatma Gandhi
Search after Sunrise

28

WHITE MURDERS

I believe that the civilization India has evolved is not to be beaten in the world. Nothing can equal the seeds sown by our ancestors. Rome went, Greece shared the same fate. . . . In the midst of all this India remains immovable and that is her glory. . . . Indian civilization is the best and the European is a nine-days wonder. . . . I bear no enmity towards the English, but I do towards their civilization.

—Mahatma Gandhi (1909)
Hind Swaraj

The Satyagraha movements in India were different in shape and scope than those in South Africa. In South Africa, a miniscule Indian minority resorted to Satyagraha against another minority, a ruling white government. The rest of the masses were mainly untouched. In India, that was not the case; the "nonviolent movement" was seeking to take power. In South Africa, Satyagraha was remarkably peaceful until the last stages, whereas, in India, it was bloody from its inception. In South Africa, the Satyagraha movement was financed by the Gujarati Moslems, but in India, it was financed by capitalist Hindus, who also financed Gandhi quite lavishly. The Satyagraha in South Africa was exclusively for the Indian elite (mainly the Moslems and a few upper-caste Hindus), to gain better racial positioning among the whites. In India, it was *against* the British white ruling elite, for the exclusive benefit of elite Hindu capitalists and the Hindu orthodoxy. So Gandhi's many Moslem friends in both India and South

273

Africa abandoned him as a consequence. The ultimate price tag of the Satyagraha in India was millions of lives massacred needlessly.

But there was something else that was strange and unique about Satyagraha in India. We know that in South Africa, Satyagraha had underpinnings of racism directed against blacks. Now, in India, the racism was against whites. We have already witnessed in previous chapters that in Gandhi's own speeches and writings from the South African period, one can vividly see his racism against blacks. In India, there was a remarkable change. Gandhi's speeches and writings (compiled in the *Collected Works*) were not only of a "nonviolent" character but also conspicuously devoid of any racism, even against whites. However, the Indian masses resorted to violence during the Satyagraha campaigns in spite of Gandhi's instructions. Why? Ironically, Gandhi loved the Satyagraha-prone emotional masses and in return they loved him. An explanation is needed here.

Before Gandhi was incarcerated in March 1922, two nationwide Satyagraha movements against the British had already taken place. These Satyagrahas involved riots, and the killing of Indians by Indians. There were also white killings that many Gandhi scholars, for unexplained reasons, have continued to ignore. The constant barrage of Gandhi's nonviolence and noncooperation message seemed to mean a license to loot, plunder, and kill. This happened too often. You would think he might have wondered what was going wrong, but he never questioned it. Gandhi was playing a game, the rules of which were already in place. The masses themselves became the scapegoat every time there was a killing. A peaceful, remorseful Gandhi languished with fastings and other types of penances for the crimes. Then he would get up and start all over again. The violent cycle continued after the crowds heard another sermon on nonviolence. How do we explain this dichotomy? When the scholars of today read Gandhi's speeches and find nothing violent in them, but the crowds who actually listened to him (including his National Volunteer Corps) somehow took the message differently and turned bloody, not once but many times. I have a possible answer. I believe Gandhi's rhetoric had changed since South Africa. It incorporated a coded script, like the language of *Bhagavad Gita*,* which he had mastered. The crowds knew their man and the man knew his large audience. In this chapter, we will explore those white killings. Relatively speaking the evidence on white killings is weak quantitatively, meaning that the whites were not and could not be killed in the thousands by the Indian masses. Having said that, let there be no second thoughts on the nature of the evidence being presented as you will read it: It is very strong, qualitatively speaking.

Edward VIII (1894–1972) was a handsome, charismatic, and popular king. He is most familiar to Americans for having abdicated his kingdom to marry an American divorcée, Wallis Simpson. As Prince of Wales, he visited India in the midst of

---

*Expounds a doctrine to "transform" a person into a killer as Lord Krishna did to Arjuna.

Gandhi's second nationwide Satyagraha movement. In his book *A King's Story: The Memoirs of the Duke of Windsor*, Edward recorded the following:

> Yet, for all that, Gandhi's ominous shadow fell often across my path; and especially in the native sections of the swarming cities the struggle for the loyalties of the masses seemed to me to be a bidding match between the Government of India on the one hand and Gandhi on the other. The Indians love a tamasha. Whatever their feelings on the injustices of British rule, they found it hard to resist the great public shows being organized in my honor. In an effort to overcome simple curiosity and scatter the crowds that otherwise would be hailed as proof of the loyalty of the Indian masses to the British Raj, *Mahatma Gandhi and his followers went to rather unusual lengths of intimidation and bribery.* Storekeepers along the routes of my procession were ordered to close their shops, students to boycott their classrooms, and the rest to remain out of sight in their homes. The Party men spread the rumor that the police had been ordered to shoot any native who approached the route of my procession. It was even said that the Government would poison the food at the "feeding of the poor." The dispensing of this bounty was customary on the occasion of a visit by the Viceroy or by some other exalted person. Whenever it was proclaimed in my honor, Gandhi's lieutenants would circulate a warning among the natives that the free food had been poisoned, adding a diabolical story in explanation. This stated in essence that, having been appalled and shocked by the evidences of widespread poverty, I had commanded the Government of India to remedy the conditions without delay and that the authorities, embarrassed by my Royal command, had decided to eliminate hunger at a stroke with a mass poisoning of the poor.[1] [my italics]

Can anyone imagine Gandhi stooping so low? For those of us who are familiar with Gandhi and his tactics, Edward's allegation of "intimidation" should come as no surprise. But what about the allegation of bribery? That is something new and worth looking into.

Accidentally, I came across an incident where an American, William Francis Doherty, was murdered by Gandhi's followers. Gandhi personally got involved in a cover-up of that murder, using intimidation and bribery. Here is the evidence reproduced in full:

State of California
County of Los Angeles

ANNETTE H. DOHERTY, being first duly sworn on oath, deposes and says:
    My deceased husband, William Francis Doherty, an American citizen, was a mechanical and electrical engineer and, at the time of his death, was managing engineer and business associate of Mr. Richard J. Brenchley, engaged in sand extraction at Mumbra, adjacent to Bombay, India.
    On November 19th, 1921, as he was quietly proceeding to the Bombay

Improvement Trust work-shops, he was set upon, his eyes were gouged out and eventually he was beaten to death by a group of rioters in a public street of Byculla, a suburb of Bombay.

This was during the visit of the Prince of Wales to India, when Gandhi was at the height of his popularity as saint and political leader, and had, through his violent speeches against the British, worked his followers into a frenzy of race hatred. My husband was probably mistaken for a Britisher when he was murdered by Gandhi's followers.

Within three days following this killing of my husband, word was brought me from Gandhi that he greatly desired an interview with me, begging me to set a time when I would receive him. I was then stopping with an American family in Bombay. Gandhi's emissary was Mrs. Sarojini Naidu, the Indian poetess and politician.

Mrs. Naidu was greatly agitated, and made many statements to me that I feel she would now like to unsay. Her chief concern, however, was that the American public should never be allowed to hear of this outrage committed upon my husband; and she very frankly asked me my price for refraining from ever discussing or advertising the affair in America and from myself returning to America. Under no condition, said Mrs. Naidu, would they be willing that the American public should learn that they were killing people so promiscuously that even a white face cost a man's life.

As to Gandhi's request for an interview with me:

At that time he was going about so unclothed that Mrs. Naidu suggested I call upon him rather than that he come to the American home where I was stopping—inasmuch as this latter might prove embarrassing. It was therefore determined that I should see him at his own headquarters in Bombay, which I did, a motor car having been sent by him to fetch me.

Upon this occasion of my visit with Gandhi he repeated to me in substance what Mrs. Naidu had said, but even more emphatically stressed the point that Americans, because they were so much in sympathy with him in his political views, must on no account learn the details of the murder of my husband lest it hurt the success of his movement in America and prejudice our people against him.

ANNETTE HELEN DOHERTY.

Subscribed and sworn to before me this 4th day of January, 1929.

W.J. SCHISEL
Notary Public in and for the County of
Los Angeles, State of California. My
commission expires Jan. 18, 1931.[2]

Mrs. Doherty's deposition is not hearsay. She is a firsthand witness. Gandhi tried to intimidate and bribe her. Also, notice carefully that Mrs. Doherty has brought allegations of *racism against whites* practiced by Gandhi. I read of this incident in *After Mother India*, which I read in 1992—seventy-one years after the murder. I wanted to check the accuracy of Mrs. Doherty's deposition, which had also suggested new possibilities for Gandhi research, particularly racism against whites. This is what I unearthed:

Mr. Doherty's murder took place at the time the Prince of Wales was visiting Bombay in 1921. It would be easy to check; at least that's what I thought. It does not appear in *Collected Works*, nor in the writings of Mrs. Sarojini Naidu. I also checked C. F. Andrews's chapter "The Bombay Riots"[3] and browsed through Mahadev Desai's (Gandhi's Chief Secretary) *Day-to-Day with Gandhi: Secretary's Diary from November 1917 to March 1927*.[4] There was nothing. I searched everywhere (biographies included), but I could find no mention of this incident. I checked volumes 1 and 2 of *Seven Months with Mahatma Gandhi: Being an Inside View of the Non-Co-Operation Movement (1921–1922)*.[5] There were two relevant chapters: "Bombay Riots—I" and "Bombay Riots—II." Another relevant book, *Gandhi and Bombay*, was also thoroughly checked.[6] I began to suspect that perhaps Mr. Doherty's murder never took place and Mrs. Doherty's deposition was a fake. However, at last I got a lucky break in an unexpected place, the work titled *A Lamp for India: The Story of Madame Pandit*. Madame Pandit is Madame Vijaya Lakshmi Pandit (1900–1990), sister of Jawaharlal Nehru. Regarding the incident in question, it reads:

> The accusation [referring to Mrs. Doherty's deposition] stunned Sarojini Naidu, who said Gandhi and all his followers would let themselves be killed rather than be guilty of killing or of condoning it, and that color had nothing to do with the freedom crusade, "any more than caste or creed."[7]

Here Madame Pandit is speaking for Sarojini Naidu, which is not the best way to handle this problem. The statement above is terribly inadequate. It doesn't say whether the murder actually took place; it doesn't tell us if Mrs. Sarojini Naidu went to see Mrs. Doherty. We learn nothing here about Gandhi's tactics of intimidation and bribery. Nonetheless, at least now I had meager evidence that someone like Madame Pandit, with open access to Gandhi, had known about Mr. Doherty's murder. If serious criminal allegations were ever made, I expect Gandhi was clever enough to refute them. But, as I have said earlier, there is nothing in the Gandhi literature. I was stranded again, but got lucky. What I came across shocked me to take a closer look into the white murders.

Nirad C. Chaudhuri, writing in 1988, placed the number of deaths during the Bombay riots to a total of thirty-six; of which two were Europeans, three Parsi, fourteen Hindu, and seventeen Muslim.[8] Notice, there is no American in this count. A police officer who saw Gandhi during the riots in Bombay reported that, when he was in danger, Gandhi ran with an agility remarkable in a man of his age.[9]

The *New York Times*, under the heading "Gandhi Blames Disciples," reported 36 killed, including 2 Europeans, and 150 injured and taken to the hospital.[10] Two days earlier, the *New York Times* had reported, "A dispatch to the *Morning Post* today from Bombay says that William Francis Dogherty, an American engineer, was killed in the course of last week's rioting in that city. The verdict of the coroner's inquest, says the dispatch was that he died of injuries from sticks thrown by the rioters."[11] The *New York Times Index* (July–December 1921), on page 240, recorded "W. F. Dogherty, Amer, was killed in Bombay riot."[12] So we have confirmation of Mr. Doherty's murder, even though the *Index* and the *Times* made an error in spelling his last name. About twenty days later, the *New York Times* reported the official casualty list, "One American, William Francis Doherty; two Europeans and two Parsees killed; three Europeans and an unknown number of Parsees wounded, eighty-three police wounded, fifty-three rioters killed, and 298 wounded."[13] This time they got his name right.

Sir C. Sankaran Nair, a high Indian official at the time, in his compelling book, *Gandhi and Anarchy* (1922), has tabulated a "list of riots or disturbances since the year 1919." The number of casualties in Bombay from November 17 to November 20, 1921, are listed as: "Two Europeans, one American and two Parsis were killed. Three Europeans and an unknown number of Parsis were wounded. Of the rioters 53 were killed and 298 wounded."[14]

Nair (1867–1934), formerly a judge of the Madras High Court, was a member of the government of India till July 1919 when he resigned. Soon thereafter he also resigned as a member of the Viceroy's Executive Council in protest. So this is an account coming from a top official, well versed in Gandhi politics. The figures quoted are more reliable because of their timeliness. We know who the one American is. Who were the two Europeans? Also Sir Nair has listed a total of 58 killed, not 36.

A reporter named Gertrude Emerson, in a 1922 *Asia* article, "'Non-Violent Non-Cooperation' in India" offered the following:

> In Bombay the rioting that followed the Prince's arrival grew out of the desire of the Parsis, a small, wealthy group of Indians, originally of Persian extraction and followers of Zoroaster, to present an address of welcome on behalf of their community to the Prince. Non-coöperators objected and vented their animosity by attacking in the streets Parsis, Christians and Jews who were returning from welcoming the Prince. The police, who attempted to interfere, were stoned. Tram-cars were set on fire, carriages and motor-cars stopped, shop windows broken, Parsi temples burned and persons wearing European clothes assaulted in the streets. Out of the death toll of fifty-eight, four Englishmen and one American were killed, the latter a young engineer who happened to be walking along the street and was so unfortunate as to meet a mob who turned on him and savagely beat him to death with sticks.[15]

Here we have a few corroborations of Nair. The total number killed is fifty-eight. The details of one American killed corroborate Mrs. Doherty's deposition. Instead of two Europeans, now we have four Englishmen killed. Most likely the Europeans killed were the British. Whether they were two or four, I am not certain. Or, it could be that two of the wounded Europeans died later. Also, there are no details about how they were killed, or even what their names were. Did Gandhi attempt to cover up their murders, too, through intimidation and bribery? These are some of the questions that I am still pursuing. However, in Gertrude Emerson's report there is no mention of Gandhi's attempt to buy Mrs. Doherty's silence. Is there corroboration of that? Yes.

Professor C. H. Van Tyne, head of the history department at the University of Michigan, was on a fact-finding mission to India at the time of the Prince of Wales's official visitation, which included a visit to Bombay. He has reported:

> Knowing full well the race hatred with which Gandhi, willingly or not, had filled his disciples, and recalling the fate of an American in the recent Bombay riots. . . . Gandhi went to see the widow of the murdered American, actually begging her, as I heard from another American present, not to let the news get to America lest it hurt the N.C.O. (Non-coöperator) cause![16]

I think I can say with a degree of certainty that Gandhi was involved directly in a cover-up of the murder of William Francis Doherty, after the appeals of Mrs. Sarojini Naidu failed. If Gandhi was not directly involved in the murder of Mr. Doherty, I nevertheless have no hesitation in blaming him for being indirectly involved and he ought to be held accountable.

There is something more to the story that gives me an eerie feeling when this murder is placed in a historical setting of event that surround this incident. Katherine Mayo's *Mother India*, published in early summer in 1927, caused an uproar among the caste Hindus and Gandhi. Yet it seems to me Gandhi fares better in this book than his Hindu brethren. However, Gandhi couldn't resist the temptation to respond—his "Drain Inspector's Report" was more a personal attack on Ms. Mayo than anything else (CWMG 34, #452, pp. 539–47). In fact, Gandhi reported many more verbal attacks on her. Then in 1929, *After Mother India*, by Harry Field, was published and Gandhi was made to look repulsive by allegations of criminal tactics and racism. One would expect that this explosive provocation would very possibly impel Gandhi and caste Hindus to be up in arms again. But my findings are puzzling: the literature is blank. There is no attempt to refute Field; there is only one occurrence of the book's title found in Gandhi's literature. After all the commotion of *Mother India*, *After Mother India* induces total silence. Why? Could it be that Gandhi learned a lesson here: If he speaks up against Field, he may run the risk of exposing his other criminal activities, like possibly dealing with the cover-up of murders of more whites? I am sure that Gandhi knew that wisdom lay here in being selectively silent. Even more amazing is that those educated Hindus who wrote books and articles against *Mother India* and its author also opted for silence upon publication of *After Mother India*.

Apparently, a certain Indian in London, K. Srinivasan, sent Gandhi selected chapters from *After Mother India*. On October 19, 1929, Gandhi responded to Mr. Srinivasan:

My Dear Srinivasan,

I thank you for your letter and the enclosures. You are quite right in being indifferent about *After Mother India*. However, if I get some leisure I shall go through the chapters you have sent and if I find anything that I can usefully deal with I shall do so.[17]

A careful scrutiny into the literature has revealed that Sarojini Naidu was in Bombay during the time period of Doherty's murder. Mrs. Naidu (1879–1949) was a strange woman, and in popular circles was referred to as *Bulbul-e-Hind*, meaning Nightingale of India. She considered herself Gandhi's "good soldier" and would do anything possible to please her savior. In a letter dated July 17, 1924, (about three years after the efforts to buy Mrs. Doherty's silence) Gandhi applauded her for her timely labors: "Sarojini Devi [Naidu] has deliberately cultivated that special quality of her sex. She showed it to perfection at the time of disgraceful rioting in Bombay in 1921. Her personal bravery and her tireless energy had become infectious. Wherever she went, the rioters laid down their arms."[18] It is absolutely clear in the literature that Gandhi was in Bombay during the time period in question.

The story on the cover-up of the murder of Mr. Doherty gets more interesting with time: In 1999, the Indian government published the Mahatma Gandhi Compact Disk (CD), which included the *Collected Works of Mahatma Gandhi*. In this CD, the section "List of Persons"—"list of persons to whom Gandhiji wrote frequently or have been mentioned in his writings"—included the name "Doharty, Annette Helen." But it failed to reveal any further information. However, there was something more in it that caught my attention. In the main text portion of the *Collected Works*, in supplementary volume #4, (or volume 94) there appears a letter that should draw our interest. Apparently, a certain individual named O. M. Thomas, resident of Allahabad in India, wrote two letters to Gandhi, the second of which by registered mail. It appears Thomas asked Gandhi to "account for" and explain what Mrs. Doherty had written concerning her late husband's murder as recorded in *After Mother India*. Undoubtedly, Gandhi refused to answer. Instead, Pyarelal (his chief secretary by this time) responded on May 13, 1945. To dodge the issue, Pyarelal asked Thomas in a letter to produce the "authentic copy of Mrs. Annette Helen Doharty's affidavit." The implication was that to Pyarelal (and hence Gandhi), Mrs. Doherty's deposition as it appeared in *After Mother India* was undesirable. They asked Thomas to produce the "authentic copy," knowing that Thomas, who resided in India, had no way to reach Mrs. Doherty, who lived in the United States and therefore could not produce the "authentic copy." This tactic of Gandhi's must be evaluated in the context of all the letters to which he did respond. The record shows that on May 13, 1945, Gandhi responded by writing at least twelve letters to various other individuals. Of course, the only exception was the one to Thomas! Imbued with the spirit of not responding in a reasonable manner about this murder case, Gandhi exercised another evasion when he asked Pyarelal to write again for him twelve days later. In a letter dated May 25, 1945, to Mrs. Naidu, who was addressed as "Dear Ammajan" meaning "Dear Beloved Mother," Pyarelal wrote, ". . . Bapu [Gandhi] knows nothing about it. . . ."[19] This statement of Gandhi via Pyarelal is worded strangely and somewhat evasive for the following reasons: (1) the wording says that Gandhi is professing total ignorance of the incident of Mr. Doherty's murder and its cover-up; (2) the wording doesn't say by any stretch of the imagination that the incident never took place; (3) the wording doesn't mean that Mrs. Doherty's deposition is a lie; and (4) the wording expressed, however in a half-hearted manner, doesn't mean that Gandhi has denied his role in the cover-up of murder.

We must therefore ask the following nagging questions:

1. Why didn't Gandhi respond to *After Mother India* when it was published in 1929 and he knew of it through the letter of Mr. Srinivasan?
2. Why didn't Gandhi respond himself to the two letters of inquiry that Thomas addressed to him?
3. Why didn't Gandhi personally write a letter to Mrs. Naidu, his own right-hand disciple being herself implicated as a coconspirator in the cover-up saga by Mrs. Doherty?
4. Why would Gandhi use the services of Pyarelal, his secretary, to "beat around the bush" instead of coming straight out in a truthful manner?

With the evidences at hand, we are left to wonder at both Gandhi's and Pyarelal's actions. First, Pyarelal asks Thomas to produce the authentic copy of Mrs. Doherty's deposition while acknowledging that Gandhi has "no recollection of having read" *After Mother India*. Second, Pyarelal writes to Saojini Naidu expressing Gandhi's complete ignorance of the incident. This bizarre behavior resonates with the ring of more suspicions and has strengthened my level of belief that Gandhi employed desperate evasive tactics to keep the lid tight on anyone knowing about Mr. Doherty's murder and its cover-up.

Another example is reproduced here of white killings before the awful Jallianwala Bagh tragedy in Amritsar (Punjab region) on April 13, 1919, during Gandhi's first nationwide Satyagraha campaign. Sir Michael O'Dwyer, lieutenant-governor of Punjab from 1913 to 1919, has elaborated on these killings, which occurred during the period of April 10 through 12:

> The mob, which had been incited to defy the law by months of open and secret revolutionary propaganda, at once rose, endeavored to force its way into the Civil Station where the British officials and non-officials reside, and was held up by the small British picguets on the bridges over the railway which connect the city with the Civil Station. The mobs . . . at once attacked and murdered all the Europeans (five) whom they could lay hands on in the city. They attempted

to murder two Englishwomen—a lady missionary and a lady doctor working in the city, and left the former for dead in the street; set fire to the Anglican Church, to the Mission School, while the teachers and pupils were inside, and to several other Mission buildings. They then looted the two English banks, after murdering the three British managers and burning their bodies; set fire to the railway goods station and murdered a British railway official on duty. . . . Such was the manner in which the Amritsar mob in a few hours gave a display of Gandhi's "Soul Force."[20]

Even though the Moslem elites were mainly aloof, largely as a result of the ongoing "Khilafat movement," the Moslem masses considered themselves closely associated with Gandhi's movement. The Moplahs' uprising is one example. The preaching of Gandhi and the propaganda of his volunteers led elements of Moplahs' common Moslems to believe that the government was to be overthrown, which to them meant Islamic rule and the freedom to do what they pleased to their neighboring Hindus. Perceiving that the moment was at hand, they attacked white government officials, murdered a few Europeans, and, with a special ferocity, turned on innocent Hindus. How many whites were murdered during the Moplahs' bloody uprising? Such figures are not available, but the Indian casualties were in the thousands.

Is there any example available of revolutionary propaganda used by Gandhi groupies to foment the crowds? Yes, as an example, one poster said:

Blessed by Mahatma Gandhi. We are the sons of India. We shall not give way. We shall lose our lives. We shall never abide by the Rowlatt Bill.

Gandhi! We the Indians will fight to the death after you. The flag of cruelty and oppression has been fixed in the ground. Alas, British, how you have cheated us. . . . You have fired on the Indians and shot them to death. . . . The treatments meted out to our girls at Amritsar are unbearable and we cannot expose them. It is very sad, that all our brethren are keeping silent at this moment.

What time are you waiting for now? There are many (English) ladies here to dishonour. Go all round India, clear the country of the ladies and those sinful creatures and then will be the only time when we can all say together, "Blessed be the Hindus, Mohammedans, and Sikhs."[21]

At another time, posters appeared on the walls reading "KILL ALL EUROPEANS." There were "holy" men who went about in the crowds, demanding "white men's blood," and "seize the white women."[22]

In South Africa, there were Indians who were resentful of Gandhi. Similarly, in India there were those who wanted to do the right thing, irrespective of Gandhi. In the words of Sir Michael O'Dwyer, "Sikh gentlemen, Sikh soldiers, and Sikh peasants, at the risk of their lives, saved European ladies who had been attacked, conducted to places of safety others who had been in danger, and rescued wounded soldiers from the roused fury of the mob." Other Indians, too, acted in a similar manner.[23]

NOTES

1. *A King's Story: The Memoirs of the Duke of Windsor* (New York: G. P. Putnam's Sons, 1947), pp. 171–72.

2. Harry H. Field, *After Mother India* (London: Jonathan Cape and Company, 1929), pp. 42–45. This book is referenced in Sharma's *Mahatma Gandhi: A Descriptive Bibliography* at #2715 without revealing the murder case. The bibliography by Pandiri failed to mention *After Mother India*.

3. Charles F. Andrews, *Mahatma Gandhi's Ideas* (New York: The Macmillan Company, 1930), pp. 276–89.

4. Mahadev Haribhal Desai, *Day-to-Day with Gandhi: Secretary's Diary from November 1917 to March 1927*, vol. 3 (Varanasi: Sarva Seva Sangh Prahashan, 1968).

5. Krishnadas, *Seven Months with Mahatma Gandhi: Being an Inside View of the Non-Co-Operation Movement (1921–1922)*, vol. 1 (Madras: S. Ganesan, 1928). Volume 1 covers the period from September to November 1921. Volume 2 covers the period from December 1921 to March 1922.

6. K. Gopalaswami, *Gandhi and Bombay* (Bombay: Bharatiya Vidya Shavan, 1969), pp. 121–38.

7. Robert Hardy Andrews, *A Lamp for India: The Story of Madame Pandit* (Englewood Cliffs: Prentice Hall, 1967), p. 115.

8. Nirad C. Chaudhuri, *Thy Hand Great Anarch! India: 1921–1952* (New York: Addison-Wesley Publishing Company, 1987), p. 21.

9. Ibid., p. 24.

10. *New York Times*, November 25, 1921, p. 11.

11. *New York Times*, November 23, 1921, p. 1.

12. *New York Times Index* (July–December 1921): 240.

13. *New York Times*, December 16, 1921, p. 14.

14. Sanharan C. Nair, *Gandhi and Anarchy* (Madras: Tagore & Co., 1922), pp. 240–41.

15. Gertrude Emerson, "'Non-violent Non-cooperation' in India," reprinted in *The Americanization of Gandhi: Images of the Mahatma*, ed. Charles Chatfield (New York: Garland Publishing, 1976), p. 197.

16. Claude H. Van Tyne, *India in Ferment* (New York: D. Appleton and Company, 1923), pp. 97, 127.

17. CWMG 42, #24, p. 19.

18. E. S. Reddy, comp. *The Mahatma and the Poetess* (Bombay: Bharatiya Vidya Bhavan, 1998), p. 158. Also check CWMG 24, p. 386.

19. In 2000, the government of India published a new 6th revised edition of the Collected Works of Mahatma Gandhi in 100 hardbound volumes. Pyarelal's letter to Sarojini Naidu is printed in volume 86, document #726, and on page 416 of *this* edition. Out of the total of eleven letters signed by Gandhi and dated May 25, 1945, Pyarelal authored only one letter and that was addressed to Naidu. This is the only CWMG reference in this book that pertains to the volumes published in 2000.

20. Michael O'Dwyer, *India as I Knew It* (London: Constable & Company Ltd., 1925), pp. 273–74.

21. Ibid., pp. 292–93. Ahmedabad, Gandhi's home city in his home state of Gujarat, linked with other cities to perpetrate more white murders and, its own share of wall-posters inciting the crowds to murder. See *A Searchlight on Gandhi*, authored by an unnamed "British-India merchant."

22. Post Wheeler, *India Against the Storm* (New York: E. P. Dutton & Company, Inc., 1944), p. 158.

23. Verney Lovett, *A History of the Indian Nationalist Movement* (New York: Frederick A. Stokes Company, 1920), p. 218.

29
RACISM against WHITES

See me please in the nakedness of my working, and in my lim-itations, you will then know me. I have to tread on most delicate ground, and my path is destined to be through jungles and temples.

—Mahatma Gandhi
The Life and Death of Mahatma Gandhi

Katherine Mayo, following her extraordinary visit to India remarked: "The doctrine on non-coöperation with the established Power led nowhere, as all see now. The mystic doctrine of spiritual war, a war of 'soul-force,' that uses the language of hate while protesting theories of love, had logically and insistently projected itself upon the material plane in the form of the slaughter of men."[1] Anyone interested in exploring the dimensions of Gandhi's "non-violence, civil disobedience, non-cooperation," their close association with mass riots and killing, and his intricate planning of huge frauds and deceptions to dupe the masses and then financially loot them, is welcome to scrutinize the literature. The best place to start is Sir Sankaran Nair's *Gandhi and Anarchy*. Another book titled *Gandhi As I Know Him* is a fascinating text by an individual who was very close to Gandhi, and who explored his deceptions carried out on poor Indian masses.[2] Here I am interested in the race side of this complex equation, whites not excluded. Since it happened and the evidence is there to prove it, the question is how to explain it, given what we know of Gandhi's alleged nonviolent, "full of love" speeches. Gandhi is not directly responsible for the racism in India. As we have seen, it is a fundamental feature of the Hindu caste system.

Perhaps it's not out of the way to revisit A. O. Hume, who founded the Indian National Congress (the Congress Party) in 1885. A year later, he wrote to a British official named Lord Dufferin and warned him of the reality in India, that because of racism:

> You do not get the truth—that virtually when it is alleged that the cat stole the cream, you blandly say—'Pussy, you surely did not steal that cream?' The virtual indignation of that *felis domesticus* may be conceived. I said that (unless when thieves fall out) the service and race bias is so strong that you never get the truth. The race bias makes the ordinary Magistrate let off the ravisher or the murderer; the service bias makes the whole official series, more or less, uphold the erring Magistrate. . . .[3]

In the words of Professor Van Tyne:

> Although India was a land of castes and a land where color was a basis of distinction between Brahmans and lower castes long before the British set foot upon it, still the race hatred based on this very distinction, seems to a casual observer at least, the most fundamental of all the conditions which array Indian against English.[4]

Racism had long existed in India, which is no surprise. The British, to their credit, were instrumental in keeping a tight control on what has been described as "unchecked Hinduism." However, with Gandhi as the head of the Brahmin-controlled Congress Party, they were no longer able to do so. The issue of caste blossomed in the public arena with no holds barred. Since the British didn't fit into the caste system, it was only a matter of time until Gandhi's Satyagraha methods exacerbated hate toward whites in India.

The various castes existed throughout history with few contacts. With the help of the British, Western education, and Western technology, the caste was beginning to learn to adapt to a new set of circumstances without abdicating its inner core. Now with Gandhi on the scene, the different castes metamorphosed into a monster for the unprepared British—namely, the "Hindu Race."[5] Not only did whites (who were opposed to Hinduism) have to leave India, but, as Professor Van Tyne was apprised: "We are told that once more the world must be conquered by India."[6] The new Hindu political ideology, a natural outcome of the continuing maturation of modern Hinduism, was set in place. However, the British were able to "control" Gandhi and the forces of destruction he was unleashing until the Second World War. Sir H. Twynam, governor of Central Provinces and Berar, in a letter to the viceroy, wrote: "But if Gandhi is going to embark on a subversive movement with a slogan designed to arouse racial feeling, with all its dangerous possibilities. . . . I feel, myself that no progress will ever be made unless Gandhi 'Deflated' as he was in 1932. . . ."[7]

When it comes to the racist implications of Gandhi's tactics, I am not the first one to have noticed a need for an explanation and more examples. Noted author Paul Johnson says:

> The events of 1920–1 indicated that though he [Gandhi] could bring a mass-movement into existence, he could not control it. Yet he continued to play the sorcerer's apprentice, while the casualty bill mounted into hundreds, then thousands, then tens of thousands, and the risks of a gigantic sectarian and racial explosion accumulated. This blindness to the law of probability in a bitterly divided sub-continent made nonsense of Gandhi's professions that he could not take life in any circumstances.Gandhi was not a liberator but a political exotic, who could have flourished only in the protected environment provided by British liberalism. He was a year older than Lenin, with whom he shared a quasi-religious approach to politics, though in sheer crankiness he had much more in common with Hitler, his junior by twenty years.[8]

According to Johnson, thanks to Gandhi and following his second nation-wide Satyagraha, "From that point onwards, large-scale racial, sectarian and anti-government violence became a permanent feature of Indian life."[9]

Sir Michael O'Dwyer, in *Fortnightly Review*, said, "The ascetic pose of this unctuous hypocrite is nauseating to honest men, many of whom have for years seen through his gospel of mixed humbug and race hatred."[10] Michael Edwardes, regarding the first Satyagraha, commented: "Most of the rioting, which was virtually confined to the Punjab and parts of western India, was spontaneous and characterized by racial and communal hatred."[11] And Titus Lowe, a resident of New York and general secretary of the Board of Foreign Missions of the Methodist Episcopal Church, addressed the Jersey Church Conference in New Jersey. He accused Gandhi of fomenting antiwhite passions in India, "The unrest in India under the leadership of Gandhi threatens to bring about a serious situation if the antiwhite sentiment continues to increase."[12]

S. N. Agnihotri (1850–1929), founder of the religious sect *Dev Samaj* and himself an eyewitness to Gandhi's Satyagraha tactics, accused him in strong words: "No doubt this soul destroying [Satyagraha] and most sinful poisonous dose of *racial hatred* is administered with the hollow assurance of its being non-violent and harmless, yet those who can dive deep into human nature, knew full well that the feelings of *hatred* and *revenge* towards British which were being excited in the people were bound to lead to violence, disorder, rebellion and bloodshed."[13] Mr. Agnihotri continued, "Had Mr. Gandhi not been blinded by the low passion of *race hatred* he could have utilized this cloth for the poor Indian men and women, who as in Khulna (Bengal) *hardly* find *rags to cover their shame* and almost go about stark naked. . . . He is unable to see that the abominable and very horrible fire of *race hatred* which he by this and other ways is kindling into flame, will surely bring *great havoc* in India. . . ."[14]

Noted scholar Sir Valentine Chirol has also established in his book that Gandhi was successful in controlling India's political scene by inciting inflammatory racial hatred against the whites.[15] Louis Fischer, being a pro-Gandhi fan and while visiting him in India in 1942 and 1946 also noted a general pervasive antiwhite atmosphere.[16] George Slocombe, who had interviewed Gandhi in one of his papers, recounted Gandhi as an example of "Men of Turmoil": "[Gandhi's] entire adult life has been devoted to the regeneration of Indian nationality and race consciousness and to destroying the submissiveness of the conquered to the conquerer."[17]

Albert F. Bemis, an American, while visiting India in the early 1920s, couldn't help but notice Gandhi's modus operandi and described as follows:

> In directing this [satyagraha] campaign he has very cleverly fitted his acts and framed his politics so that he has appealed to the desires and prejudices of the Indian people. In the first place, he has made use of natural racial aversions to develop hatred against the British. His agents have cunningly sown the seed of hatred among the young men, yea, even among the youth and children of the land. Where murders of Britishers have occurred, the murderers have often been boyish or youthful tools of the propagandists, and often without any previous connection with their victims or knowledge of their aims or accomplishments. He has, then, been poisoning the minds of the youths of the land against the British people and government. Such doctrine would always find ready believers among ignorant and subject peoples. In the second place, having established his foundation of hatred, he has openly fostered, if not preached, sedition, by pushing his policy of passive, pacific non-cooperation. Politically this means civil disobedience or the boycott of Government.
> Commercially it means the boycott of British industrial effort.[18]

At the very beginning of the book I asserted that Gandhi had two heirs: Vinoba Bhave as his spiritual heir, and Pandit Nehru as his political heir. When Dr. Martin Luther King Jr. visited India in February 1959, he had the occasion to meet, among others, Vinoba Bhave. It has been reported that Dr. King had called Vinoba Bhave a "kook," meaning a crackpot.[19]

As events unfolded, the British left and Pandit Nehru was appointed by Gandhi to be India's prime minister in 1947. In October 1949, Nehru paid an official visit to the United States and met President Harry Truman in the White House. Based upon that meeting, Truman informed various Congressmen, "Nehru practices color prejudice in reverse, he hates white people."[20] When the Socialist leader Norman Thomas met the president, he was told, "Mr. Thomas, not very long ago, Prime Minister Nehru was sitting in the very chair where you are now sitting, and I got the impression that he doesn't like white folks."[21] What Truman said about Nehru being "racist" can be directly inferred to apply to Gandhi as well. In 1942, in his speech to the All India Congress Committee meeting, Gandhi made this clear: "Pandit Jawaharlal [Nehru] has been resisting me ever since he fell into my net. You cannot divide water by repeatedly striking it with a stick. It is just as difficult to divide us. . . . [He] will be my successor.

He says whatever is uppermost in his mind, but he always does what I want . . ."
(CWMG 75, #302, p. 224). Could it be that Gandhi had rubbed his racist emol-
lient on Nehru or did he merely endorse the Brahmin's racial superiority? Nehru
was of that highest caste.

Until now, you have read a few examples put forth by a few important figures that acknowledge Gandhi's racism against whites. Admittedly, the example
of Truman points more to Nehru than Gandhi, even though they were intimately
connected. However, it still doesn't explain their white racist ideology. For that
we have to turn to Sir Sankaran Nair. What I have presented next is based on the
analysis in *Gandhi and Anarchy*.

To answer the mystery, Nair begins with Gandhi's first manuscript—*Hind
Swaraj* (Indian Home Rule)—which he authored in South Africa in 1909. Based
upon a meticulous analysis, he reaches the conclusion that Gandhi is not only
against parliamentary government, but practically against any form of government. Instead, what he would like to see is anarchy and "soul-force." While in
South Africa, the political and demographic situation was repressive. But back in
India, once the Congress Party was under him, the situation changed dramatically,
and he had the means to bring about anarchy through "soul-force": establish a
society without government, without railways, without machinery, without hospi-
tals or schools, without lawyers, without courts, etc. In other words, take India
back to the dark ages, dictated by totalitarian Hinduism, where everybody
serenely follows a caste-ordained life. To attain that objective, the present government had to be overthrown, using the "non-violent non-cooperation" movement.
But the reins of the government were in white, British hands. And that's where
race hatred against whites had its inception. With the help of the caste system and
subcontinent Moslems, he pursued a methodical plan to destroy the government.
He created a situation in which a peaceful resolution was impossible. Bloodshed
and constant hate propaganda against the British government kept the momentum
going. The masses were too ignorant to understand the complexities. They were
given one false promise after another; they were repeatedly duped.

The British knew how to govern but were no match for Gandhi-induced
Hindu propaganda. They operated in crisis management, crawling from one desperate move to another. Gandhi's powers of delusion were breathtaking, he
swayed vast numbers of people, making them passionately intolerant. The
British authorities knew well what Gandhi was up to—overthrowing the white
government in India. In *Gandhi and Anarchy*, there are testimonies of senior officials recognizing that the Gandhi propaganda machine used racial hatred against
the British to achieve its objectives. Another major casualty of Gandhi's racial
tactics was the constitutional reforms under which all races could join hands in
unity toward a common goal.

I want to make it clear that there is no evidence in place that has convinced me
that Gandhi was a racist per se when it comes to the whites—his hatred seemed to

be exclusively focused on the British. With respect to the blacks, however, it was a different story. There the evidence is overwhelming that Gandhi is a racist. Traditionally, it has been thought among the Hindus that un-caste white people are below Untouchables. The evidence does not show whether or not Gandhi ever held those views. On the contrary, his view of the whites was quite the opposite, as evidenced by his actions and writings of South Africa. When we see the signs and symptoms of racism against whites in India, the situations were markedly different. Simply put, British whites were a roadblock to Gandhi's utopic vision; they had to be removed. The best available method was to set in motion the complex scheme to beat them by using the race card. After all, the training and experiences of South Africa came in handy in India. The Indian masses were vulnerable and easy to incite for that purpose, and in the long run, it took its toll.

Gandhi's actions created a permanent gulf between Hindus and Moslems and dangerously widened the gulf between Indians and the British. Fomenting racial (and caste) and religious differences killed, for all practical purposes, any meaningful reforms. For the British, the only solution left was to play hardball and keep tight "control" over Gandhi using the security apparatus at their disposal. But this tactic was to haunt them later on with the outbreak of World War II, which gave Gandhi a window of opportunity to play with fire—the idea of ethnic cleansing—and to overthrow the British rule. Written in 1942, the words of Sir H. Twynam, governor of Central Provinces and Berar in British India, should resonate the depth of British mistrust: "Since 1920 Gandhi has been the Hitler of Indian Politics."[22]

NOTES

1. Katherine Mayo, *Mother India* (New York: Harcourt, Brace & Company, 1927), pp. 353–54.

2. Indulal K. Yajnik, *Gandhi As I Know Him* (Delhi: Danesh Mahal, 1943).

3. Quoted in William Golant, *The Long Afternoon: British India 1601–1947* (New York: St. Martin's Press, 1975), p. 68.

4. Claude H. Van Tyne, *India in Ferment* (New York: D. Appleton and Company, 1923), p. 160.

5. Earl of Ronaldshay, *The Heart of Aryavarta: A Study of the Psychology of Indian Unrest* (Boston: Houghton Mifflin, 1925), p. 7.

6. Van Tyne, *India in Ferment*, p. 196.

7. Quoted in *The Transfer of Power* (London: Her Majesty's Stationery Office, 1971), vol. 2, pp. 195–96.

8. Paul Johnson, *Modern Times: The World from the Twenties to the Eighties* (New York: Harper & Row, 1985), p. 472.

9. Ibid., p. 47.

10. Michael O'Dwyer in *The Americanization of Gandhi: Images of the Mahatma*, ed. Charles Chatfield (New York: Garland Publishing, 1976), p. 198.

11. Michael Edwardes, *The Myth of the Mahatma: Gandhi, the British, and the Raj* (London: Constable, 1986), p. 199.

12. *New York Times*, March 12, 1922, p. 18. Also in its January 25, 1922, issue, p. 3, the *Times* reported Lord Northcliffe's comments; "I am shocked at the change of demeanor and acts toward the whites by both Hindus and Mohammedans, especially those of them who formerly were most friendly." Another statement by Lord Northcliffe points out that there was another male friend walking with Mr. Doherty on that fateful day. But he, unlike Mr. Doherty, escaped by running up an alley after being badly hurt.

13. S. N. Agnihotri, *Mr. Gandhi in the Light of Truth: A Critical Examination of Mr. Gandhi's Non-co-operation Propaganda in the Light of Facts and Principles of National Evolution* (Lahore: S. A. Singh, 1921), p. 8.

14. Ibid., p. 10.

15. Valentine Chirol, *India: Old and New* (London: Macmillan, 1921).

16. CWMG 85, #10, p. 10.

17. Quoted in *Men of Turmoil: Biographies by Leading Authorities of the Dominating Personalities of Our Day* (New York: Books for Libraries Press, 1935), p. 61. Another article authored by E. M. E. Blyth, titled "Mahatma Gandhi: A Study in Destructiveness," *Quarterly Review* 256 (1931): 388–401, is highly recommended.

18. Albert Farwell Bemis, *A Journey to India: 1921–1922* (Boston: The Merrymount Press, 1923), p. 59.

19. Jeffery Paine, *Father India: How Encounters with an Ancient Culture Transformed the Modern West* (New York: HarperCollins, 1998), p. 252. Original work was reported in *Parting the Waters: America in the King Years, 1954–63*.

20. Louis Fisher, *This Is Our World* (New York: Harper & Brothers, 1956), p. 153.

21. Ibid., p. 153.

22. *The Transfer of Power*, vol. 2, p. 196.

30

GANDHI and ETHNIC CLEANSING

My nonviolence does recognise different species of violence, defensive and offensive. It is true that, in the long run, the difference is obliterated, but the initial merit persists.

—Mahatma Gandhi (1940)
On Prejudice: A Global Perspective

With global celebrations we marked the end of the twentieth century and the beginning of the twenty-first. Much of the younger generation is ignorant of how bloody the twentieth century was. The last few months of that century witnessed the latest example of ethnic cleansing, in the Balkans. Looking even further back, the record becomes more shameful. It is incumbent upon us to draw concrete lessons from those unspeakable crimes perpetrated against humanity. The affirmation lies in the fact that human beings have made a voyage through various ethnic cleansings of one sort or another. The twentieth century started with one of those opprobrious examples of mass killings in South Africa, and Gandhi was right there. His history with respect to ethnic cleansing ranges from a pindrop silence to its outright promotion. This chapter will study that side of his life.

Gandhi was no innocent bystander to mass suffering and mass killing. In the two examples I set forth here, Gandhi's relationship to the ethnic cleansing is marked by a premeditated silence.

The first is during the Boer War of 1899 in South Africa, when Gandhi led about eleven hundred Indians and participated with them as "medic soldiers." His corps was mentioned in dispatches and Gandhi received a war medal. Before proceeding to the front, he declared in a press statement that their dream had been realized and although, unfortunately, they were not to be engaged in the fighting, he hoped they would be able to discharge their duties. Gandhi did not mention anywhere after the war that the British had set up concentration camps for women and children and had committed atrocities. Did he know about it? Yes. After a lapse of many years, long after he had removed from the scene, he wrote in *Satyagraha in South Africa*:

> Boer women understood that their religion required them to suffer in order to preserve their independence, and therefore, patiently and cheerfully endured all hardships. Lord Kitchener left no stone unturned in order to break their spirit. He confined them in separate concentration camps where they underwent indescribable sufferings. They starved, they suffered biting cold and scorching heat. Sometimes a soldier, intoxicated with liquor or maddened by passion, might even assault these unprotected women. Still the brave women did not flinch.[1]

The details of the narrative are convincing evidence that Gandhi was well aware of the war crimes being committed at that time, but decided to keep silent, even when there was an uproar and protests in England by many honest English men and women. Reports estimate that as many as twenty-five thousand Boer females and children perished in these concentration camps.

The second example is presented by Elliott Green of Philadelphia, who wrote the following letter to the editor in response to *The Gandhi Nobody Knows*:

> When Gandhi supported the Khilafat movement of the Indian Muslims after World War I, he opposed the creation of new states for the subject peoples of the Ottoman empire, which has been envisioned by the treaty of Sèvres (1920). One of the new states called for by the victors in World War I was an Armenian state to be set up in eastern Anatolia in part of historic Armenia. The Armenians had just suffered the first modern genocide at the hands of the Turks. The massacre continued after the end of the World War I in areas which France and the Russian Bolsheviks handed over to the Muslim Turkish government of Ataturk, as well as in Smyrna, conquered from Greece. By his support of the Khilafat movement, Gandhi was disregarding the national rights of the Ottoman subject peoples and especially those of the Armenians. He was saying in effect that mass murder did not bother him. Genocide, he implied, was OK. Let me add that the Armenian massacres were not an obscure event. In fact, they received worldwide attention. Surely Gandhi was aware of them from the British papers.[2]

Various information groups have reported the Armenian genocide count at a million to a million and a half.

As I have already noted, the British government put the brakes on Gandhi, and for all practical purposes his actions within India were under control. But with the outbreak of World War II in September 1939, all hell broke loose and so did Gandhi. Now he could see the light at the end of the tunnel—the fall of British rule. Lord Archibald Percival Wavell, viceroy of India from October 1943 to March 1947, confided in his diary of September 26, 1946, "Gandhi at the end exposed Congress policy of domination more nakedly than ever before. The more I see of that old man, the more I regard him as an unscrupulous old hypocrite; he would shrink from no violence and blood-letting to achieve his ends, though he would naturally prefer to do so by chicanery and a false show of mildness and friendship."[3] Michael Edwardes, the British-Indian historian, has written a provocative chapter—"Giant Killer?"—in his *The Myth of the Mahatma: Gandhi, the British and the Raj*, a must read for any serious student. By this time, as the events unfolded and the British left the subcontinent in 1947, in those dreadful hours there were 1 million to 4 million people murdered and millions of others uprooted.

Many of us are naïve, thinking that since Gandhi never picked up a gun, how could he be held responsible for any mass killings? We should realize that a gun is only one of many tools used to kill people. Second, we must keep in mind that during the decades Gandhi was fighting using "soul-force," he held no political power and the traditional killing machines were in the hands of the British officials—far removed from Gandhi's reach. The "soul-force," far from being benign, carried its own armory—alternative means to kill and the necessary tools tucked away in the appendix. World War II brought those attachments into the open; some were applicable to the Indian setting and others were honed for the European and other theaters. Let's revisit briefly to search for ethnic cleansing in the European war theatre with respect to Gandhi. A few scholars, familiar with the literature, have stated that Gandhi's recommendations were: (1) inconsistent and contradictory; (2) Hindu romanticism, if somewhat camouflaged; (3) an all-out nonviolent pitch; (4) anti-Semitic; (5) idealistic but not realistic; and (6) demented. Let's check the facts:

THE JEWS

Quite early on, Gandhi advised Jewish people facing the Third Reich of a way out of Hitler's persecution:

> [Satyagraha] can and does work in the teeth of the fiercest opposition. But it ends in evoking the widest public sympathy. Sufferings of the non-violent have been known to melt the stoniest hearts. I make bold to say that if the Jews can summon to their aid the soul power that comes only from non-violence, Herr Hitler will bow before the courage which he has never yet experienced in any large measure in his dealings with men, and which, when it is exhibited, he will own is infinitely superior to that shown by his best storm troopers. (CWMG 68, #225, pp. 191–93)

At an unknown date during the war (most probably in June 1942), he updated his advice: they [Jews] should commit collective suicide. If only the Jews of Germany had the good sense to offer their throats willingly to the Nazi butchers' knives and throw themselves into the sea from cliffs.[4] Gandhi believed that if the Jews had listened to his advice on collective suicide, "that would have been heroism."

THE FRENCH

Gandhi praised the French surrender in 1940 as brave statesmanship. Later on, in April 1942, in an interview with Eve Curie (daughter of scientist Marie Curie), Gandhi insisted that the French chart only a nonviolent course to face Nazi aggression and occupation. Apparently, Gandhi harbored negative views of the French resistance movement—men and women were active behind the lines in low-intensity maneuverings against the Nazis. Anyway, their conversations revolved in a circle, since Eve's probing questions were a bit troublesome. Her description of her frustration is eloquent:

> I felt as if he and I were moving on different floors of the same house, he on the top floor and I on the ground floor. There was no staircase I could find to join him. I never got a chance of coming across him in a passage, face to face, and saying: "Hello—I've caught you at last." One could not "catch" Mr. Gandhi: he always slipped away.[5]

THE BRITISH

With German might at its peak, Gandhi turned toward the embattled British and urged them to lay down their arms. He said:

> I do not want Britain to be defeated nor do I want her to be victorious in a trial of brute strength. . . . I want you to fight Nazism without arms, or, . . . with non-violent arms. I would like you to lay down the arms you have as being useless for saving you or humanity. You will invite Herr Hitler and Signor Mussolini to take what they want of the countries you call your possessions. Let them take possession of your beautiful island, with your many beautiful buildings. You will give all these, but neither your souls, nor your minds. If these gentlemen choose to occupy your homes, you will vacate them. If they do not give you free passage out, you will allow yourself, man, woman and child, to be slaughtered, but you will refuse to owe allegiance to them. (CWMG 72, #281, p. 230)

A few days later, he emphasized to the British people, "Herr Hitler has never dreamt of possessing Britain. He wants the British to admit defeat" (CWMG 72, #434, p. 383). Just in case the British had misunderstood the Fuhrer, Gandhi stepped forward to help them out. In a letter to the British viceroy Lord Linlithgow, he announced that the war was lost and offered his services as a mediator with Hitler. He wrote: "This manslaughter must be stopped. You are losing; if you persist, it will only result in greater bloodshed. *Hitler is not a bad man.* If you call it off today, he will follow suit. If you want to send me to Germany or anywhere else, I am at your disposal. You can also inform the Cabinet about this" [my italics].[6]

Other European countries like Czechoslovakia, Poland, Norway, Denmark, Holland, Belgium, etc., which were no match for the Nazi's ferocious onslaught, had earlier been advised by Gandhi to try the same tactics.[7] In sharp contrast, as the war accelerated in the Asian theater, he asked the Chinese not to submit to the Japanese. And when the Japanese encroached very near to the eastern frontiers of British India, Gandhi called for the defence of India by all means, including cooperation with British forces and mobilization of Indian soldiers.[8]

ANALYSIS AND CONCLUSION

The goal of Gandhi's strategy was to defeat the British, which would set India free, in his mind. There was something grotesque in Gandhi's thinking of Europeans as his new pawns, as if he could manipulate them from thousands of miles away into adopting his solution of self-induced mass killings and perishing gloriously.[9] His advice, if adopted, would have guaranteed a Nazi victory and a British defeat. I believe Gandhi saw the Jewish people as an obstruction to his goal, since so much of German manpower and assets were tied up in persecuting and killing them. Collective suicide would have quickly solved the problem and diverted precious resources to defeat the British. His advice to the British people was no less repulsive. The "ethnic cleansing" of the Jewish and British peoples would have been total—*nonviolently*, if you know what I mean. After the war, when the full extent of the Holocaust was revealed, Gandhi told Louis Fischer that the Jews died anyway; they might as well have died significantly. One can also draw another conclusion: Aryan Gandhi was doing all he could to help his cousin, Aryan Hitler! In addition to throwing the British government out of India, using Hitler's leverage, Gandhi had another main objective: to transfer the power to upper-caste Hindu hands, preferably the Brahmins. This would ensure that the modern Hinduism state nourished modern Hindu ideology, a vital ingredient for Hindu imperialism and expansionism.

Since Gandhi's ideas of ethnic cleansing did not go over well in Europe, there was another market to try: the Punjab and Kashmir regions of the subcontinent. With the likely creation of Pakistan looming on the horizon, the Punjab and Kashmir people received their Gandhi-prescribed doses of perishing gloriously. They died in wholesale numbers but not gloriously. The expansionist feature of Hindu Imperialism came in handy. Expectedly, and it should come as no surprise, all three states—Hyderabad, Junagarh, and Kashmir—were swallowed in one sequential gulp. They had the luxury to taste Satyagraha's love call with Gandhi's blessings. In January 1948, more than two years after the United States had dropped two atomic bombs on Japan, Gandhi decided to show the way of perishing gloriously—there is a proper way to die en masse. Responding to *Life* magazine photographer Margaret Bourke-White's question on how he would meet the atom bomb, Gandhi said: "I will not go underground. I will come out in the open and let the pilot see I have not the face of evil against him. The pilot will not see our faces from his great height, I know. But that longing in our hearts that he will not come to harm would reach up to him and his eyes would be opened. Of those thousands who were done to death in Hiroshima, if they had died with that prayerful action—died openly with that prayer in their hearts— then the war would not have ended so disgracefully as it has."[10] Gandhi was instrumental in exerting far-reaching pathological political influences on the budding Hindu state's polity. This is exemplified by India's action-oriented vision following the successive Hindu leaders, beginning with Mr. Nehru, in pursuit of political and ideological expansionism, have often taken shelter behind Gandhi's name as a justification for their military adventures—slaughtering people by the wholesale numbers on the way to ecstatically realizing "religiously sanctioned political self-enlightenment."[11]

There is another Satyagraha weapon ideally suited for ethnic cleansing. Untouchables and other *Sudra* people are most likely to be on the receiving end of this weapon. Any casual observer of the squalid living conditions under which most Indians live will agree with Debabar Banerji:

> The virtual breakdown of the public health system in the country is associated with frequent outbreaks of epidemics . . . of kala-azar, Japanese encephalitis, pyogenic meningitis, cholera and gastroenteritis, bacillary dysentery, infective hepatitis. . . . *[L]iterally millions of people* are allowed to die of the most elementary preventable diseases because of the inaction by the government, the same government ties up with captains of industry to develop joint ventures to cater to the high technology needs of the wafer thin uppermost class of the population of the country [my italics].[12]

Why is modern India so negligent in promoting treatments for many of the diseases that poor Indians succumb to? There are those senior Indian officials who give a sigh of relief that at least the diseases are somehow controlling the population. In this sense the Hindu elite establishment is following Gandhi's notion, expressed to Louis Fischer on June 8, 1942, regarding the only method of population control acceptable to him: ". . . *perhaps we need some good epidemics*" (my italics).[13] Unfortunately, not even these "good epidemics" have been able to control the steep population growth. India needs "better epidemics" in a true Gandhian spirit. In the meantime, Untouchables and the other low castes are the primary victims of the silent mass killings under way in post-British Hindu India. Ironically, the population keeps growing unabated. Today, India's population has exceeded a billion people with at least eighteen million added every year. For the last sixty years or so, a number of well-meaning Westerners have warned Indian leaders (Gandhi included) about the steep population growth that India had been experiencing and urged them to take measures to stem the growth. Such advice has fallen on deaf ears. It seems to me that these Hindu leaders of today are hoping that through some mysterious way, Gandhi's notion of inviting deadly diseases will take fruit and that will wipe off the undesirable Untouchables, Sudra people, the Moslems, etc.

An earlier event comes to my mind that I must share. Gandhi himself was known to view vaccination as a "dangerous and filthy habit." While he and his followers were on the long Salt March in 1930, leisurely going through various villages, it was reported that many members of his party were carrying the smallpox virus, which they had contracted earlier at Gandhi's spiritual retreat. And as they marched, they were dropped from the ranks as smallpox struck them down—meanwhile sowing the deadly seeds in the poor villages.[14]

NOTES

1. Mohandas K. Gandhi, *Satyagraha in South Africa* (1928; reprint, Ahmedabad: Navajivan Publishing House, 1972), p. 15.

2. *Commentary* (July 1983): 10–11.

3. Penderel Moon, ed., *Wavell: The Viceroy's Journal* (London: Oxford University Press, 1973), p. 353.

4. Louis Fischer, *Gandhi and Stalin: Two Signs at the World's Crossroads* (New York: Harper & Brothers, 1947), p. 50.

5. Eve Curie, *Journey among Warriors* (New York: Doubleday, Doran and Co., 1943), p. 454.

6. Robert Payne, *The Life and Death of Mahatma Gandhi* (New York: Konecky & Konecky, 1969), p. 488.

7. The cases of Czechoslovakia and Poland require somewhat different interpretations. When Nazi Germany invaded into the Bohemian heartland, Gandhi asked the Czechs to adopt unarmed nonviolent resistance. But when Hitler invaded Poland, Gandhi suddenly sanctioned the Polish army's military resistance, calling it "almost nonviolent." I believe this sudden change in Gandhi's tactics had an underlying motive. In Gandhi's mind, Hitler's military advances to the east of Germany were counterproductive to Gandhi's plans for a British defeat. It made sense, at least in Gandhi's mind, that perhaps armed resistance by the Polish army might convince Hitler to concentrate his military power to the west. Britain and the other countries in that direction were already receiving Gandhi's prescription of nonviolence, which guaranteed their defeat.

8. Stanley Maron, "The Non-Universality of Satyagraha" a chapter in *Gandhi, India and the World: An International Symposium*, p. 277.

9. I am indebted to late Richard Grenier who used the term "perishing gloriously" in his article, "The Gandhi Nobody Knows."

10. Margaret Bourke-White, *Halfway to Freedom* (New York: Simon and Schuster, 1949), p. 232.

11. In order to grasp Gandhi's blessings for India's military seizures of Hyderabad, Kashmir, and Junagarh, check the following few references: CWMG 89, #413, 433, 434, 454, 480, 481; 90, #7, and 356. In his usual characteristic fashion, Gandhi, in his interview with Vincent Sheean, recorded in *Lead Kindly Light: Gandhi and the Way to Peace*, blamed his close disciples (notably Nehru and Patel) for carrying on the invasions leading to expanisonism. Following India's military seizure in 1961 of three Portuguese colonies (Goa being the main), Prime Minister Nehru described the Goa action as "entirely in keeping" with Gandhi's principles and Gandhi's closest followers approved it. Quoted in *When a Great Tradition Modernizes: An Anthropological Approach to Indian Civilization*, p. 34.

Imbued with modern Hinduism's reinterpretation of the Hindu scriptures, Prime Minister Nehru laid territorial claims on the Himalayas and then implemented the Gandhian tactics of Satyagraha invasion to ignite a full-scale war against friendly China. Check *India's China War*, pages 127 and 175. Senior Indian officials also take shelter behind Gandhi's holy name for pursuing the building of nuclear weapons. And of course, as I have mentioned already in the introduction, Prime Minister Indira Gandhi, in her war on the Sikhs, also took cover behind Mahatma Gandhi's teaching. Further research is needed to determine if Gandhi's teachings in any fashion were the inspiration for India's annexation of Sikkim, capturing the small portion of Tibet, fomenting ethnic turmoil in Sri-Lanka, the birth of *ultra*-Hindu fundamentalism, practicing blatant human rights violations against the Untouchables and other ethnic nationalities, and the Moslem population trapped in today's political India.

12. Arthur Bonner, *Democracy in India: A Hollow Shell* (Washington, D.C.: The American University Press, 1994), pp. 227–28.

13. Louis Fischer, *A Week with Gandhi* (New York: Duell, Sloan and Pearce, 1942), p. 89. This answer was laughed off.

14. Katherine Mayo, "Gandhi's March Past," *The Atlantic Monthly* (September 1930): 328.

CONCLUSION
RECAPTURING GANDHI

Supposing an army of a lakh [one hundred thousand] of armed Afridis invaded the place [Kashmir] and a handful of people offered armed resistance in order to protect the innocent children and women and died fighting, then they could be called non-violent in spite of their using arms.

—Mahatma Gandhi
November 5, 1947

If a man fights with his sword single-handed against a horde of dacoits [robbers] armed to the teeth, I should say he is fighting almost non-violently.

Mahatma Gandhi (1940)
On Prejudice: A Global Perspective

It has taken me a full sixteen years to crack the Gandhi mystery. We need to reassess what we teach in our schools, in our history classes, on the silver screen, and on television. We need to recapture the historical Gandhi and shred the mythological, false image. Before we blame Dr. Martin Luther King Jr., Sir Richard Attenborough, and the history teachers or anybody else, for that matter, we must realize that they, like us, were victims of the Gandhi propaganda machine. Sir Richard Attenborough fell victim to the Hindu establishment, more specifically beginning with Mr. Motilal Kothari, former staff member of the

Indian High Commission in London.[1] The story of Reverend King is quite different: He fell "victim," not to the Hindu establishment, but to the American Christian propagandists, at least in the early stages. In fairness to him, in the words of Professor Keith Miller of Arizona State University, "Gandhi exerted very little direct influence on King. Instead, King learned nonviolence almost directly from American sources."[2] As for other early Gandhi lovers in the West, Professor Miller has pinpointed succinctly, "For [Stanley] Jones, for the Gandhians from Howard University, and for King, Gandhi was always a Christian. Gandhi's Hinduism never mattered."[3] In many ways, Richard Lischer (a professor at Duke University) sustains Miller's verdict: "Gandhi was foreign to King's own religious heritage and positively unintelligible to his American audience. By 1960 references to Gandhi disappeared from King's sermons and speeches."[4] More recently, another scholar, Greg Moses, has analyzed much more comprehensively the issue of Reverend King's links to nonviolence, both ideologically and tactically speaking.[5] Pulitzer Prize–winning King biographer David J. Garrow (a professor at Emory University) has consistently warned us to shy away from primary reliance on King's published books and essays, noting that these sources were largely ghostwritten by Al Duckett, Harris Wofford, Stanley Levison, Bayard Rustin, and other advisers to King.[6] Also, Professor Miller's scholarly research points out that in Dr. King's most famous speeches, Gandhi is remarkably absent. For instance, in King's "I Have a Dream," Gandhi is ignored; in "Address to Holt Street Baptist Church," which was King's first civil rights speech, Gandhi is nowhere to be found; and in "Letter from Birmingham Jail," Gandhi is conspicuously missing. In light of these modern scholarly works, it behooves us to reconsider the standard story line that has been successfully shoved down our throats and reexamine critically Reverend King's link to Sergeant-Major Gandhi. Not only is it crucial, but also fair and fitting, to protect the King legacy from being hijacked by the Gandhi propaganda machine.[7]

The evidence shows Gandhi underwent no moral reservations following the 1906 war against blacks. In his second dispatch while on board the S.S. *Armadale Castle* on his way to England, in a sequel to a Gujarati poem, Gandhi painted the white Englishmen in such glowing terms—the white soldiers as models with respect to their performance of war duties, among others.

In the minds of some scholars, Gandhi's war actions call for introspection, as if Rudyard Kipling had a Gandhilike man on his mind when he authored his famous epic poem "Gunga Din." Whether Gandhi was Gunga Din in a truly original fashion is highly debatable. There are some Indians who harbor strong feelings that Gandhi was in fact a secret British agent, planted with a purpose on the poor Indian masses to sway them in the wrong directions. I confess here that the evidence attesting to the idea of him as an "agent of the imperial Queen" thus far has been speculative at best. It is high time to chronologically catalog the critical historical events where Gandhi led us astray.

DEVELOPMENT OF COVER-UPS

After the 1906 incident dealing with the Zulu rebellion and before the birth of Satyagraha, there was some transition within Gandhi. What kind, it is hard to say. We know it was not soul-searching as we understand that term. In late December 1907 (almost a year and a half after the Zulu rebellion), Rev. Doke visited Gandhi's law office in Johannesburg and noticed that, on his office walls, among other items, was displayed a photo of the stretcher-bearer corps. As a proud testimony of combat duty, servicemen often exhibit military mementos on the walls. In that sense, Gandhi was no different—he was proud of his military action during the Zulu rebellion. Taking into consideration that after the Zulu War Gandhi underwent what can only be described as some unexplained transition, the result of which was certain: Recount the past through the modicum of storytelling. In doing so, replace the past with a new, created story—erect a pseudohistory. What I have been able to decipher is that Gandhi's greatest motivation for covering up his past was to cover the details of his involvement in the Zulu rebellion and his encounters with blacks while in prison. His strategy was to develop a pseudohistory for any given political setting. It is time to track them:

In 1909, *M. K. Gandhi: An Indian Patriot in South Africa* by Joseph J. Doke, was "dictated" by Gandhi. It was really nothing more than Gandhi using the Baptist minister's name for the purpose of "politicking" in London during his second deputation. As has already been elaborated in parts 2, 3, 4, and 5, the black-related events were twisted to a new setting. It is staggering to notice that less than one year after his prison encounters with blacks in 1908–9, those encounters were jumbled up with the 1906 Zulu rebellion pseudohistory, effectively rendering them indistinguishable. His racism against blacks was covered, but not necessarily foolproof. This pseudohistory remained in effect until the mid-1920s.

In 1914, Gandhi had a meeting with Sir Gilbert Murray in London. In all likelihood, Gandhi related his brief pseudohistory to Murray. Then, in 1918, an article titled "The Soul as It Is and How to Deal with It" was published in the *Hibbert Journal*, at the time when macho gandhi was busy promoting World War I activities. The article made it to America and Reverend Holmes read it and got hooked. From there on, a new Christ was born and church propaganda did the rest. Another layer of oral pseudohistory was spread over the 1909 pseudohistory, resulting in a phenomenon of widespread pseudohistory, mimicking as true history, unknown and unparalleled in the recorded history.

In 1919 the new Gandhi was on the horizon. Gandhi's images in India and the West needed to be reconciled. The early stages of legislation for the Rowlatt Bills provided Gandhi the political opportunity for a complete about-face against the British. One cannot overlook the earlier impact of Professor Murray's "mystical" article in the West and its likely rewards—ponderings evolved within Gandhi's "inner voice," which he equated with God's revelations to him, to benefit from the spiritual opportunity. One wouldn't be far off the mark to conclude that spiritual opportunity paved the way for political opportunity. Within India, publicity portraying him as the latest Hindu incarnation added more punch to Gandhi's growing messianic image. Sometime during this period, I believe Gandhi destroyed important papers, particularly those dealing with the 1906 war against blacks.

While incarcerated in India in 1922, a new political setting required a new pseudohistory. At that point, *Satyagraha in South Africa* was born. This new pseudohistory effectively became the Bible of Gandhi's South African period. But followers desired more. For their benefit in India and abroad (specifically in the United States) a new autobiography appeared serially. *An Autobiography, or the Story of My Experiments with Truth* was a powerful testimony shrouded in religious language. People were hooked. This new pseudohistory fully replaced the 1909 pseudohistory. From then on, many more biographies and articles appeared, making full use of *Satyagraha* and the *Autobiography* as the undisputed authorities. The cover-up was functioning. Everybody knew the humanitarian task Gandhi had performed for the poor blacks of South Africa. What a turnaround of past events—white soldiers were conveniently denigrated and ascribed with out-and-out racism. Reverend Martin Luther King Jr., decades later, described the *Autobiography* as one of the ten books that most affected his thinking.[8] Nelson Mandela, writing at the end of the twentieth century for *Time* magazine's feature coveted edition Person of the Century, repeated in essence the *Autobiography*'s pseudohistory:

> His [Gandhi] awakening came on the hilly terrain of the so-called Bambata Rebellion, where as a passionate British patriot, he led his Indian stretcher-bearer corps to serve the Empire, but British brutality against the Zulus roused his soul against violence as nothing had done before. He determined, on that battlefield, to wrest himself of all material attachments and devote himself completely and totally to eliminate violence and serving humanity. The sight of wounded and whipped Zulus, mercilessly abandoned by their British persecutors, so appalled him that he turned full circle from his admiration for all things British to celebrate the indigenous and ethnic.[9]

In both of these autobiographical accounts you couldn't help but notice an interesting feature: His first biography, *M. K. Gandhi: An Indian Patriot in South Africa* by Joseph J. Doke is mentioned nowhere. Up until the time of the *Autobiography*, or after its publication, nobody had suspected a cover-up by Gandhi encompassing his prison experiences in South Africa. In *Satyagraha in South Africa*, one reads that Gandhi had decided to forgo prison descriptions: "But I do not propose here to deal with our hardships in jail, for which the curious may turn to the account of my experiences of jail life in South Africa."[10] Here he is referring to an earlier booklet that he published in India and which detailed his jail experiences in South Africa, with racist remarks intact. Ironically, the political picture dictated new moral lessons emphasizing new *Satyagrahis* based upon his past South African prison experiences:

> I wish that the result of the perusal of these experiences would be that he who knows not what patriotism is, would learn it and after doing so become a passive resister, and he who is so already, would be confirmed in his attitude. I also get more and more convinced that he who does not know his true duty or religion, would never know what patriotism or feeling for one's own country is.[11]

By the time his *Autobiography* surfaced, the cover-up was complete. His racist tirades against blacks had been expunged in their entirety. In an updated edition of *Speeches and Writings of Mahatma Gandhi*, published by G. A. Natesan, there reappeared for the last time three subsections under the heading "Jail Experiences in South Africa," which detailed his encounters. All the derogatory and racist remarks against blacks were deleted.[12] In all probability, the decision to expunge the racist remarks was made during the time Gandhi was imprisoned. In addition to what Gandhi had written in the *Indian Opinion* columns in South Africa, which were not available in India at that time, there were at least two more versions floating around, one with and the other without racist remarks. These versions were being used carefully: the version without racist comments was more suitable for the West and the other was for Indian readers. Once his autobiographical accounts were published, all references to earlier prison experience versions were eliminated from the literature to the fullest extent possible.

Gandhi's pseudohistory (first oral and then written) depicting his South African prison experiences was remarkably successful, as was evidenced by the sermon given by John H. Holmes in April 1922, "As Gandhi moves from place to place, great multitudes of men and women follow him, as similar multitudes followed Jesus in Palestine. . . . Four times, in South Africa and in India, he has been imprisoned. Thrice he has been beaten by mobs, and once left prone in the gutter as one dead. His body bears the stripes of the whips with which he has been lashed, his wrists and ankles the marks of the chains with which he has been bound for hours together to the iron bars of his cell. Read Paul's catalogue of sufferings, and you find it a less terrible array than Gandhi's!"[13]

There was one trouble. The cover-ups were not hermetically sealed. To break them open, all it required was a skeptic to challenge his account as expounded in his *Autobiography*. There is one instance in the entire corpus of Gandhi's literature. An unnamed "British-India merchant" called into question somewhat sarcastically Gandhi's altruism in the Zulu War. His text first cited Gandhi's words followed by his own:

> I was greatly delighted on reaching headquarters to be told that our main work was to nurse the wounded Zulus. . . . The white soldiers at first would peep

through the railings that separated us from them and try to dissuade us from attending the wounds. As we would not heed them they would be enraged and pour abuse on the Zulus . . . wherever we went I am thankful that we had God's good work to do.

I fear when penning the above lines that Mr. Gandhi's vision of his "sole objective" must temporarily have become obscured—for I am convinced that in this anecdote, there is precisely the same amount of Truth as in the epic of his "heroism" under a "galling fire" in the Boer War.[14]

The original writings of *Indian Opinion* could have destroyed the entire pseudohistory. All it required was someone to go to South Africa and read the originals, but nobody did.

Gandhi may have had hopes that, in post-British India, his handpicked leaders would burn all of his documents. They didn't, but the decades of pseudo-history had already taken its toll and his followers had spread all over the globe. Gandhi, the mastermind behind his own mythmaking, died knowing that he had pulled off the greatest fraud of the twentieth century. His cover-ups were method-ical works of art. His campaign of deceptions, the lies, propaganda, misinforma-tion, half-truths, coercion, bribery, and religion as a protective shelter—were methods employed in the service of multiple cover-ups.

THE FINAL SATYAGRAHA

His death was tragic no matter how you look at it. The circumstances dictated by Hitler and the Japanese aggression during the Second World War forced the British to abdicate the subcontinent in August 1947. Finally, the white British government was overthrown! It doesn't matter who did it. Gandhi took the credit. Hindu India had new leaders: new Brahmins handpicked by Gandhi himself. And then, all of a sudden, on January 30, 1948, he himself was assassinated. What happened? In the words of Michael Edwardes:

The death of Gandhi could not have been more timely if it had been arranged by the government. In one sense, it was, for if it was not a constructive murder, it was a permissive one, encouraged by the laxity of the security services and of the police. Gandhi was already giving the appearance of opposition to those interests who now believed that they had the formulae to open the Aladdin's cave of political patronage and power. Congressmen were taking bribes from businessmen to get them licences and lucrative contracts; they were profiting from black-market activities and putting pressure upon top civil servants to arrange appointments and promotions for their friends. Sickened by this display of greed, Gandhi had made the startling suggestion that Congress should dis-solve itself and form a Lok Seva Sangh, a Servants of the People Society. Over this and other matters, even Patel [Sardar Vallabh Bhai Patel, often referred to as Gandhi's Greatest General] is reported to have said: "The old man has gone senile." For others, such "senility" posed a potential threat.[15]

The idea that Gandhi's own men were behind the plot to kill him might create strained credibility among his followers. Michael Edwardes is not alone, however. There are others who likewise point the finger in that direction. Among them is Gandhi's grandson, Arun Gandhi, and his wife, Sunanda, who, in their 1998 book stated: "Both factions (fundamentalists and the Congress Party administration) realized they had one thing in common: the belief that a martyred Gandhi was better (for them) than a living Gandhi. They were convinced that he had to be assassinated. The fundamentalists engineered the assassination plot while the administration looked the other way."[16]

Let's look below the surface. Was Gandhi really infuriated at hearing that party workers were corrupt? Gandhi himself was the most bribable of all Congress Party leaders. Why then was he murdered? The secret lay buried in Gandhi's first manuscript—*Hind Swaraj* (Indian Home Rule)—which he authored in South Africa. Let us revisit Sir Sankaran Nair's conclusion: Gandhi is not only against parliamentary government but against practically any government in any form. I would go one step further: Gandhi was against any government—even the one he himself had appointed. It was only a matter of time until his unrestrained urge for more Satyagraha surfaced. And it did—about ten days before his assassination. The final phase of Satyagraha was to be played on the home territory. No white government anymore, but his own. One would think it was an easy job. By his orders, the Congress Party workers were to be "disbanded" and taken to the villages. Gandhi was about to beat Mao Tse-tung of Communist China (who spearheaded the Great Proletarian Cultural Revolution in the 1960s) by a few years and the world was to bear witness to Satyagraha's final phase. Gandhi, the sole architect of Satyagraha, fell as its latest casualty. One would never know if he had a moment to reflect upon this strange tragedy of his. All these years, for the last forty years or so, he had been a thorn in the side of white governments, both in South Africa and India. But they put up with him in spite of all the provocations. Strange to say, his own disciples, with the reins of government power in their grip, ran out of determination to try him any further. To me the tragedy was doublefold: Gandhi didn't need to die at this time, and we, the students of Satyagraha, had every right to memorialize the final showdown: a Mao-style Satyagraha approach to usher India into a golden age like a glorious, utopic past that never was. Instead, we are left to witness its offspring—*Nuclear Satyagraha*—bone-chilling war games, the consequences of which are beyond imagination, being played by present-day Hindu leaders. Only eight months before his assassination, on May 27, 1947, the macho Gandhi resurfaced and exhorted India to reach a "higher spiritual plateau" in a speech that he delivered during a prayer meeting in New Delhi:

But today they [Sikhs] are thinking of the sword. They do not realize that the age of the sword is past. They do not realize that no one can be saved by the strength of the sword. *This is the age of the atom bomb.* [my italics][17]

Later on, tauntingly, he pointed to the Sikhs, "the sword was a rusty weapon." No sooner did the British leave than his handpicked Indian leaders jumped into the age of the atom bomb—laying the foundations for nuclear infrastructures muffled under layers of state secrecy.

RACISM

Gandhi was a racist to the bone when it came to black people. Some scholars familiar with the literature continue to harbor wishful thinking that Gandhi's antiblack tirade in South Africa merely reflected his disgust at being stranded among black criminals. They need to reread the evidence. Moreover, if we pursue that line of thought, then are we to assume that white prisoners in South African jails were somehow gentlemen, considering Gandhi didn't complain when in their company? Gandhi's relationship with whites fell into two categories: (1) First, the evidence doesn't show that Gandhi was prejudiced against whites per se. In South Africa, some of his closest disciples were whites. In India, a number of whites experienced what can only be described a "religious phenomenon" under Gandhi's shadow. However, what happened to Mr. Doherty and other whites should not be set aside. They were murdered because they were whites. Gandhi was indirectly involved in their murders and directly involved in fomenting racial hatred. Knowing the pattern of Gandhi's cover-ups, it should not surprise us that he tried to hide Mr. Doherty's murder. If he was involved in cover-ups of more white murders, perhaps more detective work will shed light on that in the future. Of particular note, British officials in India and other whites who charged Gandhi with practicing racism against the whites never knew anything of his South African antiblack racism. Dr. Ambedkar, who gathered a mountain of evidence on Gandhi's prejudices against black Untouchables, had no inkling of Gandhi's racist background while in South Africa. Such facts, coming from independent observers many years later (as compared to Gandhi's South African years), lend credence to the overall analysis of Gandhi, his racist saga, and many other less-than-honorable practices that have been presented in this book.

The evidence against Gandhi portrays a man who is virtually a pathological liar when it comes to his history. Egotism, greed, avarice, passion for power, vindictiveness and aggressiveness against anyone perceived by him to be disloyal, hostile, or standing in his way propelled him to act. When I think of Gandhi, there are two words that strike my mind: "racist" and "thug." We now know the racist side of his story. His criminal habits and other low tactics were by no means less than what is expected of a thug engaged in the sacred art of *thuggee*—that exotic Hindu practice designed to loot and kill you after first winning your confidence or even friendship.[18] Given all that we have read through these pages while investigating Gandhi the man, I think, Nirad C. Chaudhuri had a better sense of justification when he measured our "hero" against one of the twentieth century's great evils: "Mahatma Gandhi Worse Dictator than Hitler."[19]

In these last few pages I have little doubt that this book will cause considerable controversy, the intensity of which we have not seen in years. My hope is that this book will give birth to a new breed of scholars dedicated to asking difficult questions and committed to further critical research on India and Gandhi. At times, I am intrigued by those who might ask if there is something or *anything* in Gandhi that I admire. And my answer is, yes. There are certain facets of Gandhi's teachings that I appreciate. However, let me emphasize my position in the strongest possible terms so that it leaves no room for confusion: This selective appreciation of him is no different from my views of both Adolf Hitler and Joseph Stalin. The fact of the matter is that Gandhi was simply no better than them. Because of Gandhi's racially and ethnically inspired politics, he left many victims behind, the list of which comprises:

1. The blacks of South Africa were his first victims, only to be followed by a whole spectrum of south Asian residents comprising millions of innocent Hindus, Moslems, Sikhs, and, of course, the Untouchables.
2. The Sikhs were the first people who had the "honor" in the early 1920s of receiving Gandhi's blessings of *perishing gloriously*. And it got worse from there on. Beginning in early 1920, Gandhi strategically injected himself into Sikh affairs, and by employing many deceptive tactics he was successful in manipulating them. For all practical purposes, he hijacked the newly formed Sikh polity for the next two decades. The net result was huge mass killings and the uprooting of millions of Sikhs from their ancestral homes in Punjab (during the time when Pakistan was being created as a nation) at the time of the British exodus in 1947. Gandhi's Sikh friends finally smelled the rat: Their own revered Mahatma, whom they had supported wholeheartedly, was backstabbing them and had been doing so for quite a while. Gandhi, on the other hand, was quick to recognize that his own duplicitous machinations against the Sikhs were approaching a fruitful finish (from his perspective) and confessed his underhanded anti-Sikh politics. On November 28, 1947, he responded in a speech at a prayer meeting:

   > Although I have done nothing from my side, my Sikh friends are angry with me today. Of course I have tried to push a bitter pill down their throats. But that is how things go in the world.[20]

The Untouchables, too, were recipients of many of Gandhi's "bitter" pills. In their case, he never confessed his role. He didn't have to.

3. Countless Hindus facing the same tragedy and bloody consequences were no less special victims of Gandhi. One of them eventually hurled a bomb at him.

4. Many Moslems, stripped of and displaced from their homes, and others killed in large numbers, never forgot Gandhi's treacherous role-playing and they, too, were his victims.

5. We in the West are also, in a sense, Gandhi's victims, especially his orchestrated propaganda and disinformation campaigns.

Some African American friends of mine, after accepting the facts of Gandhi's antiblack racism, and overcome with expressions of utter bewilderment, ask the astonishing question: "Gandhi himself looked like a black man! Didn't he?" And this is how I answer: Gandhi was not a black man! Gandhi was not a brown man! Gandhi definitely was not a white man! The fact is he was a caste man! And given my bias toward the military ranks, I prefer addressing him as Sergeant-Major Gandhi, though, I must confess here that many of the junior-ranking military personnel have expressed their deep reservations at calling him by his rank. They believe that the rank should be earned honorably, and in Gandhi's case it was not. They are right.

Often I think: What if Gandhi's *real history* of his South African experiments had been revealed before or immediately after his triumphal return to India in early 1915? What would have been the consequences? And how would it have affected his image?

1. He would probably not have been given the apellation of "mahatma."

2. The Indian leaders in British India, many of them honorable men of both Hindu and Moslem backgrounds, would have taken preventive measures to keep Gandhi at arm's length and not let him steal the political limelight.

3. Many Indian revolutionary leaders fighting to free India from its British yoke, being already skeptical of Gandhi, would have taken decisive steps to limit Gandhi to the confines of his religious ashram.

4. Gandhi would not have evolved into an avatar. Nor would he have been inducted into the Hindu Hall of Fame as a prophet of modern Hinduism.

5. The Moslems, in the 1920s, would have never looked at him as *"Wali,"* a sacred term that comes from the pages of their holy Quran, meaning "protector" or "supporter."

6. At any rate, the British would have eventually left the region. The time for European powers to sustain colonies in the third world after the Second World War was coming to an end. However, without Gandhi and his politics, the transfer of power would have been more peaceful and

apportioned to naturally drawn ethnic nationalities and not *solely* based upon two religions, which led to the creation of the artificial states of Hindu India[21] and Islamic Pakistan.

7. The world would have been spared of the euphoria of a saint-in-the-making and all the venerations that sprang from it.

8. The social, economic, and religious plight of the Untouchables would have been alleviated. Their living conditions would have been improved and the caste system may have been eliminated from society. We have seen that Gandhi's window dressing—designed to solve the problem of Untouchability from within Hinduism—didn't work.

Throughout my many years researching Gandhi I have found several aspects of his life that need further analysis:

1. According to Gandhi, at the time he landed in South Africa and while traveling in the first-class compartment on the train from Durban to Pretoria in early June 1893, he was evicted from the train at Pietermaritzburg Railway Station. The next day, as he continued his journey, he was assaulted and faced more episodes of racial humiliation. These racial incidents, as Gandhi himself said, dramatically changed the course of his life to fight against bigotry and racism. My preliminary skeptical inquiry into these incidents has convinced me that the very historicity of these racial incidents must be questioned. A further investigation is needed.

2. We need to revisit critically those individuals who were instrumental in bringing Gandhi's good name to the West. What were their motivations and in what ways was it to their advantage to introduce and promote Gandhi to Western audiences?

3. As a corollary to the above paragraph, and as set forth in part 1, a number of Christian missionaries were heavily involved with Gandhi and disseminated his propagation abroad. We need to explore further what factors motivated these missionaries; what role, if any, various Christian denominations played behind the scenes; the role of some seminaries in teaching about Gandhi to the students; and how Gandhi's good name made it to Reverend Martin Luther King Jr. as he was himself raised within the Christian religious tradition.

4. By now it is no secret that India is and has been actively building weapons of mass destruction, in spite of its heart-breaking poverty. The difficult question we missed asking was this: Why are the Hindu leaders, who claim to be followers of the peaceful and nonviolent Gandhi, bent upon manufacturing these weapons and investing in building a huge military? Did we miss something important here when India had been supporting nuclear freeze while simultaneously developing nuclear weap-

ons? While investigating Gandhi on many fronts, we must open Hindu thought to the critical scrutiny that it deserves, the type of review it avoided in the past under the guise of a sacred religion. This process must include a political evaluation: how all this directly affects the well-being of many millions of poverty stricken Indians, its connections to the weapons of mass destruction, and the underlying psychological compulsions it causes for the India's neighbors (especially Pakistan) to pursue the same course, forcing further proliferation of these weapons. Furthermore, proliferation will intensify to engulf both the Middle East and south Asia, thereby rendering these geographical regions the Greater Middle East, for reasons of global security. The events of September 11, 2001, have taught us some bitter lessons. The challenge in the near term and in the distant future is this: How do we, as the human race, plan to face these pressing dilemmas that will confront us in the months and years ahead? Our choices will spell the difference between triumph and utter devastation. Assuming that we survive as a species, future generations will judge us.

NOTES

1. Richard Attenborough, *In Search of Gandhi* (Piscataway, N.J.: New Century Publishers, Inc., 1982), page 9.
2. Keith D. Miller, *Voice of Deliverance: The Language of Martin Luther King, Jr. and Its Sources* (New York: Free Press, 1992), page 88.
3. Keith D. Miller, *Voice of Deliverance: The Language of Martin Luther King, Jr. and Its Sources* (Athens, Georgia: The University of Georgia Press, 1998), p. 205.
4. Richard Lischer, *The Preacher King: Martin Luther King, Jr. and the Word that Moved America* (New York: Oxford University Press, 1995), p. 214. Professor Lischer never meant to suggest that there were no references to Gandhi after 1960. He specifically noted that in "Rev. King's writings and especially his sermons, which were my chief interest, Gandhi all but disappears. . . ." Personal communication with the author by e-mail on March 28, 2000.
5. Greg Moses, *Revolution of Conscience: Martin Luther King, Jr., and the Philosophy of Nonviolence* (New York: The Guilford Press, 1997). Within the King scholarship, one question, regrettably that has always been ignored is: Which books did Rev. King "read" on Gandhi? Though Rev. King himself never mentioned those titles, painstakingly, I have been able to compile the following: *The Life of Mahatma Gandhi* by Louis Fischer; *That Strange Little Brown Man Gandhi* by Frederick B. Fisher; *Mahatma Gandhi: His Own Story* by C. F. Andrews; *Mahatma Gandhi's Ideas* by C. F. Andrews; *Mahatma Gandhi at Work* by C. F. Andrews; *Mahatma Gandhi: The Man Who Became One with the Universal Being* by Romain Rolland; *Mahatma Gandhi: An Interpretation* by E. Stanley Jones; *The Power of Nonviolence* by Richard B. Gregg; *The Gandhi Reader: A Sourcebook of His Life and Writings* by Homer A. Jack; *India Afire* by Clare and Harris

Wofford; *War Without Violence* by Krishnalal Shridharani; *An Autobiography or the Story of My Experiments With Truth* by M. K. Gandhi

6. Quoted in Lewis V. Baldwin, *There Is a Balm in Gilead: The Cultural Roots of Martin Luther King, Jr.* (Minneapolis: Fortress Press, 1991), p. 11. Professor Garrow has confirmed to me his findings. According to him, "Gandhi/Thoreau overlay was a 'PR' effort aimed at 'presenting' MLK to the white American elite as someone speaking from a more intellectually 'classy' foundation than 'just' the African-American church." Personal communication with the author by e-mail on April 7, 2000.

7. Today the "King legacy" is a hot topic; it has become a drama being played out in the open, in the media, and in the courts by many actors, not to exclude the King family, the National Park Service, and others. Commercializing King has left many with bitter experiences and raised the financial stakes to millions of dollars to be harvested. For the Gandhi propaganda machine the stakes are not financial at all. They are of different nature: India's foreign policy objectives are being carried out under the disguise of "cultural diplomacy," a euphemism for modern Hinduism.

8. *The Christian Century* 79 (May 23, 1962): 661.

9. Nelson Mandela, "The Sacred Warrior: The Liberator of South Africa Looks at the Seminal Work of the Liberator of India," *Time*, December 31, 1999, pp. 124–25.

10. M. K. Gandhi, *Satyagraha in South Africa* (1928; reprint, Ahmedabad: Navajivan Publishing House, 1972), p. 201.

11. Quoted in "Mahatma's African Jail Experiences," in *Mahatma Gandhi: The World Significance* by John H. Holmes, P. G. Bridge, and F. E. James (Calcutta: C. C. Basak, The Research Home, n.d). Also quoted in *Behind the Bars*, a booklet "authored" by Gandhi himself.

12. *Speeches and Writings of Mahatma Gandhi*, 4th ed. (Madras: G. A. Natesan, 1933), pp. 209–40. The opening pages of *Speeches and Writings* in the editions of 1917, 1919, and 1922 incorporated respective issues of Polak's *Gandhi: A Sketch of His Life and Works*. However, by the time of the 1933 edition of *Speeches and Writings*, a dramatic change had occurred: The biography by Polak, with its previous editions, was brushed aside and consequently rendered useless. This action was necessary and made sense in light of the fact that Gandhi's pseudohistory in the form of the two autobiographical accounts was on the market.

Other references of importance are: *Mahatma Gandhi's Jail Experiences* (Madras: Tagore and Company, 1920[?]); "Mahatma's African Jail Experiences," in *Mahatma Gandhi: The World Significance* by John H. Holmes, P. G. Bridge, and F. E. James, the racist remarks were incorporated in this book; *Behind the Bars* (Bhadarkall, Lahore: Gandhi Publications League, n.d.); *Gandhi's Letters from Prison*, comp. R. N. Khanna (Lahore: Allied Indian Publishers [1950?]); and *Stonewalls Do Not a Prison Make*, comp. and ed. by V. B. Kher (Ahmedabad: Navajivan Publishing House, 1964).

13. Blanche Watson, comp., *Gandhi and Non-Violent Resistance: The Non-Co-operation Movement in India: Gleanings from the American Press* (Madras: Ganesh & Co., 1923), p. 38.

14. *A Searchlight on Gandhi* (London: P. S. King and Sons, 1931), pp. 95–96.

15. Michael Edwardes, *The Myth of the Mahatma: Gandhi, the British, and the Raj* (London: Constable, 1986), p. 252.

16. Arun and Sunanda Gandhi, *The Forgotten Woman: The Untold Story of Kastur*

Gandhi, Wife of Mahatma Gandhi (Huntsville, Ark.: Ozark Mountain Publishers, 1998), pp. 313–14.

17. CWMG 88, #13, page 21. Readers should note how the apologists have interpreted Gandhi's other contradictory statements to make him look antinuclear. See James W. Douglass, *Lightning East to West: Jesus, Gandhi, and the Nuclear Age* (New York: Crossroad, 1986); and Arne Naess, *Gandhi and the Nuclear Age* (Totowa, N.J.: Bedminster Press, 1967). On June 16, 1947, at a prayer speech, Gandhi made clear his position: "If we had the atom bomb, we would have used it against the British."

18. George Bruce, *The Stranglers: The Cult of Thuggee and Its Overthrow in British India* (New York: Harcourt, Brace & World, 1969), pp. 166–89.

19. Swapan Dasgupta, ed. *Nirad C. Chaudhuri, The First Hundred Years: A Celebration* (New Delhi: HarperCollins Publishers India, 1997), p. 42.

20. CWMG 90: #114, p. 124. Since 1984, beginning with the military attack on the Sikhs and their religious sites, the conservative estimate is that 250,000 Sikhs have perished in India's Gandhi-inspired bloodthirsty politics along with thousands more of them today languishing behind bars without formal charges.

21. India, as a unitary political state, never existed in history until the British finished conquering the subcontinent. As far as I know, the word "India" originated from the Book of Esther of the Hebrew Bible. Winston Churchill had a better understanding of it when he said, "India is an abstraction," and "India is a geographical term. It is no more a united nation than the Equator." The word "Hindu" cannot be found in any of the "Hindu scriptures." It came into existence in about the eighth century C.E. and the invading Moslems thrust this derogatory Persian word, meaning a thief, upon the adjoining Indian subcontinent residents. Centuries later, the British tried to give a new name of Gentoo (or Gentu). Of course, the Hindus didn't take it. Had they adopted it, what is termed "Hinduism" would have been known as "Gentuism."

GANDHI TIMELINE: THE FOUNDATION to UNDERSTANDING GANDHI

My Life Is My Message

—Mahatma Gandhi (1945)

Mohandas K. Gandhi lived to be seventy-eight years old (1869–1948) and his life was extremely complex. There are so many facets to his life that they can render even the best of minds bewildered. To fully comprehend Gandhi's racist mind, it is imperative to understand his earthly journey, which spanned the continents of Asia, Africa, and Europe.

BEFORE SOUTH AFRICA

YEAR		*DESCRIPTION*
1869		Gandhi born in Porbandar.
1880		Enters Kathiawar High School.
1882		Marries Kasturba.
1888	Spring	Birth of his first son, Harilal.
	September	Sails for England to study law.
	November	Admitted into the Inner Temple.

315

1891	June 10	Called to the Bar.
	June 12	Sails for India.
1892	May	Fails to establish law practice.
	Spring	Birth of his second son, Manilal.
1893	April	Sails for South Africa, alone, to a job as a legal advisor.

SOUTH AFRICA

1893	June	While traveling, he is ordered off the train, faces racial discrimination.
1894	August	Natal Indian Congress is established.
1896	June 5	Sails to India.
	November 30	Sails for South Africa along with his family.
	December 12	Reaches Durban.
1897	January 13	Gandhi attacked by mob upon leaving the ship.
	May	Birth of his third son, Ramdas.
1899	December	Left for the Boer War—Indian Ambulance Corps.
1900	January	Corps is active in the Boer War.
	May 22	Birth of his fourth son, Devadas.
1901	October	Gandhi leaves South Africa for India.
1902	December	Returns without his family to South Africa after having failed to establish a legal practice.
1903	February	Opens a law office in Johannesburg. British Indian Association is established.
1904	February	Plague breaks out in Indian Location in Johannesburg.
	November–December	Phoenix Settlement established.
	December 24	First volume of *Indian Opinion* issued from Phoenix Settlement.

1905	August	Natal Legislative Council passes poll tax bill. Gandhi calls for revision of the bill.
1906	January 1	Poll tax enforced on Indians over the age of 18.
	March 17	Gandhi begins to organize against the Zulu rebellion.
	June–July	Gandhi participates in war against blacks.
	September 11	Calls for withdrawal of Asiatics Registration bill in Johannesburg.
	October 3	Sails for U.K. to seek redress from the British government. Returns to South Africa on December 18.
1907	July 31	General strike after a mass meeting.
1908	January 10	Sentenced to two months' imprisonment; released on January 30. In South Africa, he went to prison three more times.
1909	June 23	Gandhi sails for England. His first biography is published.
	November 23	Gandhi writes *Hind Swaraj* on his journey back to South Africa.
1910	May 30	At Tolstoy Farm for passive resisters, the struggle continues.
1914	January 13	Gandhi and General Smuts begin negotiations, resulting in a compromise.
	July 18	Gandhi sails for England, never to return to South Africa again.
	August 4	World War I starts.
	August	Gandhi forms Indian Volunteer Corps, but falls ill with pleurisy and is unable to continue his command tasks.
	December 19	Sails for India, reaches Bombay on January 9, 1915. Awarded *Kaiser-i-Hind* medal.

INDIA 1916–1935

1916		Gandhi starts to participate in Indian politics. He takes on other nonpolitical causes dealing with religion, human rights, etc.

1918		Gandhi starts to participate actively to promote military activities for World War I.
	April 30	Promotes his past military leadership roles in South Africa to achieve present goals of recruiting more Indians for the war. He continues to play recruiting sergeant for the British government.
		World War I ends.
1919		Gandhi turns against the government.
		First nationwide civil disobedience.
		Campaign against the Rowlatt Bills in April fails. Tragedy at Jallianwala Bagh, Amritsar, and other events.
	May 7	*Young India** starts from Bombay.
	September 7	First issue of *Navajivan** in Gujarati.
	October 8	*Young India* moves to Ahmedabad, Gujarat. Gandhi assumes editorship of *Young India*.
1920		Gandhi writes his "The Doctrine of the Sword."
1921		His second nationwide non-cooperation movement fails. He decides to write an autobiography.
	November 17	Gandhi writes "Why Did I Assist In War?"
	November 19	City of Bombay experiences riots.
1922	March 10	Gandhi is arrested and sentenced to six years in jail at Yeravda Prison. His confession statement mentions the Zulu War.
	March	Interview with the *Manchester Guardian*.
1923	November 26	He begins writing *Satyagraha in South Africa*.
1924	February 4	Released from jail.
	March	Interview with *Stead's Review*.
1925	December 3	Weekly installments of his *Autobiography* appear in *Young India*.
1926	April 5	*Unity* begins to publish his *Autobiography* on a weekly basis until November 25, 1929.

* Both newspapers began publication prior to Gandhi assuming control of them.

1929	(before) March 1	Interviews with foreign visitors.
	July	"To the American Negro: A Message from Mahatma Gandhi" is published in *Crisis*.
1930	January	Indian Declaration of Independence Proclamation.
	March 12	Begins Salt March.
	April 6	Breaks salt law on the beach at Dandi.
1931	September 12	Gandhi attends Round Table conference in London.
	December 14	Meets Romain Rolland in Switzerland.
1932	August 17	Prime Minister Ramsay MacDonald hands down the Communal Award.
	September 20	Gandhi begins a fast unto death in protest of separate electorates for Untouchables.
	September 24	Poona Pact signed.
	October 26	Organizes *Harijan Sevak Sangh*.
1933	February 11	First issue of a weekly paper, *Harijan*, in English.
	February 23	First issue of *Harijan Sevak* in Hindi language.
	March 12	First issue of *Harijanbandhu* released from Poona in Gujarati language.
1935	(before) September 7	Meeting with Swami Yogananda.

MEETING THE AFRICAN AMERICAN LEADERS

1936	February 21	Interview with American Negro delegation.
1937	(before) January 10	Meeting with Dr. Benjamin E. Mays.
		Meeting with Dr. Tobias.
1939	January 1	Interview with Chinese delegation.
		Interview with Reverend S. S. Tema.
	(before) February 6	Interview with South African Indian students.
1942	May 16	Interview with the press.
	June 4	Interview with Louis Fischer.
	June 10	Interview with Preston Grover.
	July 1	Letter to Franklin D. Roosevelt.

| 1945 | May 30 | Interview with Denton J. Brooks Jr. |

1946   (after) January 21   Talk with Indonesian sailors.
                            Discussion with black soldiers.
       March 24   Statement to the press regarding South Africa's "Land and Franchise Bill."
       (after) April 1   Interview with South African delegation.
       July 17   Interview with Louis Fischer.

1947   August 15   The British leave India. The colony is divided into Pakistan and India.
       (before) August 20   Meeting with Dr. William Stuart Nelson.

1948   January 30   Gandhi is assassinated.

AFTER GANDHI'S DEATH

1948   Gandhi is officially "canonized."

1949   U.S. Congress passes a resolution to erect a monument to the memory of Mohandas K. Gandhi in Washington, D.C.

1949   Prime Minister Nehru visits the United States.

1950   Mahatma Gandhi World Peace Memorial is established in Pacific Palisades, California. (Private property of Self Realization Fellowship)

1950s–1997   Pyarelal begins to write the official biography. After his death, his sister continues with the project. A total of ten volumes are already published.

1958–1994   *The Collected Works of Mahatma Gandhi* is published as a project of the government of India in one hundred volumes, about fifty thousand pages. Also published is *Sampurna Gandhi Vangmaya*, the Hindi translation of the *Collected Works*. A translation in the Gujarati language is near completion.

1959   February   Dr. Martin Luther King Jr., his wife, and Professor Lawrence D. Reddick visit India.

| 1961 | January | Champion of Liberty issue, Mahatma Gandhi stamps by the U.S. Postal Service. Scott Catalog Numbers 1174 and 1175. |

1961   January   Champion of Liberty issue, Mahatma Gandhi stamps by the U.S. Postal Service. Scott Catalog Numbers 1174 and 1175.

1976   Gandhi Memorial Center opens in Washington, D.C.

1982   *Gandhi* movie is released.

1986   October   Gandhi statue set up in New York City.

1988   September   U.S. House of Representatives publishes House Report 100-947 for "Mahatma Gandhi Memorial" in the District of Columbia.
        October   Gandhi statue set up in San Francisco, California.
        October   President Ronald Reagan declares October 2, 1988, as "National Day of Recognition for Mohandas K. Gandhi" under Proclamation 5875.

1989–90   *Gandhi Marg*, section of Devon Avenue—conamed for a stretch of four blocks in Chicago, Illinois.

1990   October   Gandhi statue set up in Honolulu, Hawaii. Gandhi bust is installed in the Peace Garden at California State University, Fresno.

1991   October   M. K. Gandhi Institute for Nonviolence opens at Christian Brothers University in Memphis, Tennessee. Herbert Plaza renamed as Mahatma Gandhi Plaza and India Square in Jersey City, New Jersey.

1992   January   A public school in Jersey City, New Jersey, renamed Mahatma Gandhi Elementary School.
        July   Mahatma Gandhi Center opens in Saint Louis, Missouri.

1994   October   Gandhi statue set up at The Life Experience School in Sherborn, Massachusetts.

1995   July   Gandhi bust set up at Mahatma Gandhi Center in Saint Louis, Missouri.

1996	May	President Clinton accepts Gandhi bust as part of the Mahatma Gandhi World Peace Award.
1996		Construction begins of Gandhi Temple in Wayne, New Jersey.
1997	May	Gandhi bust installed in Salt Lake City, Utah.
	October	The Gandhi-Hamer-King Center for the Study of Religion and Democratic Renewal opens at the Iliff School of Theology in Denver, Colorado. In 2000, the center was renamed The Veterans of Hope Project: A Center for the Study of Religion and Democratic Renewal.
1998	January	Gandhi statue set up at Martin Luther King Jr. National Historic Site in Atlanta, Georgia.
	July	U.S. House of Representatives publishes House Report 105-666: "Memorial To Honor Mahatma Gandhi."
	October	President Bill Clinton signs a law (Public Law 105-284) allowing the government of India to establish a memorial for Mahatma Gandhi in the District of Columbia.
1999	October	Suffolk County executive unveils the Gandhi statue in the media center of H. Lee Dennison Building in Hauppauge, Long Island, New York.
2000	April	The Gandhi Institute for Reconciliation opens at Morehouse College in Atlanta, with the unveiling of Gandhi's and his wife's busts on a platform. Morehouse College awards Gandhi and Mrs. Gandhi with Doctorates of Humane Letters.
	September	Mr. Atal Bihari Vajpayee, the prime minister of India, dedicates Mahatma Gandhi Memorial in the District of Columbia.
2001	October	City of Orlando installs a Gandhi statue on the rim of Lake Eola in Orlando, Florida.

2002	May	Mayor of Tinian Island (U.S. Dependent Area in the Pacific) dedicates the World Peace Gardens to Gandhi, King, and Ikeda.*
	June	City of Denver, Colorado, installs a Gandhi statue along with the statues of Dr. Martin Luther King Jr., Rosa Parks, Frederick Douglass, and Sojourner Truth in the City Park in Denver, Colorado.
	October	Milwaukee County installs a Gandhi statue in its MacArthur Square adjoining the Milwaukee County Courthouse in downtown Milwaukee, Wisconsin.
2003	April	Gandhi bust installed at the National Civil Rights Museum in Memphis, Tennessee.
	October	Mayor Lee P. Brown of Houston and deputy chairman of upper house of India's parliament performed a ground-breaking ceremony at the Hermann Park in Houston, Texas, to eventually set up a Gandhi statue.
	November	Millsaps College set up a Gandhi statue on its campus in Jackson, Mississippi.

In addition to the United States, Gandhi statues stand tall in many other countries such as Argentina, Australia, Belgium, Bosnia, Brazil, Britain, Canada, Denmark, France, Germany, Guyana, Iceland, Italy, Japan, Kenya, Luxembourg, Malaysia, Malta, Myanmar, Mexico, Nepal, Panama, Portugal, Puerto Rico, South Africa, Spain, Russia, Trinidad & Tobago, Turkey, Uganda, and Yemen. This list is not exhaustive. Understandably, India has the largest number of these statues. But even the remote and frigid Antarctica has not been spared from serious considerations for a statue. By the end of the twentieth century, Mahatma Gandhi Park opened in south Lebanon, fully funded by the Indian government and constructed by the soldiers of the Indian Army's 2/4 Gurkha Infantry Battalion, which at the time was part of the United Nations Interim Force in Lebanon.

---

*Daisaku Ikeda is the president of Soka Gakkai International (SGI), an organization with headquarters in Japan. SGI actively espouses Nichiren Buddhism worldwide. SGI's Korea branch headquarter complex in Seoul houses the biggest Gandhi statue I have ever seen. Professor Lawrence E. Carter Sr., dean of the Martin Luther King Jr. International Chapel at Morehouse College, has joined with SGI to actively promote Gandhi.

GLOSSARY

Adi-Dravidian. Outcaste.
Afridis. Tribesmen inhabiting the Northwest Frontier Province of Pakistan.
Ahimsa. Nonviolence.
Ashram. A monastic retreat.
Atishudras. Beyond *Shudras*.
Avatar. A god incarnated in a human.

Bengali. A resident of the region of Bengal.
Brahma. Name of a major Hindu deity.
Brahmacharya. Observance of chastity.
Brahmachari. A person who practices Brahmacharya.
Brahman-rishi. A Hindu seer who has attained the highest self-consciousness.

Caste. Color. The top three castes are collectively referred to as "upper castes." Those of the Sudra caste are called "lower caste."
Charkha. Spinning wheel.
Crore. One hundred lakhs or ten million.

Dewan. Prime minister.

Gujarati. A language of the people of the state of Gujarat. Also, any person with a background from Gujarat is referred to as Gujarati.

Harijan. A new name given to the untouchables by Gandhi. Also the name given to one of Gandhi's weekly newspapers.
Himsa. Violence.
Hindustani. Pertains to a "citizen" of "Hindustan," the land of the Hindus.

Ji. When used with a person's name, as in *Gandhiji*, is an honorific suffix to show reverence.

Kaffir. The black people of South Africa. The word is also used in an insulting manner similar to the word "nigger." Since Gandhi repeatedly used the word "Kaffir" in his writings, my use only reflects what he believed.

Khilafat. Caliphate—the word corrupted to "Khilafat" in India. The movement came into existence to protest the fate of the Sultan of Turkey, who bore the title of Caliph and was regarded as the supreme head of the Moslem community and the successor of the Prophet Muhammed. World War I had come to an end, and the Turkish Empire was in ruins. The Caliph was a prisoner in his palace in Constantinople, deprived of all political and religious authority. The Khilafat movement under Gandhi's leadership in British India was designed to restore the Caliph's religious authority based on imaginary grievances.

Lakh. One hundred thousand.

Madrassis. Residents of the region of Madras Presidency.
Mahabharata. A voluminous war document, often known as a Hindu epic.
Mahatma. Great soul.
Mantra. A word or words powerful enough to carry supernatural powers.
Moksha. Liberation from the cycle of birth and death.
Muni. Another reference to a Hindu seer.

Parsee. Religious follower of the Zoroaster.
Pathan. Resident of the Northwest Frontier province of Pakistan and adjoining Afghanistan.
Punjabi. A resident of the state of Punjab.
Puranas. Name of a large number of Hindu "scriptures."

Ramayana. A Hindu epic—many in number.
Roti. A kind of wheat bread.

Sannyasi. A wandering recluse.
Sudra (Shudra). Serf—the lowest main caste.
Sadhu. A recluse; mendicant.
Swaraj. Self-rule; independence.
Samskar. Carrying the effects of our pasts in the form of unconscious tendencies.
Santhals. A black tribe living in northeast India.
Satyagrahi. One who practices Satyagraha.
Shastras. Refers to any number of Hindu "scriptures" depicting laws.

Tamasha. A spectacle; a play.
Tamil. A resident of Tamil Nadu, southern India.

Untouchable. The lowest, outcaste group.

Varna. Hindu terminology for caste.
Vishnu. Name of a major Hindu deity.

Yogi. One who practices Yoga.

Zulu. A black tribe of South Africa. Also referred to as "natives."

SELECT BIBLIOGRAPHY

BOOKS

Agnihotri, S. N. *Mr. Gandhi in the Light of Truth: A critical examination of Mr. Gandhi's non-co-operation propaganda in the light of facts and principles of National Evolution*. Lahore: S.A. Singh, 1921.

Ali, Shanti Sadiq. *Gandhi & South Africa*. Delhi: Hind Pocket Books, Pvt., Ltd, 1994.

Ambedkar, B. R. *Gandhi and Gandhism*. Edited by Bhagwan Das. Jullundur, Punjab: Bheem Patrika Publications, 1970.

———. *What Congress and Gandhi Have Done to the Untouchables*. 2d ed. Bombay: Thacker & Co., Ltd, 1946.

Andrews, Charles F. *Mahatma Gandhi's Ideas*. New York: The MacMillan Company, 1930.

———, ed. *Mahatma Gandhi: His Own Story*. New York: The Macmillan Company, 1930.

Andrews, Robert Hardy. *A Lamp For India: The Story of Madame Pandit*. Englewood Cliffs, N.J.: Prentice Hall, 1967.

Annamalai, Velu, comp. *Sergeant-Major M. K. Gandhi*. Bangalore, India: Dalit Sahitya Akademy, 1995.

Ashe, Geoffrey. *Gandhi*. New York: Stein and Day Publishers, 1968.

Attenborough, Richard. *In Search of Gandhi*. Piscataway, N.J.: New Century Publishers, Inc., 1982.

Baldwin, Lewis V. *There Is a Balm in Gilead: The Cultural Roots of Martin Luther King, Jr.* Minneapolis: Fortress Press, 1991.

Bemis, Albert Farwell. *A Journey to India, 1921–1922*. Boston: The Merrymount Press, 1923.

Bhana, Surendra. *Gandhi's Legacy: The Natal Indian Congress 1894–1994*. Pietermaritzburg, South Africa: University of Natal Press, 1997.

329

Bondurant, Joan V. *Conquest of Violence: The Gandhian Philosophy of Conflict.* Princeton: Princeton University Press, 1958.

Bonner, Arthur. *Democracy in India: A Hollow Shell.* Washington, D.C.: The American University Press, 1994.

Bose, Nirmal Kumar. *My Days with Gandhi.* New Delhi: Orient Longman, 1974.

Bosman, Walter. *The Natal Rebellion of 1906.* London: Longmans, Green & Co., 1907.

Bourke-White, Margaret. *Halfway to Freedom.* New York: Simon and Schuster, 1949.

Brittain, Vera. *Search after Sunrise.* London: Macmillan & Co., 1951.

Brown, Judith M. *Gandhi: Prisoner of Hope.* New Haven: Yale University Press, 1989.

Bruce, George. *The Stranglers: The Cult of Thuggee and Its Overthrow in British India.* New York: Harcourt, Brace & World, Inc., 1969.

Carson, Clayborne, ed. *The Autobiography of Martin Luther King, Jr.* New York: IPM, 1998.

Chadha, Yogesh. *Gandhi: A Life.* New York: John Wiley & Sons, Inc., 1997.

Chatfield, Charles, ed. *The Americanization of Gandhi: Images of the Mahatma.* New York: Garland Publishing, Inc., 1976.

Chaturvedi, Benarsidas, and Marjorie Sykes. *Charles Freer Andrews: A Narrative.* Delhi: Publications Division, Ministry of Information and Broadcasting, Government of India, 1982.

Chaudhuri, Nirad C. *Hinduism: A Religion to Live By.* Delhi: Oxford University Press, 1996 (reprint).

———. *Thy Hand, Great Anarch!: India, 1921–1952.* New York: Addison-Wesley Publishing Company, Inc., 1988.

Chitambar, Jashwant Rao. *Mahatma Gandhi: His Life, Work, and Influence.* Chicago: The John C. Winston Company, 1933.

Collins, Larry, and Dominique LaPierre. *Freedom at Midnight.* New York: Simon and Schuster, 1975.

Consul, Govind Dass. *Mahatma Gandhi: The Great Rogue of India?* Delhi: Garcon National Publishers, 1939.

Cousins, Norman, ed. *Profiles of Gandhi: America Remembers a World Leader.* Delhi: Indian Book Company, 1969.

Covey, Stephen R. *Principle-Centered Leadership.* New York: Simon & Schuster, 1992.

Curie, Eve. *Journey Among Warriors.* New York: Doubleday, Doran and Co., 1943.

DeJong, Constance, and Philip Glass. *Satyagraha: M. K. Gandhi in South Africa 1893–1914: The historical material and libretto comprising the opera's book.* New York: Tanam Press, 1983.

Desai, Mahadev Haribhai. *Day-to-Day with Gandhi: Secretary's Diary from November 1917 to March 1927.* Vol. 3. Varanasi: Sarva Seva Sangh Prakashan, 1968.

Doke, Joseph J. *M. K. Gandhi: An Indian Patriot in South Africa.* London: Indian Chronicle, 1909. Reprinted; Varanasi, 1956.

Douglass, James W. *Lightning East to West: Jesus, Gandhi, and the Nuclear Age.* New York: Crossroad, 1986.

———. *The Nonviolent Coming of God.* Maryknoll, New York: Orbis Books, 1991. Maryknoll is the Catholic Foreign Mission of America.

Dwiroopanand, Swami. *Mahatma Gandhi: Ambassador of God for Mankind in 21st Century.* Ahmedabad, India: Adhyatma Vignan Prakashan, 1992.

Edwardes, Michael. *The Myth of the Mahatma: Gandhi, the British and the Raj*. London: Constable, 1986.

Ellsberg, Robert. *All Saints: Daily Reflections on Saints, Prophets, and Witnesses for Our Time*. New York: The Crossroad Publication Company, 1997.

Erikson, Erik H. *Gandhi's Truth: On the Origins of Militant Nonviolence*. New York: W. W. Norton & Company, 1969.

Farmer, James. *Lay Bare the Heart: An Autobiography of the Civil Rights Movement*. New York: A Plume Book, 1985.

Farson, Negley. *The Way of a Transgressor*. New York: Harcourt, Brace and Company, 1936.

Field, Harry H. *After Mother India*. London: Jonathan Cape and Company, 1929.

Fischer, Louis. *Gandhi and Stalin: Two Signs at the World's Crossroads*. New York: Harper & Brothers, 1947.

———. *The Life of Mahatma Gandhi*. New York: Harper & Brothers, 1950.

———. *This Is Our World*. New York: Harper & Brothers, 1956.

———. *A Week with Gandhi*. New York: Duell, Sloan and Pearce, 1942.

———, ed. *The Essential Gandhi: An Anthology of His Writings on His Life, Works and Ideas*. New York: Random House, 1962.

Fisher, Frederick B. *That Strange Little Brown Man Gandhi*. New Delhi: Orient Longmans, 1970. Originally printed in the United States in 1932.

Gandhi, Arun and Sunanda. *The Forgotten Woman: The Untold Story of Kastur Gandhi, Wife of Mahatma Gandhi*. Huntsville, Ark.: Ozark Mountain Publishers, 1998.

Gandhi, Ela. *Mohandas Gandhi: The South Africa Years*. Pinelands, Cape Town: Maskew Miller Longman, 1994.

Gandhi, Manuben. *Last Glimpses of Bapu*. Delhi: Shiva Lal Agarwala & Co., 1962.

Gandhi, Mohandas K. *An Autobiography or The Story of My Experiments with Truth*. Boston: Beacon Press, 1957.

———. *Behind the Bars*. Bhadarkall: Gandhi Publications League, n.d.

———. *The Collected Works of Mahatma Gandhi*. 100 Volumes. Delhi: Publications Division, Ministry of Information and Broadcasting, Government of India, 1958–1994.

———. *Gandhi's Letters from Prison*. Compiled by R. N. Khanna. Lahore: Allied Indian Publishers, [1950?].

———. *Mahatma Gandhi's Jail Experiences*. Madras: Tagore and Company, [1922?].

———. *Non-Violent Resistance (Satyagraha)*. New York: Schocken Books, 1961.

———. *Satyagraha in South Africa*. 1928. Reprint, Ahmedabad: Navajivan Publishing House, 1972.

———. *Speeches and Writings of Mahatma Gandhi*. 4th ed. Madras: G. A. Natesan, 1933.

———. *Stonewalls Do Not a Prison Make*. Compiled and edited by V. B. Kher. Ahmedabad: Navajivan Publishing House, 1964.

Gandhi, Prabhudas. *My Childhood with Gandhiji*. Ahmedabad: Navajivan Publishing House, 1957.

Gandhi, Rajmohan. *The Good Boatman: A Portrait of Gandhi*. New Delhi: Viking, 1995.

Garrow, David J. *Bearing the Cross: Martin Luther King, Jr. and the Southern Christian Leadership Conference*. New York: Morrow, 1986.

Gilbert, Martin. *Winston S. Churchill*. Boston: Houghton Mifflin Company, 1986.

Gioseffi, Daniela, ed. *On Prejudice: A Global Perspective.* New York: Anchor Books, 1993.

Golant, William. *The Long Afternoon: British India 1601–1947.* New York: St. Martin's Press, 1975.

Gopalaswami, K. *Gandhi And Bombay.* Bombay: Bharatiya Vidya Bhavan, 1969.

Grant, Joanne. *Ella Baker: Freedom Bound.* New York: John Wiley & Sons, 1998.

Gray, R. M., and Manilal C. Parekh. *Mahatma Gandhi: An Essay in Appreciation.* Calcutta: Association Press (YMCA), 1931.

Gregg, Richard. *The Power of Nonviolence.* Nyack, N.Y.: Fellowship, 1959.

Grenier, Richard. *The Gandhi Nobody Knows.* Nashville: Thomas Nelson, 1983.

Gupta, S. P. K. *Apostle John and Gandhi: The Mission of John Haynes Holmes for Mahatma Gandhi in the United States of America.* Ahmedabad: Navajivan Publishing House, 1988.

Hawley, John Stratton, ed. *Saints and Virtues.* Berkeley: The University of California Press, 1987. See the chapter titled "Saint Gandhi" by Mark Juergensmeyer.

Hick, John, and Lamont C. Hempel, eds. *Gandhi's Significance for Today.* New York: St. Martin's Press, 1989.

Holmes, John Haynes. *My Gandhi.* New York: Harper & Brothers, 1953.

———. "Who Is the Greatest Man in the World Today?" New York: The Community Church, 1921. Sermon delivered on Sunday Morning, April 10, 1921.

Holmes, John H., P. G. Bridge, and F. E. James. *Mahatma Gandhi: The World Significance.* Calcutta: C.C. Basak, The Research Home, n.d.

Huq, Fazlul. *Gandhi: Saint or Sinner?* Bangalore: Dalit Sahitya Akademy, 1992.

Huttenback, R. A. *Gandhi in South Africa.* Ithaca: Cornell University Press, 1971.

Inden, Ronald. *Imagining India.* Oxford: Basil Blackwell, 1990.

Isaacs, Harold R. *Scratches On Our Minds: American Images of China and India.* New York: The John Day Company, 1958.

Iyer, Raghavan. *The Moral and Political Thought of Mahatma Gandhi.* New York: Oxford University Press, 1973.

Jack, Homer A., ed. *The Gandhi Reader: A Sourcebook of His Life and Writings.* Bloomington: Indiana University Press, 1956. Grove Press published the revised edition in 1994.

Jesudasan, Ignatius. *A Gandhian Theology of Liberation.* Maryknoll, N.Y.: Orbis Books, 1984.

Johnson, Paul. *Modern Times: The World from the Twenties to the Eighties.* New York: Harper & Row, 1985.

Jones, E. Stanley. *Gandhi: Portrayal of a Friend.* Nashville: Abingdon Press, 1983. This book surfaced after the *Gandhi* movie hit the market in 1982. Actually this book is a reprint of *Mahatma Gandhi: An Interpretation*, published in 1948.

Joshi, P. S. *Mahatma Gandhi in South Africa.* Privately printed in Rajkot, Gujarat, 1980.

Kapur, Sudarshan. *Raising Up a Prophet: The African-American Encounter with Gandhi.* Boston: Beacon Press, 1992.

Keer, Dhananjay. *Mahatma Gandhi: Political Saint and Unarmed Prophet.* Bombay: Popular Prakashan, 1973.

King, Martin Luther, Jr. *Stride toward Freedom: The Montgomery Story.* New York: Harper & Row, Publishers, 1958.

———. *Strength to Love*. New York: Harper & Row, Publishers, 1963.

King, Mary. *Mahatma Gandhi and Martin Luther King Jr: The Power of Nonviolent Action*. Paris: UNESCO Publishing, 1999.

Koestler, Arthur. *The Heel of Achilles: Essays 1968–1973*. New York: Random House, 1974.

Kovalsky, Susan Jovan, comp. *Mahatma Gandhi and His Political Influence in South Africa 1893–1914: A Selective Bibliography*. Johannesburg: University of the Witwatersrand, 1971.

Kripalani, Krishna, ed. *All Men Are Brothers: Life and Thoughts of Mahatma Gandhi As Told in His Own Words*. New York: Columbia University Press, 1958.

———. *Gandhi: A Life*. New Delhi: Published by the author, 1968.

Krishnadas. *Seven Months with Mahatma Gandhi: Being an Inside View of the Non-Co-Operation Movement (1921–1922)*. Vol. 1. Madras: S. Ganesan, 1928. Volume 1 covers the period from September to November 1921. Volume 2 covers the period from December 1921 to March 1922.

Krolick, Sanford, and Betty Cannon, eds. *Gandhi in the "Postmodern" Age: Issues in War and Peace*. Golden: Colorado School of Mines Press, 1984.

Kytle, Calvin. *Gandhi, Soldier of Nonviolence: An Introduction*. Washington, D.C.: Seven Locks Press, Inc., 1982.

Lischer, Richard. *The Preacher King: Martin Luther King, Jr. and the Word That Moved America*. New York: Oxford University Press, 1995.

Lovett, Verney. *A History of the Indian Nationalist Movement*. New York: Frederick A. Stokes Company, 1920.

Mallac, Guy de. *Gandhi's Seven Steps to Global Change*. Sante Fe, N.M.: Ocean Tree Books, 1989.

Mahar, Michael J., ed. *The Untouchables in Contemporary India*. Tucson: University of Arizona Press, 1972. See "Gandhi and Ambedkar—A Study in Leadership," an essay by Eleanor Zelliot.

Mansergh, Nicholas, ed. *The Transfer of Power*. Vol. 2. London: Her Majesty's Stationery Office, 1971.

Marks, Shula. *Reluctant Rebellion: The 1906–8 Disturbances in Natal*. Oxford: Clarendon Press, 1970.

Mathews, James K. *The Matchless Weapon: Satyagraha*. Bombay: Bharatiya Vidya Bhavan, 1989.

Mathur, D. B. *Gandhi, Congress, and Apartheid*. Jaipur, India: Aalekh Publishers, 1986.

———. *Prefacing Gandhi*. Jaipur, India: RBSA Publishers, 1988.

Mayo, Katherine. *Mother India*. New York: Harcourt, Brace & Company, 1927.

Mays, Benjamin E. *Born to Rebel: An Autobiography by Benjamin E. Mays*. New York: Charles Scribner's Sons, 1971.

Meer, Fatima, ed. *The South African Gandhi: An Abstract of the Speeches and Writings of M. K. Gandhi*. Durban, South Africa: Madiba Publishers, 1996.

Mehta, P. J. *M. K. Gandhi and the South African Indian Problem*. Madras: G. A. Natesan & Co., [1912?].

Mehta, Ved. *Mahatma Gandhi & His Apostles*. New Haven: Yale University Press, 1993. First published by Viking Press in 1977.

Miller, Keith D. *Voice of Deliverance: The Language of Martin Luther King, Jr. and Its*

Sources. New York: Free Press, 1992. The University of Georgia Press published an updated version containing a new Afterword by the author in 1998.

Mitchell, James R. *The Gandhi Image In the American Mind: 1921–1941.* Thesis presented to the graduate faculty of the University of Virginia, August 1967.

Moon, Penderel, ed. *Wavell: The Viceroy's Journal.* London: Oxford University Press, 1973.

Moses, Greg. *Revolution of Conscience: Martin Luther King, Jr., and the Philosophy of Nonviolence.* New York: The Guilford Press, 1997.

Muzumdar, Haridas T. *Gandhi the Apostle: His Trial and His Message.* Chicago: Universal Publishing Co., 1923.

———. *Mahatma Gandhi: A Prophetic Voice.* Ahmedabad: Navajivan Publishing House, 1963. Originally published as *Mahatma Gandhi: Peaceful Revolutionary* in 1953.

Naess, Arne. *Gandhi and the Nuclear Age.* Totowa, N.J.: Bedminster Press, 1967.

Naipaul, V. S. *India: A Wounded Civilization.* New York: Vintage Books, 1978.

Nair, Sir Sankaran C. *Gandhi and Anarchy.* Madras: Tagore & Co., 1922.

Nanda, B. R. *Gandhi and His Critics.* Delhi: Oxford University Press, 1993. Originally published in 1985.

———. *Mahatma Gandhi: A Biography.* Oxford: Oxford India Paperbacks, 1996. Originally published by George Allen and Unwin Ltd., 1958.

———, ed. *Mahatma Gandhi: 125 Years.* New Delhi: New Age International Publishers Limited, 1995.

Narula, Smita. *Broken People: Caste Violence against India's "Untouchables."* New York: Human Rights Watch, 1999.

Nayar, Sushila. *Mahatma Gandhi: Satyagraha at Work.* Vol. 4. Ahmedabad: Navajivan Publishing House, 1989.

Nichols, Beverley. *Verdict on India.* New York: Harcourt, Brace and Company, 1944.

O'Dwyer, Michael. *India As I Knew It: 1885–1925.* London: Constable & Company Ltd., 1925.

Omer-Cooper, J. D. *History of Southern Africa.* Portsmouth: Heinemann Educational Books, 1987.

Paine, Jeffery. *Father India: How Encounters with an Ancient Culture Transformed the Modern West.* New York: HarperCollins Publishers, 1998.

Pandiri, Ananda M. *A Comprehensive Annotated Bibliography on Mahatma Gandhi: Volume One Biographies, Works by Gandhi and Bibliographical Sources.* Westport, Conn.: Greenwood Press, 1995.

Paranjape, Makarand, ed. *Sarojini Naidu: Selected Letters 1890s to 1940s.* New Delhi: Kali for Women, 1996.

Pattery, George. *Gandhi–the Believer: An Indian Christian Perspective.* Delhi: ISPCK (Indian Society for Promoting Christian Knowledge), 1996.

Payne, Robert. *The Life and Death of Mahatma Gandhi.* New York: Konecky & Konecky, 1969.

Pillay, Bala. *British Indians in the Transvaal: Trade, Politics and Imperial Relations, 1885–1906.* London: Longman, 1976.

Polak, Brailsford, and Lord Pethick-Lawrence. *Mahatma Gandhi.* London: Odhams Press Limited, 1949.

Polak, Henry S. L. *M. K. Gandhi: A Sketch of His Life and Work.* Madras: G. A. Natesan

& Co., 1910. Later editions were published as *Mahatma Gandhi: The Man and His Mission.*

Polak, Millie G. *Mr. Gandhi: The Man.* London: George Allen & Unwin, 1931.

The Pope Speaks to India. Bombay: St. Paul Publications, 1986.

Puri, Rashmi-Sudha. *Gandhi On War and Peace.* New York: Prager, 1987.

Pyarelal. *Mahatma Gandhi.* 3 vols. Ahmedabad: Navajivan Publishing House, 1965, 1980, 1986.

Raju, J. B. *A Critical Study of the Non-Cooperation Movement in India.* Nagpur, India: Published by the author, 1920.

Randi, James. *The Mask of Nostradamus.* New York: Charles Scribner's Sons, 1990.

Rao, Raja. *The Great Indian Way: A Life of Mahatma Gandhi.* New Delhi: Vision Books, 1998.

Ray, Sibnarayan, ed. *Gandhi India and the World: An International Symposium.* Philadelphia: Temple University Press, 1970.

Reddy, E. S. *Gandhiji's Visions of a Free South Africa.* New Delhi: Sanchar Publishing House, 1995.

———, comp. *The Mahatma and the Poetess.* Mumbai: Bharatiya Vidya Bhavan, 1998.

Rolland, Romain. *Mahatma Gandhi: The Man Who Became One with the Universal Being.* New York: The Century Co., 1924.

Ronaldshay, Earl of. *The Heart of Aryavarta: A Study of the Psychology of Indian Unrest.* Boston: Houghton Mifflin Company, 1925.

Rothermund, Dietmar. *Mahatma Gandhi: An Essay in Political Biography.* Delhi: Manohar Publishers, 1991.

A Searchlight on Gandhi. London: P. S. King & Sons, 1931.

Sharma, Jagdish S. *Mahatma Gandhi: A Descriptive Bibliography.* Delhi: S. Chand, 1955.

Sheean, Vincent. *Lead Kindly Light: Gandhi & the Way to Peace.* New York: Random House, 1949.

———. *Mahatma Gandhi: A Great Life in Brief.* New York: Alfred A. Knopf, 1955.

Shirer, William L. *Gandhi: A Memoir.* New York: Simon & Schuster, 1979.

Shridharani, Krishnalal. *The Mahatma and the World.* New York: Duell, Sloan and Pearce, 1946.

Simmons, Paul D., ed. *Freedom of Conscience: A Baptist/Humanist Dialogue.* Amherst, N.Y.: Prometheus Books, 2000.

Smail, J. L. *Those Restless Years: Dealing with the Boer and Bombata Rebellion.* Cape Town: Howard Timmins, 1971.

Stuart, J. *A History of the Zulu Rebellion.* London: MacMillan and Co., Limited, 1913.

Swan, Maureen. *Gandhi: The South African Experience.* Johannesburg: Raven Press, 1986.

Tendulkar, D. G. *Mahatma: Life of Mohandas Karamchand Gandhi.* Vol. 1. Bombay: Vithalbhai K. Jhaveri and D. G. Tendulkar, 1951.

Thurman, Howard. *With Head and Heart: The Autobiography of Howard Thurman.* New York: Harcourt Brace Jovanovich, 1979.

Twain, Mark. *Following the Equator: A Journey around the World.* New York: Harper & Brothers, 1897.

Uppal, J. N. *Gandhi: Ordained in South Africa.* Delhi: Publication Division, Ministry of Information and Broadcasting, Government of India, 1995.

Van Tyne, Claude H. *India in Ferment*. New York: D. Appleton and Company, 1923.

Vivekananda, Swami. *The Complete Works of Swami Vivekananda*. Vol. 3. Mayavati: Advaita Ashrama, 1954.

Watson, Blanche, comp. *Gandhi And Non-Violent Resistance: The Non-Co-operation Movement in India: Gleanings from the American Press*. Madras: Ganesh & Co., 1923.

Wheeler, Post. *India Against the Storm*. New York: E.P. Dutton & Company, 1944.

Windsor, Edward. *A King's Story: The Memoirs of the Duke of Windsor*. New York: G. P. Putnam's Sons, 1947.

Wofford, Clare, and Harris Wofford. *India Afire*. New York: The John Day Co., 1951.

Wolpert, Stanley. *Gandhi's Passion: The Life and Legacy of Mahatma Gandhi*. New York: Oxford University Press, 2001.

Yajnik, Indulal K. *Gandhi As I Know Him*. Delhi: Danesh Mahel, 1943.

Yeats-Brown, Francis. *Lancer At Large*. New York: Garden City Publishing Co., 1939.

ARTICLES

Grenier, Richard. "The Gandhi Nobody Knows." *Commentary* 75, no. 3 (March 1983): pp. 59–72.

Hunt, James D. "Gandhi and the Black People of South Africa." *Gandhi Marg* 11, no. 1 (April–June 1989): pp. 7–24.

Mandela, Nelson. "The Sacred Warrior." *Time*, December 31, 1999.

Marty, Martin E. "Richard, Stay Home!" *The Christian Century* (August 17–24, 1983): p. 759.

Mayo, Katherine. "Gandhi's March Past." *The Atlantic Monthly* (September 1930): pp. 327–33.

———. "Mahatma Gandhi and India's Untouchables." *Current History* 32 (1930): pp. 864–70.

Murray, Gilbert. "The Soul as It Is, and How to Deal with It." *Hibbert Journal* 16, no. 2 (January 1918): pp. 191–205.

Ramchandani, R. R. "Gandhi in South Africa: A Study in Social Accounting." *India Quarterly: A Journal of International Affairs* (October–December 1993): pp. 31–48.

Rudolph, Lloyd, and Susanne Rudolph. Letter to the editor. *Commentary* 76, no. 7 (July 1983): pp. 11–33.

Switzer, Les. "Gandhi in South Africa: The Ambiguities of Satyagraha." *Journal of Ethnic Studies* 14, no. 1 (Spring 1986): pp. 122–28.

"To the American Negro: A Message from Mahatma Gandhi." *Crisis* 36, no. 7 (July 1929): p. 225.

"We Nominate Gandhi for Nobel Peace Prize." Editorial. *The Christian Century* 51 (March 14, 1934): p. 350.

GANDHI JOURNALS AND AWARDS

Gandhi Marg is the official publication of the Gandhi Peace Foundation, headquarters in New Delhi, India.

The Gandhi Message. Special Edition, volume 29, no. 1 and 2, 1995. This is a publication of The Mahatma Gandhi Memorial Foundation, Inc., located in Washington, D.C.

Other Gandhi journals: *Journal of Peace and Gandhian Studies* (India), *Gandhian Perspectives* (India), *Sansthakul* (India), *Journal of the Gandhi Smriti & Darshan Samiti* (India), *Gandhi Jyoti* (India), *Gandhian Thought* (India), *Gandhi Vigyan* (India), *Science for Villages* (India), *Vigil* (India), *Gandhians in Action* (India), *Gandhian Opinion* (Australia), *The Gandhi Way* (Great Britain), and *The Acorn: Journal of the Gandhi-King Society* (USA). The government of India and few other nongovernmental organizations confer awards on a yearly basis under Gandhi's name. The Gandhi Peace Award, the International Gandhi Peace Price, and the UNESCO Gandhi Gold Medal are just a few examples of a growing list.

NEWSPAPERS

New York Times, April 9, 1930; November 25, 1921; November 23, 1921; December 16, 1921; March 12, 1922; January 25, 1922; December 14, 1931; January 31, 1948

The New York Times Index, July–December 1921.

Time, "Foreign News," January 5, 1931.

Time, "The Roots of Violence," July 2, 1984.

The Christian Century 79 (May 23, 1962): p. 661.

INDEX

339

seven social sins, 16–17, 20n4
sexual abstinence. *See* celibacy, vow of
S. Ganesan (publisher), 48
Shaikh, Mahomed (also known as
    Mahomed), 94, 107
Sharma, Jagdish S., 26
Shastras, 258–59
Sheean, Vincent, 58–59, 239, 300n11
Sheen, Martin, 58
Shelat, Shris Umiashankar Manchharam,
    36, 94, 106, 107, 108, 115n2
Sheth Maneklal Jethabhai Pustakalya
    (library), 84
Shirer, William L., 58
Shourie, Arun, 260n1
Shridharani, Krishnalal, 48–49
Shudras (also known as Sudras), 238,
    251–52, 256–57, 258
Sidat, M. B., 109, 117
Sikh-Hindu conflicts, 15–16, 282–83, 308,
    309, 314n20
Sikh religion, 14–15, 44
Simpson, Wallis, 274
Singh, Anup, 48
sins, seven deadly, 16–17, 20n4
Slade, Madeleine, 37, 220–21
Slocombe, George, 288
Smritis, 259
Smuts, Jan C., 120, 155, 157, 317
Smythe, Mister, 92
Sojourner Truth (statue of), 323
Soka Gakkai International, 323n
Solomon Commission, 158
soul-force. *See* Satyagraha
"Soul As It Is, and How to Deal with It,
    The" (Murray), 65, 303
South Africa and Satyagraha, 147–55,
    229–31
South African British Indian Committee,
    195
*South African Gandhi: An Abstract of the
    Speeches and Writings of M. K.
    Gandhi, The* (Meer), 133
South Asia Institute (Heidelberg, Ger-
    many), 64
Sparks, Colonel, 38, 113, 206

Spear, Percival, 236
*Speeches and Writings of Mahatma
    Gandhi*, 55n9, 305
spinning wheel, 252–53
S. P. Mahomed & Co., 109
Srinivasan, K., 279–80, 281
S.S. *Armadale Castle*, 153, 302
Stalin, Joseph, 309
Star, The (newspaper), 121
Statesman (newspaper), 187
Stead's Review, 213
Stead's Review, 318
Stent, Vere, 155
Stokes, Mr., 111, 130
Story of My Experiments with Truth, The.
    *See Autobiography or The Story of My
    Experiments with Truth, An* (Gandhi)
Stretcher-Bearer Corps, 30, 31, 35–36,
    119, 210
    chronology June 21–July 14, 1906,
        109–15
    creation for Zulu Rebellion, 100
    duration of duty, 127
    duties of, 129–31
    names of, 106–108, 115n2
    numbers of, 106–107, 115n4, 127
strikes as strategy of Satyagraha, 154
Student Christian Movement of India,
    Burma, and Ceylon, 221
Sudras (also known as Shudras), 238, 298
Swan, Maureen, 40, 140, 155, 192–93,
    200–201, 202n
Swaraj, 208, 212, 250
Switzer, Les, 200

Tax on ex-indentured Indians, 196
Tema, S. S., 226–27, 319
temple access by Untouchables, 265,
    266–67
Temple Entry Bill (1933), 266
Tendulkar, D. G., 52–53, 76
Tengo Jabavu, John, 200
terrorism and Gandhi, 209
That Strange Little Brown Man Gandhi
    (Fisher), 50, 228n11
Thomas, O. M., 280, 281